THE SANCTUARY OF SILENCE

ISRAEL KNOHL

THE SANCTUARY OF SILENCE

The Priestly Torah and the Holiness School

Fortress Press Minneapolis

THE SANCTUARY OF SILENCE
The Priestly Torah and the Holiness School

Library of Congress Cataloging-in-Publication Data

Knohl, Israel.
[Miḳdash ha-demamah. English]
The sanctuary of silence : the priestly Torah and the holiness school / Israel Knohl.
p. cm.
Includes bibliographical references and index.
ISBN 0-8006-2763-6
1. P. document (Biblical criticism) 2. Bible. O.T. Pentateuch—Criticism, interpretation, etc. 3. Priests, Jewish. I. Title.
BS1181.6.K5613 1995 94-12975
CIP

The paper used in this publication meets the minimum requirements of the American National Standard for Information Sciences—Permanence of Paper for Printed Library Materials, ANSI Z3229.48-1984.

Manufactured in the U.S.A. AF 1-2763

99 98 97 96 95 1 2 3 4 5 6 7 8 9 10

Contents

Preface

This book is a revised and expanded version of my Hebrew volume מקדש הדממה (Jerusalem: Magnes Press, 1992). My former student Galit Beracha provided valuable research assistance. The manuscript was rendered into English by Jackie Feldman and Peretz Rodman. I wish to express my appreciation to all of them.

The stimuli for my interest in researching the Priestly literature in the Pentateuch are described in Excursus 5 at the conclusion of the present work. The dissertation underlying this book, "The Conception of God and Cult in the Priestly Torah and in the Holiness School" (The Hebrew University, Jerusalem, 1988), was composed under the dedicated guidance of Professor Moshe Greenberg. The Shalom Hartman Institute, along with its director Professor David Hartman, provided me with a stimulating environment.

My wife Rivka and our children Shai Menashe, Tal Shahar, and Or Yissachar, have been a source of support and love throughout.

This edition of the book is dedicated to my mother Shoshana, who, together with my late father Yissachar Dov Knohl, endowed me with a love for the Book of Books.

Israel Knohl
Jerusalem
June 1994

Abbreviations

AB	Anchor Bible
AJSL	*American Journal of Semitic Languages and Literature*
AnBib	Analecta Biblica
AOAT	Alter Orient und Altes Testament
BA	*Biblical Archaeologist*
BiOr	*Bibliotheca Orientalis*
BK	Biblischer Kommentar
BWANT	Beiträge zur Wissenschaft vom Alten und Neuen Testament
BZ	*Biblische Zeitschrift*
BZAW	Beihefte zur *ZAW*
CaRB	Cahiers de la Revue biblique
CB	The Century Bible
CBSC	Cambridge Bible for Scholars and Clergy
CBQ	*Catholic Biblical Quarterly*
D	The Deuteronomic source in the Pentateuch
E	The Elohist source in the Pentateuch
EM	*Encyclopedia Miqrait* (Hebrew)
ERE	*Encyclopedia of Religion and Ethics*
FRLANT	Forschungen zur Religion und Literatur des Alten und Neuen Testaments
H	Holiness Code
HAT	Handbuch zum Alten Testament
HKAT	Handkommentar zur Alten Testament
HS	Holiness School
HUCA	*Hebrew Union College Annual*
IDB	*Interpreter's Dictionary of the Bible,* ed. G. A. Buttrick
J	The Yahwist source in the Pentateuch
JANES	*Journal of the Ancient Near Eastern Society of Columbia University*

JAOS	*Journal of the American Oriental Society*
JBL	*Journal of Biblical Literature*
JE	The Yahwist-Elohist material in the Pentateuch
JJS	*Journal of Jewish Studies*
JSOTSup	*Journal for the Study of the Old Testament* Supplement Series
JTS	*Journal of Theological Studies*
KeH	Kurzgefasstes exegetisches Handbuch zum Alten Testament
KH	Kurzer Hand-Commentar zum Alten Testament
MT	Masoretic Text
OTL	Old Testament Library
OTS	*Oudtestamentische Studiën*
P	The Priestly source in the Pentateuch
PT	Priestly Torah
RB	*Revue biblique*
SBLMS	Society of Biblical Literature Monograph Series
TLZ	*Theologische Literaturzeitung*
TWAT	*Theologisches Wörterbuch zum Alten Testament,* ed. G. J. Botterweck and H. Ringgren
TZ	*Theologische Zeitschrift*
VT	*Vetus Testamentum*
VTSup	Supplements to *Vetus Testamentum*
WC	Westminster Commentaries
WMANT	Wissenschaftliche Monographien zum Alten und Neuen Testament
ZA	*Zeitschrift für Assyriologie*
ZAW	*Zeitschrift für die alttestamentliche Wissenschaft*

Introduction

It has long been accepted in biblical research that the Torah is comprised of four principal sources. These sources are customarily denoted as follows: J, the source using the Tetragrammaton from the beginning of the Torah; E, the "Elohist," who uses the name "Elohim"; P, the Priestly source; and D, the book of Deuteronomy.[1]

For more than a century the Priestly source, P, has been the focus of attention of biblical research,[2] but, in spite of the great interest in this topic, many central questions still lack appropriate and accepted answers. These questions refer to two principal issues—the internal literary composition of the Priestly material in the Torah and the explanation of the theological and ritual uniqueness of this source, including its several layers and its historical and social context.

Within the Priestly work in the Torah, Leviticus 17–26 stands out in its linguistic and stylistic uniqueness.[3] In some of the chapters in this group

1. For a survey of the history of pentateuchal study and a description of the various sources, see A. T. Chapman, *An Introduction to the Pentateuch* (Cambridge, 1911), as well as the concise summary in M. Weinfeld, "Pentateuch, Pentateuch Study in Modern Times," *EM* 8 (1982) 492–94.

2. See the survey in R. J. Thompson, *Moses and the Law in a Century of Criticism* (VTSup 19; Leiden: Brill, 1970).

3. For the history of research on the uniqueness of this collection, see A. Kuenen, *The Origin and Composition of the Hexateuch* (Eng. trans. P. H. Wicksteed; London, 1886) 88 n. 24; C. Feucht, *Untersuchungen zum Heiligkeitsgesetz* (Berlin, 1964) 11–12; also, more recently, H. Sun, "An Investigation into the Compositional Integrity of the So-called Holiness Code (Leviticus 17–26)" (diss., Claremont Graduate School, 1990) 1–40. For the linguistic characteristics of this collection, see A. Dillmann, *Die Bücher Numeri, Deuteronomium und Josua* (KeH; Leipzig, 1886) 637–38; Kuenen, *Hexateuch*, 89; S. R. Driver, *An Introduction to the Literature of the Old Testament* (Edinburgh, 1913) 49–50; H. Holzinger, *Einleitung in den Hexateuch* (Freiburg, 1893) 411–12; and others. Among the characteristic linguistic and stylistic elements, we should single out the closing formula (אלהיכם, מקשכם), אני ה׳, which is

the holiness of God is emphasized, and this is taken to imply a call to holiness addressed to the Israelites in general (see Lev 19:2; 20:7, 26; 21:8; 22:35). It has therefore been customary, since A. Klostermann's study, to call this section the "Holiness Code."[4] It is denoted H, to distinguish it from the other parts of the Priestly work, which are denoted P.[5] In addition to its unique linguistic features, H includes many features that match the language of P. Scholars have explained this phenomenon by suggesting that there is a collection of laws antedating P that underlies the Holiness Code and that scribes of the P school edited this early collection at the time they included it in their writings.[6]

When research on this issue was just beginning, it was found that the passages with the characteristics of H actually extend beyond the confines of the Holiness Code, that is, Leviticus 17–26. The proposals suggested for identifying the work of H outside of the Holiness Code are many and varied, each scholar having his or her own methods.[7] Some scholars explain the existence of fragments of H outside the Holiness Code by suggesting that these fragments were originally part of the Holi-

---

commonly found in the collection, as well as the personal nature of some of the כרת formulas, such as ונתתי את פני בנפש ההוא והכרתי אותו מקרב עמו (Lev 20:6; compare 20:3; 17:10; etc.). Similarly, ושמתי אני את פני באיש ההוא ובמשפחתו והכרתי אתו ואת כל הזנים אחריו (Lev 20:5). These phrases differ greatly from the uniform impersonal expression ונכרת(ה) מעמיו(ה), which is common in other parts of the Priestly stratum (see Exod 30:33, 38; Lev 7:20, 21). Another characteristic of this collection is the formulation of laws as a direct address by God to Israel in the second person, with God's self references in the first person when addressing the people. This style is not be found elsewhere in the Priestly writings (see J. Begrich, "Die priesterliche Torah," in *Werden und Wesen des alten Testament* [BZAW 66; Berlin, 1936] 82; A. Cholewinski, *Heiligkeitsgesetz und Deuteronomium* [AnBib 66; Rome, 1976] 137). Furthermore, the word אני is often employed as part of the divine speech, especially in the closing formula (אני ה׳ (אלהיכם, מקדשכם. It is used in informal speech as well (see Lev 17:11; 18:3, 24; 20:3, 23, 24; 23:10; 25:2; 26:16, 24, 28, 32, 41; see Cholewinski). In general HS's [=Holiness School; see below] language is free and exhortatory, whereas the Priestly style is uniform, measured, restrained, and dry. There are also striking similarities between HS's language and that of Ezekiel (see Driver, *Introduction,* 145–49).

4. See A. Klostermann, *Der Pentateuch* (Leipzig, 1893) 368–418. Klostermann coined the term "Heiligkeitsgesetz." Among English-speaking scholars the term "Holiness Code" is common, whereas the term "ספר הקדושה" is current in Hebrew-language scholarship.

5. According to the prevailing scholarly view, the main corpus of P contains the passages Exodus 25–31; 35–40; and Leviticus 1–16. In addition, several passages and chapters in Genesis, in the first part of Exodus, and in Numbers are attributed to P.

6. See, e.g., Kuenen, *Hexateuch,* 87; Driver, *Introduction,* 47–48.

7. See Klostermann, *Pentateuch,* 377; F. Horst, *Leviticus XVII–XXVI und Hezekiel* (Colmar, 1886) 32–36; P. Wurster, "Zur Charakteristik und Geschichte des Priesterkodex und des Heiligkeitsgesetzes," *ZAW* 4 (1884) 123–26; A. Dillmann, *Die Bücher Numeri, Deuteronomium und Josua* (2nd ed.; KeH; Leipzig, 1886) 640–41(hereafter *Hexateuch*); Kuenen, *Hexateuch,* 96, 278–79; Driver, *Introduction,* 59, 151; Holzinger, *Einleitung,* 410; M. Haran, "Holiness Code," *EM* 5 (1968) 1095; idem, "Behind the Scenes of History: Determining the Date of the Priestly Source," *JBL* 100 (1981) 329 n. 12.

ness Code but were omitted from it, or that this material had remained outside the Holiness Code when it was edited.[8]

But over the years many cracks and fissures have appeared in this theory. Aside from the lack of agreement about the identification of H fragments outside the Holiness Code, the awareness that signs of H appeared in writings spread out over the entire Priestly work led some scholars to doubt the very existence of the Holiness Code as a separate unit within the Priestly source.[9] Even among those who still believe in the separate existence of the Holiness Code (and the H layer), some reject the accepted idea of the chronological relationship between H and P. Some scholars believe that certain units of H are later than parallel units of P,[10] while others believe that the entire work of H is later than the work of P.[11]

The Holiness Code is unique not only in its language and style but also in its belief, ritual, and legal contents. Unlike the P code, which concentrates on the realm of ritual, ignoring issues of social organization and cut off from agricultural life, the Holiness Code combines laws concerning the Temple and the sacrifices with legal and social rules, and it shows real concern for agricultural life. Another difference between P and H is revealed in their connection with non-Priestly sources in the Torah (J, E, and D): the H layer shows a closeness to these sources that is absent in the P layer.

Julius Wellhausen, in *Prolegomena zur Geschichte Israels* (1882), placed the difference between H and P as a part of his comprehensive theory of the history of ritual worship among the Israelites. According to his analysis, early Israelite worship was natural, spontaneous, and involved with human life—as it appears in the J and E sources. Over the years the rituals were institutionalized and were gradually distanced from nature and

8. See the summary in Haran, "Holiness Code."

9. V. Wagner cites the names of scholars preceding him who cast doubts on the existence of the Holiness Code ("Zur Existenz des sogenannten 'Heiligkeitsgesetzes,'" *ZAW* 4 [1884] n. 2). To his list we may add D. Hoffmann's objections (*Die Wichtigsten Instanzen gegen die Graf-Wellhausen Hypothese* [Berlin, 1904]; idem, *Leviticus with Commentary* [Jerusalem, 1976] 2:10–12, 84–85, 110–11, 185–87, 258–68) as well as those of A. Toeg, *Lawgiving at Sinai* (Jerusalem, 1971) 148–49 n. 113, 149–50 n. 116, 153–54 n. 121 (Hebrew).

10. H. C. Brichto is of the opinion that the slaughter laws of H in Leviticus 17 are of a later date than the prohibition of the consumption of blood in P in Genesis 9 ("On Slaughter and Sacrifice, Blood and Atonement," *HUCA* 47 [1976] 42–43). Lohfink declares that Leviticus 26 reflects a change in the original Priestly view, as formulated in P ("Die Abänderung der Theologie des Priestlichen Geschichtswerks im Segen des Heiligkeitsgesetzes," in *Wort und Geschichte* [Festschrift K. Elliger; Neukirchen, 1973] 129–36).

11. G. H. Davies states that H was composed at the time of the Babylonian exile, whereas the P stratum was composed earlier ("Leviticus," *IDB* 3:118). K. Elliger claims that HS was composed as a supplement to P and never had an independent existence (*Leviticus* [HAT; Tübingen, 1966]). Cholewinski (*Heiligkeitsgesetz,* 138–41, 334–38) accepts Elliger's view, except that he admits to some final editing of the Holiness Code by writers of P.

from human life. This process was accelerated by the destruction of the Land of Israel and the Babylonian exile, which involved the severance of the physical connection between the people and their land. Wellhausen believed that the end of this process was expressed in the creation of P, which he considered to be a code written in exile, totally lacking the natural and agricultural context of the early ritual worship. The precisely detailed Temple ceremonies of ritual worship presented in the laws of P were, in his opinion, new, artificial ceremonies that were created within the priestly circles of the Second Temple. Therefore he believed that the historical sources of the First Temple period did not contain any real evidence of the existence of these ceremonies. Wellhausen accepted the prevalent opinion that H antedated P, and on this ground he explained the attitude of the H source to agricultural life and to the daily life of the people, as well as its link with the non-Priestly sources. He claimed that H constitutes an intermediate stage between the J, E, and D sources and the P source; thus, it still contains some of the spirit of popular ritual worship, but it also shows signs of the Priestly conception that was to reach its full consolidation in the creation of P.[12]

Wellhausen's theory captured the minds of his contempories. There were, however, several important scholars—A. Dillmann, F. Delitzsch, and G. Kittel—who refused to accept it.[13] In the following generations, the critical camp increased,[14] especially after the remains of the cultures of the ancient Near East were discovered, and it was found that customs similar to the ritual ceremonies described in P had already been prevalent in the Near East in the second millennium BCE.[15] Wellhausen's critics, who claimed that P was an early work, had to suggest an alternative explanation for P's disconnection from popular ritual and from the non-Priestly sources and for the absence of any real evidence for the existence of the ritual ceremonies described in P in the historical sources of the First Temple period. The explanation that was accepted among those who believed in P's antiquity was based on the hypothesis that in Israel before the Babylonian exile—as in other countries of the ancient East—the priests constituted a closed, isolated social elite[16] and that their work was essen-

12. See J. Wellhausen, *Prolegomena zur Geschichte Israels* (6th ed.; Berlin, 1905) 90–98, 375–78.

13. For a summary of their criticisms, see Thompson, "Moses," 60–62.

14. Ibid., 72ff. Of special importance are the critiques of Hoffmann (*Instanzen*) and Y. Kaufmann (*A History of the Religion of Israel* [Jerusalem/Tel Aviv, 1960] 1:1–220).

15. See the comprehensive formulation in M. Weinfeld, "Social and Cultic Institutions in the Priestly Source against their Near Eastern Background," in *Proceedings of the Eighth World Congress of Jewish Studies, Bible Studies, and Hebrew Language* (Jerusalem, 1981) 95–129.

16. On the creation of P and its preservation within a small circle of priests, see Dillmann, *Hexateuch*, 666–67; J. Begrich, "Die priesterliche Torah," 86; H. L. Ginsberg, *New Trends in the Study of the Bible* (Essays in Judaism 4; New York, 1967) 23; M. Weinfeld,

tially esoteric. Therefore it did not leave a noticeable impression on the life of the people until Ezra included it in the Torah.[17]

It is not easy, however, to see this theory as the solution to the problem of H's special nature within the Priestly work, for the question immediately arises: If the priesthood was really a closed circle isolated from the nation, how could it give rise to a work like the Holiness Code, which emphasizes the holiness of the entire nation, addresses its laws directly to the people, considers questions touching on social and agricultural life, and demonstrates a link with the popular sources of the Torah? It is thus not surprising that some of Wellhausen's most prominent critics, such as Y. Kaufmann and M. Weinfeld, tend to ignore the uniqueness of the Holiness Code (and the H layer in general) and to assimilate it to P.[18] In contrast, scholars such as Dillmann in his generation and Haran in our own—who asserted the antiquity of the Priestly source yet emphasized the uniqueness of H— did not succeed in providing a satisfactory explanation for the status of this layer within the entire Priestly work.[19] It thus seems

---

"Theological Currents in the Pentateuchal Literature," in *Proceedings of the American Academy for Jewish Research,* 37 (New York, 1969) 118, 122–23; idem, "Towards the Concept of Law in Israel and Elsewhere," *Beit Miqra* 8 (1964) 61–63; M. Haran, *Ages and Institutions in the Bible* (Tel Aviv, 1972) 185; idem, *Temples and Temple Service in Ancient Israel* (Oxford, 1978) 11, 143; C. Cohen, "Was the P Document Secret?" *JANES* 112 (1969) 39–44.

17. Haran also mentions in this context the utopian side of the P composition (*Ages,* 183–84; *Temples,* 11–12).

18. In his polemic against Wellhausen, Kaufmann argues that "the Holiness Code is merely a part of PT (=P). Not only is it similar to P in style and character, but it has been blended with P into a single unit" (*History,* 1:121). Weinfeld frequently contrasts and compares what he identifies as the two main theological currents composing the Pentateuch—the Priestly and the Deuteronomist (see Weinfeld, "Currents"; "The Change in the Conception of Religion in Deuteronomy," *Tarbiz* 31 [1961] 1–14; *Deuteronomy and the Deuteronomistic School* [Oxford, 1972] 179–243). For Weinfeld, the laws of the Holiness Code are included in his general treatment of the Priestly school and, with the exception of several isolated comments, merit no separate discussion.

19. Dillmann (*Hexateuch,* 637–47; Kuenen, *Hexateuch,* 279–80) proposed a theory on the composition of the Holiness Code and its origins, which outlines the place of the H stratum (which he calls S) in relation to P (which he calls A). His theory, however, is extremely complicated and was justifiably attacked and rejected by other scholars (see Kuenen, *Hexateuch,* 280–81, and the comments of his predecessors cited there). Haran sees the Holiness Code as the "secular-civil" law of the Priestly source. This, in his opinion, would account both for the Holiness Code's preoccupation with agricultural life and legislation and for its relation to non-Priestly legal compilations (Haran, "Holiness Code," 1094–95). Aside from the difficulty in referring to the Holiness Code as "secular," Haran's proposal has other, more severe weaknesses; Haran, as we mentioned, is numbered among the scholars who view the priesthood as a closed circle (see n. 16 above). What, then, would motivate those priests, sheltered within the walls of the Temple and concerned entirely with their secret rites, to write a civil "secular" laws—a law that, according to Haran, was composed prior to P? See Haran, "Holiness Code," 1098; see also chapter 5 n. 4, below for the chronological problems in Haran's system.

that the problem of the H layer's literary status and conceptual uniqueness within the Priestly work has not yet been solved. The lack of a satisfactory solution for this problem makes it difficult to understand the nature of the Priestly work in its entirety and to determine the historical period and social background within which it was composed.

In this book I suggest a new solution to the problem of the Priestly source. My suggestion undermines the accepted opinions on the relationship between P and H. In my opinion, considering H as a unit (and even a special unit) embedded within the comprehensive work of P is fundamentally mistaken. Many sections outside the Holiness Code that have hitherto been attributed to P are really part of the writings of the H school. We must therefore recognize the existence of two separate Priestly sources, P and H. These sources represent, in my opinion, the work of two independent Priestly schools: One is the P school or, as I prefer to call it, the Priestly Torah (PT),[20] while the other is the H school, which I call the Holiness School (HS).[21] I believe that the work of the HS clearly postdates the work of the PT. Moreover, in my opinion the HS is responsible for the great enterprise of editing the Torah, which included editing and rewriting the legal scrolls of the PT[22] and blending them with the non-Priestly sources.

The basis of these claims is presented in the first two chapters, in which I reclassify the corpus of Priestly writings in the Torah according to their origin in one of the two schools: the Priestly Torah and the Holiness School. This reclassification clarifies and sharpens the lines separating the theological and ritual conception of the Priestly Torah from the cultic and theological conception of the Holiness School. It reveals two streams that are so different from each other that it will no longer be possible to continue speaking in general terms about "the theology of the Priestly source"; rather, it will be necessary to recognize two separate Priestly theologies—that of the PT and that of the HS. The PT philosophy is focused on the priestly views of belief and ritual and on differentiating them from the beliefs and ritual of the masses, while the HS attempts to interweave and blend the priestly elements of belief and ritual with popular

20. The "Priestly Torah" (PT) will refer here to both the source P and the school in which it was composed.

21. Since the call for the sanctification of the community of Israel and the guarding of the sanctity of its place of residence appear in several places in the writings of this school, both in the Holiness Code and outside of it (Lev 11:44–45; Num 15:40; and elsewhere), we find the name "Holiness School" particularly appropriate. We should note that the expansion of the corpus of writings ascribed to HS in no way detracts from the uniqueness of the composition called the Holiness Code (Leviticus 17–26). This collection is the central corpus of the HS, in which its unique concepts were first formulated.

22. On the commandment scrolls of PT, see M. Haran, "Book Scrolls at the Beginning of the Second Temple Period—The Transition from Papyrus to Skins," *HUCA* 54 (1984) 115.

traditions and customs. The belief and ritual conceptions of the two schools are described in the third and fourth chapters of the book.

In the final chapter I suggest a historical and social framework for the activities of the Priestly schools. I describe the hypothesized background of the separation and isolation of the PT, and I examine the circumstances of the turning point in the priestly circles that led to the growth of the HS and the emergence of a more popular approach among the priests. I also examine the relationship between the turnabout in the Priestly philosophy and the criticism leveled against the ritual establishment by classical prophecy.

CHAPTER
1

The Sabbath and Festivals in the Priestly Torah and in the Laws of the Holiness School

Thorough confirmation of our claim regarding the relationship between the works of the Priestly Torah and those of the Holiness School requires a comprehensive study of all the Priestly material in the Pentateuch. We begin by focusing on a particular topic within the Priestly writings—the Sabbath and festival legislation. In this area of religious life are a wealth of creativity and a multiplicity of emphases; these make it an appropriate showcase for varying approaches and differing opinions, which find expression in various strata of legislation. At the center of our discussion stands Leviticus 23, which, because of its unique layered character, can be highly instructive about the relationship between the Priestly schools.

The Priority of PT over HS: A Preliminary Inquiry into the Composition of Leviticus 23

In analyzing Leviticus 23, one must constantly compare it with Numbers 28–29. These two sections are the organized and detailed lists of the festivals found in P. The talmudic sages perceptively differentiated between these two lists by saying:. "In the Torah of the Priests (Leviticus) because of their order, in the Fifth of Numbering (Numbers) because of sacrifice,"[1] that is, the list in Leviticus is primarily concerned with listing

1. *Sifre Deut.* 127 (ed. L. Finkelstein; New York, 1969) 185.

those days of the year which are "appointed times of the Lord, the sacred festivals,"[2] while the list in Numbers is intended to list the additions to the daily sacrifices prescribed for each of these special occasions.[3]

Scholars generally agree that Numbers 28–29 is wholly PT, as opposed to Leviticus 23, which, as mentioned above, is composed of elements of PT interwoven with elements of HS. This appraisal of the compound nature of Leviticus 23 is based on differences in content and style among the various constituent elements of this chapter. On one hand, there are several sections[4] in this chapter that differ from the corresponding sections in Numbers 28–29 only in the absence of information about sacrifices, as is derived from the aforementioned difference in intent between the two lists. On the other hand, there are other sections that clearly depart from the well-measured style of PT and list some ritual practices unmentioned in Numbers: the wave offering of the sheaf and the two loaves, and the "Four Kinds" to be taken on the feast of Tabernacles. Furthermore, one of the sections of Leviticus 23 which deals with the feast of Firstfruits explicitly contradicts instructions given elsewhere in PT regarding the festival offerings.[5] Since these sections conclude with the formula "I am the Lord your God" (Lev 23:22, 43), which is characteristic of HS, it is only proper to conclude that they originated in that school.

That the section regarding the sheaf and two loaves (vv. 9–22) and the second Tabernacles passage (vv. 39–43) stem from HS has been accepted by most scholars. These scholars, who (as already mentioned) assume that HS preceded PT, explain the presence of these two sections in the chapter by saying that later editors of the Priestly school somehow received some writings of the earlier Holiness School, which they wove into their festival laws.[6] This explanation gives rise to the question whether an editorial process of blending the materials written by the two schools produced the list of festivals in Leviticus 23, or whether the basis of this chapter

2. An exception to this generalization is the discussion of the sacrifices of the firstfruits festival in Lev 23:18–20. This deviation will be explained below.

3. Thus, the New Moon, when an additional sacrifice is offered, is included in this list, despite its not being a "sacred occasion" (מקרא קדש).

4. The passage treating the Passover sacrifice and the feast of Unleavened Bread (Lev 23:5–8); that treating the first day of the seventh month (23:23–25); and that treating the first feast of Booths (23:33–36).

5. Whereas Num 28:27 requires that there be offered on this day one ram, two bulls, and seven sheep as a burnt offering, Lev 23:18–19 calls for one bull, two rams, and seven sheep as a burnt offering and two sheep as a sacrifice of well-being.

6. See the discussion in J. F. L. George, *Die älteren Jüdischen Feste* (Berlin, 1835) 127ff., followed by J. Wellhausen, *Die Composition des Hexateuchs und der historischen Bücher des Alten Testaments* (3rd ed.; Berlin, 1899) 159–64; A. Kuenen, *The Origen and Composition of the Hexateuch* (Eng. trans. P. H. Wicksteed; London, 1886) 90, 282; B. Baentsch, *Exodus-Leviticus* (HKAT; Göttingen, 1903) 412–13. For additional literature, see A. Cholewinski, *Heiligkeitsgesetz und Deuteronomium* (AnBib 66; Rome, 1976) 87 n. 15.

was an independent PT list to which HS materials were added only at a later stage. There seems to be convincing evidence for the second possibility: after the first Tabernacles passage (whose origins are to be sought in PT), there comes what was clearly intended to be the conclusion of the entire portion on the festivals (23:37–38); only after this conclusion does the second Tabernacles passage (HS) appear. This means that the primary element of this chapter was a PT festivals list that ended in v. 38, that the elements stemming from HS were added only later, and that that is why the second Tabernacles passage comes after the original conclusion.

Let us now consider how that course of events has to be portrayed in accordance with the commonly accepted premise of the priority of HS over PT. In PT, there were two festivals lists. One list dealt elaborately with the sacrifices to be brought on the festivals; it has been preserved in its original form in Numbers 28–29. Another, shorter list was linguistically similar to the first list but differed in that it was concerned with presenting the calendar of festivals without detailing their sacrifices; this list formed the basis of Leviticus 23. At a later point in time, some members of the Priestly school came across Holiness writings, including one unit that dealt with the sheaf-waving and the firstfruits festival, and another unit dealing with Tabernacles and its ceremonies. Since Tabernacles was the last of the festivals mentioned in the original list, the Priestly editors could attach the HS Tabernacles passage by merely adding it to the end of the list, after the concluding verses. But since the firstfruits passage was in the middle of the original list, this method could not be employed, and therefore the editors struck out the original PT firstfruits festival passage and replaced it with that of HS, along with the introductory passage dealing with the wave offering of the sheaf.

Textually such a process is possible, but it does not seem very sensible. Can it be seriously entertained that Priestly editors would disturb their own original list of festivals, drop their own firstfruits passage, and replace it with an HS firstfruits passage that contained a ritual contradicting the sacrificial laws of PT as presented in Numbers 28?[7]

On the other hand, if we assume that PT was the earlier school, the course of events may be explained without difficulty. The original PT festival list of Leviticus 23 was at first similar in form and contents to Numbers 28–29, also a PT creation. The HS authors, in constructing their legal code, the Holiness Code, sought to include in it festival legislation. The

7. The contention of Kuenen (*Hexateuch,* 99 n. 40), and similarly Baentsch (*Exodus-Leviticus*), and Elliger (*Leviticus* [HAT; Tübingen, 1966]), that the reference to a burnt offering and a sin offering in vv. 18–19 resulted from a later (possibly mistaken) interpolation, is reasonable. But removing these alleged additions only sharpens the contradiction between the passage in Numbers, which prescribes burnt offerings for this day, and the instructions in Leviticus, which command two sheep as a sacrifice of well-being. Possibly the addition was intended to try to cover up this contradiction.

earlier PT writings included two scrolls containing directions about the festivals:[8] one was composed of the list of festivals known as מקראי קדש ("sacred occasions") and a synopsis of the theme and obligations of each, while the other (Numbers 28–29) specified the additional sacrifices to be offered on each occasion. Since the Holiness Code is directed primarily toward the nation as a whole, the first scroll, which dealt with the general theme of each festival without attention to the details of sacrifices, was the appropriate choice for inclusion in the Holiness Code. Before its inclusion, though, the PT festivals scroll underwent a process of adaptation and redaction intended to bring it into conformity with new practices that had been accepted by HS but were unknown to PT.[9] HS had introduced the ritual of the wave offering of the sheaf and its accompanying sacrifice, and the ritual of the wave offering of the two loaves and its sacrifice (which differed from the sacrifices for the firstfruits festival prescribed by PT), as well as the taking of the "Four Kinds" and their use in the rejoicing before the Lord on the feast of Tabernacles. Since their innovations regarding Tabernacles did not contradict the PT laws and the description of that festival came last in the PT list, the HS editors could avoid tampering with the original PT list by simply appending their Tabernacle section to the end of the PT Tabernacles section, after the original conclusion (vv. 37–38). On the other hand, they had to cut the original PT text regarding the firstfruits festival in order to splice in the sections reflecting their innovative practices regarding the wave offerings and the two loaves. This also explains why it is in regard to this festival alone in Leviticus 23 that there are detailed prescriptions regarding sacrifices. Elsewhere, the editors from HS could let stand the original PT references "And you shall bring an offering by fire to the Lord," which are meant to direct the reader to Numbers 28-29, as indicated by the conclusion of the festivals list (Lev 23:37): "Bringing offerings by fire to the Lord—burnt offerings, meal offerings, sacrifices, and libations, on each day what is proper to it." Here, however, the HS editors had to change the original PT reference to the sacrifices listed in Num 28:27, because they had a different conception of the sacrificial ritual to be celebrated on this

8. On PT as a collection of scrolls, see Introduction, n. 22.

9. As will be made clear below, the PT scroll of additional sacrifices for festivals, which was not worked into the Holiness Code, was reworked by HS. But, unlike the systematic editing of the festival passage in Leviticus 23, only minor changes were introduced into Numbers 28–29. The difference in the treatment of the two scrolls by the editors is due, we believe, to the late reworking of the section on additional sacrifices as part of the final redaction of the Pentateuch by HS. At that stage, the editors did not introduce major changes into the PT scrolls and instead left in place tensions and contradictions between the Holiness Code and PT, just as they preserved contradictions between other collections of laws. The redaction of Leviticus 23 took place at a much earlier stage in the activity of HS, when its own law code was formed, and it was considered necessary to bring the PT scroll into line with the HS outlook before it could be included in the Holiness Code.

day. Additionally, they had to detail the ritual of the day on which the wave offering of the sheaf was performed, as this is nowhere described in Numbers 28.

What was the original text of the Priestly description of the firstfruits festival that was presented in the PT version of Leviticus 23? Based on the parallel section in Numbers 28, the following surmise may be ventured: "On the Day of the firstfruits, when you bring a new offering to the Lord upon your weeks, you shall observe a sacred occasion; you shall not perform any manner of work, and you shall bring an offering by fire to the Lord."

Did the HS editors omit this passage entirely, or did they possibly try to integrate part of it into their own firstfruits passage? An examination of the present text—Lev 23:21—will reveal a relic of the original passage. Analysis of the verse yields the following elements:

1. וקראתם בעצם היום הזה
2. מקרא קדש יהיה לכם כל מלאכת עבודה לא תעשו
3. חקת עולם בכל מושבתיכם לדרתיכם

1. On that same day you shall hold a celebration;
2. it shall be a sacred occasion for you; you shall not work at your occupations.
3. This is an eternal law in all your settlements throughout your generations.

The first and third elements of this verse reappear elsewhere in the chapter in sections coming from HS (see 23:14, 41). On the other hand, the second element is quite characteristic of the PT sections of both Numbers 28–29 and this chapter (see Num 28:18, 25, 26; 29:1, 7, 12; and cf. Lev 23:7, 8, 24, 25, 35), while it is lacking in the HS Tabernacles passage.

The composite nature of this verse is further attested by its stylistic roughness, especially noticeable in the transition between the first and second elements.[10] If the first and third elements of the verse indeed come from HS, while the second element is derived from PT, then this verse itself is evidence for the lateness of HS relative to PT. For if PT were the later school, we would have to say that the second element was a Priestly gloss on the original verse. But a characteristic of editorial glosses is that they may be removed without disturbing the logical order of the original sentence. In this verse, however, if the second element is removed, there remains וקראתם בעצם היום הזה חקת עולם בכל מושבתיכם לדרתיכם ("On that same day you shall hold a celebration; this is an eternal law in all your settlements throughout your generations"), which is unreadable. On the other hand, the assumption that HS is later than PT and that the HS edi-

10. The composite nature of the verse and its stylistic roughness are reflected in the Septuagint and the Syriac version, which attempt to resolve this difficulty in different ways.

tors took the PT formula and surrounded it with their own formulas can provide an explanation for the formation of this verse.[11]

Let us now examine the Day of Atonement passage (Lev 23:26–32). Comparison with the parallel passage in Num 28:7–11 reveals that all the elements present in Numbers—the date, the injunction to afflict oneself, the prohibition of all work, and the instructions regarding the offering of additional sacrifices—are present here, phrased almost identically, if in a somewhat different order. Of course, in keeping with the differing intentions of the two passages, in place of the detailed description of the additional sacrifices in Numbers 28, there is in Leviticus only an allusion to the sacrifices in the phrase, "And you shall bring an offering by fire to the Lord" (v. 27), as is the case with the feast of Unleavened Bread, the first day of the seventh month, and the first Tabernacles passage (23:8, 25, 36). The elements paralleling Numbers are concentrated in vv. 27, 28a, while vv. 28aβ–32 have no parallel in Numbers. On the other hand, these last verses exhibit linguistic elements characteristic of those elements of the chapter that are of HS origin (בעצם היום הזה ["on that same day"] vv. 14, 21, 28, 29, 30; חקת עולם לדרתיכם["an eternal law throughout your generations"] vv. 14, 21, 31, 41). Moreover, the reference to "cutting off" in the first person (v. 30), "I will cause that person to perish from among his people," is a departure from the more personal type usually found in PT, but in line with HS terminology (Lev 17:10, 20:3, 6; see Introduction, n. 2). Especially instructive is the comparison of Lev 23:29–30 with 17:9–10. Both describe the "cutting off" as an impersonal process: "That man shall be cut off from his people"; "Any person . . . shall be cut off from his kin"; in immediate juxtaposition, both present first-person warnings: "I will set my face against the person . . . and I will cut him off from among his kin"; "I will cause that person to perish from among his people.

In light of the above, we are led to the conclusion that the Day of Atonement passage in Leviticus 23 is composed of materials originating in two different schools. The beginning of the passage is drawn from PT, as is demonstrated by comparison with Num 29:7 and with other materials in Leviticus 23 that belong to PT The second part of the passage—vv. 28aβ–32—originated in HS, as is demonstrated by its linguistic similarities to other passages produced by that school. As for which was the original text and which represents the additions, the answer is clear: the basic law presented in the beginning specifies the date of the holiday and its special observances, while the following verses, added by HS, essentially expand on and reinforce the instructions offered earlier. So the analysis of this

11. Baentsch (ad loc.), Elliger (ad loc.), and Cholewinski (*Heiligkeitsgesetz,* 92) recognized that the middle element of v. 21 originates in the basic substratum of Leviticus 23, while the preceding and following elements originate in a later stratum. They explained this phenomenon, however, according to their own presuppositions.

passage, too, leads to the conclusion that HS editors took PT materials and reworked them in accordance with their own ideas and style. The examination of the structure of Leviticus 23 shows the priority of PT over HS. (This argument is elaborated and supported with linguistic verification in Excursus 1.) Additional points related to this opinion will be found in the detailed discussion of the festival legislation.

THE SABBATH AND FESTIVAL LAWS IN PT AND HS

Leviticus 23 will serve as the primary axis for our analysis of the Sabbath and festival laws in PT and HS. From there we will broaden our view. Our first step is to examine the opening section of the chapter, the Sabbath passage (vv. 1–3).

The Sabbath Laws

In Lev 23:2 we find a kind of title for the list of festivals:

מועדי ה׳ אשר תקראו אתם מקראי קדש אלה הם מועדי

This title recurs (with slight differences) in v. 4, which opens the next section, regarding the Passover and the feast of Unleavened Bread (23:4–8). This difficulty, which was already noticed by the talmudic sages and medieval commentators (who attempted to deal with it in their own way),[12] brought several critical commentators to realize that the Sabbath passage was not originally part of this chapter but an addition.[13] It seems that this conclusion is correct and that the "short" list of festivals belonging to PT which underlies the present chapter began with the Passover section and did not include the Sabbath. The probable reason for this was that the list was intended to catalogue those days which were מקראי קדש, but the Sabbath was not conceived by PT as a מקרא קדש. This distinction is borne out by the list of additional sacrifices in Numbers 28–29, in which the Sabbath was included because of the additional sacrifice brought on this day. However, unlike the other festivals, the Sabbath is not there called a מקרא קדש (see Num 8:9–10).

We can reconstruct the original introduction to the list of festivals in Leviticus 23 as follows:

(1) וידבר ה׳ אל משה לאמר: (2A) דבר אל בני ישראל ואמרת
אלהם (4) אלה מועדי ה׳ מקראי קדש אשר תקראו אתם במועדם.

12. See *Sifra Emor,* beginning of chap. 10, followed by Rashi (Lev 23:4) and Nahmanides (Lev 23:2); cf. Abravanel (first question on the festivals passage).

13. See, e.g., the commentaries of Dillmann, Baentsch, Noth, and Elliger.

If this is correct, the editorial addition includes v. 2b:

מועדי ה׳ אשר תקראו אתם מקראי קדש אלה הם מועדי

and v. 3, about the Sabbath. The wording of the additional title in v. 2b is essentially similar to the original introduction in v. 4, the main difference being in the formula concluding the additional title: אלה הם מועדי. Don Isaac Abravanel had noticed in the fifteenth century that this was strange:

> And what is the meaning of that which it says: "These are my fixed times"? It is an obvious repetition, also the entire section is in the third person, and only this phrase is presented in His name, may He be blessed, as if He were speaking for Himself.[14]

It is precisely this deviation from the usual stylistic conventions used in this chapter that discloses the identity of the editors who added this passage: in the PT stratum, God when speaking to the people, speaks in the third person, while God's direct address in HS is characterized by the use of the first person. (See Introduction, n. 2.) The term מועדי in Lev 23:2b calls to mind the way in which the Sabbath is referred to in HS as שבתתי ("My Sabbaths," Lev 19:3, 30; 26:2).[15] Since the first section of this chapter has shown that HS reworked the earlier PT list in this same section, the logical conclusion is that the Sabbath passage too was added by HS. This explains the use of expressions characteristic of that school.

The form שבתתי appears also in Exod 31:13, a verse that is shown to be of HS origins by the closing words אני ה׳ מקדשכם ("I the Lord have consecrated you").[16] Notice that there follows in the Sabbath passage in Exodus 31 the following sentence: "Six days may work be done, but on the seventh day there shall be a Sabbath of complete rest, holy to the Lord" (31:15a). This recalls the language of the Sabbath passage in Leviticus 23: "Six days work may be done, but on the seventh day there shall be a Sabbath of complete rest, proclaimed holy." Similar wording is used in the Sabbath passage in Exodus 35: "Six days work may be done, but on the seventh day you shall have a Sabbath of complete rest, holy to the Lord"

14. Actually, this is not completely accurate. There are other verses in this chapter in which God addresses the nation in the first person ("which I give to you," v. 10; "I am the Lord your God," vv. 22, 43; "And I will destroy," v. 30; "I caused to dwell . . . I took out," v. 43). All these verses, as will be shown later, are the work of HS.

15. Cf. also the construction "They will observe all My festivals and sanctify all My Sabbaths" (Ezek 44:24). The linguistic and stylistic similarity between Ezekiel and HS is well known. (See Introduction, n. 3.)

16. See A. Klostermann, *Der Pentateuch* (Leipzig, 1893) 377; A. Dillmann, *Die Bücher Numeri, Deuteronomium und Josua* (KeH; Leipzig, 1886) 640; S. R. Driver, *An Introduction to the Literature of the Old Testament* (Edinburgh, 1913) 59, 151; M. Haran, "Behind the Scenes of History: Determining the Date of the Priestly Source," *JBL* 100 (1981) 329 n. 12.

(35:2a). Are these linguistic similarities coincidental, or do they indicate deeper substantive connections between these passages?

In order to answer this question, more needs to be said about the place and intent of the Sabbath passages of Exodus 31 and 35. As A. Toeg has shown, these two passages are part of a complex literary format, arranged in chiastic order, in which they serve as links between the Priestly materials dealing with the Tabernacle (Exodus 25–31; 35–40), on the one hand, and the passages on the breaking and renewal of the covenant in Exodus 32–34, on the other, which are from the JE source.[17] This means that the Sabbath passage in 31:12–17, in which Moses is commanded to instruct the people regarding Sabbath observance, and the parallel passage in 35:1–3, in which the command is fulfilled, both originated in the school that edited and arranged the Tabernacle material, the golden calf story, and the covenant renewal in conjunction with each other. Which school was responsible for this redactional activity? Not only have we found clear marks of HS at the beginning of the Sabbath passage of Exod 31:13, but also the complementary passage in Exodus 35, according to the Septuagint, concludes with אני ה׳ ("I am the Lord"), the distinguishing concluding formula of HS. Since there is no reason to doubt the authenticity of this version, we can consider the chiastic format to be complete: the first Sabbath passage begins "That I the Lord have consecrated you" and its complement concludes "I am the Lord," in good HS style.[18] An additional indication that these passages originated in HS is the strange connection of death by execution with "cutting off" in Exod 31:14,[19] which is elsewhere found only in HS (Lev 20:2–3).

Why did HS juxtapose the Sabbath injunctions to the commandments regarding the construction of the Tabernacle? There is a great deal of merit in the rabbinic and medieval suggestions that the juxtaposition emphasizes that work for the sanctuary does not supersede the Sabbath.[20] However, there also seems to be an expression here of the tendency of HS to magnify the sanctity of the Sabbath and to place it on the same level as the sanctuary. This tendency is expressed in the twice-mentioned formula "You shall keep my Sabbaths and venerate my sanctuary" (Lev 19:30; 26:2), in which HS lists the Sabbath before the sanctuary. It seems that the desire to elevate the importance of the Sabbath and to stress the importance of its observance were what led the HS editors to add the Sab-

17. A. Toeg, *Lawgiving at Sinai* (Jerusalem, 1977) 146 (Hebrew).

18. Cf. Lev 20:7–8. The possibility that the Septuagint version attests to the origin of Exod 35:3 in HS was raised by Dillmann, *Numeri,* 398.

19. The use of the verb חלל, characteristic of HS, in Exod 31:14 provides further indication that the passage is the work of that school. The parallel verb in PT is מעל (see J. Milgrom, *Cult and Conscience* [Leiden, 1976] 86–88 and n. 303).

20. *Mekhilta de-Rashbi,* ed. Epstein-Melamed, p. 222; Rashi, Rashbam, Ibn Ezra, and Seforno in their commentaries on Exod 31:13.

bath passage to the PT list of festivals, in order to teach that the Sabbath is of no less importance than any of the other holidays of the year and is also among the days of "proclaimed holiness" (מקראי קדש, Lev 23:3). The highest expression of this view is the designation of the Sabbath as a sign of the holiness with which the Lord sanctified Israel (Exod 31:13).[21]

Another passage in Exodus that deals with the Sabbath and with its forbidden labors is the story of the manna in Exodus16. Most scholars believe that the chapter, as it presently stands, is comprised of Priestly material and of older material from JE.[22] When we examine the "Priestly" materials in this chapter, however, we find linguistic indicators similar to those of the HS style. For example, the expression שבתון שבת קדש לה' ("a day of rest, a holy Sabbath of the Lord") in Exod 16:23 also appeared in Exod 31:15 and 35:2.

Also worthy of notice is the linguistic and ideational similarity between Exod 16:32 and Lev 23:43. But special attention should be paid to the formula: "And you shall know that I am the Lord your God" (Exod 16:12).[23] This combination appears in three other places in Exodus 19, and in all of them it may be demonstrated that the formula was added by editors, who are disclosed by their style as being members of HS.[24] All

21. This idea is presented in identical terms in Ezek 20:12, 20.

22. For a summary of the literature, see B. S. Childs, *The Book of Exodus* (4th ed.; OTL; Philadelphia, 1974) 274–75.

23. For the ideational significance of this construction, see W. Zimmerli, *I am Yahweh* (trans. D. W. Scott; Atlanta, 1982) 29ff.; Haran, "Behind the Scenes," 329 n. 12. See Moshe Greenberg, "Narrative and Redactional Art in the Plague Pericope (Exodus 7–11)," in *Bible and Jewish History: Studies Dedicated to the Memory of Jacob Liver* (Jerusalem, 1972) 248.

24. Exod 6:2–8 displays marked linguistic similarity to PT usage but includes the term סבלת מצרים, which is found in JE exclusively. This difficulty has exercised interpreters; see M. Greenberg, *Understanding Exodus* (New York, 1969) 149 n. 1, following Dillmann. The terminology is understandable when it is recognized that the passage was the work of HS editors who borrowed from PT and JE, blending the earlier elements while prefacing and concluding the passage with their characteristic formula, "I am the Lord," which here indicates the revelation of the Tetragrammaton to Moses. The affinity of this passage to HS has been noted by Klostermann, *Pentateuch,* 377; Dillmann, *Numeri*, 640; Driver, *Introduction*, 151; Haran, "Behind the Scenes," 8 n. 13. The account of the plague of locusts, in whose introduction (Exod 10:1–2), the formulation that "you may know that I am the Lord" appears, differs structurally from the general plan of the plague stories in the JE tradition of which it is part. In general, the description of each plague begins with God's command to Moses that he go and threaten Pharaoh (Exod 7:9–18, 26–29; 8:16–19; 9:1–4, 13–18). The fulfillment of this command—Moses' dialogues with Pharaoh—is not described, probably just to avoid unnecessary duplication. (The Samaritan Pentateuch corrects this "oversight" by mechanical repetition.) In contrast, the account of the locust plague presents the threat in the dialogue between Moses and Aaron and Pharaoh which includes bargaining over the terms of release. Seemingly, the preceding divine command to Moses was omitted in this case to avoid needless repetition. The editors took advantage of this vacuum to insert two introductory verses that do not relate directly to the locusts, but instead explain Pharaoh's exceptional obduracy. See M. Greenberg, "Narrative and Redactional Art in the Plague Pericope (Exodus 7–11)" (Hebrew), in *Bible and Jewish History: Studies Dedicated to the Memory*

this leads to the conclusion that it was in fact HS that took the ancient manna story from the JE tradition and expanded it, adding matters of belief important to its viewpoint, particularly Sabbath observance.

Yet another discussion of labors forbidden on the Sabbath may be found in Num 15:32–36, the incident of the woodgatherer. The relationship between the story of the woodgatherer and HS is indicated by the similarities between the former and the story of the blasphemer in Lev 24:10–14, and we have already demonstrated that Numbers 15 in its entirety originated with HS (Excursus 1, n. 21).

All the Sabbath passages mentioned up to this point have been shown to originate with HS, but there are two other short passages dealing with the Sabbath that are part of PT. The first is the concluding section of the creation story in Gen 1:1–2:3. The seventh day is portrayed there as a holy and blessed day on which God rested from his labors. But the name "Sabbath" is not mentioned, nor is there any command forbidding the performance of human labors. The schematic format of this passage, its measured style, and the indications of its antiquity[25] all attest to its PT provenance. The second passage dealing with the Sabbath belonging to PT is part of the list of additional sacrifices for the various holidays (Num 28:9–10), in which the Sabbath sacrifices are detailed.

Comparison of the attitudes toward the Sabbath in the two schools yields a very interesting observation. While HS goes to great lengths to stress the importance of Sabbath observance, threatens those who desecrate it with stringent punishments, and goes into the details of forbidden labors,[26] PT nowhere explicitly forbids labors on the Sabbath. The differences in approach become clearest when we contrast the two Sabbath passages in Lev 23:3 and Num 28:9–10. The Leviticus passage, which belongs to HS, is completely concerned with forbidden labors and has nothing to say about any additional sacrifices,[27] whereas the PT passage in Numbers deals only with sacrifices and makes no mention of forbidden labors, despite the fact that throughout the same pericope the labors forbidden on

---

of Jacob Liver (Jerusalem, 1972) 73. The Samaritan version, in keeping with its usual habit, inserts the threat as spoken by God. The last place where the expression appears, Exod 29:46, ends with the words "I am the Lord their God," which clearly demonstrate the affinity of the verse and of the entire passage that the verse concludes (29:38–46) with HS. On the secondary nature of the passage, see Kuenen, *Hexateuch,* 370. The relationship to HS is noted by Klostermann, *Pentateuch,* 377; Dillmann, *Numeri*, 640.

25. See M. Weinfeld, "G-d the Creator in Gen. 1 and in the Prophecy of Second Isaiah" (Hebrew), *Tarbiz* 37 (1968) 105–32.

26. Such as kindling fire (Exod 35:3) and wood gathering (Num 15:32–36).

27. This was already noted by Abravanel: "Why is the sacrifice of the Sabbath not mentioned, unlike all the other festivals, where it says, 'And you shall make an offering by fire to the Lord'—why not say this for the Sabbath?" (ad loc., second question on festival passage).

the various festivals are mentioned along with their sacrifices.[28] Additionally, HS compares the holiness of the Sabbath with that of the sanctuary and grants the Sabbath pride of place in the list of מקראי קדש, whereas according to PT the Sabbath is not a day of מקרא קדש at all.

Passover and the Feast of Unleavened Bread

The passage dealing with the Passover sacrifice and the feast of Unleavened Bread in Lev 23:5–8 is very similar in language and style to its parallel in Num 28:16–25. On the basis of this similarity, we may posit that it belongs to PT. As already noted, this passage stood at the head of the original PT list of festivals on which the present Leviticus 23 is based. Aside from these two lists of festivals, there are three further "Priestly" pericopes that deal with Passover and with the feast of Unleavened Bread.

The first such passage is Exod 12:1–20. In Excursus 1, we ascribed this literary unit in its entirety to HS, on the basis of linguistic and ideational indicators; however, we did not pay attention there to its structure and components. This passage comprises three subunits: vv. 1–14, 15–17, and 18–20. The first subunit deals with Passover; the second and third with the feast of Unleavened Bread. The repetition of the laws of the latter festival is worthy of note. On the one hand, vv. 15–17 might be viewed as the original text, with the final subunit being a later addition; alternatively, it might be posited that vv. 18–20 were earlier and that the subunit vv. 15–17 was a later gloss, bracketed by the repetitive resumption (*Wiederaufnahme*) of "For all your generations, an eternal statute" in vv. 14 and 17.

Examination of vv. 18–20, however, tilts the scales in favor of the first possibility. The opening word בראשון already indicates relative lateness, as the abbreviated dating notation (בראשון instead of בחדש הראשון) is found, outside the Pentateuch, only in Ezekiel and in the early postexilic prophetic books.[29] Ezekiel dates the feast of Unleavened Bread as in v. 18: "on

28. See Num 28:18, 25, 26; 29:1, 7, 12, 35. The New Moon is presented in terms similar to the Sabbath in that an additional sacrifice is prescribed but labor is not forbidden.

29. Ezekiel always uses the short form of dating, except for the date of the beginning of the siege of Jerusalem—"in the tenth month" (Ezek 24:1). The short form is used by Haggai (Hag 1:15; 2:1, 10, 18), but in the beginning of the book the long form is employed. In Zechariah, the dates of the prophecies are given in the long form, but the prophet himself, when speaking, uses the short date (Zech 7:5; 8:19). There is evidence for the use of short dates in Joel's statement גשם מורה ומלקוש בראשון (Joel 2:23). For the location of Joel in the beginning of the Restoration period, see G. W. Ahlström, *Joel and the Temple Cult of Jerusalem* (Leiden, 1971) 111ff. The short form appears in the Pentateuch as early as the flood narrative (Gen 8:5, 13), alongside the long form (Gen 7:11; 8:4, 14). As noted by S. E. Loewenstamm ("The Flood" [Heb.], in *The N. H. Tur-Sinai Volume* [Jerusalem, 1960]

the first, on the fourteenth day of the month" (Ezek 45:21). The similarity between these texts is not merely linguistic; there is the important fact that both begin the celebration of the feast of Unleavened Bread on the fourteenth day of the first month. That is, in both there is complete fusion of the first day of Unleavened Bread with the day of the Passover sacrifice. In the PT passages of Numbers 28 and Leviticus 23, there is complete distinction between the two: the Passover sacrifice is on the fourteenth, while the feast of Unleavened Bread begins on the fifteenth. A first step toward fusion occurs in the first part of Exodus12, as the term היום הזה ("this day") at the end of the Passover passage (12:14) and at the end of the first Unleavened Bread passage (12:17) seems to relate to the same extended day, which began on the afternoon of the fourteenth of Nisan and lasted until the evening following the fifteenth. In the second Unleavened Bread passage and in Ezekiel, full, explicit identity between these two observances has already been achieved. This fusion requires[30] that the seven days of Unleavened Bread be counted from "evening to evening," as is indeed specified by Exod 12:18.

This special reckoning is found in only one other place in the Torah, namely, at the end of the laws of the Day of Atonement in Leviticus 23: "From evening to evening you shall observe this your Sabbath" (Lev 23:32). It seems that this verse provides an additional tool to understand the second Unleavened Bread passage in Exodus 12. Above it was proposed that the Day of Atonement passage in Lev 23:26–32 is based on a PT text that was expanded by HS. Now v. 31, immediately preceding the one that mentions "evening to evening," ends with the formula חקת עלם לדרתיכם בכל משבתיכם ("It is an eternal law for all your generations in all your settlements"), a formula often used to conclude HS pericopes. (See Excursus 1.) But then comes v. 32, which recapitulates (with slight changes in wording) the laws prescribed earlier (cessation of labor and afflictions) and adds only that they are to be in force "from evening to evening." It seems that this verse is an editorial addition[31] intended to guard the proper observance of the holy day by specifying the time of its onset.[32] The relationship between this verse and the previous passage is very similar to the relationship between the final Unleavened Bread passage (Exod

16–17), the date references were added in the final stage of recension of this passage, so the appearance of signs of late linguistic usage is not surprising.

30. Being that the festival begins on the evening after the fourteenth, at which time the Passover sacrifice is slaughtered.

31. So also M. Noth, *Leviticus* (trans. J. E. Anderson; OTL; London, 1968); and Elliger, *Leviticus*.

32. The redactors, it seems, wanted to emphasize that the festival lasts from evening to evening rather than from morning to morning. The rabbis deduced from this verse that the days of Sabbaths and festivals should "extend" somewhat into the surrounding weekdays so as to "add from the secular to the sacred"; see *Sifra Emor* 14:6.

12:18–20) and its predecessor (Exod 12:15–17). In both cases, the laws of the festival are repeated using somewhat different wording—מחמצת in place of חמץ—while the major innovation is the reckoning from "evening to evening." In light of this similarity and of the closeness to Ezekiel, it seems that there is here the work of late editors, most probably also of HS affiliation.[33] In other words, in Exod 12:1–20 there are two strata of HS activity: the first, more ancient stratum in vv. 1–17, and an editorial addition in vv. 18–20. This is true as well for the Day of Atonement passage in Leviticus 23. The chiastic structure of the addition is worthy of note: the command to eat unleavened bread (12:18), the prohibition of leaven (v. 19), the prohibition of leaven (v. 20a), the command to eat unleavened bread (v. 20b). At the core of the passage stands the warning against being "cut off," directed toward the resident alien and the citizen. This too constitutes an innovation in relation to the first unleavened bread passage, in which the warning about being "cut off" is directed toward the Israelite citizen alone.[34]

Let us now examine two additional Passover passages, Exod 12:43–49 and Num 9:1–14, which end in similar fashion: "There shall be one law for the citizen and for the stranger who dwells among you" (Exod 12:49); "There shall be one law for you, whether stranger or citizen of the country" (Num 9:14). The principle of the equality of stranger and citizen is widespread throughout the Holiness Code,[35] while in PT it appears only once, in Lev 16:29, a late editorial addition, as will be demonstrated below. The presence of this idea may therefore serve as an indication of HS provenance. Moreover, in the Holiness Code the following declaration occurs: "You shall have one standard for stranger and citizen alike: for I am the Lord your God" (Lev 24:22). Combining this statement with the concluding lines of the two Passover passages (in Exodus 12 and Numbers 9) yields a proclamation of the equality of the stranger in justice, Torah, and law. Just such a formula appears in Num 15:15–16, in the middle of a chapter that, as was noted above, is of HS provenance.

Additional evidence for the HS origin of the laws of the Second Passover in Numbers 9 may be found in the expression חטאו ישא האיש ההוא (9:13). The concept of "bearing one's sin" occurring here is found only in HS passages.[36] In the narrative section that precedes the laws of the Sec-

33. See Baentsch, *Exodus-Leviticus,* on Exod 12:18.

34. An additional innovation is the extension of the requirement to eat unleavened bread to "all your settlements" (Exod 12:20). If we are correct in surmising that this passage was composed at the time of the Babylonian exile, the special emphasis on the observance "in all your settlements" bears obvious significance.

35. See Lev 17:8, 10, 12, 13, 15; 18:26; 19:33, 34; 20:2; 22:18; 24:22. On the scope of this idea and its limitations, see J. Milgrom, "Religious Conversion and the Revolt Model for the Reformation of Israel," *JBL* 101 (1982) 169–76.

36. See Lev 19:17; 20:20; 22:9; 24:15; Num 18:22, 32 (on the HS provenance of Numbers

ond Passover, there appear two linguistic indicators of lateness, both having to do with the calendar. The first is the expression בארבעה עשר יום בחדש הזה (9:3) instead of the usual לחדש. This usage is found in the works edited after the exile.[37] Later (v. 5) the date occurs as בראשון בארבעה עשר יום לחדש בין הערבים ("in the first, on the fourteenth day of the month, at twilight"). As noted above in the additional Unleavened Bread passage at Exod 12:18, the initial word is indicative of exilic or postexilic usage.[38]

The outcome of this analysis, then, is two PT units that include Passover and the feast of Unleavened Bread (Lev 23:5-8 and Num 28:16-25), and three HS passages that deal with the Passover sacrifice and with eating unleavened bread (Exod 12:1-20, 43-49; Num 9:9-14). Comparison of the PT and HS passages is instructive. PT makes cursory mention of the Passover sacrifice and its appointed time without going into details of its performance. Also briefly noted is the command to eat unleavened bread for seven days, but nothing is said of the prohibition against eating leaven! Similarly, there is no reference to the relationship between Passover and unleavened bread and the events of the exodus.[39] The only detailed discussion in PT is related to the additional sacrifices of the feast of Unleavened Bread. On the other hand, HS, apparently wishing to stress the historical dimension of Passover and the feast of Unleavened Bread, deals with many of the specifics of the Passover sacrifice, defines who is required to celebrate it, establishes a second date for making good the Passover if for some reason one was unable to offer it at the appointed time, and punishes by "cutting off" anyone who does not have sufficient reason for failing to celebrate the Passover. The customs associated with the sacrifice are grounded in the story of the plague of the firstborn. HS also deals at length with the requirement to eat unleavened bread. It strongly stresses the commandment to remove all leavened foods from one's premises, the injunction against eating leaven, and the "cutting off" penalty for those who do eat the forbidden food (Exod 12:15,19; Num 9:13). According to HS, the commandment to eat unleavened bread preceded the exodus; it was given to Israel at the same time they received

18, see Excursus 1). PT uses נשא עון only (Exod 28:38, 43; Lev 5:1, 17; 10:17), while HS has both נשא עון and נשא חטא (Lev 17:16; 19:8; 20:17, 19; Num 18:1). The latter is true of Ezekiel as well (see Ezek 4:4, 5, 6; 14:10; 23:49; 44:10).

37. See 1 Kgs 12:33; Esth 3:12; Ezra 10:9; 2 Chr 3:2, as well as Ezek 45:20 (MT). In the Pentateuch, this formula otherwise appears only in Num 10:11, at the beginning of a passage the lateness of which may also be indicated by the repeated use of the word דגל; see B. A. Levine, "Research in the Priestly Source: The Linguistic Factor" (Hebrew), *Eretz Yisrael* 16 (1982) 127-29.

38. Though v. 1 uses full dating, Haggai and Zechariah (see n. 29 above) show that both forms may be employed in the same work.

39. Since the name פסח may be explained in light of the apotropaic nature of the sacrifice without any reference to the exodus. See S. E. Loewenstamm, *The Tradition of the Exodus in its Development* (Heb.) (3rd ed.; Jerusalem, 1983) 84-90.

the instructions regarding the Passover sacrifice. While PT maintains the sharp distinction between the Passover and Unleavened Bread festivals, HS displays a trend toward fusion which reaches its climax in the final Unleavened Bread passage in Exod 12:18–20 and in Ezekiel 45.

Firstfruits Festivals

After the Passover and Unleavened Bread passage, there appears in Leviticus 23 a unit that includes the laws of the wave offering of the sheaf and of the two loaves (Lev 23:9–22). We have already demonstrated that this unit originated in HS and conjectured that HS used it to replace the older firstfruits passage of PT. We will now examine more closely the different treatments of the firstfruits rituals in PT and HS.

There are three texts relevant to the understanding of PT's approach to the firstfruits ceremonies: the passage in the list of festivals in Num 28:26–31, and two laws, located in a PT passage, that relate to the "grain offering of choice products" (Lev 2:11–12) and the firstfruits grain offering (Lev 2:14–16). The firstfruits entry in the festivals list in Numbers 28 opens as follows: "On the day of the firstfruits, when you bring an offering of new grain to the Lord upon your weeks. . . . " The fact that the term "day" (יום) of firstfruits is used, instead of "festival" (חג) of firstfruits, implies that there was no requirement to assemble at the Temple on that day.[40] The term demonstrates that the day was distinguished by the fact that it was the occasion on which the firstfruits were brought to the sanctuary, this being described as "an offering of new grain." The term "upon your weeks" (בשבעתיכם) seems to refer to some ritual that is not explained at all. The opening of the firstfruits passage is distinctly different from the passages about other appointed times in the pericope, each of which is given a clear and specific date. Clarification of the strange term "upon your weeks" would possibly shed light on the lack of a date for this festival. The author of these laws doubtless assumed that his audience understood the matter of the weeks quite clearly and therefore made no effort to explain it or offer details. Indeed, other legal-ritual collections in the Pentateuch (the shorter Book of the Covenant and Deuteronomy) do mention a festival of the firstfruits of the wheat harvest, which is celebrated at the end of a seven-week count from the beginning of the cutting of the standing grain (Exod 34:22; Deut 16:9–10). If the reference "upon your weeks" refers to this practice, the reason why no precise date is given for the firstfruits festival is because the beginning of the harvest, when the festival takes place, comes at a different time each year.

40. On the חג (festival) as a day of pilgrimage, see M. Haran, *Temples and Temple Service in Ancient Israel* (Oxford, 1978) 289ff.

What is the nature of the "new grain offering" (מנחה חדשה) brought on this day? In PT there are two laws that deal with the first-processed offering and the firstfruits offering. One says that the first-processed offering (קרבן ראשית) was to be baked leavened and therefore was not to be offered upon the altar, since leaven may not be burnt on the altar (Lev 2:11–12). The second law describes the ingredients of a firstfruits offering (מנחת בכורים): "new ears parched with fire, grits of the fresh grain"; a "token portion" (אזכרתה) of it is to be turned into smoke (Lev 2:14–16). Is the "new grain offering" offered on the day of the firstfruits and the "offering of choice products" identical, or are we to identify the "new grain offering" with the "firstfruits grain offering"? The term "upon your weeks" helps clarify this matter, as noted above. The "new ears parched with fire" are the first barley,[41] as the barley ripens early and is harvested at the time of Passover, which is celebrated in the month of Abib (אביב). The "new offering," however, was not brought at the time of the barley harvest, but at the end of the seven-week period counting from the beginning of the harvest, which comes long after the month of Abib is over. It could not, therefore, have been made of parched spring grain. On the other hand, it could definitely have been made of wheat, which is harvested at about that time. If the "new offering" indeed has anything to do with either of the offerings mentioned in Leviticus 2, it can only be the first, the קרבן ראשית.

Collation of the PT sources yields the following picture: at the beginning of the barley harvest in the month of Abib, the Day of the Firstfruits was celebrated. Farmers would bring a firstfruits offering composed of parched spring grain and grits (see 2 Kgs 4:42). Seven weeks after the beginning of the barley harvest, the Day of Firstfruits was celebrated. On this day, a "new grain offering" was brought, seemingly composed of wheat flour from the earliest wheat harvested, it being the beginning of the wheat harvest. It seems likely that the "new grain offering" is identical with the "first-processed offering" (קרבן ראשית) mentioned in Leviticus 2; that is, it was baked leavened and not consumed on the altar.[42] PT does not attempt to turn these popular practices into a mandatory procedure, as is indicated by the wording of the firstfruits passage, "If you bring a firstfruits offering" (Lev 2:14), which seems to say quite straightforwardly that the offering was understood as being voluntary.[43] Similarly, the wording of the beginning of the entry regarding the Day of Firstfruits, "when you bring an offering of new grain to the Lord" (Num

41. See also J. Milgrom, *Studies in Cultic Theology and Terminology* (Leiden, 1983) 148 n. 28, especially his inference from the absence of any reference to semolina (סלת).

42. This identification is supported by comparison of this passage with the firstfruits law in HS, which prescribes for this day a wave offering of two leavened loaves (Lev 23:17).

43. So Ibn Ezra ad loc., contrary to the classical rabbinic interpretation.

28:26), is not a command but rather the description of accepted popular practices. In the course of its technical descriptions of the various kinds of meal offerings in Leviticus, PT does provide details regarding the composition and procedures of the various firstfruits offerings. But the passage that deals with the Day of Firstfruits itself mentions the counting of weeks and the bringing of the meal offering quite briefly, and concentrates on cataloging the various additional sacrifices and accompanying offerings mandatory on that day. Only by inference can it be determined what was the "new grain offering."

Let us now examine the Day of Firstfruits passage in Leviticus 23. The broad range of ritual and linguistic elements present in this passage demonstrates its composite nature. Some scholars have recognized that at the foundation of this passage lies an ancient popular law that preceded the centralization of the cult, commanding as it did all farmers to bring their first produce to the priest at one of the sanctuary cities.[44] According to this ancient law, at the beginning of the barley harvest, the wave offering of the sheaf is brought, and at the end of seven weeks, during the wheat harvest, firstfruit loaves are offered. On the day on which the sheaf is waved, a lamb is presented as a burnt offering, and along with the two loaves, a peace offering of two lambs is to be waved. The change in the type of offering reflects the difference in the purpose and date of the two wave offerings: the sheaf is brought at the beginning of the harvest, and is waved to effect a sympathetic blessing on the harvest to come—"for acceptance on your behalf" (לרצנכם, Lev 23:11);[45] therefore, the sheaves are waved on the stalk, as a symbol of the flourishing grain.[46] The burnt offering that accompanies the sheaf also seems to be intended to appease God and to elicit his mercies and blessing.[47] On the other hand, the wave offering of the two loaves is brought at the end of seven weeks of harvest, and the combination of leavened loaves with a sacrifice of well-being provides evidence that this ritual is intended as thanksgiving for the bounties of the fields.[48]

44. Y. Kaufmann, *A History of the Religion of Israel* (Jerusalem/Tel Aviv, 1960) 1:124; Noth, *Leviticus*, 170; M. Weinfeld, *Deuteronomy and the Deuteronomistic School* (Oxford, 1972) 217ff.

45. Milgrom, *Studies in Cultic Theology*, 151; cf. *Lev. Rabbah* 23:10, ed. Margulies, p. 659; *b. Menaḥot* 62a; Tosafot ad loc. s.v. כדי.

46. This is the simple meaning of the text, rather than the traditional rabbinic view that עמר indicates a measure of volume. For a discussion of the problematics of the rabbinic interpretation, see D. Hoffmann, *Leviticus with Commentary* (Hebrew trans.; 2 vols.; Jerusalem, 1976) ad loc.

47. On this aspect of the burnt offering, see Gen 8:20–21; 1 Sam 7:9; 13:12; 1 Kgs 18:36–38; Jer 14:12. Appeasement of God is also mentioned in the laws regarding the burnt offering in PT (Lev 1:3), but the significance of the burnt offering for PT is different from that popularly attributed to it. I will deal with this issue in detail in chapter 3.

48. This is the composition of the thanksgiving sacrifice in Lev 7:13. Because the wheat

To this basic popular ritual HS added the detailed description of the various sacrifices in vv. 18–19, which is similar, though not identical, to the Day of Firstfruits ritual in Num 28:27–30.[49] Another addition is the command "It shall be a sacred occasion; you shall not work at your occupation" (v. 21), which the first section of this chapter identified as a relic of the original PT passage that has been reworked by HS (see above, p. 12.) HS editors, then, blended the popular law about harvest offerings with earlier PT firstfruits elements, adding their own terminology throughout.[50]

It is difficult to distinguish between the ancient folk elements and the editorial additions of HS in Leviticus 23. The entire unit, however, may be treated as representative of the views held by HS regarding the firstfruits observances. Immediately noticeable is the difference in the attitudes of the two schools toward the firstfruits customs. Unlike PT, the language used here is not descriptive, but specific and normative: "you shall bring . . . you shall count. . . ." Here we find added the ritual of the wave offering of the sheaf, whose purpose (as mentioned previously) is to bring blessings upon the harvest. The wave offering has an additional significance: only after the first part of the harvest is presented to the priest may one partake of the balance of the new harvest. This is fully consonant with the idea expressed by the HS law of fruit being forbidden during the first three years of a tree's life and the jubilation with the fruit of the fourth year (Lev 19:23–25). There, too, permission to eat the previously forbidden produce is related to the promise of blessing to come: "And only in the fifth year may you use its fruit—that its yield to you may be increased: I am the Lord your God." The underlying reason for the prohibition of personal use of the harvest before the first part has been offered to God[51] is the recognition of the Lord's jurisdiction over the land

harvest is still under way at this time, it can reasonably be assumed that the wave offering of the two loaves also bears an element of appeasement and supplication.

49. See Kuenen, *Hexateuch.* As several scholars have noted, this interpolation also led to the addition of the words על שני כבשים in v. 20.

50. Lev 19:23; 25:2; cf. Num 15:2, which, as noted above, is also part of HS.

51. The simple meaning of this instruction is that the fruit of the fourth year be given to the priest; so *Jub.* 7:36 and the *Temple Scroll* 60:3–4 (see Y. Yadin, *The Temple Scroll* [Hebrew edition], vol. 2: *Text and Commentary* [Jerusalem, 1977] 191). Recently, the same notion has been found in the Qumran text known at MMT (*Miqṣat Maᶜaśei Torah* (lines 57–58). See also A. Geiger, *Urschrift und Übersetzungen der Bibel* (Breslau, 1857) 182; C. Albeck, *Das Buch der Jubiläen und die Halacha* (Bericht der Hochshule für die Wissenschaft des Judentums; Berlin, 1930) 32–33; E. Itzchaki, "Jerusalem Targum 'A' and the School of Rabbi Ishmael," *Sidra* 1 (1985) 50 n. 26. Ibn Ezra, too, in his commentary (ad loc.) assigns the fruit of the fourth year to the priest. In the view of *Targum Pseudo-Jonathan,* too, the fourth year fruits are given to the priest, but the owner may redeem them from the priest (see *Tg. Ps.-Jon.* Lev 19:24; Deut 20:6). Both Josephus and the sages, on the other hand, disagree with the interpreters cited above, maintaining instead that the fourth-year fruits are to be consumed by

and its bounty,[52] an idea that lies at the foundation of the HS sabbatical year and jubilee legislation as well.[53]

The Day of Atonement

The next subject of discussion, in keeping with the calendrical order of Leviticus 23, should be the Day of Blasts, but for methodological reasons the Day of Atonement will be dealt with first.

In the preceding textual analysis, it was concluded that the laws of the Day of Atonement (Lev 23:26–32) are composed of three different strata (see above, p. 13, and the discussion of the phrase מערב עד ערב, pp. 20–21). The first stratum is the original PT passage, which has been preserved (with certain modifications) in vv. 26–28aα. The second stratum includes the initial HS addition found in 28aβ (starting: "throughout that day . . ."). The third stratum is v. 32, which was the final addition, for which later editors (also from HS) were responsible. The Day of Atonement and the yearly purification rituals are the subject of other "Priestly" passages. These will also be discussed, with an eye toward identifying their provenance in one or another Priestly school.

The ceremony for the purification of the sanctuary is described in Leviticus 16, which is the concluding chapter of the main corpus of PT. Following the detailed listing of the purification practices (vv. 1–28), commandments are given regarding self-affliction and cessation of labor on the tenth day of the seventh month (vv. 29–31) and instructions regarding the eternal performance of the purification rite (vv. 32–34). The laws regarding self-affliction and the prohibition of labor are worded very much like those parts of the Day of Atonement passage in Leviticus 23, which we have ascribed above to HS.[54] Another indication of the con-

---

their owners in Jerusalem (see Josephus, *Antiquities* 4.227 b; *m. Maʿaser Sheni* 5:2–5; see also the sermons in *Sifre Bemidbar* (ed. Horovitz), 9–10, which take issue with the contention that the fourth-year fruit is given to the priest. For a detailed, up-to-date treatment, see J. M. Baumgarten, "The Law of Hadash," *JJS* 27 (1976) 36–46; and M. Kister, "Some Aspects of Qumranic Halakha" in *Proceedings of the Madrid Congress* (Leiden, 1992) 2:571–88.

52. So Philo, *On the Special Laws* 2.175, 180. Cf. the language of the baraita in *y. Berakhot,* beginning of chap. 10: "It is written: 'The earth is the Lord's and all that it holds'; whoever enjoys anything in the world is guilty of misappropriating divine property, unless the laws allow him to do so." On the concept of God as the owner of the earth and its produce in Semitic societies, see W. Robertson Smith, *The Religion of the Semites* (New York, 1957) 93.

53. The relationship between these laws and the laws of the firstfruits gifts is also indicated by the counting of seven weeks shared by them both. This was first noted by Nahmanides in his commentary on Lev 23:15. The emphasis on the term שבתות, and not שבועות, lends a dimension of holiness to the counting itself.

54. Cf. Lev 16:30 with 23:28, and 16:31 with 23:32a. The ties to HS were noted by Elliger, *Leviticus*, 207.

nection between this passage and HS is the reference to the equality of resident alien and citizen in v. 29, since, as already noted, the subjection of the alien to the commandments of the Torah is one of the hallmarks of this school.[55] It may therefore be concluded that the chiastically structured[56] passage vv. 29–31 originated in HS. Additionally, the following verses (vv. 32–33), which deal with the eternal observance of the purification rituals, display marked linguistic affinity to HS,[57] while making use of terminology clearly different from that used in the beginning of the chapter.[58] The logical conclusion is that while the beginning of the chapter (vv. 1–28) originated in PT, the end was added by HS editors. These editors bracketed their addition with the resumptive repetition of the phrase, "And this shall be to you a law for all time" (v. 29a, and almost identically in v. 34aα). The original PT version of this passage included the complete description of Aaron's purification rites (vv. 1–28), without establishing a particular date for the ritual.[59] The HS editors added the instructions regarding self-affliction and abstention from labor on the tenth day of the seventh month and the explication of the command that Aaron's successors continue to carry out the purification ritual (vv. 29b–34a). The reason for and significance of this addition will be discussed below.

Another reference to the annual purification rite is found at the conclusion of the incense altar passage in Exod 30:1–10. The most commonly

55. See n. 35 above; cf. Ibn Ezra's comments, ad loc.

56. Self-affliction and prohibition of labor (v. 29b); prohibition of labor and self-affliction (v. 31). Above, a similar format was found in the additional feast of Unleavened Bread passage (Exod 12:18–20). In both places, there appears in the heart of the passage an injunction equating citizen and stranger regarding the prohibitions in force on this day.

57. As Elliger perceptively noted, the description of the high priest in v. 32 is similar to the one given in Lev 21:10. In PT, on the other hand, he is referred to as הכהן המשיח, "the anointed priest" (Lev 4:3, 5, 16; 6:15). In the expression מקדש הקדש in v. 33, the word מקדש serves to indicate the place of greatest sanctity. This use of the term may be found in Num 18:29, which is part of HS, as has been demonstrated (Excursus 1, pp. 53–55).

58. In the first part of the chapter, the inner sanctum is called the קדש (vv. 2, 3, 16, 17, 23, 27), while in v. 33 it is called מקדש הקדש. Although Haran (*Temples*, 172 n. 50) has shown that PT is inconsistent in its use of the terms קדש and קדש קדשים, it seems strange that different terms should be used in the same chapter to describe the same thing. In addition, we find that while the atonement for the priests is called וכפר בעדו ובעד ביתו (vv. 6, 11, 17), in v. 33 ועל הכהנים ועל כל עם הקהל יכפר is used. Here the people of Israel are called עם הקהל, which is a combination of the two terms עם and קהל ישראל, which appear earlier in the chapter (vv. 15, 17, 24). Elliger also notes the use of the preposition על in regard to the atonement of the priest and the people in v. 33, while earlier in the chapter, atonement is בעד the subject (vv. 6, 17, 24). However, in light of J. Milgrom's contention ("כפר על/בעד," *Leshonenu* 35 [1971] 16–17), that כפר בעד is used only when the performer of the act atones for himself as well, it may be said that since in v. 33 atonement for the anointed priest is not mentioned, the use of על is to be expected.

59. See *Lev. Rabbah* 21 (7), ed. Margulies, pp. 483–84; *Shemot Rabbah* 38 (8), and the comments of the Gaon of Vilna cited in Hoffmann, *Leviticus* 1:315 ff.

accepted view regarding this passage is that it (like all of Exodus 30) belongs to a secondary stratum of the account of the tabernacle,[60] but there seems to be no reason to exclude it from the general PT corpus. It seems, however, that although the main body of the passage originates with PT, the last verse is the work of later editors.[61] The original summation of the pericope seems to have been the warning in v. 9 against improper use of the incense altar. Such warnings mark the ends of passages about the anointing oil and the incense (Exod 30:32–33, 37–38). Verse 10 seems to have been added by HS editors, who were attempting to add the incense altar to the list of appurtenances that are purified in purification rites, described in Leviticus 16. This altar is not mentioned among the ritual objects that must be purified.[62] Support for this hypothesis comes from the phrase "once a year," common to our verse and the HS editorial addition in Lev 16:34.

An exact date for the Day of Atonement appears in Lev 25:9. According to that verse, it is "on the tenth day of the seventh month, on the Day of Atonement" that the horn-blasts announcing the jubilee year are to be sounded throughout the land. The jubilee laws are found at the conclusion of the main Holiness Code and are thoroughly permeated with the ideas and language of HS. There is no reason to doubt that the date of the jubilee horn-blasts should likewise be assigned to this school.[63]

Finally, the Day of Atonement passage in Num 29:7–11 may be consid-

60. See the literature cited by M. Haran, "The Censer and TAMID Incense" (Heb.), *Tarbiz* 26 (1957) 118 n. 5, and his *Temples*, 228 n. 26.

61. The secondary nature of this passage was noted by A. Dillmann, *Die Bücher Exodus und Leviticus* (3rd ed.; Keh; Leipzig, 1897) 352.

62. As Kuenen noted (*Hexateuch*, 87 n. 23), the altar referred to in Leviticus 16 is not the incense altar, as the sages interpreted, but the altar for burnt offerings, as Ibn Ezra noted (Lev 16:18). This can be demonstrated from the order of the verses: Aaron goes out from the Tent of Meeting to the altar (16:18) when he has completed making atonement for the shrine and the Tent of Meeting (vv. 16–17). It seems, therefore, that Leviticus 16 belongs to the older PT stratum, which knows nothing of the existence of the incense altar, and therefore employs the neutral word מזבח, which refers here to the sacrificial altar. On the other hand, later PT strata are familiar with the incense altar, and those strata attempt to distinguish precisely between the two altars (see Lev 4:7, 18).

63. There are many scholars who believe that Lev 25:9b is a secondary addition to the first half of the verse, which held that the tenth of the seventh month was in effect the New Year's day—the day of blasts. In my opinion, there is no foundation for this view. The contention that there is a shift from a singular addressee in the first half of the verse to a plural addressee in the second half is irrelevant, as such transitions are legion in biblical laws in places that cannot be explained as additions. Other literary and substantive reasons must be sought to explain such changes. Examples in HS include Lev 19:9, 12, 15, 19, 27, 33; 23:22; 25:14, 17, 46. See B. Schwartz, "Three Chapters of the Holiness Code" (Heb.) (Ph.D. diss., Hebrew University, Jerusalem, 1987) 48, 53, 59, 70, 103, who explains the switches in Leviticus 19. The presence of this phenomenon in extrabiblical literature was noted by M. Greenberg, "The Design and Themes of Ezekiel's Program of Restoration," *Interpretation* 38 (1984) 185–88.

ered. This, like the entire festivals list in Numbers 28–29, originated in PT. In our view, the passage reveals several HS additions (see also n. 9 above). First we will demonstrate that HS tampered with the festivals list in general, and then we will examine the Day of Atonement passage specifically.

It is immediately noticeable that the list begins with a double command: "Say to them" (Num 28:2, 3). These two commands to address the Israelites are separated by the following sentence (v. 2b):

את קרבני לחמי לאשי ריח ניחחי תשמרו להקריב לי במועדו

"Be punctilious in presenting to Me at stated times the offerings of food due Me, as offerings by fire of pleasing odor to Me."

Elsewhere in this list, the sacrifices are related to the Lord in the third person, not in the first. Thus לחם אשה ריח ניחח לה' ("an offering by fire of pleasing odor to the Lord," 28:24) and not לחמי לאשי ריח ניחחי ("an offering by fire of pleasing odor to me"). Here Abravanel's observation regarding Lev 23:2 may be recalled: ". . . the entire section is in the third person, and only this phrase is presented in His person, may He be blessed, as if He were speaking for Himself" (commentary, ad loc.). The linguistic irregularity in the introduction to the festivals passage in Leviticus 23 indicated that it was an HS editorial addition (see previously, p. 15). The same is true here, as is especially indicated by the unusual "my food" (לחמי). PT is very careful not to make any direct connection between the Lord and food; thus it will never speak of "the Lord's food," but rather of "the food of the Lord's fires" or "a fire of pleasing odor to the Lord."[64] This avoidance apparently stems from the desire to refine the idea that sacrifices are God's food. In contrast, HS readily uses the expressions "the food of your God," "the food of his God," "the food of their God" (Lev 21:6, 8, 21, 22; 22:25; cf. Ezek 44:7). This confirms the suspicion that the sentence quoted above (v. 2b) is also an HS addition. Those responsible for the addition doubled the command "Say to them" as a resumptive repetition.

Further on in this passage, we find the phrase: עלת תמיד העשיה בהר סיני לריח ניחח אשה לה', "the regular burnt offering instituted at Mount Sinai—an offering by fire of pleasing odor to the Lord" (28:6). Dillmann pointed out in his commentary that the language of this verse is at variance with accepted PT style. Even more significantly, as G. B. Gray pointed out in his commentary, the verse interrupts the topical continuity between v. 5 and v. 7. Therefore, it is to be regarded as an editorial addition. Further, as Dillmann and Gray have noted, the phrase in question alludes to Exod 29:38–42.

As we have pointed out (see Excursus 1), these verses in Exodus 29 are

64. Lev 3:11, 16; Num 28:24. This divergence from PT style was noted by Dillmann, *Numeri,* 182.

an editorial addition of HS. It stands to reason, then, that Num 28:6, which alludes to them, is itself an interpolation by HS editors. The reason for this addition and its significance will be clarified further on (see below p. 194).

We should now examine whether other verses in the festivals list in Numbers are additions by HS. In various places in the list, there occurs the note that the festival sacrifices come not in place of but in addition to the daily offering. In the first two paragraphs dealing with additional sacrifices, this is expressed (in Num 28:10,15) by the words על עלת התמיד ("in addition to the regular burnt offering"). Beginning in the fourth paragraph, the relevant phrase is מלבד עלת התמיד ("besides the regular burnt offering"). But in the third paragraph, which deals with Passover, both the first expression (28:24) and מלבד עלת הבקר אשר לעלת התמיד (28:23) occur. While the additive על is widely employed by PT,[65] the word מלבד is used as an additive only once, in Lev 9:17, and there again, as in Num 28:23, in the phrase מלבד עלת הבקר ("besides the morning burnt offering"), which means that the dedicatory sacrifices were not to displace the daily sacrifice. Various syntactical and exegetical difficulties that this phrase creates in Lev 9:17 have led to its recognition as an editorial gloss.[66] Examination of the use of מלבד in the Pentateuch shows that it appears only in what are probably the latest strata of pentateuchal literature or in the last editorial additions. Moreover, the term מלבד is found outside the Pentateuch only in exilic and postexilic works, mostly in the late books Ezra, Nehemiah, Chronicles, and Daniel.[67] It seems, then, that PT explicitly stated only that the special sacrifices of the Sabbath, the New Moon, and the feast of Unleavened Bread (those at the beginning of the festivals list) are "in addition to the daily burnt offering"; after making that comment in respect of the first annual festival, it saw no need to repeat it regarding the other annual festivals. It was the HS editors who added the instructions "besides the daily burnt offering" for all the annual festivals.[68] As often occurs in such cases, at the transition point—the

65. Lev 3:4 (see Ibn Ezra), 5, 10, 15; 4:9; 7:4, 12, 13 (see Ibn Ezra); 10:15 (see Rashi and Nahmanides).

66. See the attempts to understand this verse in *Sifra,* beginning of *Shemini,* and in Nahmanides' commentary (ad loc.). It has been accepted by scholars that these words were added at some later point in time (Dillmann, Baentsch, Noth, and Elliger).

67. In the following places: Josh 22:29; 1 Kgs 10:13; Dan 11:4; Ezra 2:65; Neh 7:67; 1 Chr 3:9; 2 Chr 9:12; 31:16.

68. It may be that the references to the goat sacrificed as a sin offering, which precede the term מלבד ("besides"), are also an editorial addition (see M. Noth, *Numbers* [trans. J. D. Martin; OTL; London, 1962] 219). This explains the odd fact of the references to mandatory libations coming after the references to the sin offering (Num 28:30–31; 29:5–6, 11), which could lead to the conclusion that the sin offering requires a libation. (This is the view of the *Temple Scroll* 25:12–15, ed. Yadin, pp. 81–82; see also Yadin's introduction, 1:114.) When we remove the editorial interpolations dealing with the sin offering and

Passover and Unleavened Bread passage—both types of formula appear, על alongside מלבד. In light of the existence of an addition by HS scribes at the beginning of the passage, as shown above, it is reasonable to conclude that the interpolation of the "besides . . ." phrase is their work as well.

Let us now examine the Day of Atonement passage in Num 29:7–11. Close inspection reveals that in PT it was originally nothing of the sort, but rather a passage that dealt with the tenth day of the seventh month. The word "atonement" appears only at the end of the passage in the instruction "besides the sin offering of expiation and the regular burnt offering with its meal offering, each with its libation" (v. 11), which is one of the HS editorial additions just mentioned.

Three editorial additions made by HS to the PT laws have thus been identified. In the first instance, HS appended an instruction for making expiation for the incense altar once a year (Exod 30:10). In the second instance (Lev 16:29–31), HS amalgamated the holiday of tenth day of the seventh month into the description of the annual purification ceremony from PT. In the third instance (Num 29:11), HS incorporated a term that carries associations of the atonement ritual at the Temple into the concluding line of a PT passage dealing with the tenth day of the seventh month. If those editorial additions are removed, the following picture appears. On the one hand, Leviticus 16 commands the performance of a purification ceremony, whose date is not specified (Lev 16:34). On the other hand, the festivals list in Numbers 28–29 ordains the tenth day of the seventh month to be a day of self-affliction on which labor is forbidden. In the main body of this law, however, there is no hint of any connection between that day and the annual atonement ceremony. Only the HS additions to each of these two laws establish the relationship between the tenth day of the seventh month and the annual atonement purification rite, a relationship embodied in the term "Day of Atonement" itself.[69]

---

daily burnt offering, we find that the word ונסכיהם ("and their libations") refers to the additional sacrifices mentioned earlier.

Indications of originality are found only in the phrase ושעיר עזים אחד לחטאת לה' ("And there shall be one goat as a sin offering to the Lord," Num 28:15a), which precedes the use of the preposition על ("in addition to") in the New Moon section. The phrase לחטאת לה' ("as a sin offering to the Lord"), which invited a variety of homiletical interpretations, is simply an improvement on לה' לחטאת ("to the Lord as a sin offering"), which appears in PT (Lev 4:3). Jewish tradition historically attributed particular expiatory significance to the New Moon festival, a feature paralleled in the cultic laws of Ugarit (see M. Weinfeld, "Social and Cultic Institutions in the Priestly Source against their Near Eastern Background," in *Proceedings of the Eighth World Congress of Jewish Studies, Bible Studies and Hebrew Language* (Jerusalem, 1981)," 108–9 and nn. 76, 77). This helps strengthen the contention that the sin offering of a goat at the New Moon is unique among such sin offerings and should be seen as an integral part of the PT scroll.

69. The construction יום הכפורים indicates that there is a special day of the year on which the expiation rites are to be carried out. In PT the expiation rites are described at length, but there is no special day set aside for their performance.

This view of the tenth day of the seventh month as the Day of Atonement is presupposed, moreover, by the Law of the Jubilee, which is also a product of HS (see below, p. 122).

Returning to the Day of Atonement passage in Leviticus 23, the motives for HS's additions to the original PT text and the process of the passage's literary development may now be ascertained. This passage, in its original form, was part of the short PT list of festivals. Comparison with the corresponding passage in Numbers 29 enables the surmise that the original version of the passage ran something like this: "And the Lord spoke to Moses, saying: (Speak to the Israelites, saying:) On the tenth day of the seventh month, you shall have a sacred occasion, and you shall practice self-denial. You shall bring an offering by fire to the Lord, and you shall do no work whatever."[70]

That is:

וידבר ה׳ אל משה לאמר: (דבר אל בני ישראל לאמר:)
בעשור לחדש השביעי הזה מקרא קדש יהיה לכם ועניתם
את נפשותיכם: והקרבתם אשה לה׳ וכל מלאכה לא תעשו

The passage deals with the fast held on the tenth day of the seventh month, which is declared a sacred occasion. Here there is no trace of any connection between this fast day and the annual atonement ceremony, as according to PT these are two separate and distinct rituals. When HS decided to unite them, it had to make corresponding changes in the festivals passage of Leviticus 23. First, it added to the beginning of the section the word אך ("however"), a term particularly favored by the school.[71] Then, in the verse that defines the nature of the holiday, it added the words "it is the Day of Atonement" (יום הכפורים הוא), which express the blending of the fast and atonement rites. The combination of fast and atonement explains the strict prohibition of labor on this day, expressed in the appended explanation: "throughout that day, for it is a Day of Atonement on which expiation is made on your behalf before the Lord your God" (v. 28b). Thereafter, HS threatens with "cutting off" anyone who transgresses the orders of the day. Finally, HS added a repetition of

70. The words in parentheses appear only in the Syriac version. Comparison with other PT passages in this chapter (Lev 23:24, 34) indicates that the omission of this phrase occurred because of similarity to the preceding phrase, and that the Syriac version added it on its own.

Here the prohibition of labor appears after the command of the burnt offering, unlike the procedure in the festivals passages in Numbers and the Passover, Day of Blasts, and feast of Booths passages in this chapter, in which the prohibition of labor precedes the sacrificial instructions. However, an arrangement similar to the one proposed here is also used in the verse dealing with the Eighth Day of Assembly (Lev 23:36b).

71. Cf. the beginnings of the second Booths passage (Lev 23:39) and of the Sabbath passage (Exod 31:13; there אך also serves to limit and to contrast the Sabbath with the commands regarding the sanctuary, which precede the Sabbath prohibitions). See also the unusual use of אך at Exod 12:15, which, in our opinion, also belongs to HS.

the prohibition of labor and concluded with its characteristic formula: "It is a law for all time, throughout the ages in all your settlements" (v. 31). As previously noted, v. 32, which stresses that the day is to be observed "from evening to evening," was added at a later stage, also by HS (see discussion above, pp. 20–21).

It is strange that PT, which is usually careful to supply the exact date of every holiday and the full instructions for the performance of all cultic rituals, was content here with providing no specific date for the performance of the annual atonement rite. Also unspecified are the nature and meaning of the fast observed on the tenth day of the seventh month, as presented in PT. No explanation is given why self-denial is to be practiced on this day, nor why such a strict prohibition of labor is in force. Only the blending of these two rituals by HS solves the difficulties. First, the date of the performance of the atonement ritual is specified, and, second, the fast day becomes meaningful and so do the special laws that apply to it. Unlike its short and obscure references to the self-denial and abstention from labor to be practiced on the tenth day of the seventh month, PT's list of additional sacrifices for that day is clear and detailed (Num 29:8–10). The annual atonement/purification ceremony is also described in detail (Lev 16:3–28). In the case of HS, however, it is precisely the self-affliction and cessation of labor that get the most attention (Lev 16:29–31; 23:28b–32). Each of these aspects of the day is repeated several times, with the addition of the threat of "cutting off" for transgressors (Lev 23:29–30), similar to the threats of "cutting off" directed against those who violate the laws of Passover and festival of Unleavened Bread (Exod 12:19; Num 9:13). HS establishes the name "Day of Atonement" for the tenth day of the seventh month and explains its unique character: "for on this day atonement shall be made for you to cleanse you of all your sins" (Lev 16:30) and "for it is a Day of Atonement, on which expiation is made on your behalf before the Lord your God" (Lev 23:28). These verses, with their emphasis on the special status of the day, provide the basis for the rabbis' dictum that the day itself has expiatory power.[72]

The Day of Blasts

Let us now turn to the laws of the "Day of Blasts" (Lev 23:23–25). Comparison of the structure and language of this passage with the corresponding one in Num 29:1–6 shows that both originate in PT. Closer examination, however, reveals that there is a significant difference between the two passages in the presentation of the first day of the seventh

72. *m. Yoma* 8:9; *Sifra Aharei Mot* section 5, chap. 8a; *y. Yoma* 8:8 (45c); *b. Yoma* 86a; Maimonides, *Mishneh Torah*, Laws of Repentance 1:3.

month. In Leviticus the day is a שבתון זכרון תרועה, while in Numbers it is a יום תרועה. This difference is especially noteworthy, since PT is usually stylistically consistent (see Introduction, n. 3). If the difference is a result of subsequent editorial activity, it is the strange construction שבתון זכרון תרועה that arouses suspicion, both because of its awkwardness and because the preceding analyses have revealed extensive HS editorial activity in Leviticus but less in Numbers, where only marginal additions have been noted (see above, pp. 29–30 and n. 9).

We are able to confirm our suspicion of later redaction of the Leviticus verse. The term שבתון, which indicates the prohibition of labor, is unquestionably derived from שבת. As noted earlier, nowhere in PT is labor forbidden on the Sabbath and it is therefore unlikely that PT would use שבתון to indicate the prohibition of labor. Indeed, all other appearances of the word שבתון in the Torah occur in texts that demonstrably belong to HS.[73] There is no problem with HS's insertion of the term here[74] even though labor is expressly forbidden in the next verse, as this school tends to add the terms שבתון and שבת שבתון even where labor is also expressly forbidden (see Lev 16:29–31; 23:3, 31–32). The term זכרון in the phrase זכרון תרועה also exhibits affinity to HS: the talmudic sages and medieval exegetes already pointed out the connection between these "commemorative blasts" and those mentioned in Num 10:9–10, which belongs to HS[75] (see Excursus 1). All these considerations suggest that in the original PT passage dealing with the first day of the seventh month in Leviticus 23, the holiday was called "the Day of Shofar Blasts," as in Num 29:1. However, HS changed the title to "a complete rest, with commemorative shofar blasts."

Seemingly, the same happened here as in the revision of the passage dealing with the tenth day of the seventh month. Just as HS provided a rationale for the fast day by making it into the "Day of Atonement," it also clarified the purpose of the Day of Shofar Blasts by its formula "a complete rest, with commemorative blasts," which implies that the purpose of the blasts was to bring about commemoration by the Lord. According to HS, trumpet calls (תקיעות) were blown on festivals and holidays, whereas times of trouble called for horn blasts (תרועות) in anticipation of salvation (Num 10:9–10). On the first day of the seventh month, accordingly, kindness and salvation were to be implored. This custom undoubtedly reflects the perception of this day as the time of judgment for

73. Exod 16:23; 31:15; 35:2; Lev 16:31; 23:3, 32; 25:4, 5. (For the reference to שבתון at Lev 23:39, see below.) This term does not appear outside the Pentateuch.

74. The secondary character of the word שבתון was already noticed by Elliger, *Leviticus*, 309.

75. See *Sifra Emor* 11:2; *Sifrei Numbers* 77, ed. Horovitz, p. 71; *Sifrei Zuta*, ed. Horovitz, p. 262; the commentaries of Rashbam and Nahmanides, ad loc.

all, a view common in the ancient Near East.[76] This view is echoed in several psalms,[77] and it found expression in the cultic practices of the Second Temple.[78] Furthermore, Num 10:8 indicates that according to HS, the shofar blasts of this Day of Commemoration were also to be sounded by the priests.[79]

The Feast of Booths and the Assembly

Leviticus 23 contains two Tabernacles passages, the first from PT (vv. 33–36) and the second from HS (vv. 39–43). Additionally, the PT festival list in Numbers also devotes several passages to the feast of Booths and to the Assembly at its conclusion (Num 29:12–38). We will turn first to an examination of the festival of Booths and Assembly passages of PT.

Whereas this first relevant passage in Numbers introduces the holiday as חג לה' שבעת ימים ("a festival to the Lord for seven days" (Num 29:12b), the Leviticus PT passage calls it חג הסכות שבעת ימים לה' ("a feast of Booths to the Lord [to last] seven days," Lev 23:34bβ). The absence of "booths" from the former verse raises the possibility that its presence in the latter one is a result of editorial addition. This suspicion is reinforced by the fact that the word can be removed from the verse in Leviticus 23 without disturbing the grammatical or contextual sequence of the verse and that the resultant wording, חג שבעת ימים לה', is nearly identical with the phrase in Num 29:12. But even if "the feast of Booths" was an original and integral part of the Leviticus passage, it does not show that PT presupposed an obligation to dwell in booths during the festival. In fact, quite the opposite is true. The PT passages in both festivals lists always begin by presenting the special rituals of the festival (see Lev 23:5–6, 24, 27; Num 28:16–17, 26; 29:1, 7). If PT had regarded dwelling in booths as a practice pertaining to this festival, we might have expected an opening formula such as "a feast of Booths to the Lord; for seven days you shall dwell in booths," just as it speaks in the Unleavened Bread passage of "a feast of Unleavened Bread to the Lord; for seven days you shall eat unleavened bread" (Lev 23:6). This indicates that the term "feast of Booths," even if

76. See Weinfeld, "Social and Cultic Institutions," 117.

77. See Kaufmann, *History*, 2:497.

78. The view of this day as the time of judgment for all is evident in the Rosh Ha-Shana benedictions "Zikhronot" and "Shofarot." These benedictions were composed during Temple times and were primarily intended to be recited in the Temple; see J. Heinemann, *Prayer in the Period of the Tannaim and the Amoraim* (Heb.) (Jerusalem, 1978) 81, and *m. Rosh Ha-Shana* 1:2.

79. Philo, *Special Laws* 2.188, and the comments of G. Alon, *Jews, Judaism and the Classical World* (Jerusalem, 1977) 128–29; but cf. Z. A. Steinfeld, "The Shofar Blast on Rosh Hashanah" (Hebrew), *Milet* 2 (1985) 125–96.

original, signifies only that there was a popular custom of building booths, but that it was not considered by PT to be obligatory. Such a situation is found in Deuteronomy, where the festival is also called "the feast of Booths," but no express commandment to dwell in booths is given (Deut 16:13).

It seems that the festival acquired this title because of the pilgrim practice of erecting booths as temporary dwellings when visiting the Temple city. This festival was distinguished by the lengthy stay in the vicinity of the sanctuary that was required of the pilgrim.[80] Aside from the requirement of dwelling in the Temple city for seven days, this festival was characterized in PT by numerous additional sacrifices. There are no hints in PT, however, of its having any agricultural or historical associations.

The agricultural context is alluded to only in connection with the eighth day of the festival, the "Assembly." The term "Assembly" (עצרת) seems to indicate a ritual gathering (see 2 Kgs 10:20; Isa 1:13; Joel 1:14; 2:15), as does the battery of sacrifices ordained for the day. In the Numbers passage, it is said that on the day of the Assembly one bull, one ram, and seven yearling lambs are to be offered (Num 29:36). A similar battery of offerings is prescribed for two other holidays: the Day of Shofar Blasts on the first day of the seventh month, and the fast day on the tenth of that month (Num 29:2, 8). If the three elements that characterize these three days—horn blasts, fasting, and assembly—are combined, they immediately recall the words of the prophet Joel: "Blow a horn in Zion, solemnize a fast, proclaim an assembly" (Joel 2:15). The similarity is not merely coincidental: Joel calls for these three responses to crisis in anticipation of salvation, these rituals being intended to stir God's mercies and to implore his lovingkindness. The presence of these customs in the holidays of the seventh month came about as a result of the belief that it was in this month that all creatures are judged and the annual rainfall is determined.[81] The understanding of the purpose of the Assembly on the eighth day as a time of supplication for rain is explicit in *Targum Pseudo-Jonathan* to Lev 23:36 and has been accepted in Jewish liturgy throughout the generations.[82]

The original PT list of festivals underlying Leviticus 23 concluded with v. 37. This verse hints at the corresponding list in Numbers, which indeed details the additional sacrifices of these festivals, "on each day what is proper to it," as Lev 23:37 says.[83] Following the original conclusion, how-

80. This explanation of the custom of erecting booths was proposed by A. B. Ehrlich at Lev 23:43 (*Miqra ki-feshuto* [Berlin, 1899]; see also *EM* 5:1041–42; H. L. Ginsberg, *The Israelian Heritage of Judaism* (New York, 1982) 60.

81. See *m. Rosh Ha-Shanah* 1:1; and cf. the Hittite text cited by Weinfeld, "Social and Cultic Institutions," 117.

82. Weinfeld, "Social and Cultic Institutions," 119–20; and cf. *Ecclesiastes Rabbah* 7:14.

83. Though this verse belongs to the original PT stratum of this chapter, it seems to have

ever, there occurs another passage that also deals with the feast of Booths (see above, pp. 9–11). Scholars have argued that there is embedded here an ancient HS folk custom to which editorial additions have been made by PT. In their view, the earliest stratum of this passage is a commandment regarding the Harvest Festival, which lasts for seven days, during which branches of trees and fruit are taken and used in rejoicing before the Lord (v. 39aβ, "when you have gathered in the yield of your land, you shall observe the festival of the Lord seven days"; also vv. 40–41). The editorial additions (by PT, in this view) are the information regarding the exact date of the festival (v. 39aα), the commandment to observe a complete rest on the first and eighth days (v. 39b), and the obligation to dwell in booths in commemoration of the exodus (vv. 42–43).[84]

These attributions are problematic. Since the commandment to dwell in booths as a reminder of the exodus concludes "I am the Lord your God"—the characteristic signature of HS—it is plausible that this school also made the other additions.[85] Additional evidence for this supposition is provided by the wording of the commandment to observe a שבתון (i.e., cessation of labor) on the first and eighth days. If this gloss had been written by PT, as some scholars believe, the verse could be expected, on the basis of parallels, to be worded negatively: "On the first day proclaimed holiness and on the eighth day proclaimed holiness, no labor shall you perform." That is:

ביום הראשון מקרא קדש וביום השמיני
מקרא קדש כל מלאכת עבודה לא תעשו

The use of the term שבתון to indicate the prohibition of labor is thus rather an indicator of HS.[86] It seems, then, that on the basis of the folk name "feast of Booths," it ordained that the people dwell in booths throughout the seven-day festival.[87] This command seems to be based on

been adjusted by HS editors. The sequence עלה ומנחה זבח ונסכים is strange: logically one would expect זבח after עולה, before the מנחה ונסכים, which are dependent on the sacrifice. At the same time, the only reference to זבח in the additional sacrifices of the festivals is in the HS Two Loaves passage (Lev 23:19). It seems, therefore, that the appearance of the word זבח in the concluding verse of the PT scroll is a result of HS editorial activity. It was inserted to refer to the sheep brought as a sacrifice of well-being on the day of firstfruits, in accordance with HS procedure. The editors may even have inserted it at the wrong place intentionally in order to emphasize their addition. Perhaps v. 38 should be attributed to the final HS editors of this section (see Excursus 2).

84. See Wellhausen, *Hexateuch*, 162; Kuenen, *Hexateuch*, 101.

85. Elliger believes that the basic command to dwell in booths for seven days (v. 42a) is ancient and that only the historical explanation was an editorial addition. In light of the development of this custom as sketched above, his view seems unacceptable.

86. See n. 73 above.

87. The fact that the requirement to dwell in booths is limited to seven days does not mean that the eighth day was not a holiday for this legislator. After all, the commandment

a hermeneutic etiology of the name of the first station of the Israelites in the exodus from Egypt.[88] It fits well with the tendency of the school to strengthen the national remembrance of the exodus and to stress its commemoration and its significance for later generations.[89]

Of central importance in the HS feast of Booths passage is the natural agricultural character of the festival, which is especially expressed by the custom of rejoicing before the Lord with the "Four Kinds." This custom seems to express more than joy and thanks for the gifts of the harvest.[90] It was also intended to affect the precipitation of the rainy season, which in the Land of Israel begins immediately after the Harvest Festival. This idea was expressed later in the Palestinian Talmud: "By these four kinds which grow near the water; therefore they serve as pleaders for water."[91] As noted previously, according to PT it was the eighth day that was singled out as

---

originated in the pilgrim custom of building temporary shelters during the festival (which is defined as a holiday requiring one's presence in the temple vicinity). This festival, according to all views, lasted only seven days. Even in the PT passage (Lev 23:34-36) there is a distinction drawn between the seven festival days and the eighth day, which is a מקרא קדש ("sacred occasion) and an עצרת ("assembly"), but clearly not a חג ("festival").

88. See Exod 12:37; Num 33:5, cf. Gen 33:17. In Excursus 2, we assign v. 38 to one of the latest editorial strata of the Torah. Since the second feast of Booths passage comes after this verse, it is possible that it was added at the same period (although not necessarily; v. 38 alone may be a later editorial addition). If the second Booths passage was indeed extremely late, this might serve to explain the confusion that reigned during the Restoration period regarding the performance of the commandment of building booths and its relation to the ritual of the "Four Kinds." The booths would have been something of an innovation–not an ancient vision– as is indicated by Neh 8:17. E. Auerbach reaches similar conclusions regarding the dating of the passage, for similar reasons ("Die Feste im alten Israel," *VT* 8 (1958) 11-14). But his contention that the event described in Nehemiah demonstrates that at the time the scriptural texts were different from our present text is not convincing. The custom of building the booths out of the materials of the "Four Kinds" could have developed as a result of *midrash halakah* (see Kaufmann, *History*, 8:327 n. 35). The fact that the practice is described as וימצאו כתוב בתורה and ככתוב (Neh 8:14, 15) does not necessarily indicate that the Torah was being quoted exactly, as the label ככתוב בתורה is also applied to the wood offering (Neh 10:35), which was only a traditional custom without any basis in Scripture. On this entire matter, see M. Fishbane, *Biblical Interpretation in Ancient Israel* (Oxford, 1985) 109-12, 213-16.

89. See Exod 12:14, 17; 16:32; 29:46; Lev 19:36; 22:33; 25:38, 55; 26:13, 45; Num 15:41.

90. For the view that taking the "Four Kinds" was a sort of praise and thanksgiving, see *Lev. Rabbah* 30:7, ed. Margulies, p. 706; *Pesikta de Rav Kahana,* ed. Mandelbaum, p. 457; and the comments of H. Yalon, *Pirkei Lashon* (Jerusalem, 1971) 84.

91. *Y. Taaniyot* 1:1 (63c); see also the sources cited by J. Milgrom, "The SOQ HATTERUMA: A Chapter in Cultic History," *Tarbiz* 42 (1973) 170 n. 38. The duality inherent in this practice is also expressed in the requirement (*m. Sukkah* 3:9) that the palm branch be shaken when reciting the verse "Praise the Lord" at the beginning and end of Psalm 118 and when reciting the verse, "O Lord, deliver us!" (118:25), both in the context of the Hallel collection of Psalms recited on festivals. This shows that the ritual of the "Four Kinds" involves both praise and thanksgiving for the harvest bounty as well as beseeching prayer for future rains.

the time for supplication for rain. This debate may be reflected in the halakic traditions of the Tannaim.[92]

In any event, the difference between the two schools regarding the agricultural context and historical associations of the festival is clear. HS spells out these connections in detail, whereas for PT the festival has no historical significance and its agricultural aspects are merely suggested, unlike the detailed treatment accorded to the festival's additional sacrifices.

CONCLUSIONS

These findings may be compared with the classic theories of Wellhausen and Kaufmann regarding the nature of festival ritual as portrayed in the Priestly legislation in the Torah. Wellhausen's scheme will be seen to prove unworkable, but many of Kaufmann's insights can be preserved, apart from his refusal to acknowledge "popular" elements in the "Priestly" corpus of writings.

The Inadequacy of Wellhausen's Scheme

Wellhausen's *Prolegomena* opens with a systematic description of the history of Israelite cult and ritual, which includes a chapter on the festivals. That chapter is based on the distinction between the character of the cult as portrayed in "Priestly" laws and the conception of the festival practices in non-Priestly sources—the Covenant Codes and Deuteronomy. In the latter, the festival ritual is free, animated, and grounded in nature and agriculture. The Priestly Code, on the other hand, is a "late" development that has lost this natural and agricultural character and replaced it with detailed specific ritual prescriptions of public sacrifices that were to be offered at fixed times during the year. The awareness of nature was exchanged for historical discussions that explained the festivals as reflecting events of national history. Wellhausen viewed the festival laws of the Holiness Code as a transition phase between the Covenant Codes, D, and P. They still displayed some connection to agricultural realities, but the firstfruits offerings took on a ceremonial-symbolic character and were fused with a set program of communal sacrifices.[93]

According to Wellhausen, an "alienation" of the cultic aspects of the festivals from their "original" agricultural foundations, which reaches its

92. See the discussion between R. Eliezer and R. Joshua (*m. Taanit* 1:1).

93. Julius Wellhausen, *Prolegomena zur Geschichte Israel* (6th ed.; Berlin, 1905) 90–98, 375–78.

zenith in P, came about during the Babylonian exile, when the people lost their ties to the land. P is the code of the Judaism of the returned exiles, which was first published at the great assembly conducted by Ezra and Nehemiah (Nehemiah 8). The consciousness of guilt, which lay so heavily on the exiles brought about the institution of an atonement fast on the tenth day of the seventh month, and this was considered to be the holiest day of the year. The ascetic tendencies of that generation are expressed also in the transformation of the Sabbath from a day of rest for farmers into a holy occasion characterized by stringent prohibition of all forms of creative activity.[94]

The discoveries of Near Eastern archaeology, which brought increasingly greater understanding of the relationship between the ritual customs of PT and the cultic practices of neighboring peoples, led to a strident critique of Wellhausen's conclusions.[95] There are many scholars, however, who still maintain similar views.

In our view, the findings of this investigation completely undermine the schematic development of the festivals as presented by Wellhausen. It has been shown that the festival legislation of HS, which is clearly conscious of the agricultural cycle, is relatively later than PT, where the natural agricultural context is indeed lacking. This means that it was not historical "lateness" that caused an "alienation from nature." Moreover, it has been demonstrated that elements presented by Wellhausen as characteristic of the postexilic orientation of the Priestly Code—such as the emphasis on the historical significance of the festivals, the establishment of the "Day of Atonement" and the strengthening of its holiness, and the severity of the prohibition of labors on the Sabbath—have nothing to do with PT but are instead the products of HS, whose laws exhibit a genuine awareness of nature and agriculture along with those innovations.

A Reevaluation of Kaufmann

Given this refutation of the theory of a historical development from a natural and agricultural worship into an artificial ritual divorced from the realities of life, some other explanation is required for the essential difference in festival worship between the "Priestly" laws and the practices prescribed by the other sources in the Torah.[96] Here help is forthcoming from Yehezkel Kaufmann's great Hebrew opus, *The History of Israelite Faith,* where two chapters of the second volume are devoted to

94. Ibid., 103–11.

95. See above, p. 3, and n. 16.

96. For Wellhausen's straightforward distinctions regarding the unique character of the cult in PT, see below, nn. 105, 106.

the description of the Priestly and popular cultic worlds and the contacts between them.[97] Kaufmann's analysis of the "Priestly" writings themselves, however, needs to be modified.

Kaufmann believes that in contrast to pagan cults, in which there was an interaction between the popular and the priestly strata, in Israel "Priestly and popular worship were two separate, coexisting cultic spheres. The popular cult thrived not in the sanctuaries but around them." He sees the uniqueness of Israelite Priestly worship as follows:

> Not only was it not intended to elicit the flow of mysterious power to the gods through magical, mythological means, it was not even intended to elicit material bounty from God for man. . . . Those acts performed in the temple itself—on the altar, in the sanctuary, and in the Holy of Holies—were all oriented towards one idea: sanctification of the place of the name of God and the symbol of His Word, purification of all who approach Him, expression of the awe of the Holy; not material requital nor even supplication for kind gifts—just awe of the holy.[98]

In his discussion of the festival rituals, Kaufmann writes:

> The special theme of each festival is not expressed in temple worship; the sphere of the festival is outside the temple precinct. . . . It was the popular cult which created the Israelite festivals out of ancient pagan materials. The historical explanations for the festivals, expressed in Israelite terms, belong to the popular sphere; they find almost no expression in the temple ceremonies.[99]

Kaufmann holds popular religion responsible for the sanctity of the Sabbath as well, claiming that its mythic underpinnings are in no way reflected by the Temple service but only in popular behavior. Also a result of popular initiation are the horn-blast customs of the first day of the seventh month and the fast on the tenth, as well as the view of both of these days as times of judgment.[100]

Finally, Kaufmann notes that the experiences of joy and sadness existed only in the sphere of popular worship: in dance, song, music, prayer, psalm and lament, and in self-affliction and mourning. All of these practices and forms of religious expression were excluded from the priestly Temple—the Temple of silence.[101]

In his analysis of the priestly festivals law, Kaufmann makes use of Leviticus 23 and Numbers 28–29 indiscriminately, making no distinction between P and H, as in his opinion:

97. Kaufmann, *History*, 2:462–532.

98. Ibid., 2:474, 476; abridged English translation (by M. Greenberg): *The Religion of Israel* (Chicago, 1960) 303.

99. Kaufmann, *History*, 2:487 (*Religion*, 305).

100. Ibid., 2:491–98 (*Religion*, 305–6).

101. Ibid., 2:477–79, 498–99 (*Religion*, 303–4, 309–10).

> H is merely part of P. Not only is it similar to P in its character and style, it has become blended with P into one whole. . . . In Lev 23 we find a mixture of sources. The editor of P used the festival laws of H and spread them throughout his work, and therefore Lev 23 expresses the festivals conception of P throughout.[102]

Kaufmann's view that P embraces H in an integrated work, expressing a single approach to the festivals, creates several serious problems when combined with his distinctions between priestly and popular worship. How can he claim that such Temple rituals as the wave offering of the sheaf and the horn blasts of the priests over the additional sacrifices are not meant to elicit blessing or salvation?[103] If the historical grounding of the festivals was part of the popular stratum of development, why does it appear so often in P specifically? Why is there such a detailed presentation in P of the popular practice of the Passover sacrifice, and why do the Sabbath prohibitions—ostensibly of popular origin—get so much attention in that work? Was there truly no rejoicing in the Temple? What about the command found in P to take the "Four Kinds" and to use them in the rejoicing "before the Lord"? The term "before the Lord" specifically indicates the Temple and its precincts.[104]

In asking these questions, it is not our intention to contest the distinctions between priestly and popular elements proposed by Kaufmann or to dispute his descriptions of the characteristic aspects of each of these spheres of religious life. Quite the contrary: Kaufmann had great intuitive insight into the varieties of the ancient Israelite religious experience and their cultic expressions. The value of his insights, however, is obscured by his lack of analysis of the Priestly source. It is a mistake to view Leviticus 23 as completely reflecting the festivals law of a single school, as Kaufmann does. In this and other chapters in the "Priestly source," there exist side by side (or in various stages of synthesis) the views of two

102. Ibid., 1:121, in the context of his critique of Wellhausen.

103. Kaufmann argues that the wave offerings of the sheaf and of the two loaves are thanksgiving ceremonies without any intent of influencing the bounty of the coming harvest (*History*, 2:143 n. 2 and p. 475 [*Religion*, 302]). He rejects the view of the Tanna R. Akiva, who explains that these offerings were a sort of *quid pro quo*, contending that there is no hint of this in the Torah (he explains the word לרצנכם in the law of the sheaf as meaning "So that Israel will be accepted by God"). It is difficult to accept Kaufmann's position, for if the sheaf offering ritual was intended as thanksgiving for the harvest, why was it performed at the beginning of the harvest rather than at its conclusion? Evidence for the sympathetic character of the sheaf offering may be adduced from the parallel command of jubilation with the fruits of the fourth year, which is explicitly said to "add to your yield of produce" (Lev 19:25). The term לרצנכם used of the sheaf offering is to be understood similarly. As regards the horn blasts sounded over the sacrifices, Kaufmann admits that they were intended to elicit God's mercies, but he attempts to resolve the difficulty by claiming that the blasts were a marginal custom (*History*, 1:475–76).

104. N. Raban, "Before the Lord" (Heb.), *Tarbiz* 23 (1952) 1–4.

Priestly schools, each of which possesses its own distinctive religious-ritual outlook. The earlier school—PT—has a "purer" Priestly cultic conception, while the laws of the later school—HS—display a priestly-popular orientation. Reexamination of the festival laws in light of this distinction confirms many of Kaufmann's basic contentions, and the boundaries between the "pure" Priestly sphere and the popular religion become much sharper.

It turns out that the festivals law of PT, once the HS editorial revisions have been removed, does not in fact contain any Priestly-cultic practice intended to elicit material blessing for humanity. PT knows of the first-fruits ceremonies and the counting of weeks but considers them to be merely popular customs, not binding commandments. Other elements originating in the popular religion—the Passover sacrifice, the feast of Unleavened Bread, the Day of Blasts and the Fast Day—do indeed appear in PT as positive commandments, but the extreme brevity, to the point of obscurity, with which they are presented indicates that in those cases PT had to incorporate popular practices with which it was not in sympathy, or which it at least did not regard as belonging to the essence of Temple worship. It maintained a basic separation between the Priestly and popular cultic spheres: it is doubtful whether the popular cultic practices were carried out in the Temple, and certainly the priests played no significant role in the performance of those rites. In one instance, PT even describes separation in time between the Priestly atonement purification ritual and the popular Fast Day. A different kind of separation is revealed by PT's attitude toward the Sabbath. The sanctity of the Sabbath is, in fact, recognized by PT, but only outside the corpus of ritual Temple laws—in the story of the creation. In ritual context, the Sabbath is represented only by an additional sacrifice. There is no hint in the PT laws of the prohibition of labor on the Sabbath. The festivals ritual in PT is divorced from nature and agriculture and also from history. It is solely a sacrificial rite, specific and exacting, the purpose of which is fulfillment of God's commandments.[105] As Kaufmann noted, in the Priestly Temple service there is no expression of any emotion, no "rejoicing before the Lord," and no grief or mourning—"And Aaron kept silent" (Lev 10:3).[106]

105. This aspect of the priestly worship was discerned by Wellhausen (*Prolegomena*, 424): "What pleases Him . . . is only the strict observance of the rite. The sacrifices must be offered exactly according to prescription at the right place, at the right time, by the right individuals, in the right way. They are not based on the inner value of what is done on the impulse arising out of fresh occasions but on the positive command of a will outside the worshipper which is not explained and which prescribes every particular." Similarly, Kaufmann writes: "The Israelite priesthood placed at the focus of the cult not the body of God or the fate of God, but rather the Word of God, the symbol of His sovereign will" (*History*, 2:476; cf. p. 478 with 1:537).

106. Kaufmann, *History*, 2:478–79 (*Religion*, 304). This was also noticed by Wellhausen, (*Prolegomena*, 424), who writes: "They no longer draw down the Deity into human life on all important occasions, to take part in its joys and sorrows."

With the festival law in HS, the picture changes completely. Cultic practices connected to nature receive great attention; the sacrifices are of secondary importance. The desire to influence the fortunes of the harvest through the wave offering of the sheaf and to induce rainfall by taking the "Four Kinds," and the anticipation of salvation expressed in the various commemorative blasts, are especially conspicuous. Historical explanations of the festivals are more common here than in any of the other legal collections in the Torah; they include not only the Passover and the feast of Unleavened Bread, which are discussed at length, but the commandment to dwell in booths, an HS invention. Here the Sabbath, the foundation of extra-Temple holiness, is put on a level with the Temple. The prohibition of labor is discussed at length, and serious punishments are specified for transgressors. Heavy penalties are also imposed on those who do not observe the popular customs of the Passover, the prohibition of leaven during the feast of Unleavened Bread, and rest and self-affliction on the tenth day of the seventh month. In the seven-day festival celebrated in the seventh month, the joyousness of the harvest is expressed before the Lord, while at the other end of the expressionist spectrum, during times of trouble and wars, the expectation of salvation was given expression through trumpet calls that were meant to bring the Lord to remember his people.

We have called the ritual outlook of HS "priestly-popular." The blending of popular and priestly elements is particularly noticeable in the HS firstfruits and feast of Booths passages. Another expression of this synthesis is the "Day of Atonement," which combines the priestly purification ceremonies with the strict prohibition of labor and the injunction to practice self-affliction on the tenth day of the seventh month, which was the creation of the popular tradition. The historical and social background of this priestly-popular amalgam in the HS texts will be explored in the last chapter of the present work.

EXCURSUS
1

"An Eternal Law Throughout Your Generations"

In order to ground more firmly the chronological conclusions reached in the analysis of Leviticus 23, I here examine a general criterion for the application of my theory throughout the "Priestly" source. An analysis of Leviticus 23 showed that the phrase "an eternal law throughout your generations" (חקת עולם לדרתיכם) is a characteristic of the HS in that chapter. Let us therefore use it as a linguistic criterion for detecting HS activity elsewhere in the Torah. For the purpose of this examination, it is necessary to divide the Priestly material in the Pentateuch into three major groupings: (1) the sequence Exodus 25–30, Leviticus 1–16, which deals with the construction of the Tabernacle, the sacrificial laws, and the laws of purity; it is clearly the central corpus of PT; (2) the sequence Leviticus 17–26: the Holiness Code; (3) the miscellaneous Priestly material outside of these two collections.

The phrase חקת עולם לדרתיכם (לדרתם) ("an eternal law throughout your/their generations") appears fifteen times in the Priestly material: six times in the Holiness Code,[1] four times in the central PT corpus, and five times in the other material. If it is characteristic of HS and HS is later than PT, then every occurrence of this phrase in the central PT corpus is an HS editorial addition. Its appearance in the miscellaneous material would indicate the possibility that the literary unit of which it is part belongs to HS. Let us test whether these hypotheses are confirmed by an examination of the text.

Because of the differences between the types of material under examination, different additional indicators of HS activity are appropriate to each type. Regarding the appearance of the phrase in the central PT corpus (Group A), the following indicators are relevant:

1. Whether the passage in which the phrase appears disturbs the sequence of the larger unit or whether it is in a passage appended to a PT unit.
2. Whether there is any contradiction between the laws in the passage and other laws in PT, of any other incongruity between the passage and PT.
3. Whether the passage displays other clear linguistic similarities to the Holiness Code (or to Ezekiel, which is linguistically very close to the Holiness Code).

1. Four in this chapter (Lev 23:14, 21, 31, 41) and two elsewhere (Lev 17:7; 24:3).

4. Whether there is an apparent ideational motive for HS's supposed addition to the passage, and whether the passage expresses the unique cultic conception of HS.

The first of these should be discernible in every passage in which the phrase appears, as it is the sure indicator of editorial activity. In addition, one or more of the others should be present.

In the miscellaneous Priestly material (i.e., in the first parts of Exodus and in Numbers), the criterion of continuity is invalid, since we are dealing not with a simple literary unity, but with random literary units. It may be, however, that these units belong in their entirety to HS. In this case the literary examination of these texts will have to reckon with this type of complex literary unity. The presence of several of the following indicators will be sufficient for us to label one of these passages a product of HS:

1. Use of language and terminology unlike that of the central PT corpus.
2. Terms or phrases characteristic of the Holiness Code or of the book of Ezekiel.
3. Literary structures absent from the central PT corpus, but present in the Holiness Code.
4. Contradictions between laws appearing in the passage under consideration and those in PT, or affinity to ideas particular to the Holiness Code.

The Central PT Corpus

The appearances of the phrase in the central PT corpus will now be examined. These include Exod 27:21; Lev 3:17; 7:36; 10:9. We will treat them in the order of their appearance in the Pentateuch.

l. Exod 27:21. The construction "an eternal law throughout your generations from the Israelites" concludes a short unit (Exod 27:20–21) commanding the people to bring olive oil to be used for kindling the eternal light. The dislocation of this passage has troubled both early and recent exegetes.[2] This commandment could be expected to appear adjacent to the description of the Menorah (25:31–40) or to the injunction regarding the preparation of spices for the oil of anointment and the incense (30:22–38), as is the case in the introduction to the list of materials for the Tabernacle (25:6). Why should this passage appear after the description of the courtyard? An additional problem is that here (v. 21) it is Aaron and his sons who are to set up the lamp, although Moses is instructed to raise them to the priesthood only later, in chap. 28. Additionally, there is a linguistically almost identical parallel to this passage in the Holiness Code (Lev 24:1–4). The conclusion indicated is that HS editors were responsible for interpolating this passage and disturbing the sequence of PT. What led them to do so?

2. See, e.g., Abravanel's commentary, ad loc.; and A. Kuenen, *The Origin and Composition of the Hexateuch* (Eng. trans. P. H. Wicksteed; London, 1886) 74.

At the end of each commandment regarding the manufacture of the implements of the Tabernacle (Exod 25:1–27:19), there is an explanation of the function of the implement in the cult. (This is true also of the commandments regarding the manufacture of the garments for Aaron and his sons: each ends with a statement of the purpose and function of the garment in the sacred service.) There are two exceptions: the Menorah (25:31–40)[3] and the bronze altar (27:1–8), where no statements of purpose and cultic function are made. It seems that the HS editors set out to correct this omission in the case of the Menorah by copying a passage from the Holiness Code detailing the proper kindling of the eternal light.[4] Since the passage about the manufacture of the Tabernacle accessories was already a completed existing entity, they did not insert the command regarding the eternal light adjacent to the Menorah passage; instead, they appended it to the scroll about the Tabernacle and its furnishings (Exod 25:1–27:19), at the "seam" between that scroll and the one following it, which described the elevation of Aaron and his sons to the priesthood. Similar treatment was accorded the bronze altar. At the beginning of the PT scroll about the daily and additional sacrifices (in our text, Numbers 28–29), the HS editors found a passage about daily worship (Num 28:3–8), on which basis they filled in the information lacking in the Tabernacle scroll. The Priestly scroll about the elevation of the Aaronides to the priesthood ended with instructions regarding the purification of the altar during the Days of Consecration (Exod 29:36–37), at which point the HS editors were able to add the passage about the daily sacrifice without disturbing the existing PT scrolls.[5] To the descriptions of the daily

3. While the lighting of the lamps is mentioned in Exod 25:37, this verse does not fully explain the ritual role of the candelabrum. It does not say that its lamps are to be kindled before the Lord, nor does it say anything about the constancy or regularity of the lighting.

4. The substance of this verse indicates that it was an editorial addition. Here one would expect a special command specifically dealing with the lighting of the candelabrum but finds instead that this idea is secondary to the command to provide oil. This becomes understandable if the author responsible for the verse did not have freedom to write as he wished but was rather constrained by what he found in the preexisting material, which dictated the literary and substantive parameters of the passage. Since the core of Leviticus 25 is the command to provide oil, that message was transferred intact from there. Also significant is the addition of the word ובניו to v. 21, which shows negligence or ignorance of the PT doctrine that the inner rites of the Sanctuary were to be performed by the anointed high priest exclusively; see M. Haran, *Temples and Temple Service in Ancient Israel* (Oxford, 1978) 209 n. 6. Haran, following Rashi and Abravanel, wishes to interpret the opening words of the verse ואתה תצוה as a reference to the future. As Rashi puts it: "You will eventually command the Israelites regarding this." Haran therefore feels that this is not a mechanical editorial addition but rather the work of a single scribe, who repeats himself stereotypically. The irregular location of the verse, however, indicates that it is indeed an editorial addition, in which case ואתה תצוה is not a hint of the future but rather just the opposite: an attempt by the editors to adjust their style to the existing material. Since the following section begins (Exod 28:1), here too the form ואתה תצוה was used (see A. Dillmann, *Die Bücher Exodus und Leviticus* [3rd ed.; Leipzig, 1897] 311).

5. For the identification of this passage as and editorial addition based on Numbers 28, see Kuenen, *Hexateuch*, 310. The passage begins in the future tense: וזה אשר תעשה על המזבח. Haran (*Temples*) also understands this as a reference to the future and therefore denies that it is an editorial addition. It seems, however, that in this case as well the editors

sacrificial rites, they added some concluding verses dealing with reasons for the construction of the Tabernacle and its rituals (Exod 29:42–46). These verses, too, bear the linguistic and ideational imprint of HS.[6]

2. Lev 3:17. The verse "It is an eternal law throughout your generations in all your settlements: you must not eat any fat or any blood" (Lev 3:17) comes at the end of a Priestly pericope dealing with the sacrifice of well-being (3:1–16). Some scholars have suggested that it is a secondary addition. Though there is some connection established by the words "any fat" in v. 17 and the conclusion of the previous verse "all fat is the Lord's," this connection seems to be a result of the late editorial activity. The passage dealing with the sacrifice of well-being is composed of three sections: offerings of cattle (vv. 1–5), of sheep (vv. 6–11), and of goats (vv. 12–16). The first section concludes with "an offering by fire, a pleasing odor to the Lord," the second with "food, an offering by fire to the Lord." Stylistic convention would lead us to expect the third section to conclude in such a way as to combine the elements of the two previous phrases, something like "food burnt in fire as an offering of pleasing odor to the Lord," the likes of which are used elsewhere by PT (Num 28:24). It seems that this was indeed the original concluding formula in v. 16, but that the editors who added v. 17 inserted the words "all fat" into the original conclusion.[7] The view that the sacrifice of well-being passage originally ended with v. 16 is strengthened by comparing the conclusions of preceding passages: those dealing with the burnt offering (1:17) and the meal offering (2:16), which both exhibit the construction "in fire to the Lord." In light of the secondary character of the added verse, we must ask why this passage was added and how it is connected to HS.

The original sections of Leviticus 3 (vv. 1–16) contained instructions that ordered the burning of the fat of the sacrifice of well-being on the altar as a "fire to the Lord." This view recurs, expounded at greater length, in the passage added to the laws regarding the sacrifice of well-being in Lev 7:22–27.[8] There it

---

wished to imitate the style of the opening phrase of the previous passage, which reads אשר תעשה להם וזה הדבר (Exod 29:1) in order to integrate the addition into the existing text, and to show that it is a command rather than a prediction.

6. The HS provenance of this passage was already noted by A. Klostermann, *Der Pentateuch* (Leipzig, 1893) 377. HS may be detected in the closing words אני ה' אלהיכם (see Introduction, n. 3). The view expressed here—that it was God who sanctified the Tent of Meeting, the altar, and the priests—is similar to that of the Holiness Code (Lev 21:15, 23; 22:9, 16). On the other hand, PT believes that Moses sanctified the Tent, the altar, and the priests (Exod 29:21, 36; 30:26–30). The present passage also highlights the pan-Israelite dimension of the Tabernacle and of the Temple rites, reflecting here, too, HS's outlook.

7. This possibility has been raised by B. Baentsch and K. Elliger. Some evidence for it may be had from the Septuagint and Samaritan versions, which indicate a reading: לחם אשה לריח נחח לה' כל חלב לה'. Even if this is a later harmonization, it indicates the unevenness of the Masoretic Text, which in our opinion resulted from editorial intervention. In Martin Noth's opinion, the words כל חלב were copied into v. 17 in error from v. 16. Even though such vertical dittography is possible, there seems to be a greater likelihood of deliberate editorial addition, intended to link v. 17 to the main body of the pericope.

8. That this passage (Lev 7:22–27) seems dislocated was already felt by Abravanel (in the twenty-second question in *Parashat Zav*). See also S. R. Driver, *Introduction*, 44; B.

is explained that the people are prohibited from consuming fat from oxen, sheep, or goats, that is, the animals that could be offered as a sacrifice of well-being. The fat from animals thay died or were torn by beasts (and are therefore unfit for sacrifice), while also unfit for consumption, could be put to use. The connection between the prohibition against eating the fat and the sacrificial use of the animal that is its source is also illustrated by the verse that threatens "cutting off" for those who transgress the commandment: "If anyone eats the fat of animals from which offerings by fire may be made to the Lord, the person who eats it shall be cut off from his kin" (Lev 7:25). The extension of this prohibition to all animals fit for sacrifice makes sense only on the assumption that all animal slaughter must take the form of sacrifices of well-being, that is, that the fat be burned and the blood sprinkled on the altar. If it is forbidden to eat the flesh of cattle or flocks other than from a sacrifice of well-being, then in any case it is forbidden to eat "any fat of an ox, sheep, or goat," since all the fat of such a sacrifice must be offered on the altar as "fire to the Lord." But the opinion that all profane slaughter is prohibited is expressed in only one place—Leviticus 17, the first chapter of the Holiness Code.[9]

Now the picture becomes clear. The original version of the sacrifice of well-being passages in PT (Lev 3:1–16; 7:11–21) included commands to burn the fat of the sacrifices of well-being on the altar, but did not prohibit the eating of all fat, as PT did not entertain the possibility of nonsacral slaughter of cattle or flocks.[10] However, after HS innovated the injunction barring profane slaughter and demanded that all appropriate animals be slaughtered only as sacrifices, the next logical step was to prohibit eating all fat and to assign it to the altar. The HS editors did this by adding to the margins of older Priestly scrolls dealing

---

Baentsch, *Exodus-Leviticus* (HKAT; Göttingen, 1903); M. Noth, *Leviticus* (trans. J. D. Martin; OTL; London, 1965); and also Elliger (*Leviticus* [HAT; Tübingen, 1966] 90, 101), who notes the connection with Lev 3:17.

9. On the prohibition of nonsacral slaughter in Lev 17:1–7 and the HS provenance of that entire chapter, see below, p. 112. On the dependence of the prohibition of all fat on the sacrificial commands of Leviticus 17, see D. Hoffmann,"Die wichtigsten Instanzen gegen die Graf-Wellhausen Hypothese I," *Jahres-Bericht des Rabbiner-Seminars zu Berlin* (1902–3) 23; M. Haran, "Foods and Beverages" (Hebrew), *EM* 4:543–58. Nahmanides in his commentary on Lev 7:25 attempts to prove, on the basis of the term בכל מושבתיכם used regarding the prohibition of fat and blood in Lev 3:17, that the prohibition is independent of the sacrificial character of the animal, as this term is not used regarding the sacrifices since they are offered in the Sanctuary, not in the people's dwelling places. This is no proof, however, since the term בכל מושבתיכם in Lev 3:17 seems to apply only to the prohibition of blood, which is also in force regarding nonsacrificial animals and birds (Lev 7:26; 17:13–14). Thus, the command may indeed apply to all dwelling places. This is borne out by Lev 7:22–27, where the prohibitions of blood and of fat are presented separately, and in which בכל מושבתיכם is used of the former only (see A. B. Ehrlich, *Miqra ki-feshuto* [Berlin, 1899] on Lev 7:26).

10. One cannot draw inferences about PT's attitude toward nonsacral slaughter from the permission given to Noah and his children to eat the flesh of all living things. PT views that permission as something allowed since ancient times, before the establishment of the cult. Just as PT does not relate to the possibility of nonsacral slaughter of an animal that can be sacrificed, it does not take an explicit stand on the isue of the centralization of the cult.

with sacrifices of well-being the new prohibition against eating any fat (Lev 3:17; 7:22–25).

3. Lev 7:36. The third appearance of the phrase is in Lev 7:36. This verse concludes a passage dealing with the portions of the sacrifice of well-being to be presented to the Lord and to the priest (Lev 7:28–36). Following it is a general conclusion to the sacrificial instructions (7:37–38). Since the preceding passage (7:22–27) has been identified as an addition made by HS editors to the PT document, it is reasonable to consider the same possibility regarding the present passage (vv. 28–36). This possibility is also corroborated by the contents and language of the passage. The ritual described here, in which the breast is waved before it is offered to the priest, whereas the thigh is not (7:30–33), stands in direct contradiction to the usual view of PT that the two are waved together (9:21; 10:15).[11] A unique linguistic feature of this passage (possibly indicative of relative lateness) is the rare use of the word "anointing" (משחה) in the sense of perquisite, portions accruing from appointment (v. 35).[12] The affinity to HS usage is displayed in the presentation of God as speaking in the first person in v. 34.[13]

4. Lev 10:9. The last appearance of the phrase in the central PT corpus occurs in Lev 10:9, in the middle of a short passage (10:8–11) treating the prohibition against priests drinking wine during their performance of the sacred service in the Tent of Meeting. This passage interrupts the story about the death of the two sons of Aaron. The rabbis who noticed this problem attempted to resolve it in their own way.[14] The passage is also unusual in being addressed to Aaron alone, as happens nowhere else in PT.[15] Furthermore, it has linguistic similarity

11. This contradiction was already noticed by Nahmanides and Abravanel in their comments on these verses. A comprehensive discussion of the problem is provided by J. Milgrom, "The SOQ HATTERUMA: A Chapter in Cultic History," *Tarbiz* 42 (1973) 5–8. He claims that the references to the wave offering of the thigh in Lev 9:21 and 10:15 resulted from secondary additions reflecting cultic reforms, while the passage in Leviticus 7, which does not prescribe that the thigh be waved, is in accordance with ancient custom as derived from the practice in small sanctuaries. Milgrom's textual evidence for the secondary character of the waving of the thigh is convincing, but why then was the text of Leviticus 7 not corrected accordingly? We believe that this passage was not known by the editors/scribes who inserted the references to the waving of the thigh into the PT story of the Days of Consecration. These editors' corrections reflect a PT reform of ancient cultic practices. Only later on, during the era of the final editing of the Torah, HS editors who adhered to the older custom of giving the thigh directly to the priest added to the PT laws of the sacrifice of well-being the passage Lev 7:28–36, which reflects the ancient practice. If this custom was indeed based on the realities of the small sanctuaries, this is additional evidence that HS drew from the popular cultic traditions.

12. See B. A. Levine, "Research in the Priestly Source: The Linguistic Factor" (Hebrew), *Eretz Israel* 16 (1982) 125–27. This form also appears in Num 18:8; the same chapter also contains the formula חקת עולם לדרתיכם!

13. This was noted by Dillmann, *Leviticus*, 496. On this usage as a linguistic identifier of HS, see Introduction, n. 2.

14. See the *derashah* of R. Ishmael in *Lev. Rabbah* 12:1, ed. Margulies, p. 255, and R. Levi's comment, ad loc.

15. This was already noted by Ibn Ezra. See the references brought by S. E. Loewenstamm, "The Investiture of Levi" (Hebrew), *Eretz Israel* 10 (1971) 172 n. 29.

to Ezekiel (44:21, 23), whose language has been noted to be close to that of HS. All these indicators show the passage to be an editorial addition of HS, which was probably intended to create, together with the preceding verses (Lev 10:6-7),[16] a collection of laws pertaining to the behavior of priests on duty.

To sum up, all the appearances of the phrase "an eternal law throughout your/their generations" in the central PT corpus show signs of being parts of secondary additions to that complex. Three of the passages (cases 1, 2, and 3) were appended at the end of PT sections, and one (case 4) is interpolated into the midst of a PT section. Three of the passages concerned (cases 1, 2, and 4) display marked similarities to HS or Ezekiel, while the fourth (case 3) contradicts PT laws.

The Miscellaneous Priestly Material

We turn now to the group of references ouside the main PT corpus: Exod 12:14, 17; Num 10:8; 15:15; 18:23. We will attempt to uncover the sources of the complete literary units. If we find tracks leading to HS in a given literary unit, we will consider that as proof that the phrase "an eternal law throughout your generations" indicates an HS text environment.

1. Exod 12:1-20. This is the Passover and Unleavened Bread passage. The elements of our phrase appear there in inverted order: לדרתיכם חקת עולם ("throughout your generations, an eternal law"). Traditional scholarly opinion assigns this passage to PT, but the language of the "cutting off" warning in vv. 15 and 19 militates against this attribution: ונכרתה הנפש ההיא מ[עדת] ישראל ("that person shall be cut off from [the community of] Israel"). This is at variance with the usual PT formula ונכרת(ה) ... מעמיו(ה) ("he shall be cut off from his people"). (See Introduction, n. 2.)[17]

Other indicators of an HS connection are also evident: the closing formula "I am the Lord" in v. 12,[18] the linguistic affinity between v. 14 and Lev 23:41, which appears within the additional HS Tabernacles passage;[19] and the inclusion of the resident alien among the community of Israel in v. 19, a uniquely HS conception (see chapter 1, n. 35).

2. Num 10:1-10. The traces of HS in this passage are clear, both in the formula "I am the Lord your God" (10:10)[20] and in the general format of the list of shofar blasts and trumpet calls. This law has two parts: the directions for organi-

16. That these verses are secondary additions was noted by Wellhausen (*Die Composition des Hexateuch und der historischen Bücher des Alten Testaments* [3rd ed.; Berlin, 1899] 140, 147). It seems that they too are a secondary addition. He wisely noted that this section is "an addition to an addition."

17. The "cutting off" formula of Exodus 12 appears in Num 19:13 as well. As is shown further on (p. 93), that verse, too, is of HS provenance.

18. See Klostermann, *Pentateuch,* 377; Dillmann, *Leviticus,* 592; and M. Haran, "Behind the Scenes of History: Determining the Date of the Priestly Source," *JBL* 100 (1981) 329 n. 12.

19. See D. Hoffmann, *Leviticus with a Commentary* (Jerusalem, 1976) 2:95.

20. On this basis, vv. 9-10 have already been shown to be HS creations. See Klostermann, *Pentateuch,* 377; Haran, "Behind the Scenes," 329 n. 12; and A. Dillmann, *Die*

zational blasts (vv. 1–8), which concludes "an eternal law throughout your generations," and the law of ritual blasts (vv. 9–10), which concludes "I am the Lord your God." This format is used in passages in Leviticus 23 of HS origin. Thus, the main section of the first fruits law (23:15–21) ends "an eternal law . . . throughout your generations," while the addition regarding the harvest gifts (23:22) ends "I am the Lord your God." The same is true of the HS Booths passage (23:39–41, 42–43).

3. *Numbers 15.* J. Wellhausen and A. Kuenen already pointed to the associations between this entire chapter and the Holiness Code.[21] To the evidence adduced by them, one may add an observation based on inspection of the law concerning the sin offering that appears in this chapter (15:22–31). The language of the "cutting off" warning here—ונכרתה הנפש ההוא מקרב עמה ("that person shall be cut off from among his people")—differs from the usual PT formula ונכרת(ה) מעמיו(ה) ("he shall be cut off from his people"). (See Introduction, n. 3.) On the other hand, frequent use is made of מקרב ("from among") in the Holiness Code "cutting-off" formulas (Lev 17:4, 10; 18:29; 20:3, 5, 6, 18).

The relationship between Num 15:22–31 and the law of the sin offering found in Leviticus 4 has been discussed at length by scholars.[22] As we shall explain in detail further on (p. 171 and n. 18), the sin offering legislation in Numbers 15 is a reworking of the sin offering legislation in Leviticus 4, transforming the views of that chapter in keeping with a unique theological and legal orientation. As background for the opinion of Numbers 15 that any sin performed willfully constitutes blasphemy, we turn to Leviticus 19, the heart of the Holiness Code, which sees all laws as being of equal importance as expressions of God's will.[23] The sin offering passage in Numbers 15 shows the relationship of that chapter to HS and, by the same token, the lateness of this stratum compared to Leviticus 4, which is part of the central PT corpus.

4. Numbers 18. This last unit deals with the roles of the priests and Levites and the benefits accruing to them as a result of their sacred service. Linguistic and stylistic motifs connect this passage to two of the passages from the central PT corpus: the word משחה is used only twice in the Pentateuch in the sense of "allotted portion," at Lev 7:35 and Num 18:8; and in only two Priestly passages is Aaron alone addressed, at Lev 10:8 and Num 18:1, 8. It is reasonable to see something other than chance in the concentration of these unique features in three pericopes in which the phrase חקת עולם לדרתיכם (לדרתם) ("an eternal law throughout your generations") appears. These phenomena presumably have a common provenance. This hypothesis is supported by noting the relationship between Num 18:9, 12–14, 20; and Ezek 44:28–30a. Even more important, how-

Bücher Numeri, Deuteronomium und Josua [2nd ed.; Leipzig, 1866] 50), who also notes that the word בארצכם ("in your land"), which appears in Num 10:9, is a common HS phrase.

21. Wellhausen, *Hexateuch*, 175; Kuenan, *Hexateuch*, 96 n. 38.

22. A. Toeg, "A Halakhic Midrash in Num. XV:22–31" (Hebrew), *Tarbiz* 43 (1974) 1–20; see also J. Milgrom, "The Two Pericopes on the Purification Offering," in *The Word of the Lord Shall Go Forth* (Festschrift D. N. Freedman; Winona Lake, IN, 1983) 211–15.

23. Toeg, "Halakhic Midrash," n. 18. While I disagree with Toeg's principal explanation (see chapter 4, n. 19), on this point he appears to be correct.

ever, is the fact that there is a substantive connection between the views of HS and one of the laws in this chapter, namely, the law concerning the redemption of the firstborn for five silver shekels (18:15–16). Classical exegetes had noticed that the basis of this ritual is the replacement of all the Israelite firstborn by the Levites and redemption of the extra firstborn for five shekels, a story presented in full in Num 3:11–51.[24] The idea of the replacement is expressed several times (3:12–13, 41, 45), and in every case a similar expression recurs: "They will be mine; I am the Lord" (v. 13); "To me, I am the Lord" (v. 41); "And the Levites shall be mine . . . I am the Lord" (v. 45). In two of these cases (vv. 13, 45), the expression "I am the Lord" ends the verse, a well-known characteristic of HS.[25] Yet more evidence for the connection with HS is the comparison of 3:13, "For every firstborn is mine: at the time that I smote every firstborn in the land of Egypt, I consecrated every firstborn in Israel, man and beast, to myself to be mine, the Lord's," with the verse concluding the jubilee laws in the Holiness Code, "For it is to me that the Israelites are servants: they are my servants, whom I freed from the land of Egypt, I the Lord your God" (Lev 25:55), where the close similarity in outlook and manner of expression is evident. It may be concluded, then, that the idea of transferring the sanctity of the firstborn to the Levites, and therefore the ritual of the redemption of the firstborn which developed from it, both come from HS.[26] Finally, it is important to take note of the construction לחלל קדש, which appears at the end of chap. 18: ואת קדשי בני־ישראל לא תחללו ("but you must not profane the sacred donations of the Israelites"). This construction, along with the similar ones חלל שם קדש and חלל מקדש, is common in the Holiness Code (Lev 19:8; 20:3; 21:12, 23, 32; 22:15, 32). It is not found, however, in PT, which prefers the term למעול מעל (e.g., Lev 5:14, 21; and see chapter 1, n. 19).

All the passages in the group of references outside the central PT corpus display marked linguistic and ideational connections to HS. Additionally, there came to light elements common to the two groups of appearances of the phrase חקת עולם לדרתיכם, indicating that both originated in a single stratum of composition. The lateness of this stratum relative to the PT complex is demonstrated by the secondary character of passages from this stratum appearing in the central PT corpus.

In summary, we can say that the formula חקת עולם לדרתיכם ("an eternal law throughout your generations") is unique to HS. It is composed of two expressions: חקת עולם ("an eternal law") and לדרתיכם ("throughout your generations"), each of which appears alone in PT[27] and each of which denotes constancy and

24. See Ibn Ezra's comment on Num 3:45.

25. The relationship with HS was already noted by Klostermann (*Pentateuch*, 377); see also Dillmann, *Hexateuch*, 640.

26. See Loewenstamm, "Investiture of Levi" (Heb.), 172, who also notes the relationship between Num 3:11 and 18:6.

27. It may be that one PT verse already evinces the tendency to conflate the two expressions. In the Masoretic Text of Exod 30:21 we read: והיתה להם חק עולם לו ולזרעו לדרתם ("It shall be an eternal law for them—for him and his descendants—throughout their generations"). M. Paran appears to be correct in his opinion that the reading חקת עולם, as in the Samaritan version, is to be preferred to חק עולם (*Forms of the Priestly Style in the Pentateuch* [Heb.] [Jerusalem, 1988–89] 232). If so, we have here a combination of the two expres-

eternality. The conflation of the two expressions is in accord with HS practice, which creates pleonastic phrases (see chapter 1, n. 58, chapter 2, n. 109). However, it may also be that the intent is to achieve clarity and emphasis: the expression לדרתיכם by itself could be taken to be solely an address to those generations present, while the additions of the expression חקת עולם points unmistakably toward the dimension of eternality.[28]

---

sions, although not directly juxtaposed. Taking into consideration the fact that Exodus 30 originates in a late stratum of PT (see chapter 1, n. 58, and chapter 2, n. 8), we seem to be witnessing a transitional stage between PT style and the language of HS.

28. Compare the language of *Mekhilta:* "'Throughout your generations.' This means that this practice should obtain for all generations. But I might understand 'throughout your generations' to mean, the minimum number of generations, i.e., two generations. Scripture, therefore, says: You shall keep it a feast by an ordinance forever" (*Mekhilta de-R. Yishmaᶜel,* Tractate *Pisha,* end of chap. 7, ed. Horovitz-Rabin, p. 27; trans. J. Z. Lauterbach [Philadelphia, 1933] 1:60).

EXCURSUS

2

The Use of the Word מלבד *in the Editorial Stratum of the Torah*

The use of the word מלבד as a preposition is limited to the editorial stratum of the Torah. It appears both in short glosses and additions and in legal and exhortative passages that were added to the Torah during the final stages of its redaction.[1] In order to prove this assertion, let us now look at the places in which מלבד is used in the Torah, in order of appearance.

1. Gen 26:1. The use of מלבד, which here refers to Gen 12:10, has long been recognized as an editorial addition.[2]

2. Gen 46:26. The end of the verse (as well as the main part of the following verse) has been recognized as the work of editors. (See above, n. 2.) It would seem that the words מלבד שני בני יעקב are also editorial, as was suggested by Dillmann.

3. Lev 9:17. The mention of the daily sacrifice in this verse has been shown to be an editor's addition.[3]

4. Lev 23:38. This verse was added to the original conclusion of the festivals passage at v. 37. The verse begins with the words מלבד שבתות ה', which refer to the additional sacrifices on the Sabbath, no mention of which occurs in the passage that HS placed at the beginning of the chapter. It appears that whoever added this verse sought to fill in what was left absent from the opening, and thus it would seem to be the work of late editors.

5. Num 5:8. The "Ram of Atonement" mentioned here (v. 8b) has been judged by scholars to be a secondary feature of the passage. I believe, however,

1. The frequent use of the term in the editorial material in the Pentateuch was already noted by A. Dillmann in several places (see *Die Genesis* [6th ed.; Leipzig, 1892] 323; *Die Bücher Exodus und Leviticus* [3rd ed.; Leipzig, 1897] 513; *Die Bücher Numeri, Deuteronomium und Josua* 2nd ed.; Leipzig, 1866] 379), but he does not consider this to be exclusively characteristic of the editorial stratum.

2. See Dillmann's commentary on Gen 26:1; S. R. Driver, *The Book of Genesis* (London, 1904) ad loc.; J. Skinner, *Genesis* (2nd ed.; London, 1912).

3. See Dillmann's commentary on Lev 9:17. On the meaning of this addition, see below, p. 169 and n. 69.

that Milgrom is correct in seeing it as an integral part of the original law.[4] I would suggest, though, that the law belongs to the last compositional stage of HS, simultaneous with the redaction of the Pentateuch, thus making the use of מלבד understandable. The intent of this law and its relation to the guilt offering legislation in Leviticus 5 will be clarified in later chapters.

6. Num 6:21. This verse is quite difficult, and many different explanations of it have been proposed by interpreters ancient and modern. In our opinion, the construction מלבד אשר תשיג ידו reflects an editorial attempt to clarify the verse, which in the end only created more confusion. The original verse probably read something like this:

> זאת תורת הנזיר אשר ידר קרבנו לה׳ על־
> נזרו כפי נדרו אשר ידר כן יעשה על תורת
> נזרו.

The beginning of the verse is really the conclusion of the laws of the Nazirite (Num 6:13–20). As in several other places in the central PT corpus, the conclusion of the group of laws is accompanied by an "escape clause," which allows for variation in the usual complement of sacrifices in certain cases.[5] However, while such provisions in PT always serve to lighten the sacrificial burden for those who are too poor to afford the prescribed offerings, here the gloss deals with additions to the standard complement:

> כפי נדרו אשר ידר כן יעשה על תורת נזרו

This statement, "In accordance with the vow which he took, he shall act, in addition to the prescribed Nazirite offerings," means that the requirements established by the law of the Nazirite—a sheep as burnt offering, a ewe as sin offering, and a ram as a sacrifice of well-being—are the minimum, but if the Nazirite took upon himself to bring additional sacrifices on the day of the completion of his Nazirhood, he must do as he promised, "in addition to the prescribed Nazirite offerings."[6] In the PT leniency clauses, poverty is offered as a reason for special consideration,[7] but here no explanation is given for deviation from the norm. The editors attempted to rectify the situation by adding the phrase מלבד אשר תשיג ידו ("besides whatever he can afford"), which attributed the additional sacrifices to the Nazirite's wealth.

7. Num 17:14. The words מלבד המתים על דבר קרח are an editorial addition, as was noted by Dillmann.[8] The reason for this addition and its role in the editorial process of the Korah story will be explained in a later chapter.

4. B. S. Jackson, *Theft in Early Jewish Law* (Oxford, 1972) 173; J. Milgrom, *Cult and Conscience* (Leiden, 1976) 106 n. 396.

5. Lev 5:7–14; 14:21–32. Most like this instance, however, is the brief note appended to the section regarding postpartum purification (Lev 12:8).

6. On the amplificatory use of על in PT, see chapter 1, n. 65. This explanation of על in the verse under consideration is adopted from the Sifrei by Rashi.

7. ואם לא תגיע ידו (Lev 5:7); ואם לא תשיג ידו (Lev 5:11); ואם לא תמצא ידה (Lev 12:8); ואם דל הוא ואין ידו משגת (Lev 14:21).

8. Dillmann, *Numeri*, 97.

8. Numbers 28–29. The many uses of מלבד in this section dealing with the festivals and their sacrifices (in the third passage, about the Passover, and in the fourth and subsequent passages) were discussed in the full interpretation of this section given above. It was argued that while the amplifications beginning with על, in the first two passages, are original, those beginning with מלבד are editorial additions. (See above, pp. 30–32.)

9. Deut 4:35. It is widely accepted that the entire chapter containing this verse belongs to the latest stratum of Deuteronomy, which explains the use of מלבדו.

10. Deut 28:69. As suggested by Dillmann, this is an editorial addition intended to establish the relationship between the covenant described in the earlier chapters of the book and the one described in chaps. 29–30.[9]

9. Dillmann, *Deuteronomium*, 379.

CHAPTER 2

The Separation of the Priestly Stratum of the Pentateuch into Its Constituent Parts

In the first chapter, which focused on the issues of the Sabbath and the cult in the Priestly stratum of the Pentateuch, we suggested that the prevalent opinion in biblical scholarship, which considers the source entitled H (Holiness Code) to be earlier than P (Priestly Torah), is fundamentally wrong. Furthermore, we demonstrated, through our analysis of the festival law, that the extent of H is far wider than hitherto assumed. As stated at the beginning of chapter 1, the validation of these claims calls for a thorough examination of the Priestly material in the Pentateuch, separating this stratum into its constituent parts and determining the chronological relation of the material originating in PT to the Scriptures of HS origin. This analysis will also yield two separate bodies of Scripture—the corpus of PT and that of HS; this will enable us, at the end of chapter 2, to compile two glossaries of words and terms, each corresponding to one of the two Priestly schools. These two listings of Scriptures will form the basis for the discussion developed in subsequent chapters—a survey of the conceptions of God and the cult in PT and HS—examining both the common elements in the two sources as well as the differences between them.

Rather than examine the entire Priestly corpus of the Pentateuch, we will restrict our attention to texts dealing with belief and the cult. We will not treat genealogical lists, census lists, and the like, nor narrative or legal units unrelated to the religious or cultic realm. Because the Scriptures related to the cult constitute, qualitatively and quantitatively, the bulk of the Priestly material in the Pentateuch, I believe that the philological conclusions derived from our analysis will be founded on solid textual ground. A special problem is posed by those pericopes in which Priestly material is blended with non-Priestly traditions, as in the stories of the flood, the ten plagues, the scouts, and others. As a rule, we will avoid the convoluted problem of separation of all sources, restricting our inquiry to identification and analysis of clearly defined, ideologically significant Priestly units embedded in those pericopes.

In identifying the components of the Priestly stratum in this chapter, we will aim to employ linguistic and literary criteria, avoiding reference to ideological characteristics of the two schools. In employing this approach, we will distinguish the first stage–identification of the various collections of Scriptures–from the later stage, in which we will investigate the concepts of belief and the cult in these sources. Our analysis will generally follow the order of the passages in the Pentateuch, beginning with the Priestly stratum of the book of Genesis.

The Book of Genesis

A large portion of the Priestly material in this book has no clear theological or cultic significance. In accordance with the guidelines we have set out, we shall discuss only those texts of immediate concern to those subjects; these are (1) the creation story (1:1–4a); (2) the introductory and concluding verses of the flood story (6:9–22; 9:1–17); (3) the covenant with Abraham (chap. 17); (4) the revelation to Jacob (35:9–13; 48:3–6). In most of these units we find no linguistic features typical of HS; thus, we may assign them to PT, as is commonly accepted. The covenant with Abraham in chapter 17 is an exception, as it contains expressions common in HS (in vv. 7–8 and 14), but, for methodological reasons, we will postpone discussion of this section to the conclusion of this chapter.

The Book of Exodus

The book opens with the story of the enslavement in Egypt, the narrative of the ten plagues, and the exodus. The narrative fabric is woven of various sources and includes several legal units. As we stated earlier, we will limit our investigation to "pure" Priestly units of theological or cultic import.

Exodus 2:23aβ–25

Biblical scholarship has regarded this passage as a continuation of the Priestly traditions on the enslavement (Exod 1:13–14). Nothing in these verses leads us to question their assignment to PT.

Exodus 6:2–7:6

This unit, which is a preamble to the narrative of the ten plagues, is composed of three major units: (1) God's revelation to Moses and the announcement of redemption (6:2–8); (2) the genealogical lists of Reuben, Simon and Levi, and their descendants (6:14–25); (3) the mission to Pharaoh and the explanation of the purpose of the plagues (7:1–6). Connecting these passages are transition verses (6:9–13, 26–30), edited in chiastic form, creating a resumptive repetition which facilitates the introduction of the genealogical list without substantially interrupting the narrative flow.[1] It would seem that, before the genealogical list was incorporated into the chapter, units 1 and 3 formed a single narrative block.[2] Indeed, the two units are linguistically related (cf. 6:6; with 7:4, 5). In the previous chapter we determined that unit 1 originates in HS;[3] thus, unit 3 belongs to HS as well. As far as the genealogical list is concerned, I believe that its inclusion was the work of a late editor—also of HS—and was designed to draw attention to the relation of the families of Aaron and Korah, as preparation for the final version of the rebellion of Korah narrative in the final editing stage of HS, as we will analyze later. In summary, the unit Exod 6:2–7:6 is entirely of HS and reflects two stages in the production of this school.[4]

Exodus 7:8–13; 8:12–15; 9:8–12

These are the "pure" Priestly units of the narrative of the ten plagues. Their common elements have already been identified by many scholars.[5] These passages are usually attributed to PT, and I see no grounds for questioning this ascription.

Exodus 11:9–10

These verses, along with Exod 7:2–6, which introduces the story of the ten plagues, form an *inclusio* containing the narrative of the ten plagues.[6]

1. See M. Greenberg, *Understanding Exodus* (New York, 1969) 143.
2. The two passages were linked, either by 6:10–12 or by the almost identical 6:29, 30. It is hard to decide which of the two pericopes is original and which was a duplicate added in order to create a resumptive repetition.
3. See chapter 1, n. 23, and the reference there to the writings of previous scholars.
4. The passage Exod 6:13 may be of PT origin. The verse may have linked the PT 2:23–25 to the PT pericope Exod 7:8–13.
5. See the summary of research in B. S. Childs, *The Book of Exodus* (4th ed.; OTL; Philadelphia, 1974) 130ff.
6. This was pointed out by Greenberg (*Exodus,* 192) and Childs (*Exodus,* 161).

We saw earlier that its entry passage, Exod 7:2–6, is a product of the Holiness School. Thus, the closing passage must have been framed by the same school. The composition is a product of the editorial activity of HS on the plagues narrative.[7]

Exodus 12–16

At the end of the plagues narrative we find the laws of the Passover and the feast of Unleavened Bread, including two markedly Priestly units: Exod 12:1–20 and 12:43–49. We have already located their origin as HS (see Excursus 1 and above, pp. 20–21). Additional Priestly units appear in the story of the parting of the Reed Sea in Exodus 14, but, in accordance with our limitations, we will not analyze this nonhomogeneous chapter. A similar blending of Priestly and non-Priestly traditions may be found in Exodus 16. Here too we will avoid detailed analysis of the sources, noting only that the Priestly material in this chapter originates in the Holiness School (see above, pp. 16–17).

The second portion of the book of Exodus tells of the revelation at Mount Sinai and related events (making of the covenant, the golden calf) and the building of the Tabernacle. We may divide this literary material into four main sections: (1) the revelation at Mount Sinai and the making of the covenant (Exod 19:1–24:11); (2) the commands concerning the construction of the Tabernacle and the sanctification of Aaron and his children for the priesthood (Exod 25:1–31:11); (3) the golden calf (Exod 32:1–34:28); (4) the construction of the Tabernacle (Exod 35:4–40:38). Units 2 and 4 are Priestly, while 1 and 3 are products of JE. These units are linked by transition passages: 24:12–18; 31:12–18; 34:29–35:3. We must

7. I think we may also attribute to HS the mention of the hardening of Pharaoh's heart in Exod 4:21b; 9:35; 10:20, 27. These verses have already been identified as belonging to the editorial stratum of the ten plagues narrative (see R. E. Friedman, "Sacred History and Theology: The Redaction of Torah," in *The Creation of Sacred Torah-Literature* [ed. R. E. Friedman; University of California Publications: Near Eastern Studies 22; Berkeley, 1981] 33). On the editorial additions of HS to Exod 10:1–2, the introductory passage to the plague of locusts, see chapter 1, n. 23. The verses in Exod 10:21–23 dealing with the plague of darkness should also be attributed to HS. Most scholars tend to attribute the plague of darkness to E, but this ascription is dubious (see M. Greenberg, "The Redaction of the Plague in Exodus," in *Near Eastern Studies – in Honor of William Foxwell Albright* [ed. Hans Goedicke; Baltimore, 1971] 248). The main heroes of the PT tradition of the ten plagues, Aaron and the magicians, are absent from these verses (ibid.). As a result of the lack of clarity surrounding these verses, W. Rudolph ("Der 'Elohist' von Exodus bis Josua," *BZAW* 68 [1938] 121) wrote that the plague of darkness was added by an unknown source. If we assume that this plague was added by the final editors of the entire ten plagues story, whom we identified as HS, then the reason for the deviation of these verses from the standard patterns of the main traditions of the ten plagues narrative becomes evident.

first determine whether the Priestly units are of PT, HS, or a blending of material of the two schools. We will then seek to identify Priestly additions to units 1 and 3. Finally, we will attempt to determine the origin of the transition passages and identify the school of editors who assembled the various sources into a single corpus.

Exodus 25:1–31:11

This unit is composed of three scrolls and is mostly of PT. The first scroll includes ordinances on the making of the ark, the table and the Menorah, the Tabernacle, the altar of sacrifice, and the court of the Tabernacle (25:10–27:19). The second section deals with the sanctification of Aaron and his sons for the priesthood and the priestly vestments (28:1–29:37). The third unit, which appears to be a later addition, includes ordinances pertaining to the altar of incense, the expiation monies, the laver, the oil of anointment, and the incense (30:1–38).[8]

In Excursus 1 we showed that the transition passages linking the first source to the second (27:20–21) and the second section to the third (29:38–46) are additions of the HS editors, and we gave the reasons for these additions. I now suggest that the introductory and closing passages of the entire unit (25:1–9 and 31:1–11) were composed by the same hand.

The main issue in the opening passage is the ordinance concerning the collection of gifts for the building of the Tabernacle, an ordinance that concludes with the statement of purpose, "and let them make me a sanctuary that I may dwell among them" (25:8). The use of the word מקדש as a synonym for the parallel word משכן is never found in PT,[9] but is common in HS.[10] Another link to the style of HS appears in the words of God, addressed to the entire community of Israel, in the second person plural,[11]

8. The secondary nature of these laws is accepted by scholars. Much attention has been focused on the question of the originality of the tradition of the altar of incense. Although I agree that the position of this scroll in the biblical narrative attests to its relative lateness, I believe it belongs to a relatively late stratum of PT. See also chapter 1, n. 60.

9. "She shall not enter the Sanctuary" (Lev 12:4) means, as Ibn Ezra has already demonstrated, that she shall not enter the sanctified area of the Tabernacle courtyard, for she may not enter the Tabernacle itself even when pure.

10. See Lev 19:30; 20:3; 21:12; 26:2, 31. J. Milgrom claims that the word מקדש is never used in PT to mean a house and that all references to מקדש in the above-mentioned verses refer to the sanctified enclosure (*Studies in Levitical Terminology* [Leiden 1983]). I am of the opinion that the simple meaning of the texts does not support this claim. These verses exhort people to venerate the sanctuary and guard its purity. Undoubtedly the primary object of this sanctity and veneration is the house itself and not the auxiliary enclosure. In any case, Milgrom too admits that in Exod 25:8 מקדש refers to the house rather than to the enclosure.

11. Although the verse begins with God's first person speech to Moses referring to the

and in God's referring to himself in the first person: "you shall accept gifts for me" (25:2). The ordinance concerning the oil for the lamps in v. 6 is in harmony with Exod 27:20–21, where HS added what was missing from PT (see Excursus 1).[12] All these signs lead us to attribute the opening section to HS.

The concluding section—Exod 31:1–11—contains unique terms that appear nowhere else in the set of instructions for the construction of the Tabernacle, but only in the unit on the actual building of the Sanctuary and in the Holiness Code.[13] The link to the language of HS is evident also in the wording of v. 6: ואני הנה נתתי אתו, "Moreover, I have assigned to him." God's speech in the first person, presenting himself as "I" is very common in H; the characteristic closing formula of this school is "I am the Lord."[14]

One idea is frequently mentioned in all the verses added by HS: unlike in PT, where the ordinances concerning the construction of the Tabernacle are addressed to Moses alone and the construction of the Tabernacle is seen as an obligation entirely incumbent on Moses himself,[15] HS em-

---

people in the third person plural, ויקחו לי תרומה, the subsequent first person divine speech, which ends with the direct address תקחו, is directed to the entire congregation of Israelites. As M. Paran explained, the preceding formulation דבר אל בני ישראל requires an address in third person plural at the beginning of the following verse (*Forms of the Priestly Style in the Pentateuch* [Jerusalem, 1989] 72). On God's addressing the community of Israel in the first person singular in H, see Introduction, n. 3. This trait is also characteristic of HS writings outside of H. See Exod 6:6–8; 12:12–13; 16:12; 29:42; 31:13; Lev 7:34.

12. This was noticed by S. R. Driver, *The Book of Exodus* (CBSC; Cambridge, 1911) 266. On the absence of this verse in the Septuagint, see the pertinent argument of Dillmann.

13. A term unique only to our passage and to the section on the building of the Tabernacle is בגדי השרד, accompanied here by the explanatory words ואת בגדי הקדש לאהרן (הכהן) ואת בגדי בניו לכהן) (31:10; 35:19; 39:1, 41; on the meaning of this expression see M. Haran, *Temples and Temple Service in Ancient Israel* [Oxford, 1978] 172–73). Another unique expression is ואת הארון לעדת in v. 7. Dillmann, who identified the unique linguistic character of the passage, also noticed its relationship to the unit on the erection of the Tabernacle. As all these unique elements are concentrated in vv. 7–10, Dillmann sought to separate vv. 1–6, which he saw as PT material, from vv. 7–11, which he viewed as a later addition. I believe that this suggestion is unacceptable, because v. 6 too deviates from the accepted PT style, as we shall show later. Because vv. 1–6 cannot stand as an independent unit, we are forced to view the entire passage as an editorial addition. (Compare M. Noth, *Exodus* [trans. J. S. Bowden; OTL; London, 1962] 239). The reason for this addition will be explained later.

14. On the divine use of אני in H, see Introduction, n. 3. Other examples from HS outside H are Exod 6:6–8; 10:2; 12:12; 16:12; 29:46; 31:13.

15. In the first verses of chap. 28, at the beginning of the scroll on the sanctification of priests, we find a group of ordinances, some addressed to individuals, others to groups. In v. 2, Moses is asked to make the holy vestments. Later, in vv. 3–6, the instructions for making the vestments were addressed to all skilled persons, whereas later in the passage, the orders are again addressed to Moses. I believe that B. Baentsch is correct in seeing vv. 3–5 as a later expansion. Evidence for this view is that if we remove these verses, 28:1–2, 43 reads as a continuous narrative. (Read ועשו instead of ועשיתי at the beginning of v. 6. The word was revised to make the added verses fit better.) We suggest that the additional verses origi-

phasizes the all-Israelite dimension of the Tabernacle. In the opening verses it is written that the Tabernacle and its vessels shall be made from the gifts of all the people. The communal activity and its goal are explicitly stated: "Let them make me a sanctuary that I may dwell among them."[16] Even the command to take oil for lighting (27:20–21) is addressed to the entire people of Israel and, at its conclusion, the words "from the Israelites" are repeated. The addition concerning the daily burnt offering (תמיד) (29:38–46) concludes with verses that describe the purpose of the construction of the Tabernacle as the dwelling of God among the Israelites and his revelation to the entire nation: "For there I will meet with you (לכם),"[17] "and there I will meet with the Israelites" (29:42–43). PT, on the other hand, maintains that only Moses may meet with God in his Tabernacle: "There I will meet with you (לך)" (25:22; 30:6, 36). The concluding passage of this unit (31:1–11) explains that Bezalel, Oholiab, and other skilled Israelites are to carry out the work of

---

nate in HS. These verses served to stress skilled Israelites' involvement in the cult, in accordance with the consistent tendency of the school. Moreover, v. 5 says that the skilled persons took the materials for the sacred vestments, a hint on the part of HS that the materials for the priests' vestments, like all the Tabernacle vessels, came from contributions of the entire congregation (compare 25:3–4; 35:5–6, 22–25; 36:3; 39:1). The HS redactors of the additional material introduced their passage with the words ואתה תדבר in order to conform with the language of the original opening verse ואתה הקרב in v. 1 (as they did in the HS editors' interpolation in Exod 27:20–21; see excursus 1, n. 4). The effort toward linguistic uniformity is also evident in the use of the special expression לכהנו לי of vv. 3, 4, following v. 1. Note the stylistic difficulties created in v. 4 by the rigid use of this expression. Correct syntax here would be לכהנם לי.

16. The difference between the two schools may shed light on the different versions of Exod 25:9–10. Whereas in the Masoretic Text v. 9 ends with the command וכן תעשו and v. 10 begins with the instruction ועשו, the Septuagint and the Samaritan version have the singular תעשה ועשית. According to our analysis, the opening passage of HS (25:1–9) was "sewed on" to the PT core scroll of the ordinances of the Tabernacle. The original version apparently opened with the command ועשית addressed to Moses, as we find in the later commands to Moses, all formulated in the second person singular. The HS opening verse, which sought to emphasize the entire people's responsibility in erecting the Tabernacle, closed with the instruction וכן תעשו. Scribes used various devices in order to smooth over the linguistic roughness created when the introductory passage was added on to the main scroll. The Masoretic Text changed the language of command at the beginning of the PT scroll from singular to plural, whereas the Septuagint and the Samaritan versions placed the singular verb form תעשה at the end of the introductory verse. This procedure may have been influenced by the use of the singular form אותך in v. 9a (Septuagint consistently reads ועשית in the introductory passage—both in v. 8 and at the beginning of v. 9).

17. In the Septuagint, לך rather than לכם. It seems likely that this emendation was part of the tendency designed to make the first part of the passage conform to the singular form of the end of the passage לדבר אליך שם. It appears that the Masoretic Text preserves the original text, and the shift in the text from plural to singular reveals the dialectic in HS's claim that God revealed himself to all Israel. After all, HS too believed that Moses alone heard the word of God in the Tent of Meeting. The formula אוועד לכם also appears in Num 17:19, which also originates in HS, as we will demonstrate later.

the construction of the Tabernacle in practice—"that they make everything that I have commanded you," "Just as I have commanded you, they shall do" (31:6, 11). The discrepancy in the identities of the participants in the construction of the Tabernacle and the natures of the groups addressed by these ordinances according to each of the two Priestly schools is indicative of widespread ideological differences between the schools, as will be described in forthcoming chapters.

Exodus 35:4–40:38

According to unit 4 as well, the materials for the Tabernacle were contributed by all Israelites, both men and women (35:4–29) and the work was carried out by skilled Israelites (35:1–39:32).[18] The finished parts of the Tabernacle were brought to Moses (39:33–43) and Moses erected it. Thus, this unit too originates in HS. This corroborates the prevalent view in biblical scholarship on the late date of composition of unit 4.[19] Additional evidence for the assignment of this unit to HS is the mention of the work of the Levites in 28:21, which is the only time they are mentioned outside of the book of Numbers! As we will see later, the functional distinction between priests and Levites is one of the innovations of HS.

Now that we have identified the origins of the major Priestly units and discussed their composition, we will turn our attention to the transition passages linking Priestly and non-Priestly material: Exod 31:12–18; 34:29–34; 35:1–3. Two elements surface repeatedly in each of the transition passages: the expression ששת ימים ... וביום השביעי ("Six days . . . and on the seventh day") (24:16; 31:15; 35:2) and the mention of the giving of the stone tablets to Moses (as a command, Exod 24:12; the giving of the tablets, Exod 31:18; descending the mountain with the tablets, Exod 34:29). Examining these elements in the order of their appearance in the transition passages, we obtain the following schema:

18. As the chief artisan was Bezalel and the names of Ohaliav and other skilled men were added on (see Exod 35:30–36:2), the execution of the work of building the Tabernacle is sometimes described in the singular ויעש and sometimes in the plural ויעשו.

19. See a summary of the literature in Childs, *Exodus*, 5:24–30, and his remarks there on the Septuagint version. V. Hurowitz has recently compared the twofold description of the command to build the Tabernacle and the description of its execution to descriptions of Temple construction in the ancient Near East ("The Priestly Account of Building the Tabernacle," *JAOS* 105 [1985] 21–30). He admits, however, that the original story of the Tabernacle may have been restricted to chaps. 24–29 (p. 29) and that these chapters are not dependent on paradigms of temple building but belong to another genre, such as that of Priestly instructions.

Transition passage 1: לחת האבן, ששת ימים ... וביום השביעי (24:12–16).
Transition passage 2: ששת ימים ... וביום השביעי, לחת העדת לחת האבן (31:15, 18).
Transition passage 3: לחת העדת; ששת ימים ... וביום השביעי (34:29–35:2).

We see here a chiasmus (a–b, b–a, a–b), including a gradual transition from לחת האבן via לחת העדת לחת האבן to לחת העדת. This observation, when combined with other literary-artistic traits of these transition passages, previously discussed by critical Bible scholars,[20] yields the full picture of a complex and sophisticated redactional enterprise.

Which school was responsible for the editing? We have already determined that the Sabbath passages—Exod 31:12–17 and 35:1–3, which account for an important part of the transition passages—originate in HS (see above, pp. 14–17). It seems probable that the entire editing project and all the transition passages are the product of this school. The frequent blending of Priestly and non-Priestly elements in these transition passages,[21] a phenomenon we remarked about in editorial passages of HS elsewhere, supports this conclusion (see chapter 1, n. 23).

Finally, let us examine Priestly additions to the JE corpus in units 1 and 3. As we explained in n. 22, the phrase לחת העדות was coined by editors of the HS school. Thus, we must credit them with its appearance in Exod 32:15. Another Priestly addition already discussed in the critical literature is the reason given for the Sabbath commandment in the Decalogue (Exod 20:11). Contrary to the prevalent view, which attributes this verse to PT, I am of the opinion that it issues from HS, because it is similar in its style and anthropomorphic flavor to the HS Sabbath passage in Exod 31:17. In the PT Sabbath passage (Gen 2:2–3), the style is different, and the anthropomorphic image of God's rest is lacking.[22]

20. See A. Toeg, *Lawgiving at Sinai* (Jerusalem, 1971) 146; M. Paran identified the chiastic structure of the Sabbath passage in Exod 31:13–17 (*Priestly Style,* 167–69). In his opinion, this structure is evidence of the HS origin of the passage.

21. This phenomenon has already been investigated by several scholars, with the following conclusions: The first part of the passage, Exod 24:12–18 is JE and the latter part (vv. 15b–18), PT. Verse 12 contains a mixture of styles (see Toeg, *Lawgiving,* 10, 79–80). The composite nature of 31:18 is accepted by all scholars, and traces of different styles are reflected in 34:29–35 as well (see A. Kuenen, *An Historico-Critical Inquiry into the Origin and Composition of the Hexateuch* [trans. P. H. Wicksteed; London, 1886] 76 n. 14; Noth, *Exodus,* 267; Toeg, *Lawgiving,* 10–11). As Kuenen showed (p. 332), the phrase לחת העדת, which appears twice in transition verses (31:18; 34:29), was composed by editors who conjoined לחת of the JE phrase לחת האבן with עדת of PT. On the other mention of לחת העדת, in 32:15, see below.

22. This difference between the Sabbath passage in Genesis and Exodus was observed by M. Cassuto, *A Commentary on the Book of Genesis* (trans. I. Abrahams; Jerusalem, 1967) 39. In spite of Y. Kaufmann's criticisms (*From the Crucible of Biblical Creativity* [Hebrew] [Tel Aviv, 1966] 233), I believe that this observation is valid and reflects the difference between the overall aims of the two Priestly schools (see below, chapter 4, n. 14).

We may then conclude that HS is responsible for combining the PT scrolls dealing with the ordinances establishing the Tabernacle and sanctifying Aaron and his sons for the priesthood (unit 2) with the JE traditions on the giving of the Torah, the making of the covenant, and the golden calf (units 2 and 4). This blending was effected through transition passages edited in chiastic form; these passages are characterized by a blending of PT language with JE expressions, with several expressions unique to HS added in.[23] The sewing together of the PT scrolls to form unit 2 is also, apparently, the work of HS. HS surrounded these scrolls with passages emphasizing the participation of all Israelites in the Tabernacle, employing linguistic devices to smooth out the transition points. The unit concluding the book of Exodus, which describes in detail the actual construction of the Tabernacle and its cult (unit 4) stems from HS, and it was added to highlight the all-Israelite nature of the Tabernacle.

The Book of Leviticus

The first part of the book of Leviticus (chaps. 1–16) includes the main corpus of PT, but several editorial additions of HS are scattered throughout the material. So far we have identified four such additions: Lev 3:17 (and the words כל חלב in v. 16); Lev 7:22–36; Lev 10:8–11 (see Excursus 1); Lev 16:29b–33 (see above, pp. 27–29). To this group we may now add three more:

Leviticus 10:6–7

In Excursus 1 we determined that the section prohibiting the drinking of wine by priests during their service in the Temple (Lev 10:8–11) stems from HS. This passage is preceded by two verses in which Moses instructs Aaron and his surviving sons not to bewail Nadab and Abihu nor to leave the entrance to the Tabernacle. Some scholars deduced from this prohibition against leaving the Tabernacle that, according to these verses, the period of ordination had not yet been completed, contrary to what is written in Lev 9:1.[24] But in his commentary, A. Dillmann rightly remarked that the contradiction is only apparent, as the prohibition against leaving the Tabernacle in Lev 10:7 is unrelated to the days of ordination. Rather, it is a standing order, as explained in the section of mourning prohibitions pertaining to the high priest in H (Lev 21:10–12). The great sim-

23. For example: אני ה' מקדשכם, Exod 31:13; אני ה', Exod 35:3 (Septuagint).

24. J. Wellhausen, *Die Composition des Hexateuchs* (3rd ed.; Berlin, 1899) 140, 147; Kuenen, *Hexateuch,* 85 n. 21.

ilarity to the HS section seems to indicate an HS origin for Lev 10:6-7 as well.[25] It appears that the editors of this school wished to anchor the prohibitions applying to the priests in the narrative of the sin and death of the two sons of Aaron, and thus introduced vv. 6-11.[26]

Leviticus 11:43-45

In Leviticus 11, the Bible discusses food taboos. The style of the section and the colophon concluding it (11:46-47) is typical of PT,[27] but directly preceding the colophon we find an auxiliary passage (vv. 43-45) which bears the distinctive traits of HS.[28] It seems that HS editors saw fit to include here the dominant reason for the purity laws that applied to all of Israel, according to their school's view.[29]

Leviticus 15:31

Chapter 15 includes ordinances concerning various bodily impurities. As is customary in PT, the chapter ends with the colophon . . . זאת תורת (15:32-33; see n. 27). Just as we found in Leviticus 11, so too here, the colophon is immediately preceded by a hortatory verse, it too, apparently formulated by HS. Evidence for this may be seen in the verse ולא ימתו

25. See A. Dillmann, *Die Bücher Numeri, Deuteronomium und Josua* (2nd ed.; Leipzig, 1886) 644. Noth also emphasizes the passage's dependence on Leviticus 21.

26. The prohibitions are directed toward Aaron and his sons, corresponding to the book of Ezekiel, in which similar prohibitions, phrased in very similar language, are addressed to the community of priests (Ezek 44:20-21, 23, 25). By contrast, the Holiness Code distinguishes between the high priest and the other priests applying prohibitions to them with differing degrees of severity. This contradiction could be resolved if we note that the sons of Aaron were also anointed with the oil of anointing; thus they would enjoy a superior status equal to that of the high priest and superior to that of lay priests.

27. Compare the concluding colophon to its parallels in the PT corpus: Lev 7:37; 12:7; 13:59; 14:32, 54-56; 15:32-33. On colophons in PT and in the Bible in general, see M. Fishbane, "Accusation of Adultery: A Study of Law and Scribal Practise in Numbers 5:11-31," *HUCA* 45 (1974) 32-35; idem, "Biblical Colophons: Textual Criticism and Legal Analogies," *CBQ* 42 (1980) 438-49.

28. The HS origin of these passages has been observed by many scholars. Some scholars claim that the two appearances of the exhortation formula (vv. 43-44a and vv. 44b-45) should be assigned to different sources. But, because both are clearly HS-style formulations, they belong to the same source; perhaps we have two alternative formulations written down side by side, as is common in ancient literature. Compare Lev 20:7-8 (Baentsch), and for the phenomenon in general, see S. Talmon, "Double Reading in the MT," *Textus* 1 (1960) 112-31.

29. We find a summary of our chapter's prohibitions in H (Lev 20:25-26) supported by the same justification.

בטמאתם בטמאם את משכני אשר בתוכם. In PT, the word משכן never appears in a possessive form or in a construct form along with the name of God. In HS, on the other hand, the forms משכן ה׳, משכני, מקדשי, and מקדש אלהיו are common.[30] This difference is not accidental but derives from differing conceptions of God in the two schools, as will be elaborated later. Furthermore, the hortatory verse (15:31) explains that the transgressors of the purity laws defile the sanctuary. This concept is also the basis for the following chapter (chap. 16), which discusses the annual expiation rite. It may be that v. 31 was meant to link the corpus of purity and impurity laws in Leviticus 11–15 with the ceremony described in chap. 16. As part of the final editing process of the HS redactor of PT, the unit on purity and impurity was inserted between chap. 10 and chap. 16, which, together, formed a single narrative unit.[31]

The redaction style of the PT corpus in Leviticus 1–16 is very similar to that of the linking passages between the Priestly units on the Tabernacle. In both cases, we find that the editors added linking verses mainly at the margins of the PT scrolls. These additions were usually made in order to introduce concepts or explanations peculiar to HS. Apparently the HS redactors received completed texts of laws and scrolls of PT; they then determined the sequence of the individual scrolls, linked them together, and thus left their distinctive intellectual imprint on them.[32]

Leviticus 17–26

This is the main corpus of HS literary creation, called the "Holiness Code" by scholars. Starting with the prevalent view in biblical scholarship that HS precedes PT, scholars have identified signs of PT redaction and adaptation of HS material. Since I am of the opinion that this view is fundamentally wrong and that HS is later than PT, I also dispute the claim that the Holiness Code was edited by PT. The reasons for my objections are specified in Excursus 3.

In my mind, the question to be posed is, Did the authors of HS incorporate into the Holiness Code—their collection of laws—earlier materials originating in PT? In chapter 1, we saw that in Leviticus 23 a PT festival scroll was incorporated and adapted by HS. But, to the best of my knowledge, this is the only chapter in the Holiness Code for which we can provide substantial evidence for a PT origin. All the other chapters of the

30. משכני (Lev 26:11); מקדשי (Lev 19:30; 20:3; 26:2); משכן ה׳ (Lev 17:4); מקדש אלהיו (Lev 21:12). As we mentioned above (n. 10), משכן and מקדש are parallel terms in HS. Both Baentsch and Noth agree that Lev 15:31 is an editorial addition.

31. K. Elliger, *Leviticus* (HAT; Tübingen, 1966) 196.

32. On PT as a compilation of scrolls, see Introduction, n. 22.

book of Leviticus contain many concepts and expressions deriving from the vocabulary and laws of PT. Although this fact attests to the continuity between the two schools, there is not a single literary unit that may be assigned in its entirety to PT.

The Book of Numbers

The book of Numbers contains many Priestly legal and narrative sections. Although we are often unable to explain properly the sequence of these units in the biblical text, we may identify several main units, each treating a specific theme.

The Levite Treatise

In the middle of the first eighteen chapters of the book of Numbers, we find the section dealing with the Levites. The discussion of the Levites and their work[33] is linked to the series of marches and encampments described at the beginning of the book.[34] As this book contains a description of the wanderings of the Israelites in the Sinai desert after the construction of the Tabernacle, it became necessary to describe the dismantling, transport, and reassembly of the Tabernacle during the wanderings period. Thus, we find, at the beginning of the book of Numbers, reference to the Levites as those responsible for these functions. Previously, the Levites were mentioned only in Exod 38:21, as part of a unit dealing with the construction of the Tabernacle, which we have already identified as a product of HS (see above, p. 66). The Levites are also mentioned in the section on the chieftains' sacrifices (see chap. 7, esp. vv. 4–9) and in the Korah narrative (chaps. 16–17, esp. 16:8–11). Henceforth, we will refer to the corpus dealing with the Levites and their work as the Levite Treatise. This treatise appears in the Bible in the form of small sections, broken up by legal and narrative units. At one time, it may have formed a single continuous narrative, which, at the stage of the final redaction of the Pentateuch, was divided into several smaller portions, while other sections, most of them unrelated to the Levites' work were

33. The assignment of the Levities to the Tabernacle, the census of the Levites and the duties assigned them, the ceremony of the Levites' wave offering and the gifts allotted to them are discussed in the following verses: Num 1:48–54; 3:5–4:49; 8:5–26; 18:1–32. To this list we might add Exod 38:21, which is, as we mentioned above (p. 66), the only passage outside the book of Numbers discussing the Levites' tasks.

34. For mention of the Levites in the encampments narrative, see Num 2:21–34 (esp. v. 17); 9:15–10:28 (esp. 10:17, 21).

added. We will attempt here to reconstruct this treatise and identify its origin.

In Excursus 1, we showed the relation between the idea of the selection of the Levites in place of the firstborn, as formulated in Numbers 3, and the law of the redemption of the firstborn in Numbers 18. Furthermore, we determined the origin of these chapters as HS. We find not only an ideological affinity between the two chapters but many similarities in linguistic usage as well:

18:2–4	3:6–7
וגם את אחיך מטה לוי שבט אביך הקרב אתך וילוו עליך וישרתוך ... ושמרו משמרתך . . . ושמרו את משמרת אהל מועד לכל עבדת האהל.	הקרב את מטה לוי והעמדת אתו לפני אהרן הכהן ושרתו אתו. ושמרו את משמרתו ואת משמרת כל העדה לפני אהל מועד לעבד את עבדת המשכן.
18:6–7	**3:9–10**
ואני הנה לקחתי את־אחיכם הלוים מתוך בני ישראל לכם מתנה נתנים ...	ונתתה את הלוים לאהרן ולבניו נתונם נתונִם המה לו מאת בני

In principle, the same language is used in both passages, but, whereas the words of chap. 3 are addressed to Moses, in chap. 18 God speaks directly to Aaron. Nevertheless, one crucial difference exists between the two passages. The central idea of chap. 3, the transfer of the historic sanctity of the firstborn to the Levites, is not explicitly mentioned in chap. 18.[35] In chap. 18, the principal mission of the Levites, which serves as the justification for their receiving of gifts, is to guard the Sanctuary so that God's wrath might be removed from Israel; there is no mention of this in chap. 3.[36] This gap is bridged by a passage describing the ceremony of purification of the Levites and their designation as a wave offering before the Lord (Num 8:5–22). This passage presents, in sequence, the principle of the substitution of the Levites for the firstborn (vv. 16–18) and the theme of expiation and the removal of the plague (v. 19). Moreover, this passage bears close linguistic affinities to passages of parallel content in Numbers 3 and 18.[37] It would seem that the three units—3:5–51; 8:5–22;

35. Even though, as we showed in Excursus 1, the law of the redemption of the firstborn (18:16–17) is derived from it.

36. As Milgrom observed, the message of chap. 18 is the charging of the priests and Levites with all responsibility for intrusion into the Sanctuary (*Studies in Levitical Terminology,* 19). They bear the sin and thus remove God's wrath from the community of Israel.

37. Compare 3:12–13 with 8:16–18, and 8:19 with 18:5–6. Noteworthy too are the linguistic and substantial affinities between 18:22–23 and 8:19, as explained at length by Milgrom (*Studies in Levitical Terminology,* 28–32).

and 18:1-32—are part of a single literary and ideological unit.[38] To this corpus we may also add Numbers 4, whose relation to chap. 3 is evident.[39]

The gradual shift from the idea of substitution to the mission of the Levites as those who remove the plague from Israel is tied to the story of the rebellion of Korah and the plague that breaks out as a result. Numbers 18 is, essentially, an answer to the fears of the people and their despair in the aftermath of the plague (see 16:27-28). It would seem that the rebellion narrative is an integral part of the narrative of the consecration of the Levites, but more careful analysis shows otherwise. The incorporation of this story into the narrative sequence results in severe difficulties in our understanding of the events. The posting of a Levite guard would have prevented Israelite intrusion into the Sanctuary but would not have solved the problem raised by Korah—the demand of the Levites that they assume functions of the priesthood. On the contrary, the appointment of Levites to guard the Tent of Meeting seems like appointing the cat to guard the cream. In the light of Korah's actions, the positive attitude toward the Levites in chap. 18 is perplexing: it seems as if they earn the gifts as a reward for their rebellion!

In order to resolve these problems, we must subject the Korah narrative to an in-depth analysis. As this matter is crucial for our understanding of the entire Levite Treatise, we will make exception to our guidelines restricting our inquiry to homogeneous passages and undertake a thorough examination of this complex tradition.

The Korah Pericope

The medieval Jewish exegetes Ibn Ezra and Abravanel already recognized that this passage contains narratives of three separate disputes: the opposition of the chieftains of the congregation to restricting the use of the Holy to the tribe of Levi, the revolt of the Levites against the greater privileges of the sons of Aaron, and Dathan and Abiram's opposition to

38. G. von Rad's claim that the passages 3:5-10 and 3:11-13 were composed by authors with differing ideologies is untenable (*Die Priesterschrift im Hexateuch* [BWANT 4; Berlin/Stuttgart, 1934] 91-92) . The explanation advanced by A. H. J. Gunneweg (*Leviten und Priester* [FRLANT 89; Göttingen, 1965] 149) and S. E. Loewenstamm ("The Investiture of Levi" [Hebrew] *Eretz Israel* 10 [1971] 17-19), that vv. 11-13 give the reasons for the command that appears in vv. 5-10, seems closer to the plain meaning of the text.

39. On the close ties among these chapters, see Milgrom, *Studies in Cultic Theology,* 64 n. 236.

Moses' leadership of the people.[40] The dominant view in biblical scholarship attributes the revolt of Dathan and Abiram to JE. According to the reconstruction of most scholars, there was, alongside the narrative of this revolt, a primitive version of the revolt of the chieftains, led by Korah, who was an Israelite and not a Levite. This version is attributed to P. On this view, a later stratum of P superimposed the story of the dispute of the Levites on the two relatively earlier traditions; in the process of fusion of the traditions, Korah was made leader of the Levites.[41] The main difficulty with this explanation is the lack of solid textual basis for the person of Korah the Israelite, as a leader of the revolt of the chieftains.[42]

Gunneweg and Loewenstamm offered an alternative solution. According to them, Numbers 16 is based on two independent traditions, neither of which was connected to the person of Korah. The first tradition recounts the revolt of Dathan and Abiram; the second, the revolt of the chieftains.[43] The establishment of Korah the Levite as leader of all the rebels occurred at the final editing stage of the chapter, when the narrative of the Levite rebellion was appended. This view seems logical to me, and I should like to use it to reconstruct the stages in the composition of Numbers 16.[44] I shall begin by suggesting a reconstruction of the textual versions of the original traditions—the revolts of Dathan and Abiram and that of the chieftains. My main guideline in reconstruction will be the creation of a consistent, continuous narrative. Afterwards, I shall offer some thoughts on how the final editing process was effected.

40. See Ibn Ezra on Num 16:1 and Abravanel at the beginning of his commentary on the passage. Note that the two exegetes differ in their evaluation of Korah's role in the rebellion. Whereas Ibn Ezra emphasizes Korah's participation in the rebellion of the chieftains, Abravanel presents him as leader of the Levite rebellion.

41. See the references to classical scholarly literature in J. Liver, *Studies in Bible and Judean Desert Scrolls* (Jerusalem, 1971) 12 n. 7. Some scholars have gone overboard in analyzing the chapter; for example, S. Lehming identifies eight different strata! ("Versuch zum Num. 16," *ZAW* 74 [1962] 291–321).

42. See Gunneweg, *Leviten,* 173–75; and J. Milgrom, "Korah's Rebellion—A Study in Redaction," in *De la Tora au Messie* (Festschrift H. Cazelles; AOAT 212; Paris, 1981) 135–46, n. 20.

43. Gunneweg, *Leviten,* 175ff.; S. E. Loewenstamm, "Korach, Sons of Korach, Korachites," *EM* 7:261. The core of this idea is already present in the commentary of Abravanel, who linked Korah only to the Levite rebellion. Abravanel, of course, does not present any critical analysis.

44. Gunneweg suggested an analysis of the chapter along these lines (*Leviten*); his analysis, however, is only partial and ignores the question of the integration of the conflict of Dathan and Abiram. I also disagree with him on several principal issues of his analysis of the stratum of the rebellion of the chieftains; thus I propose to present the first detailed analysis separating the chapter into its constituent sources.

The Rebellion of Dathan and Abiram (Num 16:12–15, 25, 27b–34)[45]

וישלח[46] משה לקרא לדתן ולאבירם בני אליאב ויאמרו לא נעלה:
המעט כי העליתנו מארץ זבת חלב ודבש להמיתנו במדבר כי תשתרר
עלינו גם השתרר: אף לא אל ארץ זבת חלב ודבש הביאתנו ותתן־
לנו נחלת שדה וכרם העיני האנשים ההם תנקר לא נעלה: ויחר
למשה מאד ויאמר אל־ה׳ אל־תפן אל־מנחתם לא חמור אחד מהם
נשאתי ולא הרעתי את־אחד מהם: ויקם משה וילך אל־דתן ואבירם
וילכו אחריו זקני ישראל: ודתן ואבירם יצאו נצבים פתח
אהליהם ונשיהם ובניהם וטפם: ויאמר משה בזאת תדעון כי ה׳
שלחני לעשות את כל־המעשים האלה כי־לא מלבי: אם־כמות כל־
האדם ימתון אלה ופקדת כל־האדם יפקד עליהם לא ה׳ שלחני:
ואם־בריאה יברא ה׳ ופצתה האדמה את־פיה ובלעה אתם ואת־כל־
אשר להם וירדו חיים שאלה וידעתם כי נאצו האנשים האלה את
ה׳: ויהי ככלתו לדבר את כל־הדברים האלה ותבקע האדמה אשר
תחתיהם: ותפתח הארץ את־פיה ותבלע אתם ואת־בתיהם ואת כל־
האדם אשר [להם] ואת כל הרכוש: וירדו הם וכל־אשר־להם חיים
שאלה ותכס עליהם הארץ ויאבדו מתוך הקהל: וכל־ישראל אשר
סביבתיהם נסו לקלם כי אמרו פן־תבלענו הארץ:

Moses sent for Dathan and Abiram, sons of Eliab; but they said, "We will not come! Is it not enough that you brought us from a land flowing with milk and honey to have us die in the wilderness, that you would also lord it over us? Even if you had brought us to a land flowing with milk and honey, and given us possession of fields and vineyards, should you gouge out those men's eyes? We will not come!" Moses was much aggrieved and he said to the LORD, "Pay no regard to their oblation. I have not taken the ass of any one of them, nor have I wronged any one of them." Moses rose and went to Dathan and Abiram, the elders of Israel following him. Now Dathan and Abiram had come out and they stood at the entrance of their tents, with their wives, their children, and their little ones. And Moses said, "By this you shall know that it was the LORD who sent me to do all these things; that they are not of my own devising: if these men die as all men do, if their lot be the common fate of all mankind, it was not the LORD who sent me. But if the LORD brings about something unheard-of, so that the ground opens its mouth wide and swallows them up with all that belongs to them, and they go down alive into Sheol, you shall know that these men have spurned the Lord." Scarcely had he finished speaking all these words when the ground under them burst asun-

45. Our reconstruction differs in its wording from the present language only in v. 32, where we replaced אשר לקרח with אשר להם. For evidence supporting the supposed reading אשר להם, see Milgrom, *Studies in Cultic Theology,* 137.

46. It is possible that this is not the original introduction of the tradition and that the original beginning of the story was truncated in the editing process.

der, and the earth opened its mouth and swallowed them up with their households [all their people] and all their possessions. They went down alive into Sheol, with all that belonged to them; the earth closed over them and they vanished from the midst of the congregation. All Israel round them fled at their shrieks, for they said, "The earth might swallow us!"

The Revolt of the Chieftains
(Num 16:2–7a, 18, 35)[47]

ויקומו לפני משה אנשים מבני ישראל חמשים ומאתים נשיאי עדה
קראי מועד אנשי־שם: ויקהלו על־משה ועל־אהרן ויאמרו אלהם
רב־לכם כי כל־העדה כלם קדשים ובתוכם ה׳ ומדוע תתנשאו על־
קהל ה׳: וישמע משה ויפל על פניו: וידבר [אליהם] לאמר בקר
וידע ה׳ את־אשר־לו ואת־הקדוש והקריב אליו ואת אשר יבחר־בו
יקריב אליו: זאת עשו קחו־לכם מחתות ותנו בהם אש ושימו
עליהן קטרת לפני ה׳ מחר והיה האיש אשר־יבחר ה׳ הוא הקדוש:
ויקחו איש מחתתו ויתנו עליהם אש וישימו עליהם קטרת ויעמדו
פתח אהל מועד ומשה ואהרן: ואש יצאה מאת ה׳ ותאכל את החמשים
ומאתים איש מקריבי הקטרת.

And men rose up against Moses, together with two hundred and fifty Israelites, chieftains of the community, chosen in the assembly, men of repute. They combined against Moses and Aaron and said to them, "You have gone too far! For all the community are holy, all of them, and the LORD is in their midst. Why then do you raise yourselves above the Lord's congregation?" When Moses heard this, he fell on his face. Then he spoke to [them] saying, "Come morning, the LORD will make known who is His and who is holy, and will grant him access to Himself; He will grant access to the one He has chosen. Do this: take fire pans, and tomorrow put fire in them and lay incense on them before the LORD. Then the man shom the LORD chooses, he shall be the holy one. Each of them took his fire pan, put fire in it, laid incense on it, and took his place at the entrance of the Tent of Meeting, as did Moses and Aaron. And a fire went forth from the LORD and consumed the two hundred and fifty men offering the incense.

At the editing stage, the account of the rebellion of the Levites was added to these two traditions, and the editors were faced with the problem of combining stories concerning different heroes (Dathan and Abi-

47. The following are the deviations from the present version: in v. 2 we dropped the conjunctive ו from ואנשים; in v. 5 we replaced אל קרח ואל כל עדתו with אליהם; at the end of v. 6 we removed the words קרח וכל עדתו and in v. 7 we dropped the ending רב לכם בני לוי. The reasons for these changes will be explained below.

ram, the chieftains, the Levites) and occurring at different places (the entrance to the Tent of Meeting, the tent of Dathan and Abiram) into a single, coherent unit. The solution was found in the person of Korah the Levite, who was made the leader of all the rebel groups and who appeared simultaneously in both sites of revolt, rebelling against Moses' authority for three different reasons. Obviously, such a monumental effort in fusing diverse texts could not be executed without avoiding stylistic pitfalls and considerable confusion.[48]

Let us, then, reconstruct the details of the editorial procedure: in the list of rebels placed at the beginning of the chapter, v. 1 adds the names of Dathan and Abiram to that of Korah the Levite,[49] while v. 2 appends the two hundred fifty chieftains, using the connective ו before the word האנשים. Korah was placed at the head of the chieftains' rebellion by substituting the words אל קרח ואל כל עדתו for אליהם at the beginning of v. 5 and by adding the words קרח וכל עדתו at the end of v. 6—an addition that created the anomalous hybrid form of an imperative followed by a lengthy address.[50] The casting of Korah the Levite as the leader of the rebellion of the chieftains facilitated the incorporation of Moses' address to the Levites in vv. 8–11. The passage was included in a sophisticated way, making the verses a transition unit linking the two earlier traditions. At the seam between Moses' words to the chieftains and his words to the Levites, the words רב לכם בני לוי were placed. This angry articulation was composed in order to emphasize the levitical dimension of the chieftains' rebellion led by Korah; furthermore, it refers us back to the original text of the chieftains' complaint in v. 3a, רב לכם כי כל העדה כלם קדשים. Moses' response to the Levites opens with the expression המעט מכם, which corresponds to the opening words of Dathan and Abiram's complaint, המעט כי העליתנו.[51] The incorporation of the tradition of Dathan and Abiram's rebellion resulted in a break in the narrative of the incense test, while vv. 16–17 are a resumptive repetition bridging this gap. This repetition, however, does not merely repeat the text of vv. 6 and 7; it adds the element of personal competition between Korah and Aaron, an element absent from the original version. The editors, in order to stress the levitical aspect of the rebellion, introduced the motives of family and personal

48. The stylistic difficulties resulting from the blending of traditions are especially salient in the opening verses, as we will demonstrate in detail below. Especially well known is the confusion surrounding the fate of Korah, which already troubled the sages (see *b. Sanhedrin* 101a). See also R. Alter, *The Art of Biblical Narrative* (New York, 1981) 133–37, on the difficulties arising from the combining of stories in this chapter.

49. On the various explanations for the mention of און בן פלתי in v. 1, see G. B. Gray, *Numbers* (ICC; Edinburgh, 1903) ad loc.

50. Gray, who observed this anomaly, was also of the opinion that it was a secondary addition.

51. See Gunneweg, *Leviten,* 178; Milgrom, "Korah's Rebellion," 141.

rivalry. The transition verses bring us to the following day, which, in v. 7 (and in v. 16), was designated the day of the incense test. The place chosen, the entrance to the Tent of Meeting, is specified in v. 18, which is part of the original tradition of the rebellion of the chieftains.[52] Verse 35 describes the results of the incense test, but the editors chose to insert the conclusion of the revolt of Dathan and Abiram prior to this verse; this was accomplished in vv. 19–24. In v. 19, the community crowds around the entrance to the Tent of Meeting awaiting the contest of the fire pans, whereas in v. 24 they congregate around משכן קרח דתן ואבירם ("the abodes of Dathan, Korah, and Abiram"), awaiting the contest that has yet to take place. Scholars have attempted to resolve this difficulty by dividing the passage into several strata, suggesting that the original text, which read משכן ה' was replaced by משכן קרח דתן ואבירם.[53] This hypothesis seems unnecessary to me, as the entire passage is of the editorial stratum.[54] In order to reconcile the geographical discrepancies and bring together the various heroes of the story, the editors placed Korah's tent alongside those of Dathan and Abiram (16:24, 27a).[55] The locale of the event was then transferred from the Tent of Meeting to the tents of the protagonists. The process was completed by substituting the words לקרח

52. Because I see v. 18 as a verse of the original tradition, I cannot accept Gunneweg's opinion that the expression איש מחתתו is an editorial innovation emphasizing the individual taking of fire-pans (this expression is also used in the tradition of Nadab and Abihu in Lev 10:1). Neither can I accept Gunneweg's distinction (*Leviten,* 177) between two different foci of conflict: the question of election and sanctification in the early stratum and the emphasis on God's bringing close to himself in the later editorial stratum. This distinction is based on Gunneweg's ascription of v. 6 to the editorial level. It seems to me, however, that this goes against the overall editorial concept in this chapter. If the editor's intention was to add the story of the rebellion of the Levites, presenting it as a conflict between Korah the Levite and Aaron the priest, why should they have placed in Moses' mouth the argument that the incense test would prove whom God brought close to himself (הקריב)? Moses himself, in speaking to Korah, says that the Levites were brought close to God (16:9)! On the contrary, it would seem that v. 5 conforms to the version of the early tradition that viewed the incense test as a confrontation between the chieftains of Israel and the entire tribe of Levi, as represented by Moses and Aaron.

53. See, e.g., Wellhausen, *Hexateuch,* 340. Many other scholars agree.

54. Cf. vv. 26–27a, which present the stages in the execution of God's command (v. 24) to disperse the congregation around the tent of Korah, Dathan, and Abiram. The secondary nature of this command is unquestionable, for in the story of the splitting of the earth (which must be original; without it the story is incomplete) it is written "All Israel around them fled at their shrieks, for they said, 'the earth might swallow us!'" (16:34). This fact conflicts with the dispersal of the congregation described in v. 27 (as pointed out by Gray in his commentary on v. 34 and Milgrom, "Korah's Rebellion," 136).

55. By contrast, in vv. 12, 25, 27b, which belong to the original stratum of the tradition, Dathan and Abiram alone are mentioned, as in the parallel tradition in Deut 11:6. The combination of Dathan and Abiram with Korah (and his company) can be seen in Num 26:9–11 as well. Those verses undoubtedly reflect the final editing stage of our chapter. On the tradition in Ps 106:16–18, see Liver, *Studies,* 17–18.

אשר for להם אשר in Num 16:32, presenting Korah as the main victim of punishment and, thus, as the main character in the story. The editors then placed v. 35, which, as we remarked, was the original conclusion of the revolt-of-the-chieftains tradition, at the end of the story.[56]

Numbers 17 describes the events following the deaths of the rebels: the plating of the altar with the copper of the fire pans (vv. 1–5), the complaints of the people and the subsequent plague (vv. 6–15), the miracle of Aaron's staff (vv. 16–25) and the desperation of the people (vv. 27–28). The concluding verse of the first unit (17:5) clearly indicates that the passage belongs to the editorial stratum, in which the character of Korah serves to unify the narrative elements. The lesson to be derived from this passage is that only Aaron may bring offerings. The passage on the contest of the staffs, on the other hand, which affirms God's choice of the tribe of Levi over all the other tribes of Israel, conforms with the original stratum of the story of the rebellion of the chieftains: the chieftains' rebellion stems from the people's objection to the privileges of the tribe of Levi, whereas the rebellion of Korah was an internal conflict among Levite families.[57] As the contest of the staffs was a response to the people's murmuring against Moses and Aaron (see 17:20), the complaint and the plague stories must also have originated in the earlier stratum,[58] while the two concluding verses of chap. 17 serve as a link to chap. 18.

In identifying the various strata in chaps. 16 and 17, we have resolved the unanswered questions raised earlier as to the continuity between chap. 18 and the chapters that precede it. We were perplexed by the reasoning in appointing the Levites as guardians of the Sanctuary and by the reasons for granting gifts to the Levites. These questions are relevant only if we accept the current order of the chapters, in which chap. 18 appears after the story of the revolt of Korah and the Levites. If we assume, however, that the chapter belongs to the earlier stratum of the tradition of the revolt of the chieftains, the plague, and the miracle of the staffs, and that it was written before the narrative of the Levite revolt and the character of Korah were appended by the editors of chap. 16, the picture becomes

56. Milgrom is of the opinion that the verse originally began with the words ותצא אש, as the story uses other verbs in the sequential *waw* ("Korah's Rebellion," 140). I believe, however, that we may accept the phrase ואש יצאה; as Paran has shown, "closing deviation" (i.e., the change of tense of a verb at the end of a legal or narrative unit) is typical of the Priestly style (*Forms of the Priestly Style in the Pentateuch* [Jerusalem, 1989] 179ff.).

57. See Gunneweg, *Leviten,* 184 n. 1. Josephus, who wrote that Aaron wrote "Levi" on his staff, also understood the miracle in this way (*Ant.* 4.64; as pointed out by Loewenstamm ["Investiture," n. 23]).

58. Thus, the added comment מלבד המתים על דבר קרח (17:14b) is an editorial addition. This accords with our findings that the use of the word מלבד is limited to the editorial stratum of the Pentateuch.

clear:[59] after the revolt ends with the death of the chieftains (16:35), the congregation complains against Moses and Aaron, accusing them: "You two have brought death upon the Lord's people!" (17:6; Eng. 16:41). As a result, a plague breaks out, claiming many victims (vv. 7–15; Eng. 16:42–50) and the contest of the staffs is held (vv. 16–26 Eng. 17:1–11). The people of Israel are in a state of mortal fear: "Lo, we perish! We are lost, all of us lost! Everyone who so much as ventures near the Lord's Tabernacle must die. Alas, we are doomed to perish!" (vv. 27–28). Chapter 18 offers an attempt to allay their fears: the responsibility for preventing the intrusion of outsiders into the Holy is removed from the people and placed on the shoulders of the priests and Levites (vv. 1–8). As recompense for the weighty responsibility they must bear, the Priests take charge of all gifts given to God (vv. 8–21) and the tithes of the people of Israel, hitherto sacred to the Lord, are apportioned to the Levites (vv. 21–24).[60]

It seems that we may now reconstruct the entire basic corpus of the Levite Treatise. The first element of this corpus is the ordinance substituting the Levites for the firstborn and its consequences, and the description of the work of the Levites (3:5–4:49). Next is the description of the Levites' ceremony of purification and waving before the Lord (8:5–22). The revolt of the chieftains breaks out in response to the selection of the Levites, as a protest against the exclusion of non-Levites from the cult.[61]

59. The link in context between the story of the miracle of the staffs and chap. 18 is strengthened by linguistic evidence—the common use of the term אהל העדת in these pericopes (17:22, 23; 18:2), a term that appears nowhere else in the Pentateuch (excepting the similar phrase המשכן לאהל העדת in 9:15; see below). We find the term elsewhere in the Bible only in 1 Chr 24:6.

60. See Lev 27:30. As the tithes were originally holy to the Lord, the Levites had to redeem them by giving a heave offering from it to the priests (Num 18:25–32; see Y. Kaufmann, *The History of Israelite Faith* [Hebrew] [Jerusalem and Tel Aviv, 1960] 1:136). On the priority of the tithe law in Leviticus 27 over that of Numbers 18, see Kaufmann, *History,* 147ff. Kaufmann's claim that the tithe discussed in those chapters is a free-will offering is not supported by biblical research (see Milgrom, *Studies,* n. 246; M. Weinfeld, "Tithe," *Encyclopedia Judaica* 15:125–26). The giving of tithes to the Levites is a kind of royal gift. See Weinfeld, "Tithe," 124; Y. Muffs, *Love and Joy* (New York, 1992) 124–30; M. Greenberg, *On the Bible and Judaism: A Collection of Writings* (Tel-Aviv, 1985) 115.

61. Ibn Ezra, in his commentary on Num 16:1, emphasizes the election of the Levites to serve in the Sanctuary as the background for the rebellion. The understanding of the chieftains' protest as directed against the special privileges of the entire tribe of Levi, rather than the priesthood of Aaron alone, helps explain the range of linguistic forms in Moses' response to the chieftains (16:5–7). We find here the phrases אשר לו, usually used in reference to the Levites (Num 3:12, 13, 45; 8:15); the title הקדש associated with the priesthood (Exod 29:1, 21; Lev 27:7) and והקריב אליו associated with the priesthood (Exod 28:1; Lev 8:6; 10:4) as well as the Levites (Num 3:6; 8:9–10; 18:2). At the end of his speech, Moses employs the phrase את אשר יבחר בו. The verb בחר appears only once more in the Priestly source, in the story of the incense test—there too in the expression האיש אשר אבחר בו (Num 17:20). Although the word בחר appears in singular form and refers to Aaron as the chosen person,

The incense test, the death of the chieftains, the popular rebellion, and the subsequent plague raise with great urgency the problem of the barriers between the Tabernacle and the people. These events give rise to popular interest in preventing outsiders from intruding into the sacred precincts (17:17–28). Chapter 18, which concludes the unit, responds to this problem by explicitly designating the Levites as responsible for guarding the Tabernacle.[62]

In Excursus 1, we proved that the beginning and end of the corpus (chaps. 3 and 18) originate in HS. The great linguistic and ideological uniformity of the various parts of this corpus lead us to conclude that the entire original corpus is a product of HS. Moreover, the units of the rebellion of the chieftains, the complaints of the people against Moses and Aaron, and the plague, the miracle of the staffs, and the people's fear (16:2–7a, 18, 35; 17:6–28) all bear clear conceptual and linguistic markings of HS. We find there words and expressions at variance with the accepted style of PT but in full accordance with the language and concepts of HS. The complaints of the chieftains (16:3) contain expressions current in the non-Priestly sources of the Pentateuch and Ezekiel:[63] רב־לכם (Deut 1:6; 2:3; 3:26; Ezek 44:6; 45:9), תתנשאו (Num 23:24; 24:7; Ezek 29:15), קהל ה' (Num 20:4, Deut 23:2, 3, 4, 9). We have already noted that HS is characterized by its similarity to the language of Ezekiel and its links to the language of the non-Priestly sources of the Pentateuch. The phrase ובתוכם ה' (16:3) accords with HS's language in its additions to the PT laws of the Tabernacle (Exod 25:8; 29:45). Moreover, the ideological content of the complaint is easily understood against the background of HS's views: the complaint of the chieftains כי כל העדה כלם קדשים, for all the community are holy, all of them," evokes the call for the sanctification of the entire people, common in the writings of HS (Lev 11:44; 19:2; 20:7, 26; Num 15:40). The phrase עם ה' in the plague passage (17:6) is absent from PT, but we find it in the JE tradition (Num 11:29) and in Ezekiel (36:20). The words ואכלה אתם כרגע (17:10) correspond to the personal punishment prevalent in HS but entirely absent from PT sources (see Introduction, n. 3). The phrase אשר אועד לך שמה in the section on the contest of the staffs (17:19) conforms to the style of the appended passage of HS in the narrative on the construction of the Tabernacle

---

Aaron represents here the entire tribe of Levi as opposed to the chieftains of other tribes; thus the word בחר here refers to the entire tribe.

62. The linguistic and substantive ties between the tradition of the rebellion of the chieftains and the incense test, on the one hand, and Numbers 18 on the other, refute the thesis (W. Baudissin, *Die Geschichte des A.T. Priestertum* [Leipzig, 1889] 34–36; R. Kittel, *Geschichte des Volkes Israel 3* [Gotha, 1916] 343) that the chieftains' revolt belongs to a Priestly stratum which recognizes no distinction between priests and Levites.

63. Dillmann, *Numbers,* on Num 16:3.

(Exod 29:42). As we wrote above (p. 65), this language form stresses the all-Israelite dimension of the revelation of God in the Tent of Meeting and the public nature of the Tabernacle in the HS material. The phrase אהל העדת (17:22, 23) appears elsewhere in the Pentateuch only in Num 18:2 (see n. 59), which is part of a chapter already proved as originating in HS (see Excursus 1). The command to place the staff of Aaron before the pact (עדות) as a token (17:25) evokes the placing of the jar of manna before the pact as a token in Exod 16:32–34; the latter passage belongs to the Priestly level of Exodus 16, which we have shown (above, p. 17) to belong to HS. The phrase משכן ה׳ in the text of the people's complaint (17:28), implies a relation of possession of the Tabernacle by God, which corresponds to the style and thinking of HS (see n. 30 above).

The editorial level of the Korah pericope also shows connections with HS. Earlier, in the course of our discussion of Exodus 6, we stated that the genealogical list was adjoined to the chapter by its final editors, who were of the HS school (above, p. 61). We remarked there, that at the focal point of the list, Aaron and Korah were presented as contemporaries of the same generation and of common lineage. The list thus serves as a prologue to the later confrontation of the two persons.[64] In the editorial stratum of Numbers 16—in the tradition of the revolt of the chieftains and the plague—we find certain expressions absent in PT but common in the non-Priestly language of the Pentateuch. We often find the expression רב־לכם (Num 16:7b), as we mentioned above. The phrase אלהי ישראל (Num 16:9) is found elsewhere in the Pentateuch in Exod 24:10; 32:27; and 34:23—all of the JE tradition. Furthermore, the word נא, which is never used in PT but is common in the JE tradition,[65] appears in our section (16:8, 26). As we mentioned, affinity to the language of non-Priestly sources is one of the hallmarks of HS. Finally, we should mention again the presence of the phrase משכן ה׳ (Num 16:9), which conforms with HS language.

The relative lateness of the editorial stratum of the Korah pericope is indicated by the cultic innovations it mentions: implicit in Moses' words to Korah in 16:9 is the characterization of the Levites as servants of the congregation. In the original body of the Korah pericope, service to the congregation is not mentioned among the Levites' responsibilities. Num-

64. In contradiction to the generalized list in Num 26:58, where Korah is placed in the generation of Amram, Aaron's father. On the early date of this list, see Wellhausen, *Hexateuch,* 184–86; K. Möhlenbrink, "Die levitischen Überlieferungen des A.T," *ZAW* 52 (1935) 191ff.; Liver, *Studies,* 27; F. M. Cross, *Canaanite Myth and Hebrew Epic* (Cambridge, MA, 1973) 206. The link between the genealogical list of Exodus 6 and the rebellion of Korah was observed by Milgrom ("Korah's Rebellion").

65. Dillmann observed that the expression אלהי ישראל is foreign to the language of PT. The absence of the word נא in PT and its prevalence in JE were remarked by Gray in his commentary on v. 8.

bers 18:2 states only that the Levites shall serve Aaron. In the legal section of Ezekiel, on the other hand, this function is cited as the true vocation of the Levites. In the course of his rebuke of the Levites who strayed from the Lord, Ezekiel says: "they shall slaughter the burnt offerings and the sacrifices for the people. They shall attend on them and serve them" (Ezek 44:11b). This vocation is also reflected in the descriptions of the Passover rituals of Hezekiah and Josiah in Chronicles.[66]

Thus we find that the tradition encompassing the revolt of the chieftains, the plague, and the miracle of the staffs, on the one hand, and the narrative of the Levite revolt led by Korah, on the other, are both products of HS but belong to different stages of the creative activity of this school. The historical and social background shaping the different traditions will be explained in chapter 5.

Finally, let us turn to the remaining parts of the Levite Treatise not included in the basic corpus: Exod 38:21; Num 1:48–54; 2; 7; 8:23–26; 9:15–10:28. I am of the opinion that these units were composed at a relatively late stage in the editing of the Pentateuch. I will cite here several indicators demonstrating the relationships among the various units and their relative lateness.

One of the central subjects discussed in this part of the Levite Treatise is the order of marches and encampments. In the verses on these topics, we frequently find the word דגל a word that appears nowhere else in the Pentateuch.[67] If we accept the hypothesis that the word is borrowed from Imperial Aramaic of the Persian period,[68] this would serve as evidence for the relative lateness of this stratum. The phrase משכן העדת is also virtually unique to this stratum (Exod 38:21; Num 1:53; 10:1), appearing only once elsewhere in the HS section on the actual building of the Tabernacle in Exod 38:21. We found (see n. 59) that the expression אהל העדת appears in the original part of the Levite Treatise, and it would seem that משכן העדת is a later development of the term. The tendency to combine the

66. See 2 Chr 29:34; 30:17; 35:4, 6, 11; cf. Ezek 6:20. The author of the *Temple Scroll* also assigns the task of slaughtering to the Levites (11QTemple 22:4, ed. Y. Yadin, p. 99; see editor's notes ad loc.). This law contradicts the laws of PT and HS which permit all Israelites to slaughter sacrificial animals (cf. Lev 1:5, 11; 17:3–5) but accords with the prevalent custom of the late Second Temple period as attested by Josephus (*Ant.* 3:226). The prevalent Mishnaic halakah permitted slaughtering by laymen (*m. Zebahim* 3:1; see also *Sifra Vayyiqra* 4:2, ed. Finkelstein, p. 36), which polemicizes against the view that only priests may slaughter sacrifices, as held by Philo (*The Special Laws,* 1:199). See also M. Fishbane, *Biblical Interpretation in Ancient Israel* (Oxford, 1985) 137–38; J. Liver, *Chapters in the History of the Priests and Levites* (Jerusalem, 1971) 32; Safrai, *Die Wahlfart im Zeitalter des Zweiten Tempels* (Neukirchen-Vluyn, 1981) Excursus 1, pp. 286–87.

67. The first appearance of the word דגל is in Num 1:52. Later, the word is common in Numbers 2 and in 10:14–25 (see chapter 1, n. 37).

68. See B. A. Levine, "Research in the Priestly Source: The Linguistic Factor" [Hebrew], *Eretz Israel* 16 (1982) 127–29.

terms משכן and אהל מועד to form the phrase משכן אהל מועד is apparent in the final chapters of the book of Exodus (see 39:32; 40:2, 29), whose late date is accepted by all scholars. Similarly, אהל העדת became המשכן לאהל העדת (Num 9:15); this awkward phrase was, at some later stage, contracted to משכן העדת.[69] The most obvious sign of late idiom is the designation of the date as בעשרים בחדש in Num 10:11. As we demonstrated in chapter 1, n. 36, the use of this form is characteristic of the period following the Babylonian exile. The content also displays marks of late authorship: the passage that fixes the Levites' age of commencement of service in the Sanctuary at twenty-five is part of a secondary stratum of the Levite Treatise (8:23–26). This regulation contradicts the order in the original stratum of the treatise (4:3, 23, 30), assigning all Levites thirty years and older to service in the Sanctuary. I accept the opinion of those scholars who see this change as a reflection of the tendency to reduce the minimum age for levitical service, as we find in the books of Ezra and Chronicles (Ezra 3:8; 1 Chr 23:24, 27; 2 Chr 31:17); this change was prompted by the small number of Levites at the time of the return to Zion.[70]

Now that we have shown that these units display elements that are both unique and relatively late, we need only determine their origin. I believe that this stratum of the Levite Treatise also derives from HS but reflects a later stage in the production of this school, a stage that also includes the editorial level of the Korah story. Typically HS characteristics are apparent in several places: the order of encampments and marchings includes the law of the sounding of the trumpets (Num 10:1–10), which we have already determined belongs to HS (see Excursus 1). The portion on the sacrifices of the chieftains (chap. 7) is unusual in that it announces, at the beginning of the section, that the event took place "on the day that Moses finished setting up the Tabernacle"; this does not conform to the order of events in the book of Numbers,[71] and refers us back to the conclusion of the book of Exodus (see Exod 40:1, 9–12, 33b). The extensive detail and the many repetitions in this section are suggestive of the style of the final chapters of Exodus,[72] which we have attributed to the editorial stratum of

69. For another interpretation of these expressions and their development, see L. Rost, "Die Wohnstätte des Zeugnisses," in *Festschrift F. Baumgärtel* (Erlangen, 1959) 158–65, and subsequently D. Kellermann, *Die Priesterschrift von Numeri 1,1 bis 10,10* (BZAW; Berlin, 1970) 26–27.

70. See Kuenen, *Hexateuch,* 308 n. 28. Other scholars followed suit.

71. Abravanel raised this problem in his first question on the verse. See also Wellhausen, *Hexateuch,* 179; Kuenen, *Hexateuch,* 94 n. 35. On various attempts at settling this problem, see Kellermann, *Priesterschrift,* 99; J. Licht, *A Commentary on the Book of Numbers (I–X)* (Jerusalem, 1985) 100.

72. The difficulties in the biblical language were already raised by Abravanel in his eighth question. For critical research on this issue, see Kellermann, *Priesterschrift,* 98 n.1; Licht, *Numbers,* 98–99.

HS (above, p. 66). This editorial stratum glossed the PT scrolls dealing with the ordinances on the construction of the Tabernacle, stressing the all-Israelite dimension of the Tabernacle and its construction. It would appear that this tendency is central to the pericope on the offerings of the chieftains, which completely ignores the PT version of the dedication of the Tabernacle in Lev 8:6-7; there it is Aaron and his sons who offer the community sacrifice.[73]

Our study demonstrates that the entire Levite Treatise originates in HS. This treatise is unique in that it alone describes class and functional distinctions among Levite families.[74] Whereas Aaron and his sons were promoted to perform cultic activities in the Sanctuary and to serve the Tent of Meeting, the other Levite families, of lesser status, were assigned the tasks of dismantling and reassembling the Tabernacle and carrying it and its vessels through the desert, guarding the sacred enclosure to prevent outsiders from entering and ministering to Aaron and his sons in their Tabernacle rites. This distinction is repeated several times in the course of the Levite Treatise (Num 1:40-43; 3:6-10, 32; 4:5-20, 28, 33; 8:5-22; 16:9-10; 17:5; 18:1-7). Among the laws of PT, we find no mention whatsoever of the Levites or their functions. According to PT, the sole servants of the Sanctuary are the priests, Aaron and his sons.[75] Because we maintain that HS is later than PT, we thus conclude that the distinction of two cultic classes—priests and Levites—and the assignment of their respective tasks were an innovation of HS.[76] To understand the presumed background for this cultic innovation, we must first discuss the historical framework of HS's literary activity. This issue will be taken up again in chapter 5, where we will also examine the historical aspects of the question of the Levites.

Legal Units in Numbers 5-15

Interspersed among the chapters of the Levite Treatise are units of Priestly law dealing with a wide range of topics unrelated to the Levites or

73. The tension between the story of the dedication of the altar with the chieftains' sacrifices and Leviticus 9 was observed by M. Noth (*Numbers* [OTL; London, 1968] 64). It will be discussed at length below, p. 194.

74. I accept Gunneweg's rejection (*Leviten,* 184ff.), of von Rad's claim (*Priesterschrift,* 88ff.) that the opening chapters of Numbers contains a stratum that fails to distinguish between priests and Levites.

75. Although Moses took part in the cult during the days of ordination (Exod 29:1-37; Lev 8:1-30), this participation was exceptional and could not serve as an example for future generations.

76. This distinction is not entirely new; a similar distinction exists in Hittite law, as demonstrated by Milgrom (*Studies,* 50-51; idem, "The Shared Custody of the Tabernacle and a Hittite Analogy," *JAOS* 90 (1970) 204-9.

their work. We will now examine these units in the order of their appearance in the biblical text.

Numbers 5:1-4

This passage discusses the removal of the impure from the camp. Several scholars have commented on the contradiction between this passage and the passage in the laws of PT, in which only the leper was required to leave the camp, and not those defiled by a corpse or discharge (Lev 13:46; 14:8).[77] Furthermore, we find in v. 3 the word אני spoken by God; this never occurs in God's speeches to Moses and the community of Israel in PT.[78] The obvious solution to these difficulties is to assign our verse to HS. The source of disagreement between the Priestly schools as to which impure persons must be removed from the camp will be explained in the following chapters.

Numbers 5:5-10

This passage appears to be mostly a repetition of the law of guilt offerings in Lev 5:21-26. In the framework of the present study, I will skirt the question of the innovations in this passage, restricting discussion to the identification of its origin. On the one hand, the linguistic and conceptual similarities to the law of guilt offerings of PT in Leviticus 5 would lead us to assign the passage to PT. A striking similarity is the use of the phrase מכל חטאת האדם, which originates in the phrase מכל אשר־יעשה האדם לחטא בהנה (Lev 5:22).[79] On the other hand, there is an essential difference in the terminology of the two laws;[80] our passage has its closest terminological affinities in the HS law of Priestly gifts in Numbers 18.[81] Thus, the

77. Wellhausen, *Hexateuch,* 174; Dillmann, *Numeri;* Gray, ad loc.

78. On the only exception to this rule—Lev 14:34—see below, n. 119. The word אני in God's speech is, however, common in the PT stratum of Genesis, where the names אלהים and אל שדי are used for God. See Gen 6:17; 9:9, 12; 17:1, 4. The significance of the change in the use of the divine אני in PT will be discussed in the next chapter. As we mentioned (above, n. 14), in HS we frequently find the word אני in God's speech to the congregation of Israel. In addition to the examples cited above, we find the divine use of the word אני in the Levite Treatise in the units displaying linguistic characteristics of HS: as אני ה׳ (Num 3:13, 41, 45; 10:10); and in the use of אני in the course of the divine speech (Num 3:11; 18:6, 8, 20).

79. This was already remarked by Ramban in his commentary. Among modern scholars who hold this opinion are Noth (*Numbers*) and Kellermann (*Priesterschrift,* 66).

80. Especially striking is the difference in the use of the word אשה. Whereas in Leviticus 5, אשה refers to the sacrifice, here it refers to monetary compensation (see Wellhausen, *Hexateuch,* 174).

81. The affinities are demonstrated in the phrases להשיב אשם עליו; והשיב את אשמו בראשו; אשמם אשר ישיבו לו (Num 5:7, 8; 18:9). Although in chap. 18, unlike here, אשם refers to the

arguments for both sides are weighted equally, and only further comparison of the style of the introductory verse of our passage (5:6) with that of the laws of PT can tip the scales.

We may divide the laws of PT into two main groups: those whose syntactical subject (whose acts are described by the law) is designated by the word נפש and those whose subject is אשה, איש or a combination of those words—איש איש or איש או אשה. A clear distinction exists between the two groups. Use of the word נפש is restricted to the laws of sacrifice (see Lev 2:1; 4:2, 27; 5:1, 2, 4, 15, 17, 21; 7:18, 20, 21), whereas the purity laws solely employ subjects of the אשה, איש group.[82] We never find the two subjects, נפש and איש mentioned in a single law in PT. Numbers 5:6 violates this rule on two counts: as our passage deals with sacrifice, we would expect the opening subject to be נפש rather than איש או אשה; in addition, the end of the verse, ואשמה הנפש ההיא, gives us two types of subject in the same verse. In HS, whose style is neither as polished nor as meticulous as that of PT, we find sacrificial laws also introduced by the word איש and mixing of the words נפש and איש in the same law.[83] We must then conclude that our verse originates in HS and not in PT. As we will see in subsequent chapters, this discovery is the key to the question that troubled both early and recent scholars: What does this law add to the law of guilt offerings in Leviticus 5?

Numbers 5:11-31

The style of the pericope of the suspected adulteress and its colophon (5:29-30) clearly testifies to its PT origin.[84] Recently, Milgrom revealed

---

sacrifice, both verses share the common idiom השב אשם, which appears nowhere else in the Pentateuch (outside the Pentateuch, it appears in 1 Sam 6:3, 4, 5, 17; see J. Milgrom, *Cult and Conscience* [Leiden, 1976] 7 and n. 26 on the importance of the phrase השב אשם for understanding the significance of the guilt sacrifice). An additional linguistic similarity (Dillmann, *Numeri*, on 18:8) between Num 5:9 and Num 18:8 is the use of the word תרומה to refer to all Priestly gifts. In addition to these two texts, we find this only in Lev 22:12 (H). Another term found only in our verse and in H is גאל as a name for a family relation (Lev 25:25-26; Num 5:8). Furthermore, the very mention of theft from someone who has no kinsman (גאל)—a law that refers primarily to resident aliens—jibes well with the concerns of HS, which often treats matters relating to resident aliens (see above, chapter 1, n. 36).

82. Obviously, in types of impurity specific to either men or women, the general term נפש cannot be employed. But even when the law is applicable to both men and women, the subject in these laws is איש או אשה rather than נפש (see Lev 13:29, 38 and compare Lev 15:5 to Lev 7:21). A general subject appearing in both purity and sacrificial law is אדם (see Lev 1:2; 13:2, 9).

83. The laws of sacrifice in Lev 17:3, 8; 22:18 begin with the phrase איש איש. In Lev 17:10; 20:5-6; 22:3, 4-6, we find a shift from איש to נפש in the text of the law. Compare 22:3 to the parallel PT law, Lev 7:20, where נפש is consistently used.

84. On colophons in PT, see above, n. 27. As Fishbane has shown, the colophon in this

the complex interior structure of the pericope, emphasizing what had already been noticed by several scholars, namely, that the carefully constructed narrative is interrupted at v. 21, which must be considered an interpolation. The verse's innovation lies in its casting of God as the direct punisher of the woman, whereas in the original version of the curse, the punishment is described in impersonal terms (5:19, 20, 22).[85] Milgrom is of the opinion that the impersonal version was originally a non-Israelite magic spell and that the addition, stressing the personal involvement of God in the punishment of the suspected adulteress, was added when it was incorporated into the Priestly Code.[86] I believe that a comparison of the punishment formulas in the two Priestly schools yields another explanation for the textual data. In PT we never find punishments directly attributed to God;[87] all punishments are strictly impersonal.[88] By contrast, HS contains many passages attributing direct punishment to God.[89] The significance and origin of this substantial difference will be discussed in later chapters; for the moment, we will merely state that the impersonal style of punishment appearing in the original version of the imprecation oath corresponds to the style of PT, which is the dominant style of the entire passage. Verse 21, on the other hand, is, in my opinion, an addition of the HS editors, who present the suspected adulteress's punishment in the accepted manner of their school.[90] The reasons for and significance of this addition will be discussed later in our study.

---

chapter repeats the opening formula in vv. 12, 14 ("Accusation," 30–35). This phenomenon is common in other Priestly תורות and has parallels in other Near East legal compilations; see Fishbane, "Accusation"; M. Weinfeld, "Social and Cultic Institutions in the Priestly Source against their Ancient Near Eastern Background," in *Proceedings of the Eighth World Congress of Jewish Studies, Bible Studies, and Hebrew Language* [Jerusalem, 1981] 101–2).

85. J. Milgrom, "The Case of the Suspected Adulteress, Numbers Redaction and Meaning" (a list of the scholarly literature appears in nn. 1, 2). The secondary nature of the passage and its significance were correctly described by Gray (*Numbers*, 53).

86. Milgrom, "Case," 72.

87. This holds true only for the name of Yahweh. אלהים, on the other hand, is often presented as a direct punisher (Gen 6:13, 17; 9:5). The difference is linked to the different aspects of the divinity represented by these names, as we shall explain below.

88. The כרת ("cutting off") expressions are impersonal (Introduction, n. 3; see Exod 30:37, 38; Lev 7:20, 21) as well as those of נגף (plague) and תבערה (fire of God). In the PT tradition of the ten plagues, we never find the plague directly attributed to God, whereas in JE, God is depicted as the perpetrator of the plagues (see Exod 7:27; 8:17; 9:3–6, 14–18, 23; 10:4, 13; 11:1, 4).

89. Although HS also contains impersonal descriptions of punishment, the personal descriptions predominate (see Introduction, note 3). This is true both of the Holiness Code (Lev 17:10; 18:25; 20:3, 5, 6; 23:30; 26:16–33) and other HS writings (Exod 7:3–5; 10:1–2; 12:12; Lev 10:6; Num 16:21–22; 17:10).

90. Milgrom claims that the interpolation was made in the early stages of the editing of

Numbers 6:1-21

The Nazirite pericope may be divided into two main sections: the first part (vv. 1-12) deals with prohibitions that apply to the Nazirite as a result of his consecration and how he is to act in the event that he is forced to defile his Nazirite status. The second part (vv. 13-21) deals with the sacrifices that the Nazirite brings at the completion of his term as a Nazirite. The structure and style of this pericope are characteristic of PT,[91] and thus, we confirm the accepted view attributing its origin to this school.[92]

Numbers 6:22-27

Although we find in PT that Aaron raises his hands to bless the people (Lev 9:22), the content of that blessing is nowhere specified. In any case, the language of the Priestly blessing in Numbers deviates from Priestly style, as many scholars have already remarked.[93] If, then, the verse derives from one of the Priestly schools,[94] we should attribute it to HS, inasmuch as God's speech in the first person, אני (v. 27), and the phrases פני ה' and שם ה' (vv. 25-27) appear elsewhere in HS, but are completely absent from PT.[95]

Numbers 8:1-4

The secondary nature of this passage and its affinities to Exod 27:21 and Lev 24:1-4 have already been demonstrated by scholars.[96] Since we

the pericope, since the expression לאלה ולשבועה בתוך עמך is repeated in v. 7b ("Case"). But perhaps v. 27b is an editorial addition as well! The two possible results of the ordeal of the suspected adulteress are adequately described in vv. 27a, 28, which are edited as a chiastic parallel to vv. 19, 20, 22. The editors were, apparently, sensitive to the right literary structure of the passage and thus added v. 27b to correspond to their addition in v. 21.

91. Note the opening and conclusion of the second verse: וזאת תורת הנזיר . . . זאת תורת הנזיר (Num 6:13, 21). This language appears in various PT legal collections: in the laws of sacrifice (Lev 6:2, 7, 18; 7:1, 11); in the laws of cattle and fowl (Lev 11:2, 46); in the laws of lepers (Lev 14:2-32). The introductory phrase of the pericope, איש או אשה, accords with the usual PT introduction to laws of purity (see above, chapter 2, n. 82); in fact, the main subject of the first passage on Nazirites deals with the purity and impurity of the Nazirite.

92. With the exception of the editorial addition at the end of the pericope in v. 21a—מלבד אשר תשיג ידו (see Excursus 2).

93. See the discussion of the verses in Gray, *Numbers,* and in Kellermann, *Priesterschrift.*

94. This may be a formula taken from the Temple liturgy (see Dillmann, *Numeri,* ad loc.) and adopted by HS.

95. See the use of the phrases: פני ה'—(Lev 17:10; 20:3, 5, 6; 26:17; cf. Lev 26:9), שם ה'—(Exod 6:3; Lev 18:21; 19:12; 20:3; 21:6; 22:2, 32; 24:11, 16). On the use of the divine אני, see above nn. 14, 76.

96. Wellhausen, *Hexateuch,* 174. Kuenen, *Hexateuch,* 93 n. 32. Gray, *Numbers,* ad loc.

have already determined the origin of those verses in HS (see Excursuses 1 and 3), we may also assign our passage to this school.

Numbers 9:1-14

The identification of the second Passover pericope as a product of HS was already discussed in the previous chapter (pp. 21-22). Our findings in this chapter corroborate our identification, as we find a shift from איש to נפש in v. 13, a phenomenon current in the language of HS (see above, p. 87), but not in PT. In our discussion in chapter 1, we called attention to late expressions in this pericope (בחדש, 9:3; בראשון, 9:5). We should stress that all the linguistic indications of late authorship are concentrated in the narrative portion of the pericope (9:1-8) that precedes the legal unit. As the legal unit may be considered an independent oeuvre, it may belong to a previous stratum of HS production,[97] while the narrative introduction may have been added only at the stage of the final editing of the Pentateuch.

Numbers 15

We mentioned earlier (Excursus 1) that this chapter originates in HS. We might add here a comment on the relation of the concluding passage of this chapter—the fringes pericope—to the story of the complaint of the chieftains which follows it. The first passage includes the demand addressed to all Israelites והייתם קדושים לאלהיכם ("and you shall be holy to your God," v. 40b). The fringes are a reminder of the sanctity of the people of Israel and its obligations.[98] The editors, by placing the fringes passage directly before the passage of the chieftains' complaint may have sought to provide a background for the plaint: "for all the community are holy, all of them, and the Lord is in their midst. Why then do you raise yourselves above the Lord's congregation?" (Num 16:3). The school that established this link is, apparently, the same one that left its linguistic and conceptual imprint on the fringes pericope—HS.[99]

The Scouts Pericope (Numbers 13-14)

One narrative unit, inserted between the chapters of the Levite Treatise, contains a Priestly stratum blended with a JE tradition—the scouts

97. On the stratum of Exod 12:1-17, 43-49, see above, pp. 20 and 21.

98. See J. Milgrom, *The Book of Numbers* (Philadelphia, 1990) 38, and the discussion in chapter 4, below.

99. Milgrom noted linguistic affinities between the fringes pericope and the scouts passage (Numbers 13-14) ("Tassels," *Beth Mikra* 92 [1982] 21-22 [Hebrew]). We may view this passage as a bridge between the narrative unit of the scouts (chaps. 13-14) and the Korah pericope (chaps. 16-17).

story. In accordance with the guidelines we set out at the beginning of this chapter, we will eschew detailed analysis of the pericope, restricting our inquiry to identification of the main Priestly units—Num 13:1-17a and 14:26-38.

The first unit includes the divine order to send out the scouts and an account of their mission. The use of the first person אני in God's command (13:1) betrays the HS origins of the unit (see nn. 14, 78).

The second unit opens with the passage of God's speech (14:26-35). This passage has aroused much confusion among scholars, as we find here Priestly idioms alongside expressions typical of JE. All attempts at separating the passage into its constituent sources have failed,[100] and I agree with those scholars who claim that all such efforts are fruitless, as the sources of the pericope too tightly connected.[101] The speech is presented as a direct address by God to Israel, and the words of God are formulated in the first person. As we have shown, this linguistic phenomenon is typical of HS, both in the Holiness Code[102] and outside it.[103] In PT, on the other hand, we never find God using this language in addressing the community of Israel.[104] In addition, the word אני also appears in God's words at the beginning and at the conclusion of his discourse. Finally, the vocabulary of the passage shows many similarities to HS and to the language of the book of Ezekiel. The expression נשא יד designating an oath (v. 30) appears elsewhere in the Pentateuch only in Exod 6:8 (HS), but is very common in Ezekiel. The oath formula אני ה' דברתי (v. 35) appears elsewhere in the Bible only in the book of Ezekiel, where we find it fourteen times! The root זנה (v. 33) does not appear in PT,[105] but is frequent in HS (Lev 17:7; 19:29; 20:5, 6; 21:9; Num 15:39) and is often used by Ezekiel. Moreover, the pairing of the words זנותיכם with פגריכם is com-

100. For a survey of the various attempts, see Gray, *Numbers,* 132; and S. McEvenue, "A Source-Critical Problem in Num. 14:26-38," *Biblica* 51 (1969) 439. The problematic nature of analysis of the passage was emphasized by B. D. Eerdmanns, "The Composition of Numbers," *OTS* 6 (1949) 163.

101. Gray, *Numbers;* recently, Paran, *Priestly Style,* 85-88.

102. As we mentioned in Introduction, n. 3, this style may be seen throughout H, especially in chaps. 19-26.

103. See above, n. 11.

104. See the comments of J. Begrich quoted in Introduction, n. 3. An exception to the rule is the phrase שמן משחת קדש יהיה זה לי לדרתיכם (Exod 30:31), but the Septuagint reads לכם instead of לי. The Septuagint reading is supported by the similar phrases קודש יהיה לכם (30:32), קדש קדשים תהיה לכם (30:36; the Septuagint reads לכם in v. 37 as well). The reading לי in the Masoretic Text may have been influenced by the word לי at the end of v. 30 (especially if the two words were written in the same position on two adjacent lines of text, as we find, for example in *Biblia Hebraica Stuttgartensia*).

105. Kuenen, *Hexateuch,* 3?4. The absence of this verb in Num 5:11-31, where only the verb שטה is used, is decisive.

mon to v. 33 of our passage and Ezek 43:7, 9.[106] Scholars have already drawn attention to further parallels between our verse and Ezekiel 4: the calculation ארבעים יום יום לשנה יום לשנה and the expression במספר הימים (Num 14:34; Ezek 4:4–6). Thus, we may determine that the passage does, indeed, originate in HS, though we still need to explain the linguistic links of this passage to the JE tradition.

In our discussion so far, we have often found that the editorial level of HS combines Priestly traditions with JE ones by borrowing JE expressions and combining them with Priestly expressions and linguistic forms unique to HS.[107] Furthermore, this stratum of HS manifests overt linguistic and substantial relations to the book of Ezekiel.[108] Thus, we may safely assume that Num 14:26–35 is a typical product of HS's editorial activity. It is thus possible that the editors of this school were responsible for the editing of the entire pericope.[109]

With this we have completed our discussion of the Priestly units of the chapters of the Levite Treatise. We will now turn to the second part of the book of Numbers, beginning with chap. 19.

The Red Heifer (Numbers 19)

The pericope of the red heifer is edited in a form characteristic of PT and is anchored in the sacrificial and purity laws prevailing in this school.[110] In some of the texts, however, we detect signs that have been identified in the course of our study as typical of the other Priestly school, HS. If our claim of the lateness of HS respective to PT is correct,

106. Thus Paran's suggestion (*Priestly Style,* 87) that זנותיכם be emended to עוונתיכם in Num 14:33, based on comparison with Ezek 4:4–6, becomes superfluous.

107. On סבלות מצרים in Exod 6:6, 7 see chapter 1, n. 23. On the editorial verses in Exodus 31, 34, see above, n. 21. On רב לכם, אלהי ישראל, and נא in the editorial stratum of the Korah pericope, see above, p. 82 and n. 65.

108. Compare Exod 6:2–4 with Ezek 20:5–6; Exod 31:13 with Ezek 20:12 and Num 16:9b with Ezek 44:11b.

109. I believe that the expression קהל עדת בני ישראל (14:5) was composed by these editors. This phrase combines three disparate elements: קהל, עדה, and בני ישראל. Though this specific form is unique, it resembles קהל עדת ישראל in Exod 12:6, which belongs to the HS editorial stratum of the ten plagues story.

110. The form of the pericope resembles that of the Nazirite pericope, which contains two main units. In this pericope, the second passage opens with the words זאת התורה (Num 19:14), whereas the second unit of the Nazirite pericope begins with וזאת תורת (Num 6:13). The relation of the red heifer laws to the sin offering was discussed at length by Milgrom ("The Paradox of the Red Cow," *VT* 31 [1981] 62–72), who later used this explanation to resolve several difficulties in the pericope. Other scholars claimed that the PT laws know nothing of purification from corpse defilement through lustration water, but this argument has been refuted by Gray (*Numbers,* 242) and Loewenstamm ("Red Heifer," *EM* 6:580).

those texts can only be an editorial addition of HS to the core passage of PT origin. The discovery of definitive proofs of the secondary nature of the verses bearing HS linguistic traits would confirm the axioms of our research and the path we have followed until now.

Features typical of HS surface in 19:10b–13.[111] This passage separates the first part of the pericope (19:1–10a), which deals with the preparation of the waters of lustration, from its continuation (vv. 14ff.), which discusses the practical law of those defiled by corpse impurity and their purification. The passage provides a summary of the "torah" of purity (see 19:11–12; compare 19:14–19), accompanied by the threat of "cutting off" from the community to those avoiding the obligation of purification (v. 13). Removal of the passage 19:10b–13 in no way impairs the narrative or syntactical continuity of the pericope. On the contrary, the law, as it reads without those interrupting verses, corresponds more closely to the style of PT.[112] The threat of punishment by "cutting off" is repeated in v. 20, which bears a deep imprint of the language of PT.[113] We may remove this verse along with its conclusion, v. 21a, והיתה לכם לחקת עולם, which refers in chiastic order to the opening of the additional passage (v. 10a), without interrupting the continuity of the passage in the slightest. The secondary nature of this material is attested not only to by structural and syntactical considerations but also by the terminology of vv. 10b–13 and 20–21a, which differs from the standard language of the other parts of the pericope. In the original pericope, the verb נזה prevails (19:4, 18, 21b), whereas here the verb זרק is used (19:13, 20).[114] Furthermore, the grammatical form of the verb יתחטא is unique to these verses.[115]

111. The equation of the religious status of the citizen and stranger in cultic laws, as expressed in v. 10b was identified in chapter 1, n. 35, as one of the identifying marks of HS. The expression משכן ה' in v. 13, (above, n. 30) is also typical of HS. The "cutting off" formula in this verse, ונכרתה הנפש ההיא מישראל, is foreign to PT but has a parallel in HS (Exod 12:15). This was pointed out in the commentaries of Dillmann, Baentsch, and H. Holzinger (*Numeri* [Leipzig and Tübingen, 1903]).

112. Many Priestly laws are made up of several units of laws, but we never find transition or mediating verses between units, as we do here.

113. Three elements that we have identified as typical of the style of HS appear in the verse: the combination of איש and נפש in a single law (above, n. 83), the use of מקדש as a synonym for משכן in v. 13 (above, n. 10), and the possessive משכן ה' (above, n. 30). The unique form of the כרת ("cutting off") expression, atypical of PT style, provides an additional proof.

114. Ezekiel too uses the word זרק in an image borrowed from the rite of purification with lustral waters (Ezek 36:25).

115. יתחטא in the *hitpaʿel* appears also in Num 31:19, 20, 23. These passages are part of the final recension of Numbers 19, as we will see later. ויתחטאו is found in Num 8:21, which belongs to the Levite Treatise of HS. Wellhausen (*Hexateuch,* 1–76) sought to derive, from the use of the *hitpaʿel,* that the verse referred to self-purification, not the purification described in v. 19. Dillmann and Gray (ad loc.) correctly remarked, however, that the phrase לא זרק עליו shows that here too the purification was to be performed by an איש טהור.

We may thus determine that these passages are an addition composed by editors belonging to the HS school. We may surmise that the editors found PT's law of the lustration waters incomplete and incorporated into the law the principle of the equality of resident aliens and Israelites, prevalent in their school, and applied the more severe punishment of "cutting off" to persons who chose to remain in a state of impurity. The formula זאת חקת התורה אשר צוה ה׳ לאמר in v. 2a is not in the style of PT. It appears that the formula is of the same HS editors who introduced the word חוקה into various sections of the pericope (19:2a, 10b, 21a) in order to emphasize its authoritative nature.

The Waters of Quarrel at Kadesh
(Numbers 20:1-13, 22-29; 27:12-13; Deuteronomy 32:48-52)

Scholars faithful to the Documentary Hypothesis see the story of the quarrel at Kadesh (Num 20:1–13) as a blend of JE traditions with Priestly traditions originating in P. Opinions are divided as to the attribution of various passages to one source or the other; there are about as many suggestions for the ascriptions of the passages as there are scholars.[116] In reading the narrative as a whole, we find no substantial syntactical difficulties that would have us consider the unit as anything but a single continuous narrative. The attempts at separation of the passage into sources are prompted by the recognition of a mixture of language forms—Priestly expressions alongside those of JE.[117] Outside of this pericope, two "pure" Priestly passages are tied to the story of the quarrel at Kadesh—the description of the death of Aaron (Num 20:22–29; see esp. v. 24) and the narrative of God's commanding the death of Moses and the investiture of Joshua (Num 27:12–23; see v. 14). In these three units, we find subtle references to the Priestly strata of the narrative of the revolt of the chieftains and the Korah pericope, both of which we have attributed to HS.[118] A decisive proof of the HS origin of the Priestly version of the quarrel at Kadesh (more precisely, its origin in the final editorial stratum of this school) can be seen in Num 20:12. We find there a direct address by God to Moses and Aaron, in which God speaks in the first person: יען לא־האמנתם לי להקדישני לעיני בני ישראל ("Because you did not trust Me enough to

116. See the survey in Kuenen, *Hexateuch,* 100–101, n. 42; Gray, *Numbers,* 258–59. The analysis has gone as far as dividing v. 1 among three different sources!

117. The link to the story of Massa and Meribah at Refidim in Exod 17:1–7 is particularly striking. See S. Lehming, "Massa und Meriba," *ZAW* 73 (1961) 72.

118. The phrase ולו גוענו בגוע אחינו לפני ה׳ refers to the plague that ravaged the people after the rebellion of the chieftains (17:6–14; note the language of 17:28). ויקח משה את המטה מלפני ה׳ (20:9) refers to the story of the staff of Aaron (17:25). The expression אלהי הרוחות לכל בשר (27:16) appears only once more in the Bible—in the story of Korah (16:22).

affirm my sanctity in the eyes of the Israelite people"). The first person pronoun appears in God's speech to Moses and Aaron in four other passages, all belonging to the editorial statum of HS.[119] In PT, the first person pronoun is used in the divine speech exclusively when God's words are addressed to Moses alone.[120] The theory that the editors of HS are responsible for the final text of the narrative of the quarrel at Kadesh explains the mixture of styles in Num 20:1–13. We have already noted that these editors often incorporated JE elements into Priestly language.[121]

Another mention of the waters of quarrel at Kadesh is Deut 32:51, a verse that serves as a repetition of Num 27:12–13, in which Moses' death is ordained. This repetition became necessary after the book of Deuteronomy was appended to the Genesis–Numbers corpus.[122] In light of the passage's connection to the story of the quarrel at Kadesh and the death of Aaron in Numbers 20 and the ordaining of Moses' death in Num 27:12–13, we may conclude that it too is a product of editors of the HS, and that it was they who added the book of Deuteronomy to the main corpus of the Pentateuch.[123] In each of these passages, the view stressed is that Moses and Aaron were punished על־אשר לא קדשתם אותי בתוך בני,

119. We first find such an address in the introduction to the pericope of eruptive plagues of houses in Lev 14:33–34, a passage that is outstanding in several respects: God addresses Moses and Aaron, who are to die in the desert, saying, "When you enter the land of Canaan which I give you as a possession (see Rambam, ad loc.). Verse 34 is the only time God refers to himself as אני in PT (except in Genesis; see above, n. 78). As the introduction as a whole shows affinities to HS's language (see Elliger, *Leviticus,* 176), it would seem that this is an editorial addition of HS. The original passage may have begun with a formula such as והבית כי יהיה בו נגע צרעת ("when scale disease occurs in a house"), like the beginning of the passage with fabric disease (Lev 13:47). The formula ארץ כנען אשר אני נתן לכם לאחוה appears again only in Deut 32:39, also a verse belonging to the editorial stratum of HS (see below). The other passages in which God employs the first person in speaking to Moses and Aaron is Lev 15:31, which has already been acknowledged (above, pp. 69–70) as an editorial addition of HS to a PT corpus. We find a similar phenomenon in Num 14:26–27, at the beginning of a speech identified (above, p. 91) as part of the HS editorial stratum of the scouts story. The fourth occurrence is in the final redaction stratum of the Korah story (Num 16:20–21), also originating in HS (above, pp. 77–78).

120. See Exod 25:21, 22, 30; 28:1, 3, 4, 41; 29:1; 30:6, 30, 36; Lev 6:10; 10:3 (quoted by Moses); 16:2.

121. We remarked earlier on the linguistic tie between the editorial level of HS and the language of Ezekiel. We find this characteristic here as well: the phrase מי מריבת קדש is included in a description of the boundaries of the country in Ezekiel's vision (47:19; 48:28).

122. This view of the function of the passage is held by Bacon (in S. R. Driver, *Deuteronomy* [ICC; Edinburgh, 1901] 383) and M. Noth (*Überlieferungsgeschichtliche Studien* [Halle, 1943] 215).

123. The traces of Deuteronomic language in the verse provide additional evidence of the editor's habit of integrating non-Priestly elements in transition and recension verses (contra M. Weinfeld, *Deuteronomy and the Deuteronomic School* [Oxford, 1972] 181 and n. 2, who infers Deuteronomic editing of the passage).

ישראל "for failing to uphold My sanctity among the Israelite people" (Deut 32:51; cf. Num 20:12). The severity of the transgression may be understood, in part, if we remember that HS sees the sanctification of God among the people of Israel as the main purpose of the commandments (see Lev 22:32).

I should clarify that I do not claim that the traditions of the quarrel at Kadesh, the death of Aaron, and Moses' ascent to the heights of Abarim are "innovations," created *ex nihilo* by the editors of HS. Certainly they possessed earlier traditions, some of which are reflected in other sources.[124] Nevertheless, we cannot ignore the intimate conceptual relationship between the editorial stratum of the scouts narrative, which we attributed to the editors of HS, and the final redaction of the narrative of the quarrel at Kadesh. In the revised version before us, these events are linked together, providing an answer to the question that has deeply troubled biblical thought for many generations: Why was the generation that left Egypt, and especially Moses, not granted entry to the Promised Land?[125]

The Story of Phinehas and the War against the Midianites (Numbers 25:6-18; 31:1-54)

A major block of JE narrative stretches from chap. 21 through chap. 25, ending with an account of the sin of Baᶜal Peor (25:1-5). Phinehas's display of passion for God, the pact of eternal priesthood granted him and the ordaining of the war against the Midianites (25:6-18) all form an epilogue to the sin of Baᶜal-Peor. The language of the passage diverges from the style of PT.[126] In PT we never read of the wrath of God or his passion, and the language "so that I did not wipe out the Israelite people" (v. 11), which assumes direct punishment by God, is foreign to the conception of this school. In HS, on the other hand, the wrath of God is mentioned several times: "I will act against you in wrathful hostility and I will discipline you" (Lev 26:28); in his anger, God even seeks to destroy Israel completely (see Num 16:21; 17:10; compare Lev 26:44). Moreover, the term כהנת עולם (v. 13) does not appear in PT,[127] but does surface in the

124. The dispute over the water is transmitted in Exod 17:1-7, which, according to many scholars, belongs to the E source. It may be that traces of other versions of this event—from J—are also present in the current version of the story of the Waters of Quarrel at Kadesh. Another description of the death of Aaron and Moses' ascension to Mount Ebarim, different in tone and detail, is found in Deuteronomy (3:27; 10:6). This attests to the presence among the people of several different traditions concerning the last days of Moses and Aaron.

125. See S. E. Loewenstamm, "The Death of Moses," *Tarbiz* 27(1958) 142-46.

126. Some of the exceptions were already identified by Dillmann (*Numeri*).

127. The parallel phrase in PT is כהנה לחקת עולם (Exod 29:9).

concluding chapter of Exodus (40:15), which is of HS origin. Thus, it seems to me that the passage must have been composed by HS editors, who expanded the early narrative on the sin of Baᶜal-Peor, replacing the main characters of the story, the daughters of Moab, with the daughters of Midian.[128] This recension then served as a basis for the claims of Phinehas and his descendants to the priesthood (see 1 Chr 5:30ff.).

The dependence of the narrative of the war against the Midianites on the story of Phinehas leads us to suggest that it, too, is a product of HS. Let us attempt to support this claim: First, we should take note of the relation of the purity laws in Num 31:19–24 to the recensional additions of HS in Numbers 19. The traces of the HS editors can be seen in the use of the *hitpaᶜel* form התחטא (31:19, 20; see also n. 115), the formula זאת חקת התורה (31:21),[129] and the ordinance to purify the captives (31:19), which presumes the application of the purity laws of the waters of lustration (in Num 19:10b) to resident aliens. The directive to encamp outside the encampment until the day of purification (31:19, 24) is based on Num 5:1–4, ordaining the removal of those defiled by corpses from the camp. All these texts have been assigned to HS. Additional proof of our passage's links to HS is the mention of the trumpets for the sounding of the blasts (31:6), referring to the HS law in Num 10:9 (see Excursus 1). The idiom עדת ה' in v. 19 appears elsewhere in the Pentateuch only in Num 27:17, which we also found to be of HS origin.[130] This phrase is similar to others, קהל ה' and עם ה', which we find in the traditions of the rebellion of the chieftains and the plague (Num 16:3; 17:6) and which were formulated by HS. In PT's language we never find a possessive relation between Israel and God. Finally, the distinction between priests and Levites—here expressed in the context of the unequal sharing of the booty (31:29–30, 41, 47)—belongs exclusively to HS. Thus, the nature of the pericope and its style reveal its origins in the editorial stratum of HS. This also explains the presence of many linguistic forms generally peculiar to the JE tradition;[131] as we already observed, this phenomenon is common in the HS editorial stratum.

128. In order to facilitate the incorporation of the Midianites into the story, the editors added "the elders of Midian" to the Balaam story in Num 22:4, 7 (see Wellhausen, *Hexateuch,* 100; Kuenen, *Hexateuch,* 134). A possible background explanation for the introduction of the Midianite element was suggested by A. Rofé, *The Book of Balaam (Num. 22:2–24:25)* (Jerusalem, 1980) 69–90.

129. The common usage of these linguistic forms was remarked by D. P. Wright ("Purification from Corpse-Contamination in Numbers 19–24," *VT* 35 [1985] 214) in the course of his discussion of the relation of the passage 31:19–24 to the corpus of purity laws in Numbers 19.

130. The phrase עדת ה' appears twice more in the Bible, both in Joshua 22, a chapter that bears a close relation to HS language and concepts (see below, p. 208 and n. 26).

131. On עבדיך, לקראת, טף, see Gray, *Numbers.*

Five chapters, 26–30, separate the Phinehas narrative from that of the war against the Midianites. Some of the material has already been discussed: the story of the empowerment of Joshua was analyzed in the framework of the passage of the Waters of Quarrel at Kadesh, and the festival pericope was discussed at length in chapter 1. The section on the daughters of Zelophehad (27:1–11) will be examined below, in the course of our discussion of its epilogue in chap. 36. The remaining material is of no clear theological or cultic significance; thus, in accordance with our opening guidelines, it will not be discussed here. In the concluding chapters of Numbers (32–36) we will examine only those units dealing with questions of belief or ritual.

The Stipulations of the Reubenites and the Gadites (Numbers 32)

We will confine our interest in this chapter to Moses' speech to the Reubenites and Gadites (32:6–15), which has a certain ideological content. Scholars have argued for the secondary nature and relative lateness of the passage[132] and have recognized its dependence on the final recension of the scouts pericope, especially Num 14:26–34.[133] As we attributed the passage in Numbers 14 to the editorial stratum of HS, Moses' speech, which is based on this, must have been composed by HS editors. This would also explain the conceptual and linguistic heterogeneity of this speech.[134]

The Ordinance on the Destruction of Cultic Sites and Dispossession of the Inhabitants of the Land (Numbers 33:50–56)

Biblical research has acknowledged the affinities of the language of this passage to HS.[135] Aside from the common vocabulary, the first person address of God to the community of Israel (33:53, 56) provides evidence for this link. It may be that the basis for this text was an early PT passage ordering the apportionment of the land to the tribes by lot (33:50–51, 54),

132. See Kuenen, *Hexateuch,* 101; Wellhausen, *Hexateuch,* 352; Noth, *Numbers;* S. E. Loewenstamm, "The Relation of the Settlement of God and Reuben in Num. XXXII:1–32—Its Background and its Composition," *Tarbiz* 42 (1973) 23–25.

133. Compare 14:28–30 with 32:10–12, and 14:33 with 32:13.

134. See the discussion of the passage in Gray, *Numbers.* The Priestly language incorporated into the last part of the chapter should also be attributed to HS editors.

135. Wellhausen, *Hexateuch,* 115; Kuenen, *Hexateuch,* 98 n. 39; S. R. Driver, *An Introduction to the Literature of the Old Testament* (Edinburgh, 1913) 69; M. Haran, "Behind the Scenes of History: Determining the Date of the Priestly Source," *JBL* 100 (1981) 329 n. 12.

but this is not certain. In any case, it is clear that the verses dealing with the destruction of idolatry and the dispossession of the inhabitants of the land (33:52–53, 55–56) are of HS origin.

The Levite Cities and the Cities of Refuge (Numbers 35)

The two pericopes of the Levite cities and the cities of refuge are adjacent and intertwined (see 35:6). We will begin our discussion with the cities of refuge and then take up the subject of the Levite cities.

The pericope of the cities of refuge manifests two clear indicators of HS activity—the equality of the Israelite and the resident alien (35:15) and the direct, first person address of God to the community of Israel, using the word אני (35:34). Another link to HS language is the phrase הכהן הגדול אשר־משח אתו בשמן הקדש, which is similar to the phrase used in the Holiness Code—והכהן הגדול מאחיו אשר יוצק על ראשו שמן המשחה (Lev 21:10)—but has no parallel whatsoever in PT, where the term הכהן המשיח is used (see chapter 1, note 56). Furthermore, the formula לחקת משפט לדרתיכם בכל מושבתיכם (35:30) reminds us of the idiom חקת עולם לדרתיכם בכל מושבתיכם, unique to HS, which we discussed at length in Excursus 1. The passage shows obvious similarities to HS on the conceptual level as well. The interdiction against defiling the land with homicidal blood (35:34) reminds us of the view expressed in the Holiness Code (Lev 18:25–29), that the land is defiled by abominable sexual relations. The emphasis on God's abiding (שכן) among the Israelites in the concluding passage of the pericope (v. 34) is also, apparently, unique to HS. This idea is expressed in Exod 25:7; 29:45–46; Lev 15:31; 26:11; Num 5:3; 16:3. All these passages have been identified, in the course of our study, as belonging to the HS corpus. PT refrains from using such phrases in referring to God; only with respect to the Tent of Meeting does it employ the phrase השכן אתם בתוך טמאתם ("which abides with them in the midst of their uncleanness") (Lev 16:16).[136] The cities of refuge pericope is thus of HS origin, and it is likely that the pericope of the Levite cities woven into it is a product of this school as well. The mention of the Levite cities and the unenclosed land around them in the Holiness Code (Lev 25:22–35) may serve as supporting evidence. We should also note the similarities in the description

136. The difference in the style of the two schools derives from their different conceptions of God, as we shall explain in the forthcoming chapters. Note the phrase ושכנתי בתוך בני ישראל in 1 Kgs 6:13. This verse completes a short passage (vv. 11–13) of God's command to Solomon to build the Temple. The language of this passage is reminiscent of the conditioned language in H (Lev 26:3–13). The entire passage is missing from the Septuagint version—might this be an addition of HS editors to the book of Kings?

of the network of Levite cities in Joshua 21 and the list of Levite encampments in Numbers 3, a product of HS.[137] I do not claim that the idea of the establishment of special cities for Levite residence was formulated by HS; perhaps what we have here is an attempt to codify an already existing reality. The law does not distinguish between different classes of Levites (Levites and priests), allotting forty-eight cities for the use of the entire tribe. Only in Joshua 21 do we find an internal division between cities allotted to the priests, the sons of Aaron, and those given to the other Levite families (21:20–38). But there, too, the term "cities of the Levites" includes both cities of the Levites and those of the priests (see Josh 21:39).

The Daughters of Zelophehad (Numbers 27:1-11; 36:1-12)

The two passages dealing with the inheritance of the daughters of Zelophehad are linguistically and conceptually interrelated (note the reference in Num 36:2 to 27:1–11 and compare 27:7 with 36:5). It would seem that these passages issue from a late stratum of HS. The most evident sign of this is the mention of עדת קרח in Num 27:3. Our research has shown that the character of Korah was made leader of the rebels' faction only at the stage of HS's final editing of the narrative. Additional clues pointing to an origin in HS are the phrase לשארו הקרב אליו (27:11), which appears in the Holiness Code (Lev 21:2); moreover, all other instances of the use of the word שאר in the sense of "family member" are in H (Lev 18:6, 12, 13, 17; 20:19; 25:49). Further, the phrase חקת משפט (Num 27:11) appears elsewhere only in Num 35:30, whose origin has been identified as HS. Furthermore, both of these verses contain expressions unusual in Priestly sources but frequent in non-Priestly ones,[138] a characteristic phenomenon of the editorial stratum of HS. Finally, we should note the reference to the HS jubilee law in Num 36:4.[139]

Summary of the Discussion of the Book of Numbers

Most of the Priestly material discussed has been identified as a product of HS. Even if we add the census chapters (1 and 26) and the desert encampments narrative (chap. 33), which were not discussed here and stem

137. See Z. Kalai, "The System of Levitic Cities—A Historical Geographical Study in Biblical Historiography," *Zion* 45 (1980) 26–27.

138. See the comments of Gray and Holzinger on the words אדני (36:2), דברת (27:7), and דברים (36:5).

139. Although some scholars see 36:4 as a secondary addition extraneous to the passage (see Baentsch and Noth), I find Dillmann and Gray's explanation of the relation of the jubilee law to the passage preferable.

mainly from PT, HS nevertheless constitutes the major portion of the book of Numbers. We may connect this fact to the heterogeneous nature of this book, which is evidence of its relatively late date. Even in legal pericopes of PT, we find traces of intervention of the editors of the HS school.[140] In our study of the Levite Treatise, we identified different stages in the literary production of HS. This phenomenon, which we find also in the books of Exodus and Leviticus, bears witness to the extended period of literary activity of this school.

General Conclusions

The study undertaken in this chapter has confirmed the basic assumptions put forth in chapter 1: that PT precedes HS and that the extent of HS's production is far broader than the Holiness Code alone. Detailed analysis of the Priestly stratum of the Pentateuch yielded much information on HS's recensional activities. Although the question of the editing of the Pentateuch as a whole far surpasses the parameters of our inquiry, I should like, nonetheless, to summarize briefly the pertinent results of our study. First, we will treat the corpus of Exodus-Numbers and then turn to the books of Genesis and Deuteronomy: we may conclude that HS is responsible for the final form of the books of Exodus, Leviticus, and Numbers. In places that contain Priestly traditions alongside those of JE, the editorial stamp of HS is evident.[141] The characteristics of this editing project are transition passages, skillfully constructed to create frameworks for the various traditions; the blending of Priestly and non-Priestly language; and marked affinities to the language of Ezekiel. Even passages belonging primarily to PT bear signs of HS's editing; this indicates that PT came into the possession of HS in the form of individual scrolls, and it was HS that edited and combined them. In most cases the additions contain ideological and legislative material that stresses the difference in the worldviews of the two schools.[142] The ideological intervention of HS in

140. On HS's involvement in the pericopes of the suspected adulteress and the red heifer, see above, p. 88 and pp. 92–95. On the HS editorial additions to the festivals pericope (Numbers 28–29), see p. 30. The editorial addition at the conclusion of the Nazirite pericope discussed in Excursus 2 apparently also originates in this school.

141. In the pericopes of the ten plagues (chapter 1, n. 24, above, p. 61), the giving of the Torah, the sin of the golden calf, and the building of the Tabernacle (above, p. 67, n. 21). The editors played a similar role in blending JE traditions on Dathan and Abiram with the first version of the chieftains' revolt, which was composed in an early stratum of HS (see above, pp. 73–85). See also above, nn. 107, 131, 138.

142. See the discussion in chapter 1 on the HS additions to the festival scrolls of Leviticus 23, Numbers 28–29, and the law of expiation in Leviticus 16. See also examples 1–4 in Excursus 1. We also mentioned HS additions in Exod 25:1–9; 28:3–5; 29:38–46; Lev 10:6–7; 11:43–45; 15:31; Num 19:2a, 10b–13, 20–21a.

the adaptation of JE material is far more modest, but we find some pericopes in which the editors of HS tendentiously revised the JE traditions.[143] Whereas HS often revises and rewrites PT legal passages, it almost never intervenes in JE legal compilations.[144] The differing attitudes of the HS editors toward the two collections of texts apparently stem from HS's consideration of PT as its guiding spiritual source; thus, they saw themselves as innovators of the basic platform of the Priestly code of PT. We complete the portrait of HS as editors of the Pentateuch by demonstrating that there are no traces of editing of the Holiness Code by PT (see Excursus 3).

With respect to the book of Genesis, except for 17:7–8, which manifest obvious ties to the language of HS,[145] we find no clear evidence of HS intervention in the PT passages of the book (see above, p. 60). In other parts of Genesis, however, we find several phrases that we identified as being relatively late and frequent in the editorial stratum of HS—for example, the conjunction מלבד[146] and the shortened formula for the calendar date (Gen 8:5, 13).[147] We should point out that the shortened date formula also appears in the editorial stratum of the flood narrative, which is the only pericope in Genesis combining Priestly and non-Priestly traditions; moreover, there exists a link between this date formula and the Septuagint version of Ezek 4:4–9.[148] The linguistic and conceptual affinities between the synoptic editorial stratum of HS and the book of Ezekiel have been previously discussed; we may conclude, in summary, that the final recension of Genesis was also done by HS, but that the editors did not

143. Exodus 16; Numbers 13–14; 20:1–13; 25:1–9; 32.

144. Except for Exod 20:11 (see above, p. 67).

145. The vocabulary and expressions in these texts are typical of HS, especially its redactional stratum. Compare לדרתם ברית עולם with Exod 31:16; את כל ארץ כנען לאחזת עולם with Lev 14:34 and Deut 32:49. The expression והייתי להם לאלהים is never repeated in PT, but is common in HS (Exod 6:7; 29:45; Lev 11:45; 22:33; 25:38; 26:12, 45; Num 15:41). We may, however, remove these verses from the chapter without affecting its syntactic continuity. There is even a certain tension between the promises here and the previous verses (see C. Steuernagel, "Bemerkungen zu Genesis 17," in *Festschrift K. Budde* [Giessen, 1920] 173). Nevertheless, I hesitate to view vv. 7 and 8 in their entirety as an editorial addition of HS; without these verses the promise of the inheritance of the land is missing from the chapter. This promise is also echoed in other Priestly passages of Genesis (28:4; 35:12; 48:4). It is hard to believe that all these passages originate in HS. We might also note that the language of "cutting off" used in v. 14 (וערל זכר . . . ונכרתה הנפש) shows a lack of agreement in gender between the sinner and the receiver of the punishment in PT (Exod 30:33, 38; Lev 7:20, 27). This lack of agreement is common in the "cutting off" exhortations of HS (see Exod 12:15, 19; 31:14; Lev 7:25; 17:10; 19:8; 22:3; Num 9:13; 19:13, 20). Thus, HS editors may have intervened in this chapter, introducing expressions typical of their school into vv. 7–8 and adding the "cutting off" warning in v. 14.

146. Gen 26:1; 46:26—see Excursus 2.

147. See above, chapter 1, nn. 29, 38.

148. See M. Greenberg, *Ezekiel 1–20* (AB 22; New York, 1983) 106.

rewrite Genesis but limited their editorial activity to arranging the existing early traditions. It seems that the reason for HS's minimal intervention here arises from its great emphasis on the importance of כל עדת בני ישראל ("the entire congregation of Israelites") and the laws given them. Thus, it was only natural that its interest in the generations preceding the exodus and the giving of the Torah was only minor.[149] It may be, however, that HS editors bear responsibility for the current form of chaps. 23 and 36 of the book of Genesis.[150]

Finally, turning to the book of Deuteronomy: Undoubtedly, the book was written and edited by the Deuteronomistic school. Only in the concluding chapters do we find the blending of diverse sources so typical of the Pentateuch. There we find the stamp of HS (see above, p. 95 and nn. 122, 123). HS is apparently responsible for attaching the book of Deuteronomy to the other books of the Pentateuch.

In conclusion, we may say that the Torah book was edited and shaped in HS circles.[151] Although the determination of the time and place of this editing lies beyond the scope of our study,[152] we will discuss the issue briefly later (see below, pp. 200–203).

149. We may compare this with the paucity of references to the period preceding the Exodus in Deuteronomy.

150. The attribution of the present form of these chapters to HS editors is based on their linguistic and substantive uniqueness (which gave rise to considerable uncertainty among scholars as to their origin) as well as the presence of the terms תושב and ומושבתם. The term תושב appears eleven times in the Pentateuch, ten times in passages that have been determined to be of HS origin (Exod 12:44; Lev 22:10; 25:6, 23, 35, 40, 45, 47 (twice); Num 35:15). The additional mention is in Gen 23:4. Genesis 23 has aroused great confusion among scholars: while some scholars attribute it to PT, others remain dubious (see Paran, "Priestly Style," 88, nn. 84, 85). Although this chapter has a decidedly Priestly flavor, it deviates from PT's style. I would attribute the chapter to synoptic editing of HS, who blended Priestly and non-Priestly expressions. The form מושבתיכם appears thirteen times in the Pentateuch, twelve of them in HS passages (Exod 10:23; 12:20; 35:3; Lev 3:17; 7:26; 23:3, 14, 17, 21, 31; Num 15:2; 31:10). The only other mention, the first in the Pentateuch, is in Gen 36:43. Although Genesis 36 closely resembles common PT style, it contains information on Esau's wives which contradicts that of PT (compare Gen 36:2–3 with 26:34 and 28:9). On the difficulty of attributing Genesis 36 to PT, see E. A. Speiser, *Genesis* (AB 1; New York, 1964) 181. These difficulties may be resolved if we assume that the chapter is based on early genealogy lists, which were adapted by HS editors whose language was close to that of PT, but who hesitated to change or take issue with PT.

151. On the distinction between the Torah literature and the Torah book, see Kaufmann, *History,* 1:185–220 (=*The Religion of Israel* [ed. M. Greenberg; Chicago, 1960] 200–211).

152. We will only mention here the use of מלבד (see chapter 1, n. 67), the shortened date formula (chapter 1, n. 29, the use of the form בחדש instead of לחדש) (chapter 1, n. 37), and the use of the word דגל (above p. 83, nn. 67–68), which all point to the period of the Babylonian exile and the first generations of the return to Zion.

Scriptural Passages of PT and HS

We assemble here a list of all the scriptural passages discussed so far, classifying them according to their school of origin. Several PT sections that were adapted and edited by HS are listed in the PT corpus column and marked with an asterisk. HS additions to the passage are marked on the same line in the parallel column. Chapters, passages, or individual verses of JE origin that were edited by HS are listed under the HS corpus and marked with two asterisks. Passages of the editorial stratum of HS based on a blending of PT material with JE are similarly marked. References to supporting arguments for the classification of a particular text are noted in parentheses.

HS Corpus		*PT Corpus*
	Genesis	
		1:1–2:4a
		6:9–22
		9:1–17
17:7–8, 14(?)[153]		17*
23(?) (chapter 2, n. 150)		
		35:9–13
36(?) (chapter 2, n. 150)		
		48:3–6
	Exodus	
		2:23aβ–25
4:21b (chapter 2, n. 7)		
6:2 –7:6 (chapter 1, n. 17)		
		6:13 (chapter 2, n. 4)
		7:8–13
		8:12–15
9:35 (chapter 2, n. 7)		9:8–12
10:1–2 (chapter 1, n. 23), 20–23, 27 (chapter 2, n. 7)		
11:9–10		
12:1–20, 43–49		
16**		
20:11		
24:12–18**		
		25–30*
25:1–9		
27:20–21		
28:3–5 (chapter 2, n. 16)		
29:38–46		

153. As we mentioned above (n. 145), the relation of those passages to HS is still unclear.

HS Corpus	*PT Corpus*
30:10	
31:1–17, 18**	
32:15**	
34:29–35**	
35–40	
Leviticus	
	1–16
1:1 (chapter 4, n. 68)	
3:17 (Excursus 1)	
6:10–11 (chapter 3 n. 7)	
7:19b[154]	
7:22–36 (Excursus 1)	
9:16b (Excursus 2)	
10:6–11	
11:43–45	
14:34 (chapter 2, n. 119)	
15:31	
16:29–34 (above, pp. 27–29)	
17–22	
	23*
23:2–3, 9–22, 28–32, 38–43[155]	
24–26	
Numbers	
1:48–5:10	
	5:11–31*
5:21, 27b (chapter 2, n. 90)	
	6:1–21*
6:21b? (chapter 2, n. 92)	
6:22 –10:28	
13:1–17a	
14:26–35	
15	
16:1–11, 16–24, 26–27a (chapter 2, n. 54), 35	
17–18	
	19*
19:2a, 10b–13, 20–21a	
20:1–13**, 22–29	
25:6–18	
27:1–23	

154. The words והבשר כל טהור יאכל בשר are, in my opinion, an editorial addition of HS. See I. Knohl and S. Naeh, "Studies in the Priestly Torah," in *The Bible in Light of Its Interpreters: Sarah Kamin Memorial Volume* (Jerusalem, 1994) 601–12.

155. Because of the complex nature of Leviticus 23, the HS additions are mentioned here only in a general way. For details, see the discussion in chapter 1.

HS Corpus	*PT Corpus*
	28–29*
28:2b, 6, 22–23, 30, 31a	
29:5–6, 11, 16, 19, 22, 25, 28, 31, 34, 38[156]	
31	
32:6–15	
33:52–53, 55–56[157]	
35–36	
Deuteronomy	
32:48–52	

Differences between the Language of PT and the Language of HS

We present here a summary of the linguistic and stylistic traits of PT and HS, as evidenced in our study so far. First, some general remarks: our new separation of the Priestly source into its component strata highlights the unique literary character of each of the schools. The schematic, measured, restrained style of PT is evident in all texts of this corpus. It appears that the narrative material of this school is even more restricted than previously supposed. In fact, the last narrative tradition of PT in the Pentateuch is the description of the death of the sons of Aaron in Leviticus 10.[158] PT's laws are scrupulous in their use of linguistic structures.[159] We find the use of title lines introducing the instructions and colophons resuming the opening title lines (see nn. 27, 84 above). On the other hand, the PT laws lack verses containing hortatory motive clauses.[160]

156. Here too HS additions are mentioned only in a general way. Included in those additions is the mention of the goats of sin offering in the passage (with the exception of the sin offering of the new moon in Num 29:15, as explained in chapter 1, n. 66).

157. As I mentioned above (p. 98), I doubt if Num 33:50, 51, 54 are of HS. Perhaps they contain an earlier command of PT, later expended by HS; thus, those verses were not included in the list.

158. Although I am of the opinion that the encampments pericope in Numbers 33 originates in PT, this is not a narrative tradition in the usual sense. Perhaps the description of the death of Moses in Deuteronomy 34 contains PT elements, but they do not link up to form a continuous narrative tradition.

159. There is a distinction between laws whose grammatical subject is איש or אשה (purity laws) and those whose subject is נפש (sacrificial laws). PT takes great care not to mix the two subjects in a single law (above, p. 87, and n. 82). Furthermore, PT is consistent in its use of "cutting off" formulas (Introduction, n. 3).

160. Since we found that all verses discussing the purpose of the construction of the Tabernacle (Exod 25:8; 29:43–46) and the reasons for the purity laws (Lev 11:43–45; 15:31; Num 19:13, 20) are editorial additions of HS.

There are no points of contact at all between PT's language and that of JE.

Our study results in a major change in the literary portrait of HS. Because prevalent opinion considered that the entire activity of this school was restricted to the Holiness Code, scholars did not attribute any literary creativity to HS. We now see that many narrative traditions, especially in Numbers, originate in HS. HS's style is similar to that of PT in many ways,[161] but HS lacks PT's precise rhythm and fastidious use of linguistic forms.[162] Moreover, the writings of this school contain moralizing passages and ideological justifications.[163] The language of HS, especially in the editing stratum, demonstrates similarities to the language of JE (see n. 21, pp. 81–82; n. 107; n. 124, p. 96; nn. 131, 134, 137, 141) and to the language of Ezekiel (see chapter 1, pp. 19–20 and nn. 27, 36, 64; Excursus 1, p. 52; chapter 2, pp. 81–82, nn. 108, 121, 148).

Our detailed analysis of the Priestly sources in this chapter reveals a radical change in PT writings in God's speech after the revelation of the name of Yahweh to Moses (in Exodus 7). In the PT stratum of Genesis, where the names אלהים and אל שדי are used, God often speaks of himself as אני, and we find direct punishment at the hands of God. After the revelation of the divine name, the use of אני in God's speech disappears completely (even from God's speech to Moses), and punishment is always depicted as indirect (see nn. 78, 87, 88, and 119). An additional indicator is the change in God's manner of addressing the congregation of Israel: we demonstrated that in speaking to the community of Israelites in PT, God never employs the first person in referring to himself (see Introduction, n. 3; chapter 2, n. 104); only in speaking to Moses does God employ the first person singular (see nn. 119, 120); before the revelation of the name of Yahweh, however, we find אלהים or אל שדי employing the first person singular regardless of who is being addressed.[164]

In this chapter, we discovered that the major literary work of HS opens with the story of the revelation of the name of Yahweh to Moses in Exodus 6. Unlike PT, HS does employ the divine אני (nn. 14, 78, 119), the first person singular in God's direct addresses to the congregation of Israelites (nn. 11, 102, 103, 119) and expressions of divine anger and

161. E.g., the "circular *inclusio*" and the "closing deviation" are techniques common to both schools, as indicated by Paran ("Priestly Style," 94–97, 122–79). Similarly, HS adopted many terms and expressions from PT; see the list of terms below.

162. E.g., the lack of consistency in the distinction between איש and נפש (above, n. 83), the variety of punishment formulas (above, p. 92), and the carelessness in grammatical agreement in the "cutting off" formulas (above, n. 145).

163. This tone is apparent throughout the Holiness Code but is also common to other HS writings: the HS additions to the PT law (see above, n. 159) and the HS pericopes and verses in Exodus and Numbers (see Exod 31:13, 17; Num 15:25–26, 30–31, 39–41; 35:33–34).

164. See Gen 1:29; 6:13, 17, 18; 9:3, 4, 9, 11–17; 17:1, 2, 4–11, 13, 14, 19–21; 35:11–12.

direct punishment by God (above, n. 89 and p. 95). The different forms of divine speech in the two writings of the two schools express divergent theological views, as we will attempt to show in subsequent chapters.

As we will see later, the differing descriptions in the two schools of the Tabernacle and its purpose and of the revelations of God are of great significance. HS establishes a relation of possession between God and the Tabernacle (n. 30, pp. 68, 82; nn. 111, 113), through a grammatical construct stage juxtaposing the sacrifices to the name of God (above, p. 30 and n. 60) and emphasizes God's dwelling amid the congregation of Israel (p. 99). In PT, the word משכן (Tabernacle) appears without any possessives attached (above, p. 70); the sacrifices are never found in a construct state along with the name of God, and God is never described as dwelling (שכן) among the people (above, p. 99). In PT, ordinances concerning the construction of the Tabernacle are addressed to Moses alone, and the aim of the Tabernacle is God's revelation to Moses. In HS, on the other hand, these commands are addressed to the entire people, and the broader, national dimension of God's revelation in the Tent of Meeting is stressed (above, p. 65). An additional stylistic and conceptual trait frequently found in HS is the mention of the equality of the Israelite and the resident alien before the Lord, which is absent from PT (see chapter 1, nn. 34, 54; chapter 2, n. 111).

We will now examine the terms, phrases, and expressions parallel or unique to each of the schools, as found in the passages we have examined. Expressions common to both PT and HS are listed in the PT column and marked with an asterisk; in the HS column, we listed only phrases and expressions unique to HS. Alongside the HS expressions, we list page and note numbers where the common or unique expressions are discussed. Where the PT expressions are unique, their references are listed in the PT column. For expressions that have not yet been discussed in detail, references to the biblical passage or to the discussion later on in the book are provided. Where references are to the notes alone, the body text of the chapter should be checked as well.

HS	*PT*
משכן אהל מועד, אהל העדת, משכן העדת המשכן לאהל העדת, מקדש(י), משכני, משכן ה׳, מקדש אלהיו (chapter 2, nn. 9–10, 30, 59; p. 83 and n. 69; chapter 3, n. 12)	משכן*, אהל*, אהל מועד*
לחת העדת (chapter 2, n. 21)	העדת*
פרכת העדת (Excursus 3, p. 116)	
המנרה הטהרה (Excursus 3, p. 120)	(ה)מנרה*

HS	PT
השלחן הטהר (Excursus 3, p. 120)	(ה)שלחן*
מזבח ה׳ (chapter 3, nn. 5-6)	המזבח*, מזבח העולה*
פרכת המסך (Excursus 3, n. 22)	פרכת*, מסך*
פרכת העדת (Excursus 3, p. 116)	
ונעדתי לבני ישראל, אועד לכם (chapter 2, nn. 16, 17)	ונועדתי לך, אועד לך (chapter 2, n. 15)
ושכנתי בתוכם (בתוך בני ישראל), ונתתי משכני בתוככם, אני שכן בתוכם (בתוך בני ישראל) (chapter 2, p. 99)	אהל מועד השכן אתם (chapter 2, p. 99)
הכהן אשר ימשח אתו (Lev 16:34) הכהן הגדול . . . (Lev 21:10; Num 35:28)	הכהן המשיח (chapter 1, n. 56; chapter 2, p. 99)
כהנת עולם (chapter 2, pp. 96–97)	כהנה לחקת עולם (chapter 2, n. 127)
בגדי השרד לשרת בקדש (ואת בגדי הקדש לאהרן הכהן ואת בגדי בניו לכהן) (chapter 2, n. 13)	בגדי קדש לאהרן (Exod 28:2; 29:29)
לרצנכם, לא לרצון יהיה לכם ן, לא ירצו לכם (Excursus 3, p. 117)	לרצנו, לרצון להם, לא ירצה המקריב אתו (Excursus 3, p. 117)
לחמי לאשי, להם אלהיו (אלהיכם) (chapter 1, nn. 60, 61)	לחם אשה . . . לה׳*, אשי ה׳*
מאשי (chapter 3, n. 7)	
ריח ניחחי (chapter 1, p. 30)	ריח ניחח לה׳*
נתן הבא . . . אשה (chapter 3, n. 32; chapter 4, n. 18)	הקטר*, הקרב* עשה* . . . אשה
זרק (chapter 2, n. 114)	נזה*
משחה (Excursus 1, pp. 51, 53)	חק*, מנח*
שבתותי (chapter 1, n. 14), שבתות ה׳ (Exod 31:13; Lev 19:3, 30; 23:28; 26:2)	יום השבת* (Num 28:29)
מועדי (chapter 1, n. 14)	מועדי ה׳ (Lev 23:4, 37)
שבתון, שבת שבתון (chapter 1, p. 34 n. 72; p. 35 n. 74)	כל מלאכת עבודה לא תעשו (chapter 1, pp. 12, 35)
	תעשו*
חלל (chapter 1, n. 18; Excursus 1, p. 54)	מעל*[165]
זנה (chapter 2, n. 105)	שטה (chapter 2, n. 105)

165. Milgrom, who distinguishes between חלל as typical of HS and מעל as typical of PT, says that the verb מעל appears once in H (Lev 26:40) (*Cult and Conscience,* 86–88). But our study shows that it also appears in HS writings outside of the Holiness Code: Num 5:6; 31:16; Deut 32:51.

PT	HS
נגף*[166]	קצף (Lev 10:6; Num 1:50; 16:22; 17:11; 18:5)
	חרי אף ה׳ (Num 32:10, 13, 14)
	חמת ה׳ וקנאתו (Lev 26:28; Num 25:11, chapter 2, p. 97)
חטא (Exod 29:36; Lev 6:19; 8:15) (Lev 9:15; 14:49, 52; Num 19:19)	התחטא (chapter 2, n. 115 and p. 97)
נשא עוון*	נשא חטא (chapter 1, n. 35)
העדה* (Lev 4:15; 8:3-5; 9:5; 10:17)	קהל עדת בני ישראל, קהל עדת ישראל (chapter 2, n. 109)
עדת בני ישראל* (Lev 16:4; Num 19:9)	
הקהל* (Lev 4:13, 14, 21)	
עדת ישראל* (Lev 4:13)	בית ישראל (Exod 16:31; 40:38; Lev 10:6; 17:3, 8, 10; 22:18; Num 20:29)
	עדת ה׳ (chapter 2, p. 97)
קהל ישראל (Lev 16:17)	קהל ה׳ (chapter 2, pp. 81, 97)
העם*, עם הארץ*	עם הקהל (Lev 16:33; chapter 1, n. 57)
	עם ה׳ (chapter 2, p. 97)
חקת עולם* לדרתיכם*	חקת עולם לדרתיכם (בכל משבתיכם חקת משפט לדרתיכם (Excursus 1)
	בכל מושבתיכם (p. 99)

Finally, we should mention several terms and phrases that we discovered in the course of our study to be unique to HS and have no parallel in PT:

אלהי הרוחות (Excursus 3, n. 24), כלי הקדש (chapter 1, p. 33), יום הכפרים (chapter 2, n. 118), לכל בשר (chapter 2, n. 118), השב אשם (chapter 2, n. 81), גאל (chapter 2, n. 81), שאר (chapter 2, p. 100), תושב, משבת (chapter 2, n. 150).

The expressions on this list are in addition to those already identified by previous scholars (see Introduction, n. 3 and references there).

166. נגף appears once in PT (Exod 30:12) and four times in HS (Exod 12:13; Num 8:19; 17:11, 12).

EXCURSUS

3

The Holiness Code Was Not Edited by PT

The prevailing opinion in biblical scholarship that the Holiness Code was edited by PT is based on the consensus that HS predates PT. Thus, scholars assume that HS is ignorant of the special cultic language developed in PT. But how, then, can scholars account for the many phrases typical of the cultic terminology developed by PT in the text of the Holiness Code? Scholars respond by positing that PT editors edited H, incorporating some of their language and concepts into it. Based on this assumption, scholars then dissect the verses of the Holiness Code in order to separate the HS core from later editorial accretions.

In my opinion, this approach is fundamentally wrong. Our intensive investigations in chapter 1 and 2 and Excursus 1 have demonstrated the priority of PT over HS. Our understanding of the chronological relationship of the two schools simplifies the analysis of the Holiness School, so that we need no longer resort to complicated parsing of verses into various sources. As we will explain in chapter 5, we believe that HS developed in PT circles as a result of an upheaval in the Priestly world. Thus, we should not be surprised to find that HS authors adopted vocabulary and concepts from their PT progenitors. The presence of PT terminology in the Holiness Code poses no problem, and the dissection of the verses of the Holiness Code in order to "peel away" later accretions becomes superfluous. The authors of the Holiness Code—the Holiness School—blended their PT heritage with expressions particular to their school. In the process, the PT terminology lost some of its precision, as the HS author added his own input through the adaptation of phrases from his PT heritage. Thus, the original character of these phrases was altered somewhat. Based on these distinctions, we will now survey the chapters of the Holiness Code in the order of their appearance in the Bible.

In our discussion, we will challenge mainly the early scholars who first raised the claims for PT's editing of the Holiness Code—Julius Wellhausen, A. Kuenen, L. B. Paton, S. R. Driver, and B. Baentsch. The prevailing tendency in later literature dealing with PT (e.g., Reventlow, Kilian, Cholewinski) has been to separate the material into several strata. Analysis of these newer theories would unnecessarily complicate the picture, inasmuch as a successful refutation of the claims of the earlier scholars would suffice to contradict the theory of PT editing of the Holiness Code.

Leviticus 17

The chapter opens with two laws dealing with animal slaughter and sacrifice, vv. 1-7 and 8-9. The prevailing opinion among scholars is that the core of these laws is of HS, with PT editorial accretions. Scholars disagree as to the precise extent of editing.[1] Most include the following among PT additions: במחנה . . . או מחוץ למחנה (v. 3); ואל פתח אהל מועד, לפני משכן ה׳ (v. 4); אל פתח אהל מועד אל הכהן (v. 5); all of v. 6; חקת עולם תהיה זאת להם לדרתם (v. 7); אל פתח אהל מועד (v. 9). The removal of all these alleged accretions yields a text which dictates that every slaughtering be performed as an offering to God, without specifying any particular place for the slaughtering. Scholars claim that this was the original form of the law, reflecting the ancient custom preceding the centralization of the cult. In their opinion, PT employed its own characteristic language in inserting the concept of the centralization of the cult into the basic law: all slaughtering was to be performed as sacrifice, and sacrifice was permitted only at the entrance to the Tent of Meeting.[2]

This claim is based on the observation that the centralization of the cult is expressed in typically PT phrases and, thus, must originate with editors of this school. But we might ask, Why should PT editors insist on the centralization of the cult here when they completely ignore the issue in their own laws?[3] Furthermore, our research in previous chapters demonstrated that the Priestly phrases requiring centralization of the cult in this chapter are not formulated in the "pure," precise language of PT, but are PT phrases adapted in the spirit of HS: the phrase משכן ה׳ in v. 4 is unique to HS;[4] the phrase מזבח ה׳ in v. 6 is

1. See the survey of scholarly research in S. R. Driver, *An Introduction to the Literature of the Old Testament* (Edinburgh, 1913) 15; J. Aloni, "The Place of Worship and the Place of Slaughter According to Leviticus: 17:3-9," *Shnaton–An Annual for Biblical and Ancient Near Eastern Studies* 7-8 (1983-84) 45-49: see also M. Haran, "Studies in the Bible: The Idea of Centralization of the Cult in the Priestly Apprehension," *Beer-Sheva* 4 (1973) 2 n. 3.

2. See L. B. Paton, "The Original Form of Leviticus XVII-XIX–Part I," *JBL* 16 (1897) 30-39; A. T. Chapman and A. W. Streane, *The Book of Leviticus* (CB; Cambridge, 1914) 168-70; L. Elliott-Binns, *The Book of Numbers* (London, 1927) 32-33.

3. On the lack of reference to the issues of nonsacrificial animal slaughter and centralization of the cult in PT, see Excursus 1, n. 10.

4. See above, p. 69. Critical scholarship is divided as to whether this phrase should be assigned to HS or PT (see A. Cholewinski, *Heiligkeitsgesetz und Deuteronomium* [AnBib 66; Rome, 1976] 24 n. 32). Paton's position ("Original Form I," 36-37), agreeing with those scholars who claim that the phrase belongs to the original stratum of the law, yet that this does not imply centralization of the cult, is difficult to accept. The claim that HS distinguishes between משכן and מקדש only when the latter term refers to a single place of worship is untenable. The two terms are synonymous in HS (See chapter 3, n. 11) and are used interchangeably. An example of their synonymy may be seen in the editorial additions to HS in Numbers 19. Verse 13 reads את משכן ה׳ טמא, whereas v. 19 has את מקדש ה׳

absent from PT and is foreign to its conceptions,[5] but accords well with HS's tendency to create grammatical construct forms consisting of cultic institutions conjoined with the name of God.[6] The formula חקת עולם תהיה זאת להם לדרתם in v. 7 is also typical of HS language (see Excursus 1). Thus, I see no reason to assign these laws or chap. 17 in its entirety to more than a single source;[7] the entire chapter bears the linguistic and conceptual imprint of HS.

In addition to the HS phrases discussed above, note the mention of the resident alien in vv. 8, 12, 15; the personalized language of "cutting off" (ונתתי פני . . . והכרתי) in v. 10 (cf. Lev 20:3, 6); the direct address of God to Israel in vv. 10, 11, 12, 14; and the use of the word אני in God's speech in v. 11 (on these phenomena as hallmarks of HS, see above, p. 107).

It appears that, unlike PT, which ignored the issues of the centralization of the cult and nonsacrificial slaughtering, HS takes a firm position prohibiting nonsacrificial animal slaughter and permitting sacrifice only at the entrance to the Tabernacle. The background for this conception and its relation to historical actuality will be discussed in chapter 5.

Leviticus 18; 20

Scholars agree in assigning these two chapters, in their entirety, to HS.

Leviticus 19

Some scholars assign vv. 5–8 to the PT redactor; I shall discuss this issue in detail later in the course of my analysis of the origin of the thank offering law in Lev 22:29–30. The accepted view assigns vv. 21–22 to PT.[8] This attribution is

---

טמא. The proximity of the terms אהל מועד and משכן ה' in v. 4 corresponds to HS's tendency to blur the distinction between them—even to the extent of coining the compound terms משכן אהל מועד and המשכן לאהל העדת (see above, p. 84).

5. The absence of the PT term was noted by Paton ("Original Form I," 37; Aloni, "Place," n. 38). We noted above that PT consciously avoids creating a relation of possession between God and the Tabernacle; this apparently is also the case for the ritual objects in the Tabernacle. The ideological background for this will be explained later.

6. E.g., לחם אלהיו, מקדש אלהיו, משכן ה' (see the glossary of HS language at the end of chapter 2). These linguistic forms illustrate the difference in theological concepts between HS and PT, as we will demonstrate later.

7. Opposition to the view that PT edited this chapter has already been voiced by scholars; see Aloni, "Place," p. 28 and n. 41; H. C. Brichto, "On Slaughter and Sacrifice, Blood and Atonement," *HUCA* 47 (1976) n. 27. In fixing the origin of the entire chapter of Leviticus 17 as HS, I do not deny the presence of several strata in the chapter; on the contrary, I believe that several stages in the development of HS are represented here. This would account for the double justification in vv. 4–7.

8. See J. Wellhausen, *Die Composition des Hexateuchs und der historischen Bücher des Alten Testaments* (3rd ed.; Berlin, 1899) 153–54; A. Kuenen, *The Origen and Composition of the Hexateuch* (Eng. trans. P. H. Wicksteed; London, 1886) 89, 277; Driver, *Introduction,* 52; B. Baentsch, *Exodus-Leviticus* (HKAT; Göttingen, 1903) 399. Paton opposes the separation of v. 20 from vv. 21–22, claiming that the entire law is a PT editorial addition ("Original Form I," 65).

supported by the relation of the language of these verses to PT and by the alleged claim that the cultic terminology employed—אל פתח אהל מועד, אשם—is unknown to HS.[9] This line of reasoning is based on the assumption that HS precedes PT; thus, HS could not have been aware of the cultic institutions and terminology developed in PT. But more careful analysis of these passages shows that the cultic language of vv. 21–22 differs from the standard formulations of PT;[10] the corpus of PT laws of guilt offerings is presented in Lev 5:14–16, 17–19, 20–26. The same language is used to describe the sacrifice in all of these passages: איל תמים מן הצאן בערכך . . . לאשם (see vv. 15, 18, 25). Two distinct instructions are included in this law: the requirement that the sacrificial victim be without blemish and the possibility of monetary redemption. Lev 19:21–22 describes the sacrificial victim only as an איל אשם or איל האשם. Both the requirement that the sacrifice be unblemished and the word בערכך, allowing for monetary redemption of the victim, are lacking. On the other hand, we find an instruction requiring that the sin offering be brought "to the entrance of the Tent of Meeting," an order missing from the passage in Leviticus 5. The omission of the term בערכך and the addition of the prescription that the sin offering be brought to the entrance of the Tent of Meeting may reflect the legislator's intent to eliminate any possibility of monetary redemption of the victim, as part of an effort to emphasize the uniqueness of this case:[11] the guilt offering here atones for a sin committed intentionally, even though no regret or confession takes place. But if this were so, we would expect an explicit statement requiring that the victim be unblemished, especially since no monetary redemption is possible.

It appears that any explanation focusing on the uniqueness of the particular case is not sufficient to explain the many deviations from the model for sin offerings as described in Leviticus 5. A better explanation lies in the recognition that these verses were composed by HS, whereas the corpus of sin-offering laws in Leviticus 5 originates in PT. HS is later than PT and recognizes and accepts the cultic terminology of its predecessor;[12] but, whereas PT is precise in its for-

9. Wellhausen seeks to prove from Lev 22:14 that HS knows nothing of the guilt offering (*Hexateuch*). One who accidentally eats sanctified food must return the principal plus one-fifth of the value to the priest, but is not required to bring a guilt offering, as is the case in the parallel PT law in Lev 5:15.

10. As noted by B. Schwartz, "A Literary Study of the Slave-girl Pericope—Leviticus 19:20–22," in *Studies in Bible* (Scripta Hierosolymitana 31; Jerusalem, 1985) 78.

11. Ibid.

12. According to critical scholars who assign vv. (20) 21–22 to PT, the phrase אהל מועד is unknown to HS. But in fact this phrase is common in the unit on the execution of the ordinances on construction of the Tabernacle (Exodus 35–40) and in the Levite Treatise at the beginning of the book of Numbers, both of which we have shown to belong to HS. The guilt offering, too, is known to HS and appears in the laws of Num 5:5–8 and 18:9, whose HS origins have been proved above. Wellhausen's claim (above, n. 9; cf. Baentsch, *Leviticus,* 410) has been countered by A. Dillmann and D. Hoffmann in their commentaries on Lev 22:14 and J. Milgrom (*Cult and Conscience* [Leiden, 1976] 66). They explain that the two laws treat of different matters; whereas the law in Leviticus 5 deals with misuse of objects sanctified to God, Lev 22:14 discusses the eating of sacred donations belonging to the priest—a far less grievous transgression, for which a sacrifice is not

mulation of terms, HS frames its laws with far greater freedom. Thus, the law of sin offering in Lev 19:20–22,[13] as well as the HS law of sin offering in Num 5:5–8,[14] combines a firsthand knowledge of the cultic law of PT with an independent approach to the formulation and adaptation of the earlier Priestly material.

Leviticus 21

Scholars claim that the following phrases and passages are editorial additions of PT: אמר אל הכהנים בני אהרן (v. 1); אשר יוצק על ראשו שמן המשחה ומלא את ידו ללבש את הבגדים (v. 10); כי נזר שמן משחת אלהיו עליו (v. 12); all of v. 16; דבר אל אהרן לאמר, מזרעך לדרתם (v. 17); מזרע אהרן הכהן (v. 21); מקדשי הקדשים ומן הקדשים (v. 22); אל הפרכת לא יבוא (v. 23); all of v. 24.[15] This claim is based, of course, on the assumption that HS could not have known the basic terms and cultic principles developed by PT. Those scholars are of the opinion that HS does not recognize the priesthood as unique to Aaron and his descendants; that it does not know of the ceremony of anointing or the donning of clothes sanctifying Aaron for the priesthood; that HS does not distinguish between holy (קדש) and the most holy (קדש קדשים),[16] and that the common PT designation of sacrifices as אשי ה׳ is unknown to HS. Furthermore, they claim that the curtain, mentioned in v. 23, is known only to PT.[17]

Our study refutes all these scholarly claims. We showed previously that the units Exodus 35–40 and the chapters of the Levite Treatise in Numbers 1–18 were composed by HS. These chapters emphasize the election of Aaron and his descendants to the priesthood and describe the ceremony of anointing and the

---

required. Some scholars interpret the phrase עוון in Lev 22:16 as a hint to bring a guilt sacrifice (see Milgrom, *Cult,* n. 233; and G. Wenham, *The Book of Leviticus* [Grand Rapids, 1979] 295).

13. According to our theory, there is no need to separate between the first part of the law (v. 20)—allegedly HS—and the latter part (vv. 21–22), allegedly PT.

14. As we will see later (chapter 4), the law of Num 5:5–8 is based on the PT law of guilt offerings in Lev 5:20–26 and derives many phrases from this law while adapting them in the spirit of the new conceptions of HS.

15. See Wellhausen, *Hexateuch,* 156–59; Kuenen, *Hexateuch,* 89, 277; L. B. Paton, "The Original Form of Leviticus XXI, XXII, II," *JBL* 17 (1898) 150–59; Driver, *Introduction,* 53–54; Baentsch, ad loc.

16. See in particular Wellhausen, *Hexateuch,* 158–59, who claims that HS distinguishes between the offering of לחם האלהים and the priests' eating of the sanctified foods, rather than between different degrees of holiness in sacrifice. Thus, the division between the holy and the most holy in v. 21 must be seen as a PT editorial addition. Paton ("Original Form II," 158) accepts the main lines of Wellhausen's argument but takes exception to the assignment of the words מן הקדשים in v. 22 to PT.

17. Paton doubts if the mention of the curtain in v. 23 is to be assigned to PT ("Original Form II," 159). Though he admits that the curtain is not mentioned outside of PT, he suggests that this might be because there was no other occasion to mention it. Furthermore, he argues, how can we be certain that the author used the word פרכת here in the same sense as it was used in PT?

donning of the holy vestments.[18] We need not wonder that HS uses the expression הכהן הגדול מאחיו unknown to PT,[19] in Lev 21:10, alongside the formula כי נזר שמן משחת אלהים עליו borrowed from PT.[20] Thus, we see that HS derives many of its terms and expressions from PT, while coining many new phrases and cultic terms.

The distinction between the holy and the most holy is mentioned in Numbers 18, whose attribution to HS requires no further proof. In Numbers 18 and 15, also of HS, the term אשה also appears (15:3, 10, 13–14, 25; 18:17). HS uses the sacrificial terminology of PT; thus it is perfectly plausible that those terms appear in Lev 21:21, 22. We need not posit any editorial accretions of PT. Here, too, however, HS lends its own nuances to the PT expressions. Whereas the formulation לחם אשה . . . לה׳ is common in PT, HS created construct forms such as לחם אלהיו (see above, p. 30).

As for the curtain, it is mentioned several times in HS compositions outside of H: Exod 35:12; 36:35; 38:27; 39:34; 40:3, 21, 22, 26 and Num 4:5; 18:7.[21] There is no reason to attribute its mention in Lev 21:23 to PT. Furthermore, the compound clause אל הפרכת לא יבא ואל המזבח לא יגש closely resembles Num 18:7 (HS): לכל דבר המזבח למבית לפרכת. Both passages summarize the exclusive functions of the Priests—the duties in the interior of the sanctuary, necessitating an approach to the curtain (אל הפרכת, ולמבית לפרכת[22]) and the duties in the exterior areas, at the altar. The only difference is that our verse, formulated in the negative—לא יבא, ולא יגש—begins with the more severe restriction אל הפרכת and then mentions the less severe one, אל המזבח. Num 18:7, formulated in the positive voice (תשמרו, ועבדתם) begins with the less severe דבר המזבח and ends with the more severe למבית לפרכת. Furthermore, in Numbers 18 there is another verse, 18:3, formulated in this same way, which presents the prohibition addressed to the Levites אך אל כלי הקדש ואל המזבח לא יקרבו. Here too, where the command is

18. On the exclusive gift of the priesthood to Aaron and his descendants, see Exod 35:19; 39:41; 40:13–16; Num 3:1–10, 38; 4:5–20; 8:19–22; 16:3–11, 16–18; 17:5; 18:1–20. The ceremony of anointing and the donning of the vestments is recounted in Exod 40:13–16.

19. As we mentioned (chapter 1, n. 56, and above, p. 99), PT uses the term הכהן המשיח.

20. Compare Lev 8:9, 12; Num 6:7. The significance of the relation established between the description of the priest and the Nazirite will be discussed in chapter 3.

21. In this stratum, representing the final stage of HS's literary activity (see above, pp. 66, 84), we find the phrase פרכת המסך (Exod 35:12; 39:34; 40:21; Num 4:5). In PT, on the other hand, a clear distinction is drawn between פרכת and מסך: the פרכת divides the holy area from the Holy of Holies (Exod 26:33), whereas the word מסך designates the barriers at the entrance to the Tent of Meeting and at the entrance to the courtyard (Exod 26:36; 27:16). The coining of the phrase פרכת המסך by late HS writers reflects their fondness for conjoining PT terms, even at the expense of repeating or muddling the original idioms. (Compare our discussion of the phrases משכן אהל מועד [n. 4, above] and קהל עדת ישראל [chapter 2, n. 109]).

22. Compare the duties described in Lev 4:6, 17; 16:12–17. See also J. Milgrom, *Studies in Levitical Terminology*, n. 154; M. Haran, *Temples and Temple Service in Ancient Israel* (Oxford, 1978) 206 n. 1.

phrased in the negative (לא יקרבו), the verse begins with the more severe prohibition—אל כלי הקדש[23]—and ends with the less severe one—ואל המזבח.[24]

Leviticus 22

The following verses and phrases in this chapter have been assigned to PT: דבר אל אהרן ואל בניו (vv. 2, 17), מזרע אהרן (v. 4), לרצנכם (v. 19), and vv. 29–30 except for the words אני ה׳ at the end of v. 30.[25] The reasons for our rejection of the attribution to PT of these verses referring to the priesthood of Aaron and his descendants have already been provided in our treatment of Leviticus 21. The assignment of the word לרצנכם to PT was based on the school's frequent use of the verb רצה to signify the acceptance of the sacrifice by God;[26] this also resolved the stylistic difficulty in the transition from the third person singular and plural of v. 18 to the second person plural in v. 19. The assignment to PT of the law in vv. 29–30, requiring that the thank offering be consumed entirely on the day of sacrifice, is based on the law's harmony with the PT law distinguishing between thank offerings, which must be eaten within a single day, and vow and free-will offerings, which may be consumed over a two-day period (Lev 7:16–17). According to some scholars, the HS does not distinguish between different types of offerings of well-being, fixing two days as the period of permissible consumption for all those offerings (see Lev 19:5–6).

23. The term כלי הקודש refers here to vessels used in the holy and most holy areas of the sanctuary, as opposed to the altar, which was used only for external rituals (see the formula את משמרת הקדש ואת משמרת המזבח in v. 5). The sanctity of the sacred vessels is greater than that of the altar, as the material gradation shows (see Haran, *Temples,* 159). We should note that every mention of the expression כלי הקודש in the Pentateuch is in passages of HS origin (Num 3:31; 4:15; 18:3; 31:6), more specifically, in later strata of this school's writings (see above, pp. 84, 97). This phrase appears outside the Pentateuch in 1 Kgs 8:4; 1 Chr 9:29; 22:19; 2 Chr 5:5. Since the mention of אהל מועד and כלי הקודש in 1 Kgs 8:4 is, apparently, a Priestly accretion (see Haran, *Temples,* 141 n. 11), we may make the general claim that the phrase כלי הקודש was coined at a late date.

24. In his commentary on Lev 21:23, Noth claims that the curtain mentioned in this verse is not the same curtain that is mentioned in Exod 26:33, which separates the holy area from the most holy. In his opinion, the order of events in Scripture—coming behind the curtain followed by approaching the altar—indicates that the verse refers to some kind of veil at the entrance to the holy enclosure. But comparison with Num 18:3, 6–7 shows that HS seeks formulas that could include all the Priestly duties—whether performed inside or outside (compare Haran, *Temples,* 206, and n. 1)—and is not concerned with the exact order of the Priestly activities or the hierarchy of sacred space. Thus, there is no reason not to identify the curtain of Lev 21:23 with the one mentioned in Exodus 26. The observation that the altar in these verses represents work done outside of the sanctuary refutes the theory of the Bekhor Shor, who believes that the altar mentioned in Lev 21:23 is the golden altar of incense. Compare Milgrom, *Studies,* nn. 154, 158.

25. See Paton, "Original Form II," 167–73; Kuenen, *Hexateuch,* 89, 277; Driver, *Introduction,* 53–54; Baentsch, ad loc.

26. On the meanings of רצה in sacrificial laws see R. Rendtorff, "Priesterliche Kulttheologie und prophetische Kultpolemik," *TLZ* 81 (1956) 339–42; idem, *Studien zur Geschichte des Opfers im Alten Israel* (WMANT 24; Neukirchen, 1967) 253–60.

The word לרצנכם appears four times in the Bible, all of them in the Holiness Code (Lev 19:5; 22:19, 29; 23:11). If we are to attribute this expression to PT, as some would have it, it seems strange that this form appears only in the Holiness Code. It seems more likely that this form was coined in HS as a development of the PT use of the verb רצה in the sense of the acceptance of sacrifice. As HS often employs the language of direct divine address to the community of Israel (see above, p. 107), it does not hesitate to deviate from the fixed PT forms (לרצון להם, לרצנו, לא ירצה המקריב אתו, Exod 28:39; Lev 1:3; 7:18), replacing them with the second person plural forms לרצנכם, לא לרצון יהיה לכם (Lev 22:19, 20, 25). Similarly, the shift from the third person singular and plural in v. 18 to the first person plural in v. 19 is not evidence of later accretions (compare chapter 1, n. 61).

The claim that vv. 29–30 originate in PT is not sustained by critical analysis. A comparison of the language of these passages with the parallel law in PT, Lev 7:12–15, reveals major differences in style and formulation. The law in Leviticus 7, like the other sacrificial laws at the beginning of the book of Leviticus, is formulated in the third person: אם על תודה יקריבנו (v. 12), לא יניח ממנו עד בקר (v. 15). Here, however, we find a direct address in the second person plural: וכי תזבחו זבח תודה, לרצנכם תזבחו (v. 29); לא תותירו ממנו עד בקר (v. 30). We explained above that the word לרצנכם came about through an HS adaptation of a PT cultic term, in the spirit of HS's preference for the direct address of God to the community of Israel. A similar explanation could account for the formulation of the law in vv. 29–30. HS knew the legal language of PT but rephrased it in its own particular style, adding its hallmark ending אני ה' at the close of v. 30.

A similar relation obtains between the law of vows and free-will offerings in Lev 7:16–18 and the law of offerings of well-being in Lev 19:5–8. The third person singular formulation in Lev 7:16 (ביום הקריבו את זבחו יאכל וממחרת . . .) is replaced by the second person plural in Lev 19:6 (ביום זבחכם יאכל וממחרת). The change in person also expresses a change in the identity of the persons to whom the laws are addressed. Whereas in PT, the ordinances are directed toward the priest—Aaron or his sons—who is responsible for the sacrificer's offering (see Lev 6:18), in Leviticus 19 the law is addressed directly to the congregation of Israel.[27] Here, too, HS adapted the earlier PT law in its own style. HS language is evident in the phrase לרצונכם תזבחו (19:5) and in the expression את קדש ה' חלל (19:28).[28]

A comparison of the laws in Leviticus 7; 19; and 22 lays bare the editing process: HS received the PT law of offerings of well-being, as it was formulated in Lev 7:11–18. The law consisted of two parts: thank offerings (vv. 12–15) and free-will and vow offerings (vv. 16–18). These parts were presented in ascending order: first, the law of thank offerings, which were to be eaten during a single-day period only, followed by the laws of vow and free-will offerings, which might be eaten for two days. HS took this law, separated its two parts, revised it, and changed the order of the parts. The part discussing the offerings of well-

27. Later on in the passage (v. 8), the author shifts to third person singular. The reasons for this shift are explained by B. J. Schwartz, "Three Chapters of the Holiness Code" (Ph.D. diss., Hebrew University, Jerusalem, 1987) 130.

28. On חלל as a sign of HS language, see chapter 1, n. 19.

being was placed at the beginning of chap. 19,[29] whereas the part dealing with thank offerings was placed at the end of chap. 22. Thus, HS joined chaps. 19-22 into a single unit enclosed by a ring structure (*inclusio*).[30] The order of the law was reversed to hint at its origins elsewhere.[31]

Leviticus 23

The composition of Leviticus 23 and the relations among its constituent strata were discussed at length in chapter 1. We recall our conclusion: the chapter is based on a PT legal scroll, adapted and enlarged by HS.

Leviticus 24

According to scholars, most of the chapter is of PT.[32] Scholars support their assignment of vv. 1-9 to PT by pointing out the linguistic resemblances of the ordinances on the setting out of the lamps and the shewbread here to the laws concerning the construction of the Tabernacle in PT (Exodus 25-30). The penal laws later in the chapter are part of a narrative framework comprising vv. 10-14, 23. This framework is viewed by scholars as a late addition of PT editors. Several parts of verses of the law itself, whose language, in their opinion, resembles that of PT, are also assigned to this school: רגם ירגמו בו כל העדה כגר כאזרח בנקבו שם יומת (v. 16), משפט אחד יהיה לכם כגר כאזרח יהיה (v. 22).

Let us investigate the scholars' arguments in detail. The unit Lev 24:1-9 may be divided into two subunits: (1) the ordinance to mount the lamps (vv. 1-4); (2) the ordinance to arrange the shewbread (vv. 5-9). Unit 1 has a parallel in Exod 27:20-21, in the command to take oil for the eternal flame. We already determined that this verse is a HS editorial addition at the margins of a PT scroll on the construction of the Tabernacle. Since, however, the argument for the secondary nature of Exod 27:20-21 was based on its relation to Lev 24:1-4, among other things, to assign Lev 24:1-4 to HS based on this parallel would result in circular reasoning. For similar reasons, we will not construct our argument around the phrase חקת עולם לדרתיכם, even though we have shown in

29. The use of the general term זבח שלמים (offerings of well-being) in Lev 19:5 does not reflect the legislator's ignorance of the distinction between thank offerings and vow or free-will offerings (as in Kuenen, *Hexateuch,* 90, 277; and others). Since the HS writer was well aware of the Leviticus 7 law, and, as most זבחי שלמים (offerings of well-being) were, however, vow or free-will offerings, the HS writer chose a general term. (See Haran, *Temples,* 331 n. 31; Schwartz, "Three Chapters," 133 and n. 26.)

30. See Schwartz, "Three Chapters," 134.

31. On the chiastic relation between the original text and its citation in biblical literature, see M. Seidel, "Parallels between the Book of Isaiah and the Book of Psalms," *Sinai* 19 (1955) 149-76, 229-40, 272-80, 333-55; R. Weiss, "Chiasm in the Bible," in *Studies in the Text and Language of the Bible* (Jerusalem, 1981) 259-73.

32. See Wellhausen, *Hexateuch,* 163-64; Kuenen, *Hexateuch,* 90, 278; Driver, *Introduction,* 56; commentaries by Baentsch and Noth.

Excursus 1 that this phrase is a linguistic hallmark of HS. Nevertheless, I believe that we may demonstrate this paasage's relation to the language and concepts of HS on other grounds. The verse opens with a command to take oil for the lamps from the children of Israel. This order accords with HS's view that the materials for the construction of the Tabernacle and the daily sacrifice are to come from the contributions of the community of Israel (see above, pp. 62–65). Furthermore, we find in the writings of this school an explicit command ordering that the oil for the mounting of the lamps be taken from the children of Israel (Exod 25:6; 35:8, 28; 39:37). The phrase פרכת העדת in v. 3, though a *hapax legomenon,* reminds us of the tendency in HS to create construct forms with the word עדת—for example, אהל העדת, לחת העדת, משכן העדת (see chapter 2, nn. 21, 59, 68); in PT, the only construct phrase is ארון העדת. The description of the Menorah as המנורה הטהורה in v. 4 appears only twice more in the Pentateuch, both times in HS passages—Exod 31:8 and 39:37; in the PT account in Exod 25:31–40, the Menorah is not described as טהורה. Thus, we may determine that the passage Lev 24:1–4, like its parallel passage, Exod 20:20–21, was written by HS.

The second passage, Lev 24:4–9, deals with the arrangement of the shewbread and complements the command on the construction of the table in Exod 25:23–30, which is of PT origin. In our passage, however, the table is referred to as השלחן הטהור, a phrase absent from the PT description of the table in Exodus 25 but in harmony with the HS description of the Menorah.[33] Verse 8 states that the shewbread is brought מאת בני ישראל, in accordance with the unique HS conception that everything required for the daily sacrifice come from the contributions of all of Israel, as we find in the HS passage on the lamps in Exod 27:21.[34] We saw in Excursus 1 that the precise functions of the Menorah and the bronze altar were not described in the PT description of the manufacture of the Tabernacle implements, and that HS editors added what they felt was missing at the "seams" between the PT scrolls. To this determination we may add the laconic PT command concerning the arrangement of the shewbread in Exod 25:30. HS provides details on the execution of the order of the mounting of the lamps and the arrangement of the shewbread by placing in its own legal compilation—the Holiness Code—verses dealing with the lamps and the bread.[35] It may be that these verses were deliberately placed in Leviticus 24 so that the details of the

33. The designation השלחן הטהור also appears in the description of the Temple service in 2 Chr 13:11.

34. As we indicated earlier, the passage Exod 27:20–21 was composed by late HS editors (see Excursus 1). The editors apparently composed the passage from expressions taken from the texts pertaining to the lamps and the bread in Leviticus 24, as follows: Exod 27:20 from Lev 24:2. The beginning and majority of Exod 27:21 (באהל . . . לדרתם) are taken from Lev 24:3, with the order of its elements reversed: באהל מועד מחוץ לפרכת אשר על העדת instead of מחוץ לפרכת העדת באהל מועד (see the rule in n. 31); the closing words of Exod 27:21, מאת בני ישראל, were taken from Lev 24:8.

35. Since these scriptures were designed to fill in gaps left in PT laws, it seems that the ritual described here is not a HS innovation, but a reflection of customs already accepted by PT.

daily sacrifice would be in proximity to the festival pericope discussed at length in chap. 23.[36]

The next unit in Leviticus 24 includes penal laws (vv. 15–22), inserted into the narrative of the blasphemer, the son of Shlomit bat Divri (vv. 10–14, 23). The claim that the mention of the equality of the citizen and the resident alien (vv. 16b, 22) was added by PT editors is based on the theory that this principle is an innovation of PT. We have shown, however, that every mention of the equality of citizen and resident alien originates in HS (see chapter 1, n. 34; chapter 2, n. 111). In addition, scholars attribute the legal fragment רגם ירגמו בו כל העדה in v. 16 to the narrative framework (vv. 14b, 23b), which they also attribute to PT. I believe, however, that the assignment of the narrative framework to PT is totally unjustified. The narrative indicates that the punishment to be meted out to the blasphemer was unclear, making divine judgment necessary: ויניחוהו במשמר לפרש להם על פי ה׳ (v. 12). This mode of judgment is repeated in the law of the Second Passover (Num 9:8), in the incident of the wood gatherer (Num 15:34—note the linguistic resemblance to our passage: ויניחו אתו במשמר כי לא פרש מה יעשה לו, and in the narrative of the daughters of Zelophehad (Num 27:5). Now, we have shown that Numbers 15 is entirely of HS, as is the law of the Second Passover, while the story of the daughters of Zelophehad also bears the imprint of HS. Thus, it is probable that the model of bringing judgment before God was developed by HS,[37] and that the narrative frame of our chapter, in which divine judgment is an integral element, was also composed by this school.[38]

Leviticus 25

This chapter presents an exhaustive, detailed exposition of the laws of the sabbatical and jubilee years. The complexity of this chapter has generated many theories among scholars as to its sources and subsequent adaptations.[39] Rather than grapple with the details of the many hypotheses, I prefer to show that the entire chapter, in all its constituent elements, bears the imprint of the language and the ideals of HS. While I do not claim that the entire chapter was composed by a single hand—it may well contain several strata—I maintain that all its elements are of HS, and that the chapter contains no signs whatsoever of PT editing.

36. See the commentaries of Ibn Ezra and Abravanel, ad loc.

37. On the significance of this juridical form, see M. Fishbane, *Biblical Interpretation in Ancient Israel* (Oxford, 1985) 98–105.

38. We wish to emphasize that we do not claim that the narrative frame and the legal ordinances were composed at the same time; it may well be that the law was composed first, and the narrative frame—that of the blasphemer—later. (Compare above, p. 90 and n. 97 on the relation of the law to the narrative frame in Num 9:1–14.) In any case, both the law and the narrative frame are of HS origin.

39. See the discussions in Wellhausen, *Hexateuch,* 164–67; Kuenen, *Hexateuch,* 90–91, 278; Driver, *Introduction,* 57; Chapman and Streane, *Leviticus,* 172–73 and in Baentsch's commentary. For more recent research on this subject, see M. Paran, *Forms of the Priestly Style in the Pentateuch* (Jerusalem, 1989) 34 and n. 16.

The chapter begins with the laws of the sabbatical year (vv. 1-7), formulated as an address by God to the entire community of Israel. God speaks in the first person, and the text employs the pronoun אשר אני נתן לכם—אני (v. 2). As we have shown, these are salient stylistic traits of HS. In vv. 4 and 5 we find the idioms שבת שבתון and שנת שבתון, which are also unique to this school (see above, chapter 1, n. 73). The description of the sabbatical year as a Sabbath is also consistent with HS's conception; as we saw above, HS assigns great importance to the prohibition of work on the Sabbath, whereas PT ignores this aspect completely (above, p. 18).

The following passage, vv. 8-13, presents the subject of the jubilee. The counting of seven Sabbaths of years and the sanctification of the fiftieth year reminds us of the counting of seven Sabbaths and the sanctification of the fiftieth day in the law of the two loaves in HS in Lev 23:15-21 (see chapter 1, n. 52). Verse 9, in which the Day of Atonement is fixed as the day on which the horn inaugurating in the jubilee year is to be sounded, has been viewed by scholars as a PT addition. We have demonstrated, however (chapter 1, n. 62), that this claim is unfounded; on the contrary, we have shown that the term יום הכפרים originated in HS and does not exist in PT (see chapter 1, n. 69).

Verses 13-17 establish a procedure for the sale of land based on the number of years remaining before the jubilee year. The conclusion, ויראת מאלהיך כי אני ה׳ אלהיכם, clearly testifies to the HS origin of these words (compare Lev 19:14, 32).

In vv. 18-24, God's blessing on the sixth year is promised to those who observe the sabbatical year, and the prohibition on the selling of land for eternity and the requirement to allow for its redemption are described and justified. Here, too, we find the direct address of God to the community of Israel and the use of the first person in divine speech (חקתי ומשפטי, צויתי, ברכתי, לי, עמדי), both typical of HS but contrary to PT usage. The strophe ועשיתם את חקתי ואת משפטי תשמרו is also typical of HS (see Lev 18:4, 26; 19:37; 20-22).

Verses 25-34 discuss the details of the practical application of the prohibition against permanent sale of land and the requirement to redeem the land mentioned in vv. 23-24. Since the general rules are of HS origin, I see no reason for assigning the legal details to any other source. Although some scholars attribute the mention of the Levite cities in vv. 32-34 to PT,[40] I disagree; I maintain that the law of the Levite cities in Num 35:1-8 is from HS (see above, pp. 98-100).

The next three passages, concluding the chapter (vv. 35-38, 39-46, 47-55), present the interdictions against lending with interest, against treating an Israelite as a slave or ruling over him ruthlessly; they state laws on purchase of male and female slaves from other nations and from resident aliens and their transfer through inheritance to the descendants of the purchaser as an eternal inheritance, as well as the requirement to redeem the Israelite sold to a resident alien. The warnings ויראת מאלהיך (vv. 36, 43), the concluding אני ה׳ אלהיכם . . . להיות לכם לאלהים in v. 38 (compare Lev 22:32-33; Num 15:41), אני ה׳ אלהיכם in v. 55, and the use of the first person singular in the divine speech (עבדי הם אשר הוצאתי אותם, vv. 42, 55) all attest to the HS origin of these verses.

40. Kuenen, *Hexateuch;* and others.

Thus, we have completed our textual analysis, ascertaining that the entire chapter is imbued with the language of the Holiness School.

Leviticus 26

Most scholars assign the entire chapter to HS.

Summary

We have shown that the prevailing scholarly opinion that PT revised and did the final redaction of the Holiness Code is unfounded. The arguments were based on the assumption that HS predates PT, and therefore cannot possibly know of PT's terminology. Thus, every phrase in the Holiness Code that bore linguistic or ideological affinities to PT language or concepts was considered to be an editorial accretion of PT. But sustained analysis of those expressions revealed that they do not correspond entirely to PT language. If PT editors did, indeed, coin these phrases, it seems odd that they would deviate, only in the Holiness Code, from the precise linguistic usage so meticulously observed in their other writings.

The textual data can be adequately accounted for only if we recognize that HS is later than PT. The authors of the Holiness Code knew the writings of PT well and utilized PT's language and concepts; but, as founders of a new school, they felt at liberty to revise and adapt PT's cultic terms in accordance with their own style and worldview. This accounts for the Holiness Code's linguistic and conceptual resemblances to PT as well as its conceptual and stylistic divergences. In most chapters of H, the relation to PT is expressed through the borrowing and development of terms and expressions. Chapter 23 is exceptional, in that it is based on a PT festival scroll, adapted by HS.[41]

41. Among all the laws and rituals in HS that are based on PT laws and rituals, the laws regulating the consumption of sacrifices of well-being (Lev 19:5–8; 22:29–30) are exemplary. In these laws, the PT core is preserved (Lev 7:12–18) and we may reconstruct the process of revision and editing, as described above.

CHAPTER
3

The Concept of God and the Cult in the Priestly Torah

The schema of the names of God in PT will serve as a key to our understanding of PT's thought. Through it we may understand the entirety of divine–human relations in PT; this schema will lead us to focus on the Priestly Temple and will enable us to distinguish that Temple from the sphere of popular worship outside it.

THE NAMES OF GOD

It is known that PT adopts a "historic" scheme to describe the revelation of the names of God: during the days of creation and in the times of Noah, the name אלהים is used; the name אל שדי is revealed to the patriarchs, whereas the name Yahweh was made known to Moses. According to the commonly accepted division of the Pentateuch into its sources, we frequently find, in PT material, the name אלהים used in texts that appear after the revelation of the name Yahweh. Often the two names are combined in phrases such as ה' אלהים. But if we examine the distribution of the names of God in PT, according to our new definition of this corpus (as we described in the previous chapter), we find a clear-cut distinction among the names of God employed: the name אלהים is never juxtaposed to the name of Yahweh in PT.[1] Furthermore, the revelation of the name of

1. An exception to this rule is the saying "any of the things which by the commandment of the Lord his God ought not to be done" (Lev 4:22), since all the other verses in this chapter commence with the words "any of the Lord's commandments about things not to be done" (Lev 4:2, 13, 27), dropping the word אלהיו—"his God." It appears that the word אלהיו was added by a later writer. If this is not simply an accidentally included common phrase, it may be an emendation made in the spirit of Deut 17:19 (see *Sifra,* ad loc.; *m. Horayot* 3:3; compare Y. Kaufmann, *A History of the Religion of Israel* [Jerusalem/Tel Aviv, 1960] 1:139–40).

Yahweh marks a complete end to the use of the name אלהים (as well as an end to the use of the name אל שדי). It is later mentioned only in three passages—Exod 8:15, Lev 2:13, and Num 6:7b[2]—which are all exceptions that prove the rule, as we shall see later.

PT apparently believes in two periods of divine revelation: the era preceding Moses, which we will call "the Genesis period"—in which God reveals himself through the names אלהים and אל שדי, which are found side by side[3]—and the subsequent "period of Moses," in which the name of Yahweh is used exclusively.

Personality and Impersonality

The distinction between the different forms through which God reveals himself in the Genesis period and in the period of Moses is linked to other, linguistic phenomena, which we discussed previously. We noted above (p. 107) the absence of the use of the first person in God's speech in the period of Moses, though it is common in the Genesis period. Furthermore, punishment of sinners is described in a personalized way in the Genesis period, but impersonally in the period of Moses. We might add that this distinction applies not only to descriptions of punishment but to all accounts of God's activities.

In the Genesis period, a wide range of activities is attributed to God,[4]

2. The other places in "Priestly" writings after Exodus 6 in which the name אלהים appears in various forms, whether adjoined to the name of Yahweh or not, are, according to our division of sources, in HS, and not in PT (Exod 6:7; 16:12; 29:45, 46; 31:3; 35:31; Lev 11:44–45; Num 10:10; 15:40–41; 16:9, 22; 25:13; 27:16).

3. In Gen 17:1, the name אל שדי is revealed to Abraham, but later in the chapter, the name אלהים is used (on the appearance of the name of Yahweh at the beginning of the chapter, see E. A. Speiser, *Genesis* [AB 1; New York, 1964] 124). Similarly, when speaking to Jacob, God reveals himself through the name אל שדי, but in the description of the revelation, the name אלהים is used (Gen 35:9–13). I do not intend to discuss here the question of the origins of the names אל שדי and the name of Yahweh. I accept Speiser's conclusion (ibid.), that although many explanations have been proposed, we still do not have a satisfactory answer to this question.

4. Aside from the actions of speaking, ordaining, and reading in the PT Genesis passages, we find that the following verbs are assigned to the deity: ברא (1:1, 21, 27; 2:3); ויבדל (1:4); ויעש, עשה, נעשה (1:7, 25, 26, 31; 2:2); וירא, וראיתיה (1:4, 12, 18, 21, 25, 31; 6:12; 9:16); אתן, ויתן, נתתי, נתתיך, נתתיו, אתננה (1:17, 29; 9:3, 13; 17:5, 6, 8 (dependent on chapter 2, n. 145), 20; 35:12; 48:4; ויברך, וברכתי (1:22, 28; 2:3; 9:1; 17:16, 20; 35:9; 48:3); ויכל (2:2); וישבת, שבת (2:2, 3); משחיתם, מביא . . . לשחת (6:13, 17); אדרש, אדרשנו (9:5); בענני (9:14); וזכרתי (9:15); והרביתך, וארבה, והרביתי (17:2, 20; 48:4); ויעל (17:22; 35:13). In the PT verses of the book of Exodus which precede the revelation of the name of Yahweh we find the following verbs: וירא, וידע, וישמע, ויזכר (Exod 2:24, 25). The wide variety of direct actions attributed to God in the 180 verses of PT which precede the revelation of the name of Yahweh is in striking contrast to the paucity of actions directly attributed to God in those sections of PT following the revelation of the name of Yahweh—which comprise 750 verses!

whereas in the period of Moses, the number of actions attributed directly to God is reduced to a minimum. This is achieved through the use of special mediating phrases. Sometimes the preposition לפני is used to create distance between God and the object.[5] Thus, we find the phrase לזכרון לפני ה׳ (Exod 28:12, 29; 30:16), which avoids attributing the act of remembering directly to God. This is in contrast to the texts preceding the revelation of the name of Yahweh, in which אלהים is described as remembering his covenant (Gen 9:15; Exod 2:24). In a similar fashion, distance is placed between God's name and the act of volition (Exod 28:38; Lev 1:3). Another means serving the same purpose is the use of the passive conjugations of verbs (נפעל, הופעל) instead of the active ones (קל, הפעיל). God no longer forgives, cuts off, or shows; rather, the sin is forgiven (Lev 4:20, 21, 31, 35; 5:10, 13, 16, 18, 26); the sinner is cut off (Exod 30:33, 38; Lev 7:20, 21); Moses is shown the Tabernacle and its vessels (Exod 25:40; 26:30).[6] Where we do find descriptions of God's activity, explicit mention of his name is absent (Exod 27:8; Lev 10:17).

Only in one area do we find a series of actions directly attributed to God—in verbs of speech, talk, meeting, and command. All of these appear in the description of the relation of God and Moses.[7] We have already observed that in PT, after the revelation of the name of Yahweh, God uses the first person and direct speech only when speaking with Moses (above,

5. In the Aramaic translations of the Pentateuch, the phrase קדם ה׳, which corresponds to the Hebrew לפני ה׳ is quite common. The prevailing opinion among scholars is that this phrase too is designed to remove anthropomorphisms; recently, though, M. L. Klein argued with this view ("The Preposition 'קדם'—'before'—Pseudo-Anti Anthropomorphisms in the Targumim," *JTS* 30/2 (1979) 502–7. His argument is based on the unsystematic use of this phrase in the Aramaic translations and on its use in connection with human beings. This is not the case in PT, where לפני is used to avoid direct action only when referring to God, and then only after the revelation of the name of Yahweh. Thus, this is indeed a systematic means of emphasizing the impersonal aspect of the divinity.

6. It is of interest to note that at the conclusion of the editorial addition of HS at the beginning of the Tabernacle pericope (Exod 25:1–9), an identical activity is phrased as the direct action of a personal God—"exactly as I show you—the pattern of the Tabernacle and the pattern of all its furnishings" (v. 9). The difference in the conception of God as viewed by the two schools is embodied here in the language used to refer to God.

7. Besides the verbs of telling, speech, meeting, and commandment, direct action is attributed to God in the giving of the עדות (pact) to Moses (Exod 25:16, 21). But, as we will see later on, the giving of the עדות symbolizes God's commandment. On the exception in Exod 9:12, see below, n. 54. As for the phrase חלקם נתתי אתה מאשי (Lev 6:10), it would seem, as A. Dillmann has already remarked, that this passage (and the subsequent passage) was edited at a late date. The editor—apparently of HS—added in the forms מאשי, נתתי, which appear in other editorial additions of HS (Lev 7:34; Num 28:2b) but are never found in PT. When PT mentions the giving of the flesh of the sin offering to the priests, it avoids attributing the giving directly to God (see Lev 10:17), usually referring to the offerings in the third person: אשי ה׳ and not אשי (Lev 2:3, 10; 4:35; 5:12; 10:12, 13). In the textual version reflected in the Septuagint and the Samaritan text, we find מאשי ה׳—but this is apparently an emendation made to bring the text in line with the usual PT formula.

p. 107). Thus, the personal language applied to God is particularly appropriate to describing the communication between two persons. But even Moses' contact with God does not bear the same personal, unmediated quality that often characterizes the relation between God and humans in the Genesis period. Unlike in the Genesis period, God does not employ the pronoun אני in his contacts with Moses, and their discussion is blatantly one-sided: God appears to Moses, speaks with him, and has him command the people of Israel (Exod 25:22). We never find in PT a single instance of Moses' addressing God! In addition, the personal language is limited to verbal communication; insofar as other actions of God are concerned, we find a tendency toward impersonal communication, even in his contact with Moses (see Exod 25:40; 26:30).

PT does, however, sharply distinguish between God's relation to Moses and God's relation to the Israelite community. The PT description of the receiving of the Torah on Mount Sinai in Exod 24:15-18 is particularly striking in this regard.[8] Moses alone enters the cloud to *hear* the word of God; the people do not directly hear the word of God, and their participation in the revelation is limited to *seeing* the Presence (כבוד) of God. Similarly, during the dedication of the Tabernacle, the Presence (כבוד) of God appears to the people (Lev 9:3-4, 6, 23) but the meeting with God, in which God makes his commandments known, takes place inside the Tent of Meeting, with Moses alone present (Exod 25:22; 30:6, 36; Lev 1:1).

Admittedly, Aaron enters the Tent of Meeting along with Moses during the ceremony of the dedication of the Tabernacle, but God does not communicate with them at that time. Moses is the supreme hearer of the word of God, and he alone attains the highest level of closeness to God.[9] The difference between the two persons is made evident through the way in which they enter the sacred enclosure—the Holy of Holies—where the presence of God is made manifest. Moses communicates with God frequently in the Tent of Meeting,[10] whereas Aaron is warned not to approach at will but only after painstaking preparations (Lev 16:2-13). The texts stress the danger of death inherent in approaching the Holy of

8. Although these verses are integrated in a transition verse of the editors of HS, I see no reason not to accept the prevailing opinion among scholars that these verses are PT's version of the revelation at Sinai (see chapter 2, n. 21; for a refutation of A. Toeg's arguments [*Lawgiving at Sinai* (Jerusalem, 1971)] against the PT origin of this verse, see below, n. 17).

9. For Moses' superiority over Aaron in approaching God, see also H. Holzinger, *Einleitung in den Hexateuch* (Freiburg, 1893) 383. The greater closeness of Moses to God is explicitly mentioned in non-Priestly sources (see Num 12:8; Deut 34:10); those verses, however, are full of anthropomorphic images that run counter to the views of PT. PT does not describe any frontal encounter between God and Moses and greatly restricts the anthropomorphic elements in the description of their encounter.

10. See Toeg, *Lawgiving,* 155–57, on the significance of the frequent revelation in the Tent of Meeting in PT's thought.

Holies in which God is revealed. This tone is completely absent from descriptions of God's communication with Moses.

Whereas in the period of Moses we find a distinction between the revelation of God through hearing and his revelation through sight, in the Genesis period God (who identifies himself as אל שדי) reveals himself to Abraham and Jacob through sight and speech (Gen 17:1; 35:9). The revelation to the eye and ear lends the contact between God and the patriarchs a direct, nonmediated quality, like that of a conversation between friends. Indeed, a dialogue takes place between Abraham and God: Abraham expresses his doubts and God responds, affirming that he will maintain his covenant with Isaac (Gen 17:18-21). The nonmediated relation with God of the Genesis period is not restricted to the patriarchs. Adam, Noah and his children, and all living things are privileged by God's direct address and his blessing (although God does not reveal himself to them).[11] There is a direct correlation between the nonmediated contact with God and the personalized description of his actions in the Genesis period.

Anthropomorphism and the Suppression of Anthropomorphism

The direct relation between God and his creatures in the Genesis period is expressed not only through personalized descriptions of God's actions but also through anthropomorphic expressions, which serve the same ends: "Biblical anthropomorphisms are all expressions of encounters between God and Man."[12] The first and most important of these is the idea of the creation of human beings in the image of God, which stresses human dignity and closeness to the Creator.[13] After the flood, the spilling of human blood is prohibited, "for in his image did God create man" (Gen 9:6). God enters into a covenant with Noah and his sons and with all living beings, promising not to wipe them out or destroy the world again. He informs them that he is presenting the rainbow as a sign of the covenant and that, on seeing the rainbow, he will remember his covenant (Gen 9:13-16).[14] At the close of his communication with Abraham and Jacob, God is described as ascending from them (Gen 17:22; 35:13). A

11. See the references in chapter 2, n. 163. On the unmeditated contact between God and humans as reflected in all strata of Genesis, see F. M. Böhl, *Das Zeitalter Abrahms* (Leipzig, 1931) 41; N. Söderblom, *Das Werden des Gottesglaubens* (Leipzig, 1916) 273.

12. F. Rosenzweig, *Kleinere Schriften* (Berlin, 1957) 528; see the similar conception in Kaufmann, *History*, 1:440–42.

13. See S. E. Loewenstamm, "Man as Image and Son of God," *Tarbiz* 27 (1958) 1–2.

14. On the image of the bow of God and its adaptation in PT, see M. Weinfeld, "God the Creator in Gen. 1 and in the Prophecy of Second Isaiah" (Hebrew), *Tarbiz* 37 (1968) 116, 120.

series of anthropomorphic expressions describes God's reaction to the suffering of Israel in Egypt: וישמע ("he heard"), ויזכר ("he remembered"), וירא ("he saw"), וידע ("he took notice") (Exod 2:24-25).

In the period following the revelation of the name of Yahweh, the number of anthropomorphic expressions in PT diminishes,[15] and only the direct contact between God and Moses is described, using verbs normally applied to interpersonal contact, for example, ונועדתי לך שם ודברתי אתך ("There I will meet with you and I will impart to you") (Exod 25:22). By contrast, the description of the Presence (כבוד) of God, as it is revealed to all of Israel, lacks all human dimension: "Now the Presence of the Lord appeared in the sight of the Israelites as a consuming fire at the top of the mountain" (Exod 24:17).[16] The passages describing God's revelation during the days of ordination also connect God's Presence (כבוד) with fire: "and the Presence of the Lord appeared to all the people. Fire came forth from before the Lord and consumed the burnt offering and the fat parts on the altar" (Lev 9:23-24).[17] Fire plays a major role in the deaths of Nadab and Abihu, described several verses later: "And fire came forth from the Lord and consumed them; thus they died at the instance of the Lord" (Lev 10:2). PT thoroughly removes here any anthropomorphism or personalized description, both in its description of the punishing agent—the fire—and through the avoidance of direct attribution of the fire to God: the fire comes forth מלפני ה׳, "from before the Lord."[18] Com-

15. The minimal anthropomorphism and anthropopathism in the descriptions of God in PT was already noted by A. Dillmann (*Die Bücher Numeri, Deuteronomium und Josua* (2nd ed.; Leipzig, 1886) 653.

16. The impersonality of the concept of God's Presence—כבוד in PT—was already remarked by Holzinger (*Einleitung,* 379, and in the introduction of his commentary on Exodus [p. x]; see also W. Eichrodt, *Theology of the Old Testament* (Eng. trans. J. Baker; London, 1961) 1:408–9; and J. Milgrom, "The Alleged 'Demythologization and Secularization' in Deuteronomy," *IEJ* 23 (1973) 158. The arguments advanced by Kaufmann (*History,* 1:228) and Weinfeld ("G-d the Creator," 116) on the anthropomorphism inherent in the image of the Presence of God are applicable to the descriptions in the book of Ezekiel (see Ezek 1:26–28 and compare Exod 33:18–23; Isa 6:1–3), but not to PT. The differences in the description of the "כבוד" in the two writings were described by J. Morgenstern ("Biblical Theophanies," *ZA* 28 [1913] 45–46); G. von Rad, "*kavod*" in *TWAT* 2:244; R. E. Clements (*God and Temple* [Oxford, 1965] 114), as well as by W. Zimmerli and M. Greenberg in their commentaries on Ezekiel.

17. See Rashbam, ad loc. This resolves the difficulties posed by Toeg (*Lawgiving,* 10) on the Priestly origin of the symbol of the consuming fire in Exod 24:17. Hoffmann (*Leviticus with Commentary,* I,220) seeks to prove from 2 Chr 7:1, 3 that the fire and the כבוד are separate entities, but, in spite of their many affinities to the Priestly traditions of the Pentateuch (see S. Japhet, *The Ideology of the Book of Chronicles and Its Place in Biblical Thought* [Eng. trans. A. Barber; Frankfurt, 1989] 73), these Chronicle writings differ in several crucial ways from PT (ibid., 63–64); thus they cannot be used as evidence on questions related to PT.

18. The impersonality and lack of anthropomorphism in the punishment descriptions of PT were noticed by A. Rofé, "Israelite Belief in Angels in the Pre-Exilic Period as Evidenced by Biblical Traditions" (Ph.D. diss., The Hebrew University, Jerusalem, 1962)

pare, for example, this description to a similar event, the breach of Uzzah, described in 2 Sam 6:7: "The Lord was incensed at Uzzah. And God struck him down on the spot for his indiscretion, and he died there beside the Ark of God."

As we mentioned, the tendency toward impersonal description and limitation of anthropomorphic language is dominant in PT's descriptions of events subsequent to the revelation of the name of Yahweh. This tendency is expressed not only in the descriptions of the day of dedication of the altar and the Tent of Meeting, but throughout the entire cultic Temple sphere. We have already mentioned the syntactical structures employed by PT in order to avoid attributing directly to God any actions of memory, volition, or forgiveness in the cultic realm. These structures serve both to stress the impersonal aspect of divinity and to avoid anthropomorphic imagery. Another expression of the latter tendency is PT's avoidance of any mention of a relationship of possession between God and the Tabernacle: we never find in PT forms such as משכני or משכן ה׳ (see above, p. 70). It seems that the aversion to such forms was part of the tendency to avoid the anthropomorphic association of the Tabernacle with the residence of God. Thus, the verb שכן is never attributed to God (see above, p. 99). PT even avoids reference to the dwelling (שכן) of God's Presence (כבוד) in the Tent of Meeting, preferring the verb יעד (directed toward Moses) in describing God's permanent presence in the Tabernacle.[19] PT does, however, refer to the dwelling (שכן) of the Presence (כבוד) of God on the mount during the revelation at Sinai (Exod 24:16). It

---

172–76, but he found inconsistencies in the direct attribution of the verbs כלה, קצף, נגף, הכה, and קנא in several "Priestly" sources—Exod 12:12–13; Lev 10:6; Num 16:22; 25:11. Our theory eliminates this difficulty, since all of the verses mentioned above originate, in our opinion, in HS, whose approach on these matters differs from PT. Moreover, based on our classification of the writings of the two schools, as detailed at the end of the previous chapter, we find that the anthropomorphic images of חמה, קצף, and קנאה do not appear at all in PT, not even in impersonal formulations (see the comparative table of words and expressions in chapter 2, pp. 108–10). With respect to נגף, see chapter 2, n. 165.

19. See above, p. 99 and n. 136; see also A. Geiger, *Urschrift und Übersetzungen der Bibel* (Breslau, 1857) 182. We should mention here the difference between PT and HS in their descriptions of the appearance of God in the Tabernacle upon its completion. Whereas HS writes "the cloud covered the Tent of Meeting and the Presence of the Lord filled the Tabernacle" (Exod 40:34, 35), PT describes here only the appearance of the Presence of God to the people (Lev 10:23). I do not accept the argument that the very use of the words מועד ("meeting") and the verb יעד indicate that PT is of the opinion that God does not permanently reside in the Tent (see G. von Rad, "The Tent and the Ark," in his *The Problem of the Hexateuch and Other Essays* [Eng. trans. E. W. Trueman; New York, 1966] 105–6; idem, *Old Testament Theology* [trans. D. M. G. Stalken; Edinburgh, 1973] 1:239). It is entirely plausible that God calls Moses to meet with him in his permanent dwelling place. A similar example would be the tent of the Canaanite El—his permanent dwelling place—in which he also meets with the heavenly retinue (see R. J. Clifford, "The Tent of El and the Israelite Tent of Meeting," *CBQ* 33 [1971] 224–27).

may be that, for PT, the dwelling of the Presence on Mount Sinai is less obviously anthropomorphic than its dwelling in the Tent of Meeting, which leads directly to the association with a physical home.

I should like to stress that the problem that PT grapples with in avoiding the image of the God who dwells in his sanctuary is not the concept of a permanent divine presence in the sacred precincts; that concept is accepted by PT, as the frequent use of the expression לפני ה׳ shows.[20] Indeed, without this presence, the significance of the sacred area is unintelligible.[21] The difficulty lies in the form that this idea takes in a cultic system which, by its nature, contains much imagery of the satisfaction of the daily needs of the divinity. PT adopted the ancient cultic tradition, including its anthropomorphic imagery,[22] but sought to refine that imagery wherever possible. As part of its effort to avoid anthropomorphic description of the presence of God,[23] it prefers to use the verb יעד rather than שכן to refer to the presence of the divinity in the Tent of Meeting.[24]

20. See von Rad, "Tent and Ark," 104–5. As for Exod 16:10 and Num 17:7, which von Rad uses to prove the existence of the view that denies the idea of God's permanent presence, according to our analysis, they originate in HS and not in PT.

21. On the centrality of the idea of the permanent presence of God, see M. Haran, "The Symbolic Significance of the Complex of Ritual Acts—Performed Inside the Israelite Shrine," *Yehezkel Kaufmann Jubilee Volume* (ed. M. Haran; Jerusalem, 1960) 39; idem, *Temples and Temple Service in Ancient Israel* (Oxford, 1987) 226–27; Clements, *God and Temple,* 43ff. Note, however, that many of the texts that serve as the basis for Clements's arguments originate, in fact, in HS. Moreover, for chronological and other reasons, I reject his developmental schema, which sees PT's view as a dialectical consequence of Deuteronomic thought. Compare the current criticism voiced by Haran, "The Divine Presence in the Israelite Cult and the Cultic Institutions," *Biblica* 50 (1969) 251–67.

22. See Haran, "Symbolic Significance," 35–38; idem, *Temples,* 221–25.

23. This tendency is also expressed in PT's avoiding any description of God as seated on the cherubim; instead PT describes God meeting with Moses and speaking with him from between the two cherubim (Exod 25:22); in Lev 16:2, God appears in a cloud upon the mercy-cover. See also von Rad, "Tent," 110, 120; *Theologie,* 1:239; Kaufmann, *History,* 2:353–54. On the image of the cherubim as the seat of God and the mercy-cover as his footstool, see M. Haran, "The Ark and the Cherubim: Their Symbolic Significance in Biblical Ritual," *IEJ* 9 (1959) 30–38.

24. Opposed to the tradition describing the Tent of Meeting is the tradition of E. There the Tent of Meeting is described as a temporary meetingplace at whose entrance God descends; at the end of his revelation he ascends from it (see M. Haran, "The Nature of the 'Ohel Moed' in the Pentateuchal Sources," *Journal of Semitic Studies* 5 [1960] 50–65; idem, *Temples,* 260ff.). I am of the opinion that we cannot determine which of the models of this institution is original. E reflects the prophetic view, which rejects the idea of a permanent place of God in the cultic enclosure (on the prophetic character of the Tent of Meeting in E's tradition, see Haran, *Temples,* 267–71; S. E. Loewenstamm ,"Tabernacle of God," *EM* 5:544–46). This rejection is explained in Exod 35:3–5, which provides the background for the removal of the tent outside the camp in Exod 33:6–11 (see also W. Beyerlin, *Origins and History of the Oldest Sinaitic Traditions* [Eng. trans. S. Rudman; Oxford, 1965] 114; Loewenstamm, "Tabernacle," 546). The connection of the rejection of a permanent residence for God and the erection of the prophetic tent outside the camp to the sin of the golden calf

The tendency to eliminate anthropomorphisms is expressed also in PT's attitude toward the ritual acts taking place in the Tent of Meeting and its courtyards. The central image at the core of these rituals, as we find throughout the Bible[25] and as was practiced among the surrounding nations, was the satisfaction of the needs of the divinity. PT's struggle against this concept is most forcefully expressed through the removal of all instruments for the consumption of food from the interior of the tent. The burning of an animal sacrifice, the bringing of a meal offering or the pouring out of a libation in the interior of the Tent of Meeting might easily be understood as the nourishing of God in his home. Thus, PT expressly forbids the sacrificing of burnt offerings, meal offerings, or libations on the inner altar, which is to be used solely for incense (Exod 30:9). Among the table vessels are bowls, ladles, jars, and jugs "with which to offer libation" (see Exod 25:29). But these vessels, which were certainly used originally to place food and drink on the table, here have no function at all in PT and remain empty![26] The only food brought inside the Tent of Meeting was the shewbread placed on the table, but this ritual too was very different from those practiced in the temples of neighboring nations. In Mesopotamian temples, for example, the table of the god was set four times a day and the loaves of bread were replaced at each meal.[27] Furthermore, great efforts were made to give the impression that the deity feasted on the food.[28] The shewbread,[29] on the other hand, was

---

leads us to think that this tradition may reflect the opposition of prophetic circles among the Northern tribes to the official golden calf cult of the kingdom of Israel (see A. W. Jenks, *The Elohist and North Israelite Traditions* [SBLMS 22; Missoula, MT, 1977] 54).

The opposing, Priestly view is that the cultic Tent of Meeting is in the middle of the camp and serves as the permanent dwelling place of God and the locus of the revelation of the divine command. R. de Vaux's attempt (*The Bible and the Ancient Near East* [Eng. trans. D. McHugh; New York, 1971] 140–51) to mediate between the texts and reconcile the conflicting views is unconvincing. We should mention that the opposition between the two descriptions of the Tent of Meeting was already noted by the sages. In order to resolve this difficulty, they posited the existence of "two tents, the tent of the cult and the tent of the commandments" (*Sifre Zuta,* ed. Horowitz, p. 292).

25. See W. Herrmann, "Götterspeise und Göttertrank in Ugarit und Israel," *ZAW* 72 (1960) 205–16; and Haran, "The Symbolic Significance of the Complex of Ritual Acts Performed Inside the Israelite Shrine" (Hebrew), in *Yehezkel Kaufmann Jubilee Volume* (Jerusalem, 1960) 35–36 and nn. 22–25.

26. See U. Cassuto, *Exodus,* 234; Haran, "Cultic System," 31 and n. 17; *Temples,* 216–17, nn. 13–14.

27. See J. B. Pritchard, ed., *Ancient Near Eastern Texts Relating to the Old Testament* (Princeton, NJ, 1969) 3:343.

28. See A. Leo Oppenheim, *Ancient Mesopotamia* (Chicago, 1964) 192–93.

29. The uniqueness of the custom of setting out the shewbread once a week is expressed in the *derasha* of Rabbi Berakhya, who speaks of the blasphemer who mocks God saying, "is it the custom of the king to eat warm bread or cold?" (*Lev. Rabbah* 32:3, ed. Margaliyot, p. 741). Although Rabbi Yehoshua ben Levi sought to learn from the verse לחם חם ביום הלקחו (1 Sam 27:1) that "a great miracle occurred so that the shewbread, when removed, was in

placed on the table only once a week, and it was ordained, upon removal, to be eaten entirely by the priests (Lev 24:8-9).[30]

The outer altar, to which the sacrifices and the libations were brought, was detached from the inner cultic area.[31] Therefore, this could not signify the feeding of God in his house. We do find, however, that with respect to the meat of the burnt offerings and the fat of the other sacrifices brought to the outer altar, apparently anthropomorphic expressions do appear in PT. I refer here to the terms "bread" (לחם) and "pleasing odor" (ריח ניחח) in their various forms, such as לחם אשה ריח ניחח לה' (Num 28:24). Careful investigation of the distribution and the formulation of these expressions shows that here too PT attempted to mute the more sharply anthropomorphic expressions in the cultic vocabulary. This becomes clear if we compare PT's language to other strata in the Pentateuch and the Bible that employ the same imagery. We already mentioned (chapter 1, n. 64) that HS and Ezekiel create construct states consisting of the word לחם (denoting sacrifice) along with the name of God; we find there forms such as לחמי, לחם אלהיך and others, whereas PT systematically avoids such forms. In PT, the word אשה always divides between the word לחם and the name of God. The form לחמי is also absent from PT. To the word אשה,[32] the figurative expression ריח ניחח לה is often appended;

---

the same state of freshness as when it was set out" (*b. Menahot* 96b), nevertheless, this is not the simple meaning of the text. M. Noth's (in his commentary on Lev 24:8) and P. A. H. De Boer's argument ("An Aspect of Sacrifice," in *Studies in the Religion of Ancient Israel* [VTSup 23; Leiden, 1972] 28) for the secondary nature of the ordinance to set out the shewbread once weekly is completely unfounded. The proof Noth seeks to bring from the appearance of the word תמיד in Exod 25:30 is inconclusive, since the meaning of תמיד, in the cultic context, is regular recurrence and not daily custom (see Dillmann and Hoffmann on Lev 24:8; and Haran, "Cultic System," 22–25).

30. Although theses verses are, in our opinion, of HS, it seems likely that they reflect the common practice in PT (see Excursus 3, n. 35).

31. See Haran, "Cultic System," 33–34.

32. On the meaning of the term אשה, see J. Hoftijzer, "Das sogenannte Feueropfer," in *Hebräische Wortforschung: Festschrift zum 80. Geburtstag von Walter Baumgartner* (VTSup 16; Leiden, 1967) 129ff.; J. Greenfield, "Un rite religieux Arameen et ses paralleles," *RB* 80 (1973) 50–52. PT's use of this term may also reflect its aim—to moderate the anthropomorphic imagery. Thus, PT avoids the use of the verbs הבא and נתן with אשה. As a result, we find in PT phrases like הקטר אשה לה' (Exod 29:18, 25; 30:20; Lev 1:9 , 13, 17; 2:2, 9, 11, 16; 7:5; 8:21, 28); הקרב . . . אשה לה' (Lev 3:3, 9, 14; 23:8, 25, 27, 36, 37; Num 28:3, 11–13, 36); עשה . . . אשה לה' (Num 28:8, 24; 29:2–6). But not הבא . . . אשה לה'. The phrase על אשי החלבים יביאו להניף תנופה לפני ה' (Lev 10:15) is no contradiction, since, unlike the passages mentioned above, this verse does not deal with the offering of the אשה upon the altar, but with its waving along with the shank bone and the breast, which were not offered up. Thus, the use of the word הבא here is appropriate. If the original meaning of the word אשה is a gift, then the phrases נתן אשה or הבא אשה (which are common in HS; see below, chapter 4, n. 18) conserve this meaning better than the verbal phrases in PT. Perhaps PT's avoidance of these phrases results from its desire to blur the resemblance between the offering of sacrifice and the giv-

the literal meaning of this phrase indicates God's pleasure with the odor of the sacrifices.[33] Although this expression has anthropomorphic overtones, the attribution of the sense of smell to God is far more refined than the images of God's eating or drinking.[34] Furthermore, PT avoids attributing the act of smelling directly to God; one never encounters in PT expressions such as וירח ה׳ את ריח הניחח (Gen 8:21), אריח בריח ניחחכם (Lev 26:31), ריח ניחחי (Num 28:2) . . . only the indirect formulation, אשה ריח ניחח ה׳.[35]

The examination of the contexts of the phrase ריח ניחח in PT yields several extremely interesting results. In other biblical strata, we find the theme of God's smelling the odor of the sacrifice mainly as a means or sign of satisfaction and appeasement of divine wrath; God's anger with humans and his rejection of sacrifice are represented through God's unwillingness to smell the odor of the sacrifice.[36] This principle, if applied to PT, would lead us to expect to find the phrase ריח ניחח attached primarily to the explicitly atoning sacrifices—the sin offering and the guilt offering, which, apparently, are both designed to appease God and remove his anger from the sinner. But in PT, this expression occurs primarily in the laws of burnt offerings and whole offerings,[37] whereas it is completely absent from the laws of guilt offerings and appears only once in connection with sin offerings (see Lev 4:31).[38] This perplexing phenomenon is found also in the passages dealing with meal offerings. It is known that the word מנחה in non-Priestly sources applies to animal sacrifices as well as meal offerings. In those sources, מנחה is often mentioned alongside the incense offering, and, like the incense offering, the מנחה is seen as an effective means of appeasing the deity.[39] In PT's language, on the other

ing of a gift to God (compare M. Greenberg, *On the Bible and Judaism: A Collection of Writings* [Tel Aviv, 1985] 200–202).

33. See J. Licht, "Odour, Pleasing Odour," *EM* 5:582–83.

34. See Maimonides, *Guide of the Perplexed* 1.47; compare also Kaufmann, *History* 1: 442.

35. See Licht, "Odour."

36. For examples of the placation of God through odor, see Gen 8:21 (see U. Cassuto, *A Commentary on the Book of Genesis,* vol. 1 [trans. I. Abrahams; Jerusalem, 1967] for a parallel in the Gilgamesh epic); 1 Sam 21:19; Ezek 20:41. For examples of God's refusal to smell the offering, see Lev 26:31; Amos 5:21; cf. Sir 45:16; see also Licht, *The Rule Scroll* (Jerusalem, 1965) 173–74.

37. Burnt offerings: Exod 29:18; Lev 1:9, 13, 17; Num 28:8, 13, 24, 27; 29:2, 6, 8, 13, 36. Whole offerings: Lev 3:5, 16. R. Dussaud is of the opinion that the motif of the pleasing odor is secondary in these passages as well (*Les origines cananeennes du sacrifice Israelite* 2 [Paris, 1941] 73, 93). His position seems untenable to me.

38. G. B. Gray (*Sacrifice in the Old Testament* [2nd ed.; New York, 1971] 79–81) and K. Elliger (*Leviticus* [HAT; Tübingen, 1966] 35–36) wondered at the absence of the phrase ריח ניחח specifically in the case of the atoning sacrifice. A. Knobel and Baentsch, in their commentaries, argued that the mention of ריח ניחח in Lev 4:31 also results from a faulty text or a secondary addition.

39. See M. Weinfeld, "*minḥah,*" *TWAT* 4:997–99.

hand, מנחה is always a meal offering, but here too is usually accompanied by frankincense. The frankincense is taken in a handful along with some fine flour and oil, and this handful, called אזכרה, is offered on the altar. In connection with this offering, the phrase ריח ניחח is mentioned several times (see Lev 2:2, 9, 12; 6:8, 14). But surprisingly, in the case of sin meal offerings, no frankincense is added; their אזכרה consists of flour alone, and the phrase ריח ניחח is absent from the description of their offering (see Lev 5:11–12; Num 5:15, 26).[40]

I believe that the explanation for this phenomenon lies in PT's desire to eliminate anthropomorphic overtones specifically from those portions of the cult in which they are most likely to appear. The image of a God calmed from his wrath by the pleasure that he derives from the savor of the sacrifice provided by the sinner was such a blatant anthropopathism, that PT felt it necessary to obliterate all reference to pleasing odor from the atoning sacrifices and the meal offerings of sinners. The focus of the atoning ritual was shifted to ceremonies of cleansing through sprinkling of blood, which bear a distinct technical-impersonal character. The sprinkling of blood on the altar was not designed to satisfy and appease the divinity, but to cleanse the impurity created through the act of sin.[41] The passive נפעל form (ונסלח (להם/לו at the close of the description of the cleansing procedure (Lev 4:20, 26, 31, 35; 5:10) also expresses, in linguistic form, the impersonal nature of the ritual: forgiveness is, as it were, independent of God's response, but an automatic and necessary consequence of the cleansing act performed by the priest.[42]

40. The connection between the absence of ריח ניחח in the sin offering and the lack of frankincense in the sinners' meal offerings was established by A. Knobel (*Die Bücher Exodus und Leviticus* [KeH; Leipzig, 1857]) in his commentary on Leviticus 4–8. The explanation he offers, however (in his commentary on v. 31)—that the sinner is not deemed worthy of offering up a pleasing odor before God—seems improbable. Isaiah 1:13, upon which Knobel bases his idea, and also Lev 26:31 and Amos 5:22, express disgust and total rejection of all ritual; in their view, the sinner is unworthy of sacrificing anything at all. P. D. Schoetz also drew the connection between the absence of pleasing odor from the sin and guilt offerings and the omission of frankincense from the sinner's meal offering (*Schuld- und Sündopfer im Alten Testment* [Breslau, 1930] 54). But he cannot accept the lack of appeasement through odor in the sacrifices of atonement. Consequently, he attempts to explain this difficulty through a developmental schema which, in my view, is not sustained by criticism.

41. See J. Milgrom, "The Function of the Hattat Offering," *Tarbiz* 40 (1971) 1–8.

42. Milgrom deduces from the *niphʿal* form ונסלח that the forgiveness is dependent on the will of God ("Function," 4 n. 9). I find his reasoning difficult; if the passage were meant to emphasize this dependence, a formula like וה' יסלח לה (cf. Num 30:9) would be preferable to the impersonal formulation ונסלח. PT is full of ritual actions whose results arise from the action itself, without any intervention of external forces. This is particularly true in the penal actions (see chapter 2, nn. 87–88; and von Rad, *Theology* 1:265ff.). A striking example of this is the incantation of the suspected adulteress: according to the original version—that of PT—the woman's ordeal results from the power contained in the waters of bitterness, which take effect without divine intervention (see chapter 2, p. 88).

Our identification of PT's tendency to stress the impersonal dimension of the act of atonement may help us understand several other peculiarities in its sacrificial laws. In non-Priestly biblical strata, the sacrifices of placation and atonement are the burnt offering (עולה) and the מנחה,[43] both of which are offered to God through being entirely consumed by fire.[44] In PT, on the other hand, the sin offering and the guilt offering, which are not consumed by fire at all, serve as the principal means of atonement. In some cases, the sin offering is brought as a מנחה, but then, too, it is not consumed on the altar but is eaten by the priests, as are most of the meal offerings. The Priestly sources explicitly state that the sin offering, guilt offering, and meal offering, which were originally destined to be entirely burned on the altar, were granted by God to the priests for their own consumption.[45] It seems that the opposition to the anthropomorphic coloring of the acts of atonement, as described in non-Priestly sources, is at the heart of PT's system. In those non-Priestly sources, the עולה and the מנחה—which "create" much pleasing odor, as they are completely consumed by fire—are the sacrifices capable of satisfying the deity and appeasing his anger. PT seeks to avoid anthropomorphism and thus places the extremely impersonal ceremonies of cleansing through the sprinkling of blood at the heart of the atoning process. This ritual is particularly developed in the case of the sin offering,[46] which becomes the main atoning sacrifice in PT. The burnt offering is no longer the principal atoning sacrifice,[47] as the amount of meat consumed by fire becomes irrelevant.[48] Because the focus of atonement, according to PT, is the blood and not the burned flesh, PT ordains that the main portion of

43. On the meal offering as a sacrifice of propitiation, see Weinfeld, "*minḥah.*" The elements of propitiation and atonement in the burnt offering in non-Priestly sources were thoroughly documented by R. J. Thompson, *Penitence and Sacrifice in Early Israel outside Levitical Law* (Leiden, 1963). Compare R. Rendtorff, *Studien zur Geschichte des Opfers im Alten Israel* (WMANT 24; Neukirchen, 1967) 82–83; J. Milgrom, "Sacrifices, Sacrificial Laws," *EM* 7:243.

44. See Haran, "Minha," *EM* 5:26–27.

45. Ibid. See also M. Haran, "Priesthood," *EM* 4:1069–86.

46. See Rendtorff, *Studien,* 217–20; Milgrom, "Function."

47. On the significance of the theme of atonement in Lev 1:4, see below in chapter 3. Although we do find, in several places, that the burnt offering atones along with the sin offering (see Lev 5:7–10; 12:6–8; 14:19–20; 15:14–15, 29–30; 16:24; Num 6:10–11), there is no instance in PT of the burnt offering atoning by itself for sin or specific impurities. Some of these passages clearly indicate that the sin offering is the main sacrifice and the burnt offering is the less important one (note the formulation of Lev 14:19–20 and the secondary nature of the burnt offering in the Day of Atonement ceremony in Leviticus 16).

48. This aspect of PT's law of sacrifices was described in a general way by J. Wellhausen at the end of his *Prolegomena:* "The worshipper no longer thinks that in his gift he is doing God a pleasure, providing Him with an enjoyment: what pleases Him and is effectual is only the strict observance of the rite" (*Prolegomena to the History of Ancient Israel* [Edinburgh, 1885] 424).

the flesh of individual sin offerings, guilt offerings, and sinners' meal offerings is to be eaten by the priests.[49]

The Faith of Genesis and the Faith of Moses: Morality and Cult—עדות and ברית

We demonstrated earlier the major change in the nature of the encounter between God and humanity from the Genesis period to the period of Moses. In the Genesis period, God speaks directly and without intermediaries to all creatures, and especially to humans. Abraham and Jacob even obtain the privilege of seeing God. The closeness to humanity is symbolized through personal and anthropomorphic description of God and his actions. After the revelation of the name of Yahweh, a dramatic change takes place. God no longer speaks directly to the community of Israel, and even in speech mediated by Moses, God addresses the people using the third person plural rather than the second person plural. God's direct address to Moses is entirely one-sided: Moses' role is limited to listening and obeying the divine command. The change in the relationship is expressed through religious language and through the cult: God and his actions are described thereafter in impersonal, indirect language, and anthropomorphic imagery is absent from the descriptions of God and his cult.

The change in the character of divine revelation and in the descriptions of God and his actions reflects a revolution in the content of God's demands and in the very nature of his relation to humanity. In the Genesis period, God was perceived through his creation and through his deeds for the welfare of his creatures, especially humans. His actions were based on the principles of providence, morality, and recompense.[50] At the completion of the act of creation, God provides for the sustenance of his creatures and establishes the order of the universe (Gen 1:22, 28–30). The violation of the social-moral order leads God to decide to destroy the created world,[51] but he establishes a covenant with the righteous Noah, who

49. This act was, undoubtedly, significant in increasing the income of those serving in the Temple, but it also emphasized the superior status of the priests, as they could partake of the table of the Most High. For Mesopotamian parallels, see Oppenheim, *Ancient Mesopotamia,* 189ff.

50. On the centrality of the ethical dimension in PT's description of the Genesis period, see Holzinger, *Einleitung,* 384–85; Eichrodt, *Theology,* 1:418.

51. The word חמס, which summarizes the sin of the generation of the flood (Gen 6:11, 13) refers primarily to the violation of the social-moral order (see the commentary of Ramban, ad loc., as well as von Rad, *Theology,* 1:157 n. 34; Speiser, *Genesis,* 117; C. Westermann, *Genesis* [BK I/1; Neukirchen-Vluyn, 1974] 559; H. Haag, "*Hamas,*" *TWAT* 2:1056–59). Brichto's suggestion (*Sacrifice,* 20) that the reference is to the violation of the command of

"walked with God," and God saves Noah, his family, and the animals in the ark from the catastrophe (Gen 6:9–13, 17, 18). After the flood, God establishes a new order in creation, permitting humans to eat meat but severely outlawing the spilling of blood, while providing a reason for this interdiction (Gen 9:1–7). God fulfills his covenant with Noah, his descendants, and all living beings, and promises that he will never destroy the earth again (Gen 9:8–17). Righteousness and "walking with God,"[52] which saved Noah from the flood and earned him the covenant, are demanded from Abraham as a condition for the covenant (Gen 17:1–2). God's covenant with Abraham includes the promise of fertility and numerous progeny, kingship and the land of Canaan as an eternal inheritance (Gen 17:1–8). These promises are repeated in God's revelation to Jacob (Gen 35:9–12). The covenant with the patriarchs is last repeated in PT on the eve of the revelation of the name of Yahweh, in the texts describing God's reaction to Israel's suffering in Egypt (Exod 2:24–25).

With the revelation of the name of Yahweh, the situation changes completely. The Ten Plagues narrative does not portray a righteous judge seeking to rescue his people from the iron crucible of Pharaoh. God's main purpose in smiting Egypt is to make his name known in the midst of the land.[53] In order to achieve this, he even hardens Pharaoh's heart, prolonging the suffering of slavery (see Exod 9:12).[54] After the exodus from Egypt, God's Presence is revealed to the people at Sinai and Moses is called to the mountain and hears God's commandments (Exod 24:16–18). Here, in the description of the revelation at Sinai, as well as later on in the accounts of the Tent of Meeting, a major principle of PT's thinking is shown; the commandments[55] are not at all designed to establish social

Gen 1:29–30 is interesting. (This conception is reflected in *Jubilees* 5:2.) On the moral aspect of the flood story, see N. Sarna, *Understanding Genesis* (New York, 1966) 52.

52. On the Mesopotamian parallels to this expression, see M. Weinfeld, "The Covenant of Grant in O.T. and Ancient Near East," *JAOS* 90 (1970) 186.

53. See M. Greenberg, "Ezekiel 20 and Spiritual Exile," in *Oz Ledavid: Jubilee Book for David Ben-Gurion* (Jerusalem, 1974) 436.

54. This is an exceptional attribution of an action directly to God. It may be that this exception is intended to emphasize the numinous, amoral dimension represented by the name of Yahweh and his actions.

55. This foreignness of the social law to the Priestly Torah was already noted by J. Begrich, "Die priesterliche Torah," in *Werden und Wesen des alten Testament* (BZAW 66; Berlin, 1936) 68ff. Compare M. Weinfeld; *Deuteronomy and the Deuteronomic School* (Oxford, 1972) 187. The formula "any of the Lord's commandments about things not to be done" (Lev 4:2, 3), refers to a relatively restricted corpus of negative commandments in the cultic-ritual sphere (such as Exod 30:32, 37; Lev 7:15, 19; 11:4-5, 11–20; 12:4). Although the accepted view is that the Holiness Code is the civil law of the Priestly source (M. Haran, "Sefer Hakedusha," *EM* 5:1094), this conception is based on the assumption that the Holiness Code is early and contained within PT; we have rejected this view in previous chapters. For the relation of PT to the Ten Commandments, see below chapter 3. The theory that PT originally contained moral commandments that were eliminated in the editing

order, righteousness or justice; they all relate exclusively to the ritual-cultic sphere.[56]

The fundamental division that PT makes between morality and social justice, on the one hand, and the cultic realm, on the other, is most clearly expressed, interestingly, in the only regulation among the cultic laws that contains an element of redressing of social injustice. The law of guilt offerings in Lev 5:20–26 deals with monetary damages inflicted by one person on another, which result in one party's swearing a false oath.[57] This false oath results in sanctification of the monies, which must, as a result, be reimbursed along with an additional fifth, as in the case of misappropriation of sanctified objects. The monetary restitution is followed by the bringing of a guilt offering, atoning for the sin of swearing falsely. The text of the law implies that the Priestly authors deemed the subject worthy of their consideration and required the bringing of a sacrifice, only because, in addition to the monetary damages, a false oath had been sworn. Had there been no oath sworn, the case would have been consid-

---

process to avoid duplication of other legal collections is extemely tenuous. Moral-social laws such as the law of slavery, gifts to the poor and others, reappear in different formulations in the corpora of PT, HS, and D in spite of some repetition. Why, then, should only the PT laws of social morality be dropped?

56. The requirement that the witness bring a sin offering (Lev 5:1) results from his ignoring the אלה, the oath that he heard. This is a sacral sin. As far as the suspected adulteress is concerned (Num 5:11–31), it has already been proved that the Bible views the sin of fornication as an offense against God (see M. Greenberg, "Some Postulates of Biblical Criminal Law," in *Y. Kaufmann Jubilee Volume* [ed. M. Haran; Jerusalem, 1961] English section, pp. 12–13).

57. That each case mentioned in the law is accompanied by the swearing of a false oath is made clear from the literary structure of the introductory passage to the law:

A. When a person *sins*

B. and *commits a trespass* against the Lord

C. by *dealing deceitfully* (כחש) with his fellow in the matter of a deposit or a pledge, or through robbery, or by defrauding his fellow, or by finding something lost and *lying* (כחש) *about it;*

B′. if he *swears falsely*

A′. regarding any one of the various things that one may do and *sin* thereby (Lev 5:21–22).

This structure clearly indicates the combination of two sins: (1) a sin committed by one man against his fellow man, like the sins detailed in part C, a list opening and closing with the word כחש; (2) the social-moral sin is accomplished by a false oath, as stated in part B′. In other words, the thief swears that he has not stolen. It is the addition of the false oath to the social-moral sin that makes the action a trespass against the Lord. The words in v. 24 "or anything else about which he swore falsely" make no sense unless we assume that an oath was sworn in each of the cases referred to by the law. B. S. Jackson's arguments (*Theft in Early Jewish Law* [Oxford, 1972] 245–46) on the secondary nature of the sections mentioning the oath cannot be sustained. If, as he claims, a guilt offering is required for fraud or deceit, even if no false oath had been sworn, why did the legislator bother to mention an oath, which could not affect the outcome of the law?

ered like that of any other sin committed by one man against his fellow man, and would have been of no concern to the priesthood, who were interested only in the ritual-cultic sphere.[58]

Just as the ritual experience is detached from the sphere of social morality, so too it is independent of faith in providence and divine reward for the observance of the commandments. Among all the cultic ordinances, there is not a single one designed to bring blessing or salvation, nor is there any direct request to fulfill human needs.[59] Especially striking is the absence of any sacrifice or other ritual device for assuring victory in times of war,[60] and PT's exception to ceremonies symbolizing expectation of a bountiful harvest.[61] The punishment for the violation of the commandments is described as a necessary consequence of sin, rather than the act of a personal God who punishes those who transgress his will.[62]

58. See the detailed analysis of Milgrom (*Cult and Conscience,* 89–108), which is summarized in the following words: "The understanding of Lev 5:20ff. is based on the realization that it concerns religious and not civil law . . . all that matters to the Priestly legislator is to enumerate those situations whereby the defrauding of man leads, by a false oath, to the 'defrauding' of God." N. M. Soss's argument ("Old Testament Law and Economic Society," *Journal of the History of Ideas* 34 [1973] 327) that this passage reflects the removal of barriers between civil law and cultic law results, in my opinion, from an imprecise reading of the law and from a failure to identify the necessary presence of a false oath as a component of every case discussed.

59. See Kaufmann, *History,* 2:473–76 and our discussion above, pp. 43–45. The case of the אזכרה sacrificed from the meal offering is not a contradiction to this statement. As is known, scholars disagree in their explanations of this term (see the summary in H. Eising, "זכר," *TWAT* 2:589–91. But even if we accept the opinion that the taking of the אזכרה from the meal offering and incense offerings expresses the will of the offender to be favorably remembered (זכר) before God (as is implied by the Septuagint and *Sifra,* Nedaba 9:12), this offering is still not a request for fulfillment of any specific needs. The אזכרה is taken from all meal offerings, in many different situations, and usually without any relation to the needs of the sacrificer. On this, see also below nn. 122 and 157, which discuss the inquiry of God through the oracle of the Urim and Thummim in PT. The blessing with which Aaron blesses the people after the offering of the sacrifice of the eighth day (Lev 9:23) is not seen by PT as an integral part of the cult. Thus, we find in PT no command to the priests to bless the people. Only HS, whose theological view was different, made the Priestly blessing a commandment (Num 6:22–27). On its assignment to HS, see above p. 89).

60. Its absence is striking, especially when seen against the background of the description of cultic ceremonies in other biblical strata. Those ceremonies were designed to arouse God's salvation in times of war. See the description of the assembly at Bethel on the eve of the battle at Gibeah (Judg 20:26) and at Mizpah, just before the battle of Eben Ezer (1 Sam 7:6, 9), as well as the description of the fast and the assembly convened by Jehoshaphat before marching out to war (2 Chr 20:3–14). The sounding of the horns in times of affliction (and in times of joy) is part of the HS corpus and is absent from PT (see above, pp. 35, 52; compare also n. 132 below).

61. See above, pp. 23–26, on the customs of the feast of the Firstfruits; and pp. 36–40 on the customs of the feast of Booths and the convocation of the Eighth Day.

62. On impersonal and automatic punishment in PT, see above, pp. 128–29, 134–35 and nn. 18 and 42.

In PT's conception, God ordains Moses to institute a cultic system detached from social arrangements or ways of justice; God does not intend to satisfy the needs of the individual or the congregation—neither their physical needs nor even their spiritual ones.[63] The demand to worship God is set forth without justification;[64] no recompense is offered to those who obey. Thus, we may conclude that the Genesis period has, as its central theme, God's concern to provide for human needs and to improve the order of creation and humanity according to the laws of morality and retribution, which God explained to humans through his deeds and laws. In the period of Moses, on the other hand, we find an emphasis on God's commands to Israel, commandments that demand the worship of God without any expectation of reward; these commands are totally divorced from human needs and rational concepts.

The revolution in the relationship of humanity and God that accompanied the revelation of the name of Yahweh is represented by PT through its selective use of the terms ברית and עדות. The link between God and Noah and his descendants is established through the making of the covenant (ברית) (Gen 6:18; 9:9–17; 17:2, 4, 9–13, 19, 21; Exod 2:24). The concept of ברית in these passages refers primarily to the promises and obligations of God to humans;[65] but these obligations are conditioned, as we mentioned above (p. 138), on the fulfillment of the moral demands God makes of Noah and Abraham.[66] Moreover, both covenants are accompanied by the giving of laws anchored in the covenant: Noah and his sons are ordered, "You must not, however, eat flesh with its life-blood in it," and are forbidden to spill human blood, whereas Abraham and his male progeny are commanded to practice circumcision.[67] The bilateral nature of the covenantal relation, as seen by PT, is represented by the phrase ביני וביניכם (וביניך), which is frequently repeated in connection with

63. The detachment of PT's picture of the worship of God from the "joys and worries of life" was described by Wellhausen and Kaufmann. See chapter 1, n. 99.

64. On the lack of supporting reasons in the cultic laws of PT, see above, pp. 106–7 and n. 160.

65. On ברית as a divine promise in PT's terminology, see J. J. P. Valeton, "Bedeutung und Stellung des Wortes ברית im Priestercodex," *ZAW* 12 (1982) 501–12; Haran, *Temples,* 143 n. 12.

66. As opposed to the views of Valeton ("Bedeutung") and J. Begrich ("Berit—Ein Beitrag zur Erfassung einer alttestamentlichen Denkform," *ZAW* 60 [1944] 7), who see the PT ברית as a unilateral obligation on the part of God. In light of the demands made on Abraham as preconditions for the ברית with him, it seems unjustified to call this covenant "a covenant of grace," as is commonly done. This ברית does not correspond to the standard form of a "covenant of grant" either (see Weinfeld, "Covenant of Grant," 186 n. 15).

67. On the link of these prohibitions to the Noachide covenant, see R. Krätzschmar, *Die Bundesvorstellung im Alten Testament* (Marburg, 1857) 194; on the commandment of circumcision as an obligation resulting from the Abrahamic covenant, see F. M. Cross, *Canaanite Myth and Hebrew Epic* (Cambridge, MA, 1973) 270–71.

the covenants of Noah and Abraham (Gen 9:12, 13, 15, 16; 17:2, 7, 10, 11).[68]

After the revelation of the name of Yahweh, the concept of covenant (ברית) disappears from PT,[69] to be replaced by the notion of pact (עדות). Unlike ברית, the word עדות never denotes bilateral obligation in the Bible.[70] Its main implication is commandments, orders.[71] The change in terms reflects the change in the relations between God and humans resulting from the revelation of the name of Yahweh. The unilateral character of עדות is illustrated by the prepositions juxtaposed to it. Unlike in the case of ברית, we never find the words בין ובין in connection with עדות; instead we have the formula העדת אשר אתן אליך (Exod 25:16, 21).[72]

A remarkable parallel to the shift from ברית to עדות, as an expression of the transition from a network of mutual obligations to a unilateral commitment, came to light in the political documents of the kingdom of Assyria. In the second millennium B.C.E., in Assyria as well as in other areas

68. E. Kutsch distinguishes between human communication, in which the prepositions בין ובין refer to reciprocal obligation, and the use of these words to refer to the relations between God and humans, where, in his opinion, they designate one-sided obligation ("Gesetz und Gnade: Probleme des alttestamentlichen Bundesbegriffs," *ZAW* 79 [1967] 32 and n. 54; idem, *Verheissung und Gesetz* [BZAW 131; Berlin, 1972] 25). In light of our discussion of the mutuality of the Noachide and Abrahamic covenants, it would seem that this distinction is invalid. For Kutsch's general view that the concept of ברית involves one-sided obligation, see the present criticism of James Barr, "Some Semantic Notes on the Covenant," in *Festschrift W. Zimmerli* (Göttingen, 1977) 36–37.

69. Although the ברית is mentioned in several passages that are customarily attributed to PT (Exod 6:4, 5; Num 18:19; 25:12–13), our classification of texts in the previous chapter, based on criteria independent of the concept of ברית, shows that these verses originate in HS. The only mention of the ברית in the PT corpus (as we have defined it) following the revelation of the name of Yahweh, is in Lev 2:13. The reason for this exception will be explained later in this chapter.

70. See S. E. Loewenstamm, "*Edut*," *EM* 6:89. J. Greenfield sees the passage עדות ביהוסף שמו (Ps 71:6) as referring to the making of a covenant ("Studies in West Semitic Inscriptions I: Stylistic Aspects of the Sefire Treaty Inscriptions," *Acta Orientalia* 29 [1965–66] 9); his view has, however, been contested by Loewenstamm (ibid.) and M. Parnas ("'Edut', 'Edot', 'Edwot' in the Bible, Against the Background of Ancient Near East Documents," *Shnaton—An Annual for Biblical and Ancient Near Eastern Studies* 1 [1976] 228 n. 26).

71. For a discussion of the meaning of the עדת, see Loewenstamm, "*Edut.*" Although B. Volkwein ("Masoretisches 'Edut, Edwot, Edot'—'Zeugnis oder Bundesbestimmungen," *BZ* 13 [1969] 39) and Parnas ("Edut," 236–39) also noted the extensive use of the word עדת to designate law and commandment, they were misled by the parallelism ארון/לחת־הברית to ארון/לחת העדת, viewing עדת as a term primarily designating a covenant and its commands. Volkwein did, however, distinguish between the differing uses of ברית and עדת in PT, concluding that there was a substantial difference between the two terms ("Edut," 39–40). As for the former לחת העדת, we suggested earlier (chapter 2, n. 21) that it originates with late HS redactors who sought to blend the various traditions. We never find לחת עדת in PT, only עדת. This עדת is essentially different from the לחת הברית of non-Priestly sources.

72. See n. 7 above and see our discussion of the one-sided nature of God's encounters with Moses above, pp. 127–28.

of the ancient Near East, a number of legal terms served to designate the treaties contracted between various nations.[73] These agreements—even though not always concluded between parties of equal status—dealt with matters of concern to both parties and generally specified mutual obligations.[74] The same legal terms describe, in the tradition of the Assyrian chronicles, the relations of equality prevailing between the kingdoms of Assyria and Babylon from the fifteenth century B.C.E. until the early eighth century B.C.E.[75] The founding of the Assyrian empire under Tiglat-Pileser (745-727 B.C.E.) and the rise of the Assyrian king to supreme ruler—the sole sovereign of western Asia—made changes in the texts of international agreements necessary. These changes were to reflect the unconditional sovereignty of the Assyrian emperor. The previous set of ancient covenantal terms was replaced by the *ade*[76]—an oath of loyalty and unilateral obligation, imposed by the Assyrian ruler on his vassals, with no promise of reward for their loyalty.[77] This term was borrowed by the Assyrians from the Aramaic word עדי, which is the cognate of the Hebrew word עדת![78]

Many biblical scholars have noted the lack of any covenantal ceremony or mention of the term ברית in PT's description of the revelation at Sinai.[79] Several solutions have been proposed to resolve this difficulty, but I do not find any of them acceptable.[80] I believe that only a thorough

73. On the terms referring to ברית relationships in the second millennium B.C.E. and on the nature of international relations in the ancient Near East in that period, see, recently, H. Tadmor, "Treaty and Oath in the Ancient Near East: A Historian's Approach," in *Humanizing America's Iconic Book—Society of Biblical Literature Centennial Addresses* (ed. G. M. Tucker and D. A. Knight; Chico, CA, 1982) 149–63.

74. Ibid., 162–63.

75. Ibid., 165–66.

76. Although we found an *ade* document dating from 755 B.C.E.—before the establishment of the Assyrian empire—the main use of this term dates from the period following the establishment of the New Assyrian empire (see Tadmor, "Treaty and Cult," 166–67).

77. The one-sided nature of the *ade* was emphasized by I. J. Gelb, "Review of D. J. Wiseman, "The Vassal-Treaties of Esarhaddon" (in *Iraq* 20), *BiOr* 19 (1962) 160–62. Compare also Tadmor, "Treaty and Cult," 165. On the difference between the international communications of the Hittite kings and those of the Assyrian emperors as an expression of the differing self-perceptions of these rulers, see A. Goetze as cited in Weinfeld, *Deuteronomy*, 68.

78. See Parnas, "Edut," 239–45; H. Tadmor, "The Aramaization of Assyria: Aspect of Western Impact," in *Mesopotamien und Seine Nachbarn* (ed. H. J. Nissen and J. Renger; Berlin, 1982) 455.

79. To the best of my knowledge, the first to notice this phenomenon was Valeton ("Bedeutung," 1ff.). Shortly thereafter, Krätzschmar (*Bundesvorstellung*, 183ff.) broached the subject, and subsequently, many others as well.

80. We may divide the solutions offered to this problem into three main categories: (1) *Solutions focusing on the editorial level.* The description of the ברית at Sinai was omitted, or never composed by PT, since the JE descriptions were sufficient (see von Rad, *Theology* 1:135; Cross, *Myth*, 318–20). The forced nature of such explanations was pointed out by W.

comprehension of PT's unique view on the essence of the revelation at Sinai and a recognition of PT's distinction between ברית and עדות can provide an acceptable explanation for this state of affairs.

In other biblical strata, the relationship between God and Israel is portrayed as a bilateral network of obligations and rewards. In such a worldview, the essence of the relationship between God and his people at Sinai is truly exemplified by the notion of covenant. Thus, the tablets presented at Sinai are called לחת הברית and the ark containing them is called ארון ברית ה'.[81] On the literary level, the collection of laws that, according to non-Priestly sources, originates in the revelation at Sinai are arranged in the form of a ספר ברית—a covenant book, ending with the promise of divine reward to those who uphold the covenant and the warning of divine punishment for its violators.[82] PT, on the other hand, considers the laws given at Sinai to be an עדות, a unilateral demand imposed on Israel,

Zimmerli ("Sinaibund und Abrahambund," *TZ* 16 [1960] 277). (2) *Ideological explanations.* Some scholars find a fundamental objection in PT to the Sinai covenant and a preference for the Abrahamic covenant of grace (see Zimmerli, "Sinaibund"; and, subsequently, R. E. Clements, *Abraham and David* [London, 1967] 74–75; N. Lohfink, "Die Priesterschriftliche Abwertung der Tradition von Offenbarung des Jahwenamens an Mose," *Biblica* 49 [1968] 1; D. J. McCarthy, *Old Testament Covenant* [Oxford, 1972] 48; H. Cazelles, "Alliance du Sinai, Alliance de l'Horeb et Renouvellement de l'Alliance," in *Beiträge zur Alttestamentlichen Theologie* [Festschrift W. Zimmerli; Göttingen, 1977] 69ff.). We may categorically reject this view, since, as we discussed earlier (n. 66), the Abrahamic covenant was not, according to PT, a covenant of grace either. Moreover, to attribute the opposition to the divine dimension of command to PT, which places the fulfillment of the divine command at the heart of its system, would be a great distortion (see Toeg, *Lawgiving,* 149 n. 114). Another ideological explanation was proposed by M. Noth (*The Laws in the Pentateuch and Other Studies* [trans. D. R. Ap-Thomas; Edinburgh, 1966] 91–93). Noth argues that this was an expression of the tendency prevalent in the Second Temple period (at which time, in his opinion, PT was composed), to detach the laws from their historical context in order to ensure that they would withstand the vagaries of time. Although I completely agree with Noth's emphasis on the absolute nature of the laws of PT and their presentation as the incontestable will of God, I find hard to accept the theory that the removal of the element of ברית (from the laws) could ensure their independence from transient historical institutions. After all, PT ties its laws to the cultic institution of the Tent of Meeting, an institution far more susceptible to the changes wrought by time than the relation to a divine covenant. (3) The denial that the element of ברית is missing from PT. This theory relies on Exod 31:13–17, in which the Sabbath is ordained as a sign of the covenant, immediately following the Sinaitic covenant (see Haran, *Temples,* 143 n. 12). I cannot accept this argument either, since these verses originate, in my view, in HS; thus they are of no help in determining the question of PT's attitude to the concept of ברית.

81. The expression לחת הברית appears in Deut 9:9, 11, 15. The phrase ארון ברית is found in many places throughout the Bible.

82. See Exod 23:22–31 (the conclusion of the Covenant Book); Lev 26:3–46 (the conclusion of the Holiness Code); Deuteronomy 28 (the conclusion of the Deuteronomic Book). On the common elements in the arrangement of these three collections, see S. Paul, *Studies in the Book of Covenant in the Light of Cuneiform and Biblical Law* (in VTSup 18; Leiden: Brill, 1970) 34.

without any commitment on God's part to reward or punish. Thus, PT never uses the term ברית, nor does it make mention of any covenant-founding ceremony in its account of the revelation at Sinai. The Ten Commandments, written on the לחת הברית (Deut 5:19; 9:10–11) are not part of PT's tradition.[83] These commandments contain laws of cult and morality, accompanied by promise of direct recompense by a personal God (see Exod 20:5, 6, 7, 12)—all these principles are at variance with PT's worldview. Corresponding to the לחת הברית, we find in PT העד(ו)ת; similarly, אר(ו)ן העדות appears in PT instead of ארון הברית.[84] Unlike the other legal compilations of the Pentateuch, the laws of PT are not arranged in the form of a ספר ברית, a covenant book, nor do they terminate with a list of blessings and curses.

The word ברית is mentioned in PT only once after the revelation of the name of Yahweh (see n. 69): Lev 2:13 includes an instruction to place salt on the sacrificial meat, "(so that) you shall not omit from your meal offering the salt of your covenant (ברית) with God; with all your offerings you must offer salt." Salt appears as a symbol of the covenant with God elsewhere in the Pentateuch as well as in neighboring ancient cultures (see Num 18:19; 2 Chr 13:5).[85] As the symbol מלח ברית is itself the reason for the law requiring the salting of sacrifices, PT is compelled to mention it explicitly, although it stands in contradiction to its system. The PT authors were aware of this deviation from their ideology and thus employed, exceptionally, the name אלהים (מלח ברית אלהיך) rather than the name of Yahweh (מלח ברית ה').[86] Otherwise, PT employs exclusively the name of Yahweh in its sacrificial laws.[87] Through this choice of the divine name, PT expressed its view that the concept of ברית was inappropriate in describing the nature of God's revelation to Moses (which is always presented in the name of Yahweh), and that the concept properly belongs to the terms used to describe the relation of God and humanity in the Genesis period, when the name אלהים was employed.

The systematically selective use of certain specific names of God in the Genesis period and others in the period of Moses and the replacement of

83. This was noted by Krätzschmar (*Bundesvorstellung,* 185–86). Even if we admit signs of Priestly editing in Exod 20:11, this does not change the picture, as this editing was, in our opinion, done by HS (see above, p. 67).

84. See Exod 25:16, 21, 22; 26:33, 34; 30: 6, 26, 36. Although the nature of the עדת remains unclear, it seems that it refers to the scrolls containing the cultic ordinances (see Knobel, *Exodus,* 264.

85. See also M. Weinfeld, "Berit," *TWAT,* 1:761; Japhet, *Ideology of Chronicles,* 457.

86. But in Num 18:19, which according to our classification, is of HS, we find the words ברית מלח עולם היא לפני ה'.

87. The exclusive use of the name of Yahweh in the sacrificial laws was already noted by the sages. See *Sifre Numbers* 143, ed. Horowitz, p. 191. The exceptional use of the name אלהים in this passage was pointed out by the Rambam (ad loc.), who explained it in his own fashion.

the term ברית by עדות are indications of PT's view that the revelation of the name of Yahweh resulted in profound changes in religious awareness. According to PT, this event marked a turning point in the development of faith and resulted in a reappraisal of the status of humanity before God; a deep chasm lies between the faith of Genesis and the patriarchs and the faith of Moses and Israel.[88]

In the primary level of faith—that of Genesis—humanity perceives itself as the summit and purpose of creation. Contrary to the Babylonian epos, which views humans as tools for the use of the gods, the PT creation story presents the submission of heaven and earth and all their array to human control and use as the purpose of the creation of the universe.[89] Thus, God himself is portrayed primarily through his actions vis-à-vis his creatures, and vis-à-vis humans in particular. God is primarily a creator, supervisor, legislator, and righteous judge. Human beings, the crown of creation, stand erect before God, experiencing a direct, bilateral relationship with the Creator based on comprehensible principles of morality and recompense. This relation of closeness determines the descriptions of the encounter between God and humanity in the Genesis period: God is depicted as manlike in his image and his actions.

The revelation of the name of Yahweh results in a Copernican revolution. Moses and, following him, Israel learn to recognize the essence of divine nature, which is unrelated to creation, or to humanity and its needs. This dimension cannot be fully comprehended by humans and surpasses the limits of morality and reason, since morality and its laws are only meaningful in relation to human society and human understanding. The aspect of divine essence that surpasses reason and morality—the "numinous" element—is represented in PT by the name of Yahweh.[90] Just as the personal and anthropomorphic descriptions of God in the Genesis period express the closeness of humans to their Creator, so the impersonal, nonanthropomorphic language of the period of Moses

88. The deep gap between the faith of the patriarchs and the faith of Moses, according to PT's thinking, was emphasized by M. Haran, who commented that it is for this reason that we never find in PT the formulation ה' אלהי אבותיכם, which is common in other sources (*Ages and Institutions in the Bible* [Tel Aviv, 1972] 24).

89. On this contrast, see N. Sarna, *Understanding Genesis,* 14–16; Greenberg, *On the Bible and Judaism: A Collection of Writings* (Tel Aviv, 1985) 16–20.

90. For a definition of the numinous element of God and the experience of the encounter with him, see R. Otto, *The Idea of the Holy* (trans. J. W. Harvey; Oxford, 1958) 1–40. In his discussion of the numinous expressions in the Bible, Otto insisted on the strength of the numinous dimension of the name of Yahweh, as opposed to the strongly rational and moral content conveyed by the name אלוהים. But he claims that the division is not complete and that the numinous and rational-moral elements are integrated in the Bible (pp. 74–75). I am of the opinion that, while such integration may be found in many of the biblical strata, PT clearly distinguishes between the two dimensions of God, by attributing a different name to each.

expresses the majesty of the holy and its awesomeness.[91] Human beings, when faced with the holy, no longer see themselves as the center of the universe, nor do they evaluate God from the narrow point of view of the satisfaction of their own needs and desires. Thus, we never find in the sacred sphere, centered on the cultic enclosure, any explicit request of humans for the fulfillment of their needs or any expectation of divine salvation.

Although PT concentrates on the experience of the encounter with the majesty of the holy and places the revelation to Moses and the sacred enclosure in the realm of the numinous, this does not imply alienation from the religious value of morality and social justice. PT presents the Genesis and patriarchal period as a universal, eternal realm regulated by principles of justice and righteousness.[92] In this sphere, morality is the law of creation, binding on all created beings and supervised and enforced by God. The revelation of the name of Yahweh to Moses neither invalidates the moral order nor detracts from its importance. No new moral command is entrusted to the nation at Sinai,[93] since the revelation focuses on the dimension of God that surpasses morality. But this only reinforces the validity of the universal moral laws of Genesis; Israel, as part of humanity, is subject to these moral laws, just as Abraham, its founder, was obliged to uphold the moral perfection exemplified by Noah, the father of antediluvian humanity (see above, p. 138). The faith of the Genesis and patriarchal period is the foundation on which the content of the revelation to Moses is built; the latter revelation is designed to deepen and broaden religious understanding.

Unlike the faith of Genesis, which is the heritage of all mankind,[94] the revelation of the name of Yahweh to Moses and its faith content are the sole possession of Israel. According to PT, the Gentiles do not know the name of Yahweh or the divine dimension symbolized by it. This is expressed in the words PT places in the mouths of the magicians in their response to the plague of lice: "it is the finger of God (אלהים)" (Exod 8:15). God is called by the name אלהים, even though the name of Yahweh

91. קדושה (holiness) is the concept in Israelite faith which parallels *abstraction* in philosophical religion (Kaufmann, *History,* 1:247). On the link between the Priestly concept of holiness and the tendency toward an impersonal understanding of God, see Eichrodt, *Theology,* 1:407.

92. The conception of the moral law as a universal obligation is common in the Bible (see Kaufmann, *History,* 2:438–41). PT is unique in that it recognizes no other moral commands. In this respect, PT's view approaches that of wisdom literature, which also does not limit morality to an Israelite national framework. See Kaufmann, *History,* 2:574ff.

93. In this respect, PT differs from the other biblical strata which hold that a national moral law was given to Israel at Mount Sinai. See Kaufmann, *History,* 2:558, 571–73.

94. The description of the Genesis period of humanity as a multigenerational group expressing ethical monotheism is common to all the strata of the book of Genesis. See Kaufmann, *History,* 2:434–35, 438–41.

has already been revealed to Moses and Israel: this indicates that the name is unknown to the Gentiles and is not meant to be used by them. The description of God's actions, employing the extremely anthropomorphic image אצבע אלהים ("the finger of God"), accords with the anthropomorphic language used to describe the acts of God in the Genesis period.

The Sanctuary of Silence

The recognition of the numinous dimension of God, represented, according to PT, by the name of Yahweh, illuminates several other aspects unique to the cultic system constructed around this theme. Y. Kaufmann directed our attention to the unique phenomenon of the silence of the Priestly cult, which he adeptly entitled "the Sanctuary of Silence."[95] Unlike the custom we generally find in temples of the ancient Near East and in descriptions of the Israelite cult in other biblical strata, in which the sacrificial act was accompanied by prayer, song, and praise,[96] the PT Temple cult was performed in almost total silence.[97] According to Kaufmann, the desire to break away from the magical and mythological foundations of the cult resulted in the rejection of all idolatrous explanations and in the reign of silence in the Priestly Temple.[98]

I believe that this explanation is not sustained by criticism. PT does provide speeches that accompany the ritual and thus explain cultic actions, *precisely* for those cultic practices which, externally, most closely resemble idolatrous ritual (see Lev 16:21; Num 5:19–22).[99] Prayer and song, on the other hand—which are not necessarily linked to magic or mythological formulas—are completely absent from PT's cultic system.[100] It seems to me that the suppression of prayer and song arise from PT's desire to shape the Priestly cult in a way that would express humanity's

95. Kaufman, *History*, 2:476–77.

96. On the accompaniment of sacrificial worship with prayer and song, see Greenberg, *On the Bible*, 180; idem, "Prayer," *EM* 8:910, 912, 916–17.

97. Exceptions to the rule are the priest's confession on the scapegoat (Lev 16:21) and the oath of the suspected adulteress (Num 5:19). The Priestly Blessing (Num 6:22–27) originates, according to our classification, in HS.

98. Kaufmann, *History*, 2:477–78.

99. The resemblance of the incantation text of the suspected adulteress to magic incantations becomes evident when we remove Num 5:21, which, in our opinion, is an editorial addition of HS (see above, p. 88 and n. 90; cf. J. Milgrom, "The Case of the Suspected Adulteress, Numbers 5:11–31," in *The Creation of Sacred Literature* (ed. R. E. Friedman; University of California Publication: Near Eastern Studies 22; Berkeley, 1981) 72; M. Fishbane, "Accusation of Adultery: A Study of Law and Scribal Practise in Numbers 5:121–31." *HUCA* 45 (1974) 33.

100. For the difference between prayer and magic incantation, see Greenberg, "Prayer," 915.

status vis-à-vis the holy—that is, in the spirit of the divine element abstracted from its practical functions in the world. Such a conception leaves no room for petitional prayer, in which humans request fulfillment of their needs from God; nor does it allow a role for songs of praise in which humans thank God and recount God's wonders and mercies. The structural model of prayer, a direct address by humans to their God, as well as the frequency of anthropomorphic images in the language of prayer and song, is at odds with PT's aim in emphasizing God's loftiness. This school, which does not even allow Moses the possibility of directly addressing God and which systematically purges religious language of all anthropomorphic expressions, has no choice but to accept that לך דמיה תהילה ("to You silence is praise," Ps 65:2).[101] We should clarify here that we do not claim that song, praise, and prayer were absent from Israelite temples; in the Temple courtyards outside the Priestly areas, the sounds of prayer and psalmody were often heard. The PT description is an idealized approach, which apparently was never put into practice outside the limited area in which the Priestly cult was performed.[102]

As we mentioned, the cultic relation between humans and the dimension of God represented by the name of Yahweh is detached from all aspects of mutual dependence.[103] Instead, two principles are at the heart of the ideal cultic system—holiness and commandment.[104] The inner cul-

101. Jewish tradition generally interprets the word דמיה as "silence." See Maimonides, *Guide of the Perplexed,* I, 59.

102. Many passages in Scripture testify to the existence of a large collection of prayers, songs, and instrumental music in temples. See N. Sarna, "The Psalm Superscriptions and the Guilds," in *Studies in Jewish Religion and Intellectual History* (ed. N. Stein and R. Lowe; University, AL, 1979) 282ff.

103. For the elimination of references to the satisfaction of the deity's needs in the cult, as found in PT, see pp. 130–37; for the rejection of the element of the satisfaction of human needs by God, see pp. 140–41. Otto ascribes the strangeness of the element of dependence to the numinous dimension of God (*Idea of the Holy,* 20–21). In its elimination of the relationship of mutual dependence from the cult, PT differs from the attitudes toward the cult which were prevalent in the surrounding cultures as well as in Israel. There, the worship of God was understood in terms of reciprocal utilitarian relations (see Greenberg, *On the Bible,* 182ff; J. J. M. Roberts, "Divine Freedom and Cultic Manipulation in Israel and Mesopotamia," in *Unity and Diversity* [ed. H. Goedicke and J. J. M. Roberts; Baltimore, 1975] 182–85).

104. "The purpose of the cult in the ideal temple is to sanctify it . . . so that God may appear there to Israel and its prophet; . . . the actions performed in the temple itself . . . are all directed towards a single goal: the sanctification of the place, in which the name of God dwells and where the symbol of his word is to be found; . . . the Israelite Priesthood . . . placed the *word* of God, the symbol of his sovereign will, at the center of the cult (Kaufmann, *History,* 2:474, 476). Kaufmann's view that the sovereign will of God and sanctification are the primary symbols of Israelite faith in general (*History,* 1:245, 247) is particularly instructive. In this sense, the Tabernacle is the essence of all existence, a kind of microcosm (for the view of the Tabernacle as a symbolic microcosm, see Josephus, *Antiquities* 3.180–87, and the midrashic parallels cited by A. Schalit in his edition of Josephus (*Antiqui-*

tic enclosure and its vessels are imbued with a "contagious" substantive holiness and may be neither touched nor seen.[105] Thus, the priests, who alone may approach the holy, must first undergo purification, atonement, and anointing, which grant them an envelope of sanctity.[106] But even after they have donned this protective "armor," they are still greatly endangered by their service in the sanctuary. The frequency of the warnings of death in connection with service in the sacred enclosure provides evidence of this.[107] The sacred enclosure is a kind of minefield, in which the cultic ordinances serve to mark a narrow path where the slightest deviation may be fatal. This is the main lesson to be learned from the story of Nadab and Abihu, who died near the holy upon bringing an alien fire[108] "which He had not enjoined."[109] There is no room for the slightest deviation from the divine command in the PT Temple, even if it is done out of religious enthusiasm.[110]

The relation between the symbols of holiness and the commandments finds concrete expression in the heart of the cultic system—the Holy of Holies. The cover (כפרת) above the ark flanked by cherubim is the symbol of God's presence in the sanctuary. There God appears in a cloud (Lev

---

tates Judaicae in linguam hebraicum [Jerusalem, 1944] n. 133; see also R. Patai, *Man and Temple* [New York, 1967] 105–17).

105. See M. Haran, "The Tabernacle: A Graded Taboo of Holiness" in *Studies in the Bible presented to M. H. Segal* (Jerusalem, 1964) 33–35; idem, *Temples,* 175–88. For a slightly different view, see J. Milgrom, "Sancta Contagion and Altar/City Asylum," in *Congress Volume: Vienna 1980* (ed. J. A. Emerton; Leiden, 1980) 278–99.

106. See Haran, "Tabernacle," 23; idem, *Temples,* 177; cf. Otto, *Idea of the Holy,* 57.

107. See Exod 28:35, 43; 30:20–21; Lev 16:2, 13. As demonstrated by J. Milgrom, the text refers to death through divine action (*Studies in Cultic Theology and Terminology* [Leiden, 1983] 6–8).

108. According to the simple meaning of Lev 10:1, it seems that their sin was that they did not take from the holy fire burning upon the altar, as we find written in the Targumim and in the writings of the sages (see A. Shin'an, "The Sins of Nadav and Avihu in Rabbinic Literature," *Tarbiz* 48 [1979] 207) as well as in Ibn Ezra, Rashba, and several modern commentators (see M. Haran, *Temples,* 232 n. 4; J. C. H. Laughlin, "The 'Strange Fire' of Nadab and Abihu," *JBL* 95 [1976] 561 and n. 11). Lev 16:1-2, on the other hand, seems to indicate that the sin was in the very approach to the holy.

109. "For the Priest, the gravest sin is disobedience to the commands of God. . . . The greatest danger is present among those closest to the earthly center of holiness. There, the slightest deviation is of incomparable seriousness. In this view, the sin of Nadab and Abihu is patently clear . . . their sin was disobedience, the serious provocation of penetrating to the locus of holiness though not commanded to do so" (Toeg, *Lawgiving,* 151).

110. The offering of the incense in the fire pans is, by its nature, a spontaneous act (see M. Haran, "The Censer and TAMID Incense," *Tarbiz* 26 [1957] 124). In this sense, Philo's explanation shows insightful depth. He writes that the "strange fire" brought by Nadab and Abihu was an expression of their passionate desire to join themselves to God; fire is strange and foreign to created beings but close to God (for a view proposing a midrashic background for Philo's explanation, see D. Flusser and S. Safrai, "Nadav and Avihu in the Midrash and in Philo's Writing," *Milet* 2 (1984) 79–84.

16:2). At the same time, it is also the locus of the verbal revelation of the ritual commands. The symbol system is completed by the עדות inside the ark, under the cover.[111] As we explained, the עדות emphasizes the centrality of the element of commandment in PT's thought. The location of the עדות near the place of God's Presence and his revelation expresses the aim to unite the two poles of holiness and commandment.[112]

The concept of holiness in PT has a ritual character devoid of any moral content;[113] thus, holiness is imparted to objects and to people in the same way (Exod 30:26–30; Lev 8:10–12)—through ceremonies of sanctification which combine rituals of purification, atonement, and anointing (Exod 29:1–37; 30:26–30; Lev 8:10–30). The ritual of purification and atonement plays a central role in other ceremonies described in the ritual code as well. Wellhausen and his followers, who were of the opinion that PT was composed by the exiles after their return from Babylon, attempted to explain this phenomenon by referring to the consciousness of guilt and the pressing need for atonement felt by this community.[114] But it seems to me that there is no need to explain these phenomena through reference to any particular historical circumstances, since they spring directly from the theological conceptions at the root of the cultic system. PT's cult expresses humanity's position vis-à-vis the sublime holy. Such an encounter necessarily engenders feelings of guilt and the need for atonement. This guilt is not associated with any particular sin; rather, it is a result of human awareness of insignificance and contamination in comparison with the sublimity of God's holiness.[115]

Indeed, we find in PT an atonement formula unrelated to recognition of any single defined sin: this is the meaning of the statement "that it may be acceptable in his behalf, to atone for him" (Lev 1:4), in the case of

111. On the symbolic meaning of the placing of the עדת under the mercy-cover, see N. H. Tur-Sinai, *The Language and the Book* (Jerusalem, 1955) 60–61; Haran, *Temples,* 255 and n. 11.

112. The placing of the symbols of holiness and commandment together in the Holy of Holies weakens, to some extent, the tension between the two dimensions represented by them: the holiness of God leads to an emphasis on the impersonal aspect of God, which, in turn, leads to a denial of divine volition. On this tension and PT's attempts at alleviating it, see Eichrodt, *Theology,* 1:407, 410–11.

113. PT's position on this matter resembles that of the majority of biblical sources, in which the concept of holiness is also devoid of any moral content (see H. Ringgren, *The Prophetical Conception of Holiness* [Uppsala, 1948] 22–23). PT's conception is unique in that it emphatically grants moral content to holiness, as we will explain in the next chapter.

114. See Wellhausen, *Prolegomena,* 422–23. For a refutation of his views, see Kaufmann, *History,* 1:120, 202–3, 217–18; M. Weinfeld, "Theological Currents in the Pentateuchal Literature," in *Proceedings of the American Academy for Jewish Research* 37 (New York, 1969) 118; idem, *Deuteronomy,* 179; idem, Social and Cultic Institutions in the Priestly Source against their Ancient Near Eastern Background," in *Proceedings of the Eighth World Congress of Jewish Studies, Bible Studies and Hebrew Language* (Jerusalem, 1981) 105ff.

115. See Otto, *Idea of the Holy,* 34–50.

a whole offering which is unrelated to any particular act of sin.[116] This expresses the idea that the very approach to the holy requires atonement and appeasement.[117] The law of guilt offerings too, in Lev 5:17–19, is based on the sense of general, undefined guilt. The law provides relief for this obscure sense of anguish by channeling it into the categories of violation of sacred things, which may be remedied through the bringing of a guilt offering.[118] The procedures of purification, atonement, and sanctification are most intensive during the days of ordination (Exod 29:1-37; Leviticus 8), on the ceremonies of the eighth day (Lev 9:7–11, 15) and in the annual atonement ritual (Lev 16:1-28). Through these ceremonies, the priests prepare themselves to serve in the sacred area and prepare the Tent of Meeting for the revelation of God's Presence. From the moment that God's Presence appears in the Tent, the holiness and purity of the sacred area must be guarded. This responsibility is delegated to the priests serving before the Lord. The foremost concern of the priests is the maintenance of the Presence of God, which is the main focus of the cult taking place in the Tent of Meeting.

The Priests and the People

The cultic system of PT takes place in a sacred sphere far removed from the masses. Barriers are maintained through taboos prohibiting the people from entering the area of intense and contagious holiness in the Tabernacle (above, n. 105). Furthermore, PT assigns the people no role in the erection of the Tent of Meeting (see above, p. 65). Admittedly, the entire congregation is present at the ceremony of the dedication of the Tabernacle on the eighth day of ordination and participates in the experience of the revelation of כבוד ה', God's Presence (Lev 9:3–6, 23–24). Thereafter, however, God's Presence remains hidden inside the sacred precincts; entrance to this area is permitted only to the anointed priest—and then only at certain times (Lev 16:2). No outsider's eye may witness the mysterious ceremony in the depths of the holy, and only vague bits

116. The sages already deliberated the question of the nature of the sin for which the burnt offering atones. See *t. Menahot* 10:12; *Leviticus Rabbah* 7:3, ed. Margaliot, p. 153, and redactor's notes, ad loc. According to Rava, the burnt offering is a gift, a *doron* (see *b. Zebahim* 7b).

117. Explanations similar to those given for the atoning function of the burnt offering may be found in Knobel, *Leviticus,* 355; Elliger, *Leviticus,* 30. For another explanation of the atonement of the burnt offering, see B. A. Levine, *In the Presence of the Lord* (Leiden, 1974) 73 n. 51.

118. See Milgrom, *Cult and Conscience,* 74–76. In the Second Temple period, we find evidence for the use of this sacrifice in circles that placed emphasis on the numinous dimension of God to relieve a generalized source of guilt (see I. Knohl, "A Parasha Concerned with Accepting in the Kingdom of Heaven," *Tarbiz* 53 [1984] 25).

of information on the cultic system filter out of Priestly circles.[119] The Priestly Torah is also essentially esoteric.[120] All the activities of the priests take place in the Tent of Meeting and in its courtyard. The hangings of the courtyard of the Tabernacle are the border of the sacred enclosure; beyond it is the encampment of Israel. According to PT, the camp has no intrinsic sanctity whatsoever. Thus, PT ordains that those bearing corpse impurity or those who have had a seminal issue may remain within the camp; only the leper need be removed.[121]

We need not, however, view the priesthood as an elitist sect, completely alienated from the masses and focused solely on the sanctification and religious uplifting of its own members. On the contrary, PT believes that the priests are responsible for the spiritual well-being of the entire nation and for the perfection of each of its individuals. The greatest responsibility is borne by the anointed priest. This is expressed even through the sacred vestments he wears: the names of the tribes of Israel are inscribed upon the lapis lazuli stones in the ephod and the stones in the breastpiece. Thus, the priest brings the names of the tribes of Israel into the holy as a remembrance before God (Exod 28:9–12, 21, 29). On the breastpiece are the Urim and Thummim: "Inside the breastpiece of decision you shall place the Urim and Thummim, so that they are over Aaron's heart when he comes before the Lord. Thus Aaron shall carry the instrument of decision for the Israelites over his heart before the Lord at all times" (Exod 28:30).[122] By means of the golden frontlet on his forehead,

119. See Haran, "Symbolic Significance," 21, 36; idem, *Temples,* 206, 225.

120. Although there are some Priestly laws directed toward the congregation as a whole, as they contain instruction which must be carried out by the people (see Leviticus 1:2; 4:2; 7:29; 11:2; 12:2; 15:2), the details of the rituals performed within the sacred enclosure are given exclusively to the Priestly circle (see Lev 6:2, 18; 13:1; 14:1, 33; 16:2). On the esotericism of PT and parallels to this phenomenon in other ancient Near Eastern priestly writings, see Weinfeld, "Towards the Concept of Law in Israel and Elsewhere," *Beit Miqra* 8 [1964] 59, 61; M. Paran, *Forms of the Priestly Style in the Pentateuch* (Jerusalem, 1987) 242 and n. 15.

121. See above, p. 86. Because of the uncertainty in identifying what the Bible calls leprosy (see J. Tass, "Leprosy, The Identification of Human Leprosy," *EM* 6:776–78; S. J. Brown, *Leprosy in the Bible* [London, 1970]; E. V. Hulse, "The Nature of Biblical 'Leprosy' and the Use of Alternative Medical Terms in Modern Translations of the Bible," *PEQ* 107 [1975] 87–105), it is difficult to know if the special care taken to isolate the leper (see Lev 13:44–46; cf. Num 12:14–15; 2 Kgs 7:3; 15:5) results from fear of contagion. If this was not a contagious disease, the isolation would seem to be a result of revulsion from the anomaly of the physical condition of the leper (see D. Davis, "An Interpretation of Sacrifice in Leviticus," *ZAW* 89 [1977] 396). In any case, the emphasis in Lev 13:45–46 is not on the holiness of the camp in which God is present—as is stated explicitly in Num 5:3 and Deut 23:15—but on the isolation of the leper from society.

122. U. Cassuto drew attention to the brief and unclear reference to the Urim and Thummim in this passage (*A Commentary on the Book of Exodus* [trans. I. Abrahams; Jerusalem, 1967] 267). In his opinion, the passage does refer to the use of the Urim and Thummim to inquire of God, even though the attitude toward its use is ambivalent. The remainder of

the priest carries into the sacred area "any sin arising from the holy things that the Israelites consecrate, from any of their sacred donations; it shall be on his forehead at all times, to win acceptance for them before the Lord" (Exod 28:38).[123]

The anointed priest thus serves as the representative of the entire nation during his daily service in the Sanctuary; he acts to ensure remembrance, justice, and goodwill before God. In addition, there are special actions performed by the priests as emissaries of the nation and the individual. In the annual atonement ritual, the anointed priest takes two he-goats from the congregation, and with them he purifies the Sanctuary and the altar from the impurities of the people of Israel and atones for their sins. He then sends the goat, bearing all their sins, away to the wilderness (Lev 16:5–10, 15–22). Similarly, the anointed priest atones for the unintentional sins of the entire community through the bull of the sin offering that he accepts from them (Lev 4:13–21).[124] The errors, guilt,

---

the passage, "they shall be over Aaron's heart. . . . Thus Aaron shall carry the instrument of decision for the Israelites over his heart before the Lord at all times" (Exod 28:29, 30) refers to the stones of oracle in the breastpiece, which were mentioned previously in v. 29. This explanation hardly seems acceptable: on the stones of the breastplate, as on the lapis lazuli stones on the shoulder-pieces of the ephod, the names of the tribes of Israel were inscribed, so that when the priest carried them into the holy, he brought the remembrance of the Israelites before God (Exod 28:11–12, 21, 29; see Haran, "Symbolic Significance," 28; idem, *Temples,* 213–14). Verse 30 speaks of bringing the decision of the Israelites, which is put into practice through the carrying of the Urim and Thummim (compare the phrase משפט האורים in Num 27:21). Haran explains that the phrase נשא משפט refers to the Urim and Thummim. But, according to Haran, the Urim and Thummim are placed in the breastpiece only on special occasions, that is, when the particular need arises to inquire of God, and Scripture refers to just such instances. A difficulty for this explanation is, however, the instruction תמיד at the end of the verse. Haran is forced to reply that the word תמיד determines that the inquiry be made at the time of the priest's offering of the תמיד sacrifice. But the simple meaning of Scripture, without doubt, is that the carrying of the Urim and Thummim was not an exceptional action but part of the daily worship, just like the wearing of the stones for setting and the frontlet, where the word תמיד also appears (see Exod 28:29, 38). Evidence of this may be found in Lev 8:8, in which the placing of the Urim and Thummim in the breastplate is part of the process of the priest's getting dressed. On PT's attitude toward inquiry of God through the Urim and Thummim, see below, n. 157.

123. On the working of the frontlet, see Haran,"Symbolic Significance," 30; idem, *Temples,* 215.

124. One aspect of the national responsibility of the anointed priest is illustrated through the words "if the anointed priest has incurred guilt so that blame falls upon the people" (Lev 4:3). Even if we reject the explanation that every sin of the priest is reckoned as part of the nation's guilt, and limit the responsibility to sins committed in the framework of his public office, we nevertheless find here an intimate connection between the continuous performance of the Temple cult and the religious situation of the nation as a whole. On the narrower interpretation of Lev 4:3, see Knobel, *Leviticus,* ad loc. Compare the detailed criticism of D. Hoffmann in his commentary on this verse as well as A. B. Ehrlich, *The Bible in Its Plain Meaning* 1 (Berlin, 1889) and P. Heinisch, *Das Buch Leviticus* (HS; Bonn, 1935).

and impurity of individuals are mediated by the priests, who atone for them (Lev 4:26, 31, 35; 5:6, 10, 13, 16, 18, 26; 12:8; 14:18–20, 31; 15:15, 30; Num 6:11). Scripture explicitly states that the priests are responsible "to bear the guilt of the community and to make expiation for them before the Lord" (Lev 10:17).[125]

Thus, the priesthood is an elite group that, though separated and isolated by its special functions, bears a consciousness of public mission and a sense of national responsibility. We may even speak of a certain mutual responsibility, as the people, through their observance of the purity laws and the atonement practices, enable the Priestly superstructure to exist.[126]

Although the sacred sphere contained within the holy enclosure is a kind of independent kingdom headed by the anointed priesthood, who wear the trappings of royalty,[127] they in no way serve as a replacement for civil-political rule.[128] PT recognized non-Priestly political leadership, whose representatives are the chieftains of the congregation; it seeks, however, to maintain an interior "holy kingdom" alongside the broader political structure.[129] This "holy kingdom" disregards not only the sphere of political power, which is assigned to the chieftains, but the entire social-judicial realm as well. As we explained above, the complete separation of morality from the cult is at the root of PT's thought; the restriction of Priestly activities to sacred-ritual areas is a direct consequence of this separation.[130] This trait, too, distinguishes PT's view from those of

125. For an explanation of the language of the verse, see Ehrlich, *Bible.*

126. As J. Milgrom demonstrated, the atonement procedures in PT are based on the perception that the impurities and sins of the people render the sanctuary impure ("The Graduated Hattat of Leviticus 5:1–13," *JAOS* 103 [1983] 249–54). PT even warns the Israelites to avoid contact with certain impurities (see Lev 11:8, 11) and the contact with impurity is viewed as a sin requiring atonement through sacrifice (Lev 5:2–3). For an explanation of these verses, see Milgrom, "Hattat," 143. Note, however, that we cannot be certain that PT was of the opinion that the nation's impurities and sins could lead to the destruction of the Temple. This view is explicitly put forth in Ezekiel 8–10 and in the Holiness Code (Lev 26:31), but not in PT.

127. On the signs of royalty in the image of the anointed priest, see Wellhausen, *Prolegomena,* 143–44 ; M. Haran, "Priesthood, Priests," *EM* 4:20–21.

128. As viewed by Wellhausen, *Prolegomena,* 143–45.

129. See A. Dillmann, *Hexateuch,* 659; Kaufmann, *History,* 1:137–42.

130. The phenomenon of the restriction of Priestly action to the sacral-ritual realm is common among priestly circles throughout the ancient Near East (see Weinfeld, "Towards the Concept of Law," 58–63); in those cultures, however, social justice is considered as part of the secular realm, whose authority derives from the royal powers (ibid., 62–63). In Israel, on the other hand, social justice also derives from the divine command (ibid.; Kaufmann, *History,* 1:67; Eichrodt, *Theology,* 1:74–76; Greenberg, "Some Postulates of Biblical Criminal Law," in *Y. Kaufmann Jubilee Volume* [ed. M. Haran; Jerusalem, 1960] 19–20; L. Finkelstein, "Justice, Justice in the Ancient Near East" *EM* 5:609–10); thus, the priesthood may be integrated into the judicial structure. Moreover, we do find such views expressed in the Bible (see below, n. 131). According to PT, although the moral imperative originates in the divine command, its observance is not the particular area of Priestly concern, since,

other biblical sources, which assign priests functions in the domain of civil law.[131]

Just as the priesthood is detached from society, so too is it unrelated to the difficulties of daily human existence or the crises of the nation. PT does not hint at any participation of the priests in the wars of Israel,[132] nor do they assign the priests any active role in popular ceremonies in expectation of the blessing of rain and abundant harvest (above, pp. 43–45). PT's concentration on the interior space of the desert Tabernacle is the ultimate expression of its total lack of concern with basic human needs or social legislation. The desert, in which the inheritance of the land, agriculture, kingship, and administrative regulation are all absent, serves as an ideal platform for the presentation of PT's utopian vision.[133] The clear lines of the image of utopian desert life reflects the concerns of a social circle unconcerned with daily worries, who were, as a result, able to invest all their efforts in ritual activity and the pursuit of spiritual elevation.[134] The priests of this school prepared themselves through sanc-

---

in its view, social morality is universal and based on the faith of Genesis, which is detached from the cultic-temple experience. The definition of the Priestly roles in PT corresponds to that of non-Israelite priesthoods, though the ideological worldviews are different.

131. Cf. Deut 17:8–13; Exod 44:24. I disagree with Kaufmann's argument that the lack of judicial duties for the priests in PT's law is merely a literary oversight (*History,* 2:476; but see also *History,* 1:138!). I believe that this indicates a particular ideological approach. The link between the holiness of the priests and their consequent isolation from the people and separation from judicial activity was noted by Haran ("Priesthood," 28). Soss's statement ("Old Testament Law," 326–28) that, in the Pentateuch as a whole, the priest-Levites are in charge of judgment is based on a faulty understanding of the law of guilt offerings in Leviticus 5 and on lack of discernment in analyzing the differences of opinion among the various pentateuchal sources dealing with this question.

132. In contradiction to other biblical sources which assign the priesthood a significant position in war ceremonies (on the lack of such ritual in PT, see above, p. 140 and n. 60). In HS we find the priests sounding the trumpets in times of war (Num 10:8–9; 31:6). Deuteronomy has the priests addressing words of encouragement to the people (Deut 20:1–4). It was a common Israelite custom to take the ark out to the battlefield (see Num 14:44; Josh 6:6–13; 1 Sam 4:3–11; 14:18; 2 Sam 11:11 (some are of the opinion that the taking of the כלי הקדש, "sacred utensils," mentioned in the HS account of the battle against the Midianites in Num 31:6 refers to the bringing of the ark to the battlefield; see *t. Sotah* 7:17; Rashi; Ibn Ezra, ad loc., Milgrom, *Studies,* n. 186; but compare Kaufmann, *History,* 2:468). In PT, on the other hand, the removal of the ark to the battlefield would be unthinkable (see Kaufmann, ad loc.; Haran, "Priesthood," 24); by the same token, PT ignores the custom of inquiring of God through the Urim and Thummim before going out to battle (see n. 157).

133. On the utopian aspects of PT, see M. Haran, "Behind the Scenes of History: Determining the Date of the Priestly Source," *JBL* 100 (1981) 331–32; idem, *Temples,* 11, 142.

134. As in R. Shimon ben Eliezer's saying: "The Torah was only given to manna-eaters, and heave-offering eaters are their equal" (*Mekhilta de Rabbi Ishmael,* Horowitz-Rabin edition, p. 76). Compare Maimonides' words on the tribe of Levi in his great judicial compilation, at the end of the laws of sabbatical and jubilee years.

tification, atonement, and purification, to approach the mysterious God who reveals himself in the hidden recesses of their Temple.

The Attitude of PT toward Popular Religion and Its Institutions

In his discussion of the image of God in popular worship, Y. Kaufmann remarks:

> Wherever we find in the pagan world a sublime religious faith, whether philosophical or mysterious, there we find a sharp contrast between that faith and popular belief. The higher faith either denies the popular belief or builds its structures above it, viewing the popular religion as an inferior state. . . . In Israel of the Biblical Period, however, we find no such phenomenon. The prophets and scribes of the Bible do not combat popular legend or condemn it, nor do they attempt to purify it of mythological elements. The battle of the authors of the Bible and the people takes place entirely on cultic grounds. But there is *no conflict whatsoever regarding the image of God* or the description of his essence . . . the faith of the prophets was not the "esoteric faith" of selected individuals who possessed knowledge of higher things and secret teachings. On the contrary, their faith was based on and nourished by popular belief; it was organically and fundamentally linked to popular belief and shares in its essential nature.[135]

Unquestionably, this was true of the faith of the prophets, but does it hold true of the conceptions of PT as well? It would seem that PT is an Israelite manifestation of that esoteric faith which is the inheritance of the few "who possess knowledge of 'higher things'" and, professing a sublime faith, seek a new religious truth which is not contained and does not spring from the popular faith and is, at best, complementary to it.

PT disagrees with all strata of the popular faith (including prophecy) in three fundamental matters: in its description of the essence of God, in its views of the content of the revelation to Moses, and in the shaping of the relations between God and Israel. While popular legends and prophetic visions attribute images to God, PT avoids all use of anthropomorphism in describing God or his cult.[136] In contradiction to the other sources of

135. Kaufmann, *History,* 1:610–12.

136. As part of his aim to emphasize the intuitive origins and popular nature of Israelite monotheism, Kaufmann declared: "All of Biblical literature, irrespective of source or stratum, attributes a form to God and sees no defect in doing so" (*History,* 1:226). I believe that this general statement is not applicable to PT. Kaufmann himself noted PT's tendency to remove such imagery but minimized its importance, explaining the phenomenon as reflecting dry style rather than any ideological principle. As evidence, he notes that it is this very "spiritual and abstract" source that provides us with the idea of the creation in God's image, "which carries decisive weight in our case" (ibid., 227). Our study shows that the

the Pentateuch and the prophetic writings, which claim that the revelation to Moses included a moral code, PT restricts the revelation to the cultic sphere. As opposed to the other strata of the Pentateuch and the prophetic writings, which assert the bilateral relationship between God and Israel based on the making of a covenant (ברית), PT espouses a one-sided relationship represented through the term "pact" (עדות). But, according to PT, the concepts and values absent from the revelation to Moses were present in the faith of the period of Genesis and the patriarchs. There we find God described in anthropomorphic terms; God establishes social order, sees that morality is observed and builds his relations with humanity on the basis of a bilateral covenant (ברית). Thus, the faith concepts prevalent in the other strata of the Pentateuch and in the words of the prophets serve, for PT, as the basic religious experience. Upon this basis, PT constructs its higher level of faith—an experience characterized by the recognition of the name of Yahweh. Thus, PT does not deny the popular faith in an anthropomorphic God—providential,

---

metaphor of the creation in the image of God accords well with the dominant religious language of the Genesis period in PT, in which God is described in personalized and anthropomorphic terms, but not of the period of Moses, in which anthropomorphizing imagery is suppressed. The sharp differences in the religious language used in the two periods in PT clearly indicate a fundamental theological distinction: it is unimaginable that the store of imagery suddenly became impoverished with the transition to the period of Moses. I do accept, however, Kaufmann's argument that no Jewish literary sources, before contact with Greek philosophy, contain speculative abstraction (ibid., 227ff.) The systematic suppression of anthropomorphism in PT does not result from an abstract analysis seeking to place God beyond the realm of space and time, but is, rather, an expression of the desire to exalt God; this, in the words of Kaufmann himself (ibid., 247), is the Israelite term which parallels the abstraction of philosophical religion. Weinfeld is of the opinion that the common Deuteronomic expression לשכן שמו שם indicates the desire to remove the anthropomorphism and materialization, which, in his opinion, are present in the Priestly view that maintains that God is permanently present in the Temple (see M. Weinfeld, "The Change in the Conception of Religion in Deuteronomy," *Tarbiz* 31 [1961] 10–16!; idem, *Deuterononomy,* 191–209). This argument is difficult to accept. As we discussed, PT removes any overtones of materialization and personalization from the symbols of God's presence in the Tabernacle, whereas it is Deuteronomy that contains blatantly anthropomorphic and anthropopathic expressions (see, e.g., Deut 9:19; 13:18; 20:4; 23:15; 28:63; 29:19). Weinfeld's proof from the reason given for the prohibition against making idols in Deut 4:15—"since you saw no shape when the Lord your God spoke to you at Horeb, out of the fire"—is not decisive. The verse does not state that God has no visible image but rather that, as the image of God was not revealed to the people at Horeb, they should not try to make an image of God (see M. Greenberg, "The Decalogue Tradition Critically Examined," in *The Ten Commandments in History and Tradition,* ed. B. Z. Segal [Jerusalem, 1990] 80–81). The argument between the Priestly view, maintaining that God's כבוד is permanently present in his Temple, and the Deuteronomic literature, which rejects such presence, does not devolve around the question of personification and materialization; rather, the struggle is over the forms of God's revelation, whose roots go back to the period preceding the book of Deuteronomy (see above, n. 24).

righteous in judgment, and rewarding faithful servants—but sees this as only the first step in the development of the religious personality, which can attain perfection only through recognition of the sublime dimension of God represented through the name of Yahweh. With the revelation of this aspect of the divinity—which cannot be described through any anthropomorphizing imagery, and which transcends reason and morality and is independent of the relation of reward and punishment—humans recognize their true status and are transformed into people who "worship through love," without expecting any recompense for their deeds.[137]

In the sphere of non-Priestly faith, several types of leaders arose and popular cultic institutions were developed. The aim of PT in focusing religious life around the complex of the Tent of Meeting, which was entirely controlled by the priesthood, raises several questions as to its views of the status and role of popular religious institutions. We will begin by discussing PT's attitude toward the Nazirite and the prophet, who represent sources of religious authority independent of the Temple-cultic sphere.[138] We will then examine the status of the Sabbath and the festivals, institutions that are also rooted in popular religious experience.[139]

In non-Priestly sources, the prophet and the Nazirite are described as figures of spiritual inspiration and religious authority that derive from their election and calling by God.[140] Among the prophets, we find a great degree of spiritual freedom and independence of the cultic establishment. In fact, the prophets often find themselves in severe confrontation with the priesthood and its institutions. The ambivalent attitude of PT toward the phenomenon of prophecy may be seen in its description of

137. We find a similar process of development of religious consciousness in the book of Job. Nevertheless, PT and Job disagree on several fundamental points. (On this, see Excursus 4).

138. Although we do, occasionally, find in the Bible prophecy related to the Temple, the two are not inherently linked. See B. Uffenheimer, *Ancient Prophecy in Israel* (Jerusalem, 1984) 706–7; Haran, *Temples,* 274; I. Gruenwald, "The Impact of Priestly Tradition on the Creation of the Mysticism and Shiur Komah," in *Proceedings of the First International Conference on the History of Jewish Mysticism—Early Jewish Mysticism* (Jerusalem Studies in Jewish Thought 6; Jerusalem, 1987) 71–73. As for the Nazirite, Samson's case demonstrates the independence of the Nazirite from the cultic establishment. The person of Samuel, which shows aspects of naziritism, cannot serve as evidence (explicit evidence of his naziritism may be found in the Septuagint and Qumran versions; see Z. Weissmann, "The Biblical Nazirite, Its Types and Roots," *Tarbiz* 36 [1967] 212 n. 27), since this character combines, exceptionally, the traits of priest-Levite, prophet, and Nazirite (see Kaufmann, *History,* 2:104; Uffenheimer, *Early Prophecy,* 143.

139. On the Sabbath and festivals as expressions of the popular faith, see Kaufmann, *History,* 2:486ff.

140. The consciousness of election and mission is made explicit in Israelite prophecy and requires no proof. On the election and vocation of the Nazirite of God, see Weissmann, "Nazirite," 211–12.

God's revelation to Moses. Unlike in non-Priestly sources, PT refrains from attributing to Moses the character of a prophet.[141] In JE the Tent of Meeting is not a prophetic refuge located outside the camp, at whose entrance God occasionally reveals himself. In PT, on the other hand, the Tent of Meeting is at the center of the camp and is the permanent resting place of God's Presence and the center of cultic-Temple worship.[142] God's meeting with Moses in the Priestly Tent of Meeting is not described as a revelation experience of prophetic vision; it is merely a listening to the commandments of God. It is in the revelation to the patriarchs that we find the characteristic traits of prophetic revelation: God *appears* to Abraham and Jacob and speaks with them. Moreover, in the account of the revelations to the patriarchs, God is said to ascend when departing from them (above, p. 128); this is reminiscent of the descent of God in the cloud to his place of meeting with Moses, Aaron, and Miriam in the non-Priestly tradition.[143] Thus, we may conclude that PT removes all visual phenomena from the prophetic revelation in the Tent of Meeting, concentrating on the hearing of the word of God.[144] Nevertheless, Moses does carry out the prophet task in transmitting the word of God to the people: "I will impart to you . . . all that I will command you concerning the Israelite people" (Exod 25:22).

PT also seeks to fit the Nazirite into the cultic framework. It makes no reference to the Nazirite of God (נזיר האלהים), who draws his strength from his election by God and whose period of naziritism is lifelong; rather it restricts its discussion to vows of temporary naziritism which terminate in a ritual ceremony performed in the Tent of Meeting under supervision of the priest (Num 6:1–21).[145] The image of the Nazirite is formed in accor-

141. See Haran, *Temples,* 272.

142. See Haran, "The Nature of 'Ohel Moed' in the Pentateuchal Sources," *JSS* 5 (1960) 50–65; idem, *Temples,* 264–73; see above, nn. 20, 24.

143. See Exod 33:9; 34:5; Num 11:17, 25; 12:5.

144. Note that in the Second Temple period the priesthood was assigned the privilege and the capacity to hear the divine voice while they served in the holy (see lately, Gruenwald, "Impact of Priestly Tradition," 79–82).

145. A commonly accepted scholarly view explains PT's ignorance of permanent naziritism and its focus on individual naziritism by its late date of authorship (see Gray, "The Nazirite," *JTS* 1 [1900] 210–11; idem, *Numbers* [ICC; Edinburgh, 1903] 60). But A. Dillmann (*Die Bücher Numeri, Deuteronomium, und Josua* [KeH; Leipzig, 1886] 32) and M. Haran ("Nazirite," *EM* 5:796) correctly comment that the two kinds of naziritism could exist simultaneously at a later period as well. Dillmann and Haran explain PT's ignorance of the permanent Nazirite by the independence of this form of naziritism from the Temple cult; as a result, it remained beyond the realm of interest of the priesthood. I believe that we may have here a polemic against a view that would assign permanent sanctity to someone outside of Priestly circles. The entire matter, however, requires renewed investigation, as recently some scholars have questioned the very existence of permanent naziritism in Israel (see Y. Amit, "Lifelong Nazirism–The Evolution of the Motif," *Teᶜuda* 4 [1986] 23–26).

dance with the priesthood and its symbols: just as the anointed priest wears the crown of consecration upon his head and therefore is not allowed to defile himself through contact with the dead, so too the Nazirite consecrates the crown of his head and must avoid corpse impurity.[146] Nevertheless, the Nazirite remains an exceptional figure in PT's laws. We already mentioned that, according to this school, the sacred area is restricted to the cultic enclosure, whereas the camp of Israel bears no sanctity whatsoever. By merely taking a vow of naziritism, however, any Israelite, man or woman, may temporarily take on the highest level of sanctity, which must be preserved through the most severe purity restrictions.

In spite of the link forged by PT between the Nazirite and the cultic system, it is clear that the qualities and holiness of the Nazirite are not derived from the Temple-cultic sphere; rather, they result from the Nazirite's special relation with God. This special relationship is summarized in the words כי נזר אלהיו על ראשו (Num 6:7), which serves as a reason for the Nazirite's avoidance of corpse impurity. As the Targumim and medieval exegetes properly explained, the meaning of the word נזר in this context is "crown" and not נדר נזירות, a Nazirite vow.[147] The meaning of the passage is that the spiritual level of the Nazirite and the severe holiness requirements he is to observe derive from the crown of God that is upon his head.[148]

In ancient Near Eastern literature the king's special virtue is said to derive from his being created in the image of the god and from his being crowned with the crown of the god.[149] We see that just as PT made

146. The linguistic and ideological relation of the prohibition against the Nazirite's defilement (Num 6:17) and the HS law forbidding the high priest from contracting corpse impurity (Lev 21:11–12) is clear. The midrashic exegetes already commented on the similarity of the two passages (see *Numbers Rabbah* 10:11 and *Sefer Pitron Torah,* ed. Urbach, p. 134).

147. See the commentary of Ibn Ezra (ad loc.). An interesting suggestion put forth by Y. M. Grintz (*Biblical Studies* [Jerusalem, 1979] 35) and Weinfeld ("Kavod," *TWAT* 1:30) links the Hebrew נזר to the symbols of the fire-spitting snake on the Pharaohs' heads (see M. Noth, *Exodus* [trans. J. S. Bowden; OTL; London, 1962] 226; M. Weinfeld, "Divine Intervention in War in Ancient Israel and in the Ancient Near East," in *History, Historiography and Interpretation* [ed. M. Weinfeld and H. Tadmor; Jerusalem, 1984] 126 nn. 27–28).

148. While one might explain the expression נזר אלהיו as referring to the crownlike hair, which was consecrated to God, the literal translation—the crown of God placed on the head of the Nazirite—seems more likely. This conception, in my opinion, underlies the words of Rabbi (Jo)nathan, who teaches that one must respect the holiness of a bald Nazirite, based on the words כי נזר אלהיו על ראשו, "whether he has hair or not" (*Sifre Numbers* 25, 26; ed. Horowitz, pp. 31, 34). The meaning of this explanation is that even one who has no hair—נזר—of his own, is holy, since the נזר, the crown of God, is on his head.

149. On creation in one's image as the exclusive prerogative of the king, see Weinfeld, "God the Creator," 114–15 and references there. On the divine dimension of the royal crown in Mesopotamia and Egypt, see H. Frankfort, *Kingship and the Gods* 7 (Chicago, 1971) 107, 245–47; S. Kramer and M. Weinfeld, "Prologomena to a Comparative Study of

creation in the image of God the reason for the uniqueness of all humanity,[150] so too it adapted the image of coronation with the crown of God to describe the sanctity of the Nazirite, which may be attained, if only temporarily, by all Israelites.[151] The anthropomorphic image of the creation in the image of God reflects, as we mentioned, the special closeness of God and humanity in the Genesis period. Similarly, the symbol of the crown of God, which has blatant anthropomorphic overtones,[152] expresses the unique relation between the Nazirite and God. It would seem that in order to stress the extraordinary nature of the Nazirite, which is not in harmony with the accepted network of concepts and beliefs in the cultic realm, PT made an exception to its usual practice, using the name אלהים (נזר אלהיו) rather than נזר ה׳, even though in the period of Moses PT otherwise uses the name of Yahweh exclusively. The exceptional use of the name אלהים and the anthropomorphic image נזר אלהים reflect the religious language usually employed in the Genesis period; PT apparently intended to place the image of the Nazirite of God in that sphere.[153]

PT's relation to the Sabbath and the festivals reflects the tension between its desire to shape a cultic system completely detached from anthropomorphic images of God—creator, supervisor, and savior—and the

the Book of Psalms and Sumerian Literature," *Beit Miqra* 19 (1974) 154–56. This type of imagery is also common in the psalms (see Kramer and Weinfeld, ad loc.; Weinfeld, "God the Creator," 132). Of special interest are the Septuagint and Peshitta versions of Ps 132(131):18. Most manuscripts of these translations indicate that their Hebrew source text read ועליו יצ״ץ נזרי—that is, the crown of God shines from the king's head. This motif is stated explicitly in midrashim: "In the future, God will place his crown upon the head of the anointed king" (*Tanhuma, Ve'era* 8; *Exodus Rabbah* 8:1, ed. Shin'an, p. 200).

150. On the democratization of the metaphor of creation in the image in Israel and Egypt, see Weinfeld, "God the Creator," 113–14.

151. In the midrashim of the sages, a divine crown is presented to the righteous in the world to come (see *b. Megillah* 16b; *b. Shabbat* 104a). The Agaddah speaks of wreaths that were placed on the heads of Israel when they said "נעשה ונשמע" and were removed when they committed the sin of the golden calf (see the sources in L. Ginzberg, *The Legends of the Jews* [New York, 1911] vol. 11, nn. 203, 207). Here we find the Mesopotamian motif of the removal of the divine Presence from one who has lost favor in the eyes of God, which is also hinted at in the Bible (see Weinfeld, "God the Creator," 144).

152. Describing God as a crowned king is common in the ancient world; see Oppenheim, *Ancient Mesopotamia*, 184; Pauly-Wissowa, "Corona," *RE* IV (2) 1636–37. In the Aggadoth of the sages, too, the image of Israel crowning the creator is common (see *b. Hagiga* 136; *Leviticus Rabbah* 24:8, ed. Margaliot, p. 564; *Exodus Rabbah* 21.

153. It would seem that in the three events in which PT deviates from its schema for the names of God and uses the name אלהים in the period of Moses, this resulted from the necessity of referring to concepts and expressions typical of the Genesis period: the introduction of the concept of ברית in Lev 2:13 (see above, p. 145); the description of the direct and active action of God in the world, as spoken by the Egyptian magicians, using the anthropomorphic image "finger of God (אלהים)" (Exod 8:15; see above, p. 147); the symbolizing of the closeness of God and the Nazirite using the anthropomorphizing language נזר אלהיו, "the crown of his God."

heritage of popular cultic practices which developed around the faith in God as the providential Creator who rewards the righteous. As we mentioned, PT develops faith in God the providential, rewarding Creator in the Genesis period; thus, in that sphere, PT presents the Sabbath day as a blessed and sanctified day on which God rested from the acts of creation (Gen 2:1–3). In light of the divine example presented in PT's own writings, we would expect to find an order to rest from work on the Sabbath day among its cultic laws—as a remembrance of the days of creation.[154] But the cultic system of PT concentrates on the essential numinous dimension of God, which is completely divorced from the image of God as providential creator; thus, the prohibitions of work on the Sabbath day, in remembrance of God's rest, have no place in this framework. As a result, there is no explicit mention of the prohibition against Sabbath work in the legal system of PT.[155] The only cultic expression of the Sabbath day is the additional sacrifice offered then.[156]

PT does not, however, reject completely the popular customs deriving from faith in God as Creator and providential supervisor of the world. It does not delegitimize the people's expectation for God's blessing and salvation at key moments and allows some room for popular practices which express this expectation: the ceremonies of the bringing of the firstfruits and the counting of weeks are present in its laws, although they are not formulated as obligations (see above, pp. 23-27). The laws of the Day of the Sounding of the Horn and the Fast Day are formulated as obligatory commandments, but, as we mentioned, PT seeks to create a division between those observances and the "pure" ceremonies of priestly ritual (see above, pp. 32–34). The popular ceremonies of the paschal lamb offering and the feast of Unleavened Bread do appear as obligatory commandments, but are mentioned very briefly and in a general way, which indicates PT's exception to these rites (see above, p. 22).

In the purely Priestly worship as well, we find expressions beseeching God's grace, but these are formulated in a very refined and concealed way. We already remarked the hint of expectation of God's blessing among the details of the sacrifices of the festivals of the seventh month (see above, pp. 36–38), and we mentioned (above, p. 153) that the garments of the anointed priests included symbols expressing the people's desire to be remembered before God and to bring their judgment before him. But inasmuch as these symbols are to be worn by the priests *perma-*

154. As explicitly stated in Exod 20:11; 31:17. Both passages have already been identified as originating in HS.

155. Above, p. 18. I do not claim that PT was of the opinion that there was no prohibition against work on the Sabbath at all; this seems unlikely. The very name of the day, יום השבת (Num 28:9), hints at a prohibition of work. (But see Ezek 22:26.)

156. This was already noticed by Kaufmann, *History*, 2:491.

nently, their supplicative aspect, the calling forth of God's response to specific human needs (see Exod 28:29, 30, 38),[157] is attenuated.

157. PT's attitude toward inquiry through the Urim and Thummim is instructive: the common Israelite custom was to inquire of God in times of distress, especially before going out to war (see Judg 1:1; 20:18, 23, 27–28; 1 Sam 14:36–37; 22:10, 13, 15; 23:2, 4, 9–12; 28:6; 30:7–8; 2 Sam 2:1; 5:19, 23). The questioning was done with the assistance of the priest who carried the Urim, as we find in the narrative of Joshua's appointment: "But he shall present himself to Eleazar the priest, who shall on his behalf seek the decision of the Urim before the Lord. By such instruction they shall go out and by such instruction they shall come in" (Num 27:21). We have already determined the origin of this story as HS. PT briefly mentions the Urim and Thummim placed in the breastplate (Exod 28:30), which, according to its teaching, is permanently worn by the priest (see above, n. 122). This wearing of the Urim, is, of course, not to be understood as an inquiry of God, which, obviously, takes place only on exceptional occasions of special need. PT intentionally omits the inquiry of God in times of need and ordains instead the permanent wearing of the decision of the Israelites before God. I believe that this omission results not from the mantic nature of this custom, as argued by Cassuto (*Exodus,* 381); on the contrary, such customs are common enough in PT, and PT seems to pose no objection to them (see Lev 16:8; Num 5:17–28; 34:13). Rather, it is an expression of PT's opposition to viewing the cult as a means to obtain God's help and intervention in times of distress. The permanent wearing of the Urim counters the aspect of need request inherent in this custom and turns it into a constant nonexplicit wish for God's response to Israel's needs.

EXCURSUS 4

The Priestly Torah and the Book of Job

The book of Job depicts a dynamic process—the refinement of the faith consciousness—generally similar to the shift that transpires in PT. PT relates the transition between the level of elementary faith of the Genesis period to the faith of Moses and Israel. In the Genesis period, faith was founded on a worldview that placed humanity at the center of the universe and was grounded in the laws of morality and the belief in reward and punishment. The faith of Moses and Israel, however, was founded on an awareness of the centrality of God, an awareness deriving from the discovery of a divine dimension beyond the moral, beyond reward and punishment. Similarly, the book of Job distinguishes between the fear of the Lord possessed by Job—who, avoiding evil, expects reward for his righteousness, an attitude that brings him to speak insolently toward heaven with the demand for the realization of divine justice—and the religious insight gained by Job after God revealed himself out of the tempest and uncovered to him divine foundations, beyond the grasp of human insight and not limited by the bounds of reward and punishment. Divine revelation brings Job to the awareness of humanity's true station in the world, and Job gives expression to the illumination he merited by declaring: "I had heard You with my ears, but now I see You with my eyes; therefore, I recant and relent, being but dust and ashes."[1]

Even though there are similarities in the faith dynamic, there are some fundamental differences between PT and the book of Job. As we have stated, PT holds that exalted faith consciousness is rooted in knowledge of the Tetragrammaton. Hence, it is the legacy of Israel alone; Gentiles have no share in it (see above, p. 147). In the book of Job, however, the attainment of the most exalted level of faith is ascribed to a man who is not of Israel and who does not know of the

1. Regarding this interpretation of the meaning of the revelation to Job, see R. Otto, *The Idea of the Holy*, 77–80; J. Jacobson, *The Problem of Reward and Punishment in the Bible: Essays and Questions for Study* (Tel Aviv, 1978) 45–59; Y. Leibowitz, *Judaism, Human Values, and the Jewish State* (Cambridge, MA, 1992) 48–53; M. Greenberg, *On the Bible and Judaism: A Collection of Writings* (Tel Aviv, 1985) 238–39.

Tetragrammaton: the Tetragrammaton is used only by the narrator, not by Job and his friends;[2] they use the names אל, אלה, and שדי, which resemble the names of God used in PT of the Genesis period and the times of the patriarchs.[3] The Gentile angle of the book of Job reflects a general tendency on the part of biblical literature to treat moral questions in a non-Israelite framework, in order to emphasize the universal aspect of the discussion.[4] Since, however, the book ranges beyond the realm of a wisdom discussion of morality and has revelation at its climax,[5] the choice of a Gentile protagonist is tantamount to adopting a positive position on the possibility, for a non-Israelite, of experiencing a full-fledged divine revelation.[6]

This difference between the two books ties in with their dispute about the nature of the various spheres of revelation of divinity. According to PT, the numinous element in divinity and the exalted faith-insight bound up with it come to expression only through the complex of ritual and Sanctuary, which was established after the revelation of the Tetragrammaton to Moses, and whose statutes are directed exclusively to the community of Israel. In the pre-Mosaic period, the Genesis period, the conception presented in PT is one that places humanity at the center of the universe and emphasizes the rational and moral dimension of divinity. This is conveyed by the structured description of the works of creation, with the human being as the crowning achievement, and by the portrayal of God's deeds as lawgiver, source of providence, and moral judge. The faith of Genesis is conceived of as the legacy of all of humanity (see above, p. 146). According to the book of Job, however, one can encounter the numinous dimension of divinity and can attain exalted faith consciousness even if one is not of Israel. Access to the discovery of this dimension can be gained through reflection on the acts of creation. Sacrificial worship is mentioned in the book only at the stage of Job's early faith level: Job, who fears God, seeks to secure, through sacrifice, his own happiness and the welfare of his family.[7]

This dispute would explain the striking difference in the way the two works portray creation: PT portrays, in Genesis, a step-by-step, rational creation, with each and every stage bearing a purpose and defined meaning. In the divine revelation in the book of Job, however, the mysterious, bizarre, and unfathomable

2. Exceptions are two passages, 1:21 and 12:9. In these passages, however, the Tetragrammaton appears within well-known formulations; hence, they are not refutations (see E. Dhorme, *Commentary on the Book of Job* [trans. H. Knight; London, 1926] introduction, pp. 55–62).

3. N. H. Torczyner claims that in God's answer to Job (38:1ff.) the Tetragrammaton was revealed to Job (*The Book of Job* [Jerusalem, 1941] 536–37). For this reason, he understands the book of Job to be "a song of proselytism." Y. Kaufmann, however, was correct in rejecting this theory. He claimed that there is no hint of it in the text, pointing to the lack of any mention of the Tetragrammaton in God's words to Job (*A History of the Religion of Israel* [Jerusalem/Tel Aviv, 1960] 2:620 n. 16).

4. See Kaufmann, *History*, 2:283, 440, 574–75, 620–21.

5. Ibid., 2:615.

6. See M. Weiss, *The Story of Job's Beginning* (Studies for Teachers and Group Leaders; Jerusalem, 1983) 22 n. 5.

7. See Job 1:5; cf. Weiss, *Story of Job*, 44–45.

elements of creation are emphasized.[8] PT presents the human being as the apex of the works of creation and places under human dominion all living things (Gen 1:28). The book of Job, on the other hand, makes no mention at all of the creation of humans; what is stressed is humanity's inability to rule over the beasts of creation (Job 39:9–12; 40:25–32; 41:18–21). The crowning achievement of creation, according to the book of Job, is not the human being but Leviathan, whom "no one on land can dominate. . . . He is king over all proud beasts" (Job 41:21–26).

From the language and style of the book of Job it is clear that the author wished to assume the atmosphere of the Genesis period and the times of the patriarchs.[9] This serves to magnify his argument with PT, since the implication is that the most exalted religious conception had already come into the world, even before the appearance of Moses and the revelation of the Tetragrammaton, outside of Israel!

The attainment of exalted faith consciousness is not dependent, then, according to the book of Job, on national belonging; it is not tied to the revelation of a particular divine name, nor to the giving of the teaching and the commandments, nor to the observance of a Temple ritual. Rather, any person can, by reflecting on creation, attain insight into the fullness of God's being and arrive at an understanding of humanity's true standing before God.

8. See the comments of the authors cited in n. 1 and of M. Tsevat, "The Meaning of the Book of Job," *HUCA* 37 (1966) 99.

9. See S. R. Driver and G. B. Gray, *Commentary on Job* (ICC; Edinburgh, 1921) introduction, p. 56; Dhorme, *Job*, 20–21; Kaufmann, *History*, 2:619–20.

CHAPTER

4

The Concept of God and the Cult in the Holiness Schools

The relation of HS to its PT heritage is marked by deep dependence, on the one hand, and sharp polemic, on the other. Through the affinities and the disagreements between the two sources, we may clearly discern the characteristic traits of a creative editorial Priestly school, which infused the fundamental Priestly concepts with new content. Therefore, HS's creative enterprise will be analyzed by comparing it with the concepts of its parent school, PT.

THE NAMES OF GOD

HS opens with the verses describing God's revelation of the name of Yahweh to Moses (Exod 6:2–3).[1] The passage stresses that the name of Yahweh was not known to the patriarchs and that God revealed himself to them through the name אל שדי. The sole mention of the name אל שדי in HS is found in these transition verses; moreover, we find here the exclusive use of the word אלהים as a proper name for God: "And God (אלהים) spoke unto Moses." Henceforth, HS will never use any name except Yahweh when referring to the God of Israel.

HS accepts, in principle, PT's common scheme in employing the names of God. There is, however, a fundamental difference between the two schools on this issue. In PT, after the revelation of the name of Yahweh to Moses, the name אלהים almost never appears again, and we never find the two names, אלהים and ה' in combination (see above, p. 124 and nn. 1, 2). In HS, on the other hand, the name אלהים continues to be used in the period of Moses, but as an adjective adjoined to the name of God, rather

1. Except, perhaps, for several recensional additions in Genesis; see chapter 2, nn. 145–50.

than as a proper name for God. We find there phrases such as ה' אלהים[2] in possessive constructions preceded by prepositional particles or prepositions[3] or as a noun following the dependent word in construct states: שם אלהיך, לחם אלהיך, קרבן אלהיכם, etc. We also find it used as a dependent word in construct states, such as אלהי הרוחות, אלהי ישראל.[4] Outside of construct states, inflections, or prepositional phrases, the name אלהים appears only once, where it is employed in a derivative sense, in Exod 7:1.[5]

As we will explain in this chapter, the difference in form of the names of God expresses the profound difference between the two Priestly schools in their understanding of God and his relation to humanity.

Personal and Impersonal Language

In previous chapters, we demonstrated the differences between PT and HS in their descriptions of the contact between God and humanity (see Introduction, n. 3 and p. 107, above). Whereas PT assigns direct speech to God only when He communicates with Moses, HS describes unmediated contact between God and the entire community. Whereas in PT, we never find God employing the personal pronoun אני, during the period of Moses we often find the word אני used in God's speech in HS writings.[6] Whereas in PT, punishment is strictly impersonal, personalized accounts of punishment appear in HS.[7] HS did, however, adapt some of the imper-

2. This phrase is common both in the Holiness Code and in other parts of HS writings; see Introduction, n. 3; and Exod 6:7; 16:12; 29:46; Lev 11:44; Num 10:10; 16:41.

3. לאלהים, לאלהיהם(כם), לאלהיו (Exod 6:7; 29:45; Lev 11:45; 21:6, 7; 22:33; 25:38; 26:12, 45; Num 15:40, 41; 25:13). מאלהיך (Lev 19:14, 32; 25:17, 43); לפני אלהיכם (Num 10:10).

4. שם אלהיך (אלהיהם) (Lev 18:21; 19:12; 21:6); לחם אלהיהם (אלהיך, אלהיו, אלהיכם) (Lev 21:6, 8, 17, 21, 22; 22:25); שמן משחת אלהיו, מקדש אלהיו (Lev 21:12); קרבן אלהיכם (Lev 23:14). In the writings of HS outside of the Holiness Code we find the phrase רוח אלהים (Exod 31:3; 35:31). In the HS strata in the book of Numbers we find two additional phrases in which אלהים serves as the object of a construct phrase: אלהי ישראל (Num 16:9) and אלהי הרוחות לכל בשר (Num 16:22; 27:16).

5. We should note that in non-Priestly traditions, the word אלהים appears as the proper name of God after the revelation of the name of Yahweh as well. See Exod 18:1; 20:1; Num 21:5; 22:12; among others.

6. As a closing formula (אני ה', אלהיכם, מקדשכם, etc.), as well as in the course of fluent speech on the part of God. Having identified the HS verses in chapter 2, we can present a complete listing of all the places in which the divine אני appears in the fluent speech of God in the writings of HS (see Exod 6:5; 7:3; 10:1; 25:9; 31:6; Lev 11:44; 14:34; 17:11; 18:3, 24; 20:3, 5, 22, 23, 24; 23:10; 25:2; 26:16, 24, 28, 32, 41; Num 3:11; 5:3; 6:27; 13:2; 14:28; 15:2, 18; 18:6, 8, 20; 25:12, 35:34; Deut 32:49, 52).

7. See also chapter 3, nn. 18, 42. We should mention, especially, the recensional addition of HS in Num 5:21. In the original core of the law, which originates in PT, the punishment of the suspected adulteress is described as resulting from special properties of the water itself (see Num 5:22, 24, 27). In their recensional additions, HS editors attribute the act of punishment to God (see above, p. 88).

sonal language prevalent in PT passages on God and his ways. We occasionally find in HS the juxtaposition of descriptions of personal and impersonal punishment,[8] as well as descriptions of impersonal punishment in many passages. Witness, for example, the forms (ה)(ת)יכרת, ונכרת(ה)(ו)[9] and the words describing impersonal actions of anger, punishment, and plague.[10] The account of the death of the rebellious chieftains, for example (Num 16:35), displays many similarities to the impersonal description of the deaths of Nadab and Abihu in PT (Lev 10:6). Moreover, we do find in HS several expressions designed to remove anthropomorphic overtones from the description of God, by turning the active descriptions of God's deeds into the passive mode. In general, though, HS depicts God's actions as direct, active, and personal.[11] We might mention, as illustrations, the use of the *niphʿal* form ונסלח (Lev 19:22; Num 15:25, 26, 28) and the use of the *niphʿal* form and the mediating phrase לפני ה' in Num 10:9–10 (as well as in Lev 19:22; Num 15:25; 31:50, 54). The fact that these linguistic forms surface only in sacrificial contexts leads us to surmise a specific influence of PT's sacrificial terminology. For example, in Lev 19:22, we may isolate the impersonal expressions of atonement effected through the ram of the guilt offering from the generally personal tone of the words of God in the nonsacrificial contexts of the chapter[12] (compare also the speech referring to God in the third person and using the *niphʿal* form ונכרתה in vv. 5–8). It would seem that in the realm of sacrificial law, HS adopts linguistic forms originating in PT, even though it does not accept the general, impersonal conception of God maintained by this school. But, in spite of their affinities to PT terminology, the sacrificial laws of Leviticus 19 diverge from the terminology and conceptual framework of this school; thus, we must consider them an inseparable part of HS's production (see Excursus 3).

Anthropomorphizing God

Unlike PT, which systematically attempts to remove all anthropomorphisms from the name of Yahweh, HS is not at all averse to using anthro-

8. See Lev 17:9, 10; 23:29–30.

9. Exod 12:15, 19; 31:14; Lev 7:25, 27; 17:4, 14; 18:29; 19:8; 20:17–18; 22:3; Num 9:13; 15:30, 31; 19:13, 20.

10. Exod 12:13 (here, too, we find an impersonal punishment description—נגף למשחית—alongside a personal one—בהכתי); Num 1:53; 8:19; 17:11; 18:5; 31:16.

11. In the writings of HS, we find a wide range of actions attributed directly to God. Though we cannot list all of them, we might mention, as an example, the blessings and curses in Leviticus 26, which are all described as the direct actions of God.

12. This was pointed out by B. Schwartz, "A Literary Study of the Slave-girl Pericope—Leviticus 19:20-22," in *Studies in Bible* (Scripta Hierosolymitana 31; Jerusalem, 1985) 253.

pomorphic expressions. Its literary production mentions various bodily parts of God,[13] and attributes to him human actions, states and emotions.[14] The disagreement between the two schools in this matter is clearly reflected in their differing uses of the verb שכן in referring to God: unlike PT, which avoids attributing this verb directly to God[15] (see above, p. 99), HS does apply this word directly to God and employs the forms משכני and משכן ה׳, which clearly associate the place of worship with the residence of God.[16] Moreover, HS does not hesitate to describe the sacrifices as the bread of God, calling them ריח ניחוחי, "my pleasing odor."[17]

In the course of our discussion of PT's sacrificial laws, we claimed that this school intentionally demoted the whole offering from its status in non-Priestly sources, establishing the sin offering as the main atoning sacrifice in its stead. We explained this process as part of PT's aim to extirpate the personalized, anthropomorphic image of atonement achieved through the pleasing odor of the sacrifice; this image was particularly applicable to the whole offering (see above, p. 136). It is interesting to compare the law of the community sin offering of PT (Lev 4:13–21) with the parallel law in HS (Num 15:22–26) in light of this distinction:[18] PT determines that the unintentional sins of the community are atoned for through the bull of the sin offering, whereas HS requires a bull of the

13. Exod 6:6, 8; 7:4, 5; Lev 17:10; 20:3, 5; 26:11, 17, 30; Num 6:25, 26; 14:30, 32:10, 13, 14.

14. Exod 12:12, 13; 20:11; 31:17 (see chapter 2, n. 23); Lev 26:9, 11, 12, 13, 24, 28, 30, 31, 42, 44, 45; Num 14:28; 25:11; 32:10, 13, 14.

15. Exod 25:7; 29:45, 46; Num 5:3; 35:34.

16. Lev 15:31; 17:4; 26:11; Num 16:9; 17:28; 19:13.

17. Lev 21:6, 8, 21, 22; 22:25; 26:31; Num 28:2.

18. On the attribution of Numbers 15 to HS, see above, Excursus 1 and p. 90. Although there is a tradition of interpretation that sees the two laws as referring to different cases—the violation of prohibitive laws in Numbers 4 and a failure to observe positive laws in Numbers 15, this interpretation does not fit the language of the passage in Numbers 16 (see A. Toeg, "A Halakhic Midrash in Num. XV: 22-31" [Hebrew], *Tarbiz* 43 [1974] 3–4). The absence of the word ואשמו from the passage in the book of Numbers does not point to any difference whatsoever in the circumstances of the two laws. Although we generally find this language in the laws of sin and guilt offerings in PT, there is one exceptional case in PT in which this term is absent—Lev 5:15. Thus, it would seem that the absence of the word ואשמו from Numbers 15 is of no great significance—it accords with HS's carelessness in its employment of terminology borrowed from PT. An additional HS deviation from PT's precise terminology is the verse והם הביאו את קרבנם אשה לה׳ in v. 25. Had the verse been formulated by PT, it should have read "והם הקריבו את קרבנם אשה לה׳," as in Lev 3:14. As we mentioned (chapter 3, n. 32), PT avoids using the verbs הבא or נתן when referring to אשה apparently in order to avoid having sacrifices resemble presents given to God in any way. HS uses common PT phrases like הקטר . . . אשה (Num 18:19); הקרב . . . אשה (Lev 23:18; Num 15:9, 13; 28:2); הבא . . . אשה (Exod 29:41; Num 15:3, 14). But it also uses the verbs נתן and הבא in combination with אשה (Lev 22:22; Num 15:25). HS even calls certain sacrifices מתנותיכם אשר תתנו לה׳ . . . (Lev 23:38; for the evidence of the HS origin of this verse, see Excursus 2)!

herd as a whole offering and a he-goat as a sin offering. Verses 24 and 25 in Numbers 15 mention, exceptionally, the whole offering before the sin offering.[19] It seems that HS attempted to combine the popular sacrificial tradition, centered on the appeasement of God through the pleasing odor of the whole offering, with the Priestly practice of atonement through sprinkling with the blood of the sin offering.[20] Precedence is given to the popular custom: whereas the whole offering is mentioned first, and the more important victim—the bull—is assigned to it, for the later-mentioned sin offering, a he-goat may suffice. The editors emphasize the different natures of the two processes of atonement through selective use of language: for the whole offering they employ the phrases לריח ניחח לה' and אשה לה', which have personalized, anthropomorphic overtones; for sin offerings the impersonal, indirect formula לפני ה' is used (see above, p. 126).

God and Israel— The Unique Covenant

The attribution of anthropomorphic expressions and imagery to the name of Yahweh in HS reflects its disagreement with PT on the nature of the divine revelation symbolized by this name and on the nature of the relationship between God and his people. We witnessed in PT a sharp distinction between God's relationship with humanity in the Genesis period and in the period of Moses. The Genesis period, when God revealed himself through the name אלהים, is characterized by the un-

19. This oddity was already noted by the sages and has preoccupied many scholars: see A. Toeg, "Halakhic Midrash," 5–6; A. F. Rainey, "The Order of Sacrifices in Old Testament Ritual Texts," *Biblica* 51 (1970) 491, 494; J. Milgrom, "The Two Pericopes on the Purification Offering," in *The Word of the Lord Shall Go Forth* (Festschrift D. N. Freedman; Winona Lake, IN, 1983) 212–13. The solution proposed by Toeg (pp. 8–9) and subsequently M. Fishbane (*Biblical Interpretation in Ancient Israel* [Oxford, 1985] 223–24), is that Num 15:24 is a midrashic interpolation. This solution, though very ingenious, does not, in my opinion, fit the textual situation (see I. Knohl, "The Sin-offerings Law in the 'Holiness School,'" in *Priesthood and Cult in Ancient Israel* [ed. G. A. Anderson and S. M. Olyan; JSOTSup 12; Sheffield, 1991] 194–95).

20. The relation between the bullock of the whole offering in Num 15:24 and the popular custom documented in non-Priestly sources was identified by R. Rendtorff (*Studien zur Geschichte des Opfers im Alten Israel* [WMANT 24; Neukirchen, 1967] 22–23, 81–83) and Milgrom ("Two Pericopes," 213-14). The explanation they offered was that the earlier version of the law in Numbers 15 included an instruction to sacrifice a bullock as a whole offering, while the injunction to offer up a goat as a sin offering was added later, to make the text agree with Priestly law. I disagree. The fluent and uniform style of the passage and the fine linguistic distinctions in the descriptions of the various sacrifices witness, in my opinion, to a single literary unit that is influenced by both popular and Priestly cultic traditions and seeks to harmonize them.

mediated relationship between God and man, as reflected through the personal, anthropomorphic description of God. The period of Moses, in which the name of Yahweh is used exclusively, is characterized by distance and lack of direct contact between God and the community of Israel. God's apartness and loftiness are expressed through the impersonal and nonanthropomorphic language (see above, p. 132).

We saw earlier that, while HS accepts, in principle, PT's schema of the revelation of the names of God, it does not completely isolate the name אלהים from the name of Yahweh and often combines them in various linguistic forms. Thus, HS expresses its opposition to the total disjunction of the two modes of divine revelation, as described in PT. Unlike PT, HS is not of the opinion that the revelation of the name of Yahweh created an entirely new sphere of faith. The God who reveals himself to Moses and speaks directly to the people retains many of the dimensions of the God of Genesis, who is near to his creation and supervises his creatures personally. The very use of the common HS phrase ה' אלהיכם expresses the relation of intimacy between God and Israel. This same closeness is apparent in God's direct address to his people. The direct contact and feeling of intimacy are also expressed in the personal and anthropomorphic descriptions of God common throughout HS. It is this closeness which makes possible the demand that the people should strive to resemble God: "You shall be holy, for I, the Lord your God, am holy" (Lev 19:1).[21]

As we mentioned, the term ברית is limited in PT to the Genesis period. In establishing the ברית, God commits himself to rewarding his creatures if they observe the moral commandments. The revelation of the name of Yahweh to Moses signals the replacement of the covenant (ברית) by the pact (עדות) in the realm of Israelite faith. According to PT, the relationship between God and Israel is no longer defined through providence and recompense, nor is it related to the observance of moral laws and the practice of justice. The center of the religious life is henceforth to be the divine command—the עדות—demanding the worship of God without any expectation of reward—a worship completely detached from basic needs or the shaping of the social order. The universal moral covenant—the ברית—remains in force in the realm of relations between a man and his fellow man; it determines the Israelite social order as well.

HS rejects this conception. It maintains that a special covenant (ברית) exists between God and Israel, based on a unique relation of reciprocity.[22] At the end of the Holiness Code, which is edited as a covenant book,

21. On anthropomorphism as a necessary prerequisite for the demand to imitate God, see B. Uffenheimer, "Utopia and Reality in Biblical Thought," *Immanuel* 9 (1979) 5–15.

22. See Lev 26:9, 15, 44, 45; the difference between PT's and HS's relation to the ברית was noted by N. Lohfink ("Die Abänderung der Theologie des Priestlichen Geschichtswerks im Segen des Heiligkeitsgesetzes," in *Wort und Geschichte* [Festschrift W. Zimmerli and K. Elliger; Neukirchen, 1973] 134–35); and W. Zimmerli ("'Heiligkeit' nach dem sogenannten

we find a list of rewards and blessings the people will earn if they observe God's commandments (Lev 26:3–13), along with severe punishments they will incur if they should violate the covenant and fail to observe all the commandments (Lev 26:14–45). Lev 18:5 even applies the covenant on the level of the individual: if one observes the laws of God, one will earn life.

The expectation of divine blessing and reward in return for the observance of the commandments comes to the fore even in the minor details of ritual in HS's law. Unlike PT, which attempted to shape a ritual system completely detached from daily needs and from the expectation of God's salvation, HS includes in the ritual framework the farmer's wish for abundant rain and crops as well as the people's request for victory in times of war. The firstfruits are given to God "that its yield to you may be increased" (Lev 19:25). The same reason is given for the waving of the sheaf and the practice of taking the four species (see above, pp. 25, 39, 42, and n. 99). The expectation of God's blessing and salvation is expressed through the series of horn blasts sounded on the first day of the seventh month, in times of war, and upon offering the additional sacrifices (above, p. 35; chapter 3, n. 60).

HS's cultic practices also express thanks for the blessings and salvation granted by God to Israel. The waving of the two loaves (chapter 1, n. 47) and the taking of the four species (chapter 1, n. 89) both express thanks for the produce of the fields; the national and historical memory of redemption and salvation is concretely expressed through the ceremonies of Passover, the feast of Unleavened Bread and the feast of Booths (above, pp. 22, 39, 45). In HS's view, Yahweh, the God of Israel, reveals himself through his intervention in Israel's national history, and the memory of his deeds is to be preserved for future generations, so that the people may know their God. This idea is frequently repeated in HS: "that you may recount in the hearing of your sons and of your sons' sons how I made a mockery of the Egyptians and how I displayed My signs among them—in

---

Heiligkeitsgesetz," *VT* 30 [1980] 510), as I stated earlier (chapter 3, n. 80), I cannot accept Zimmerli's explanation for PT's avoidance of any mention of the Sinai ברית. HS also mentions the ברית of the forefathers, which remains in force for their descendants (Exod 6:4–5; Lev 26:42). The concept of ברית is linked to the Sabbath, which, in this school, is understood as a sign of the "covenant for all time" (ברית עולם) between God and Israel (Exod 31:16–17). The arranging of the shewbread on the Sabbath is also ordained as a "covenant for all time" (ברית·עולם) (Lev 24:8); the gifts of sacred things were given to Aaron and his descendants as a ברית מלח עולם (Num 18:19) and God grants Phinehas and his descendants "my pact of friendship . . . a pact of priesthood for all time" (Num 25:12–13). We should mention, though, that the concept of ברית does not play a critical role in HS's thinking, unlike in the book of Deuteronomy. Deuteronomy places ברית at the center of the relation between God and his people, whereas HS grants greater importance to the relation of reciprocal holiness, as we will explain in detail later.

order that you may know that I am the Lord" (Exod 10:2); "Moses said, 'This is what the Lord has commanded: Let one omer of it be kept throughout the ages, in order that they may see the bread that I fed you in the wilderness when I brought you out of the land of Egypt'" (Exod 16:32); "in order that future generations may know that I made the Israelite people live in booths when I brought them out of the land of Egypt, I the Lord your God" (Lev 23:43).

Morality and the Cult

Just as HS opposed PT's complete isolation of the cult from elementary human needs, so too it objected to PT's total disjunction of the cultic system, centered on the name of Yahweh, from the moral commands that regulate social order. These commands, according to PT, are grounded in the Genesis sphere in which the name אלהים is used. In HS's doctrine, Yahweh, the God of Israel (אלהי ישראל), ordained on Mount Sinai the observance of both the ritual laws and those governing moral behavior. The moral element in HS's cult is especially remarkable in Leviticus 19, which combines social-moral commands with cultic instructions. Another example of this blending is Lev 24:15–22, which, after determining the punishment for the blasphemer, immediately proceeds to detail punishment for sins committed by a man against his fellow man.[23] The passage concludes with the words אני ה׳ אלהיכם, a formula commonly used to support the laws in Leviticus 19: ה׳ אלהי ישראל—Yahweh, the God of Israel, in whose name the conceptions of the period of the patriarchs and the period of Moses are combined, ordains both the practice of the cultic laws and the observance of moral behavior and justice.

As we remember, PT's conception of the total separation of the cult from morality is clearly expressed in its law of guilt offerings in Lev 5:20–26 (above, p. 139). This law states that when a moral crime is accompanied by a false oath, a sacrifice is required. The Scriptures seem to indicate that had no oath been sworn, the priests would have considered the matter to be outside their domain. In HS, on the other hand, we find warnings concerning most of the sins mentioned in Lev 5:21–22, but with one crucial difference. Unlike PT, which discusses only sins combining

23. Lately, R. Westbrook suggested that there was a practical legal tie between the various ordinances in this chapter ("Biblical and Cuneiform Law Codes," *RB* 92 [1985] 264); even so, there is an ideological meaning conveyed by the inclusion of all these commands in a single passage. This passage is redacted in chiastic form: vv. 15–16a is parallel to 23; 16b to 22; 17 to 21b; 18 to 21a; 19 to 20b. The alien resident (גר) is mentioned as an equal person with respect to the cultic (v. 16) and moral sins (v. 22), thus combining the cultic and the moral parts of this pericope (see G. Wenham, *The Book of Leviticus* [NICOT; Grand Rapids, 1979] 312).

moral injustice with a false oath, HS warns against commission of moral sins, while consecrating a separate prohibition to the swearing of false oaths (Lev 19:11–12, 13a). At the conclusion of the series of admonitions, we find the formula אני ה׳. Yahweh himself warns against both the breach of social justice and the swearing of false oaths; both transgressions are offenses against the God who ordained them.[24]

The fusing of the realms of cult and morality, an innovation of the Holiness School, made modification of PT's law of guilt offerings (Lev 5:20–26) necessary. Num 5:5–8 is, in my opinion, the revised version of that law. Although this passage is usually explained as a supplement to the law of Leviticus 5, adding the law applying to theft from someone who has no heirs,[25] I find this explanation difficult: why, then, did the codifier add the law in another passage, when he could have appended it directly to Leviticus 5![26] I believe that the key to understanding this passage, its location in the text, and its innovation lies in the recognition of its HS origin, as we already determined through linguistic criteria (above, p. 86). Once we recognize that the two versions of the law were composed by two different schools who disagree as to the relation between morality and the cult, we may identify the essential difference between the version in Leviticus and the text in Numbers.

Let us first compare the description of the sinner in the two passages. The Leviticus passage opens with the general category "when a person sins and commits a trespass against the Lord," followed by a listing of moral crimes, and ending with the false oath sworn as a result—"if he swears falsely regarding any one of the various things that one may do and sin thereby." It is the false oath accompanying the moral transgression that makes the act a breach (מעל) against God. In the parallel in Numbers 5, the description of the sin is shorter—"when a man or woman commits any wrong toward a fellow man, thus breaking faith with the Lord." As Nahmanides wrote in his commentary on the verse (see chapter

24. HS views the violation of various commandments ביד רמה, "with upraised hand," as a profanation of the name of God (see below, nn. 45–46). Thus, it may be that the concluding formula "profaning the name of your God" in Lev 19:12 applies to all of the sins listed in 19:11, 12, and not just to the false oath in v. 12. See Noth's commentary (ad loc.).

25. We already find this in the homily at the beginning of *Sifre Numbers,* Piska 2, ed. Horowitz, pp. 4–5.

26. Kellermann claims that the text of Leviticus was already finalized and that nothing could be added to it (*Priesterschrift,* 68). This claim, however, is not supported by criticism. We find recensional interpolations, usually at the margins of the priestly *toroth* of Leviticus (see Excursus 1; chapter 2, n. 142 and chapter 5, n. 5). J. Licht's attribution ("Some Consideration Concerning the Law of Restitution, Num. V:5-8," *Te*ʿ*uda* 2 [1982] 201) of this to the difficulties in distributing the text of the supplement to the original law is unconvincing. One might inquire why, if this were true, the editors did not hesitate in adding to the law in other cases. Furthermore, Licht's assumption that the PT scrolls were scattered among the priests of different temples before the editing of the Pentateuch, is doubtful.

2, n. 82), the phrase מכל חטאת האדם, "any wrong toward a fellow man," is based on the language in Leviticus, מכל אשר יעשה האדם לחטא בהנה. אשר יעשה האדם לחטא בהנה, "any one of the various things that one may do and sin thereby," includes the various kinds of monetary injury mentioned at the beginning of the text of that law: lying, embezzlement, robbery, and fraud. The phrase מכל חטאת האדם, which hints at the language of the verse in Leviticus, also refers to such deeds. But it seems that the phrase conveys an additional overtone: its relation to Leviticus 5 indicates that the חטאת האדם are the same sins that Leviticus 5 refers to by אשר יעשה האדם. But the elimination of the verb יעשה seems to hint at the meaning of "all sins committed against man." The codifier deliberately employed this ambiguous phrasing in order to emphasize that the text refers to sins committed by a man against his fellow man.[27]

As we mentioned, the essential difference in the definition of the sin in the two versions is that in the law in Leviticus the false oath is the key element that transforms the monetary injury into a breach against God, thus necessitating a guilt offering. In the law in Numbers, on the other hand, the false oath is not mentioned at all![28] I find difficult the argument that the codifier relied on the version in Leviticus and used the general formula למעל מעל בה' to refer to the false oath.[29] The syntactical form of Num 5:6 indicates that the legislator was of the opinion that the commission of "any wrong toward a fellow man" (מכל חטאת האדם) is considered "breaking faith with the Lord" (מעל בה').[30] Unlike PT, which distinguishes between cultic and moral sins and sees a breaking of faith with God (מעל בה') only in cultic trespasses that require atonement in the Temple, the HS legislator believes that a transgression against morality and social justice is also a breaking of faith with God (מעל בה'), even if no false oath accompanies it.

The essential difference between the law of guilt offerings of PT and

27. As the Midrash *Numbers Rabbah* 8:5 says, "'Of all the sins of man'—that are between man and his fellow man"; as the RaDaL explains "the Midrash understood 'the sin of man' as the sins committed by man against man."

28. As we mentioned, B. S. Jackson claims that the false oath in Leviticus 5 refers only to the denial of the finding of the lost object, whereas in other cases mentioned in this law, the transgressor is required to bring a guilt offering even if he has not sworn a false oath (*Theft in Early Jewish Law* [Oxford, 1972] 245–46; see chapter 3, n. 57). He cites as evidence the law in Numbers 5, in which no false oath is mentioned. We are of the opinion that an oath accompanies each of the cases of the law and that the editors of Numbers 5 intentionally omitted the oath in accordance with their differing ideology.

29. See J. Milgrom, *Cult and Conscience* (Leiden, 1976) nn. 300, 395; cf. Licht, "Law of Restitution," 199.

30. In their commentaries (ad loc.), G. B. Gray and L. Elliott-Binns explained the verse in the same spirit but failed to recognize the innovation in this law, as compared to the parallel in Leviticus. See further I. Knohl, "Between Cult and Morality," *S'vara* 2,2 (1991) 33 n. 16.

the law of guilt offerings of robbery in HS is evident in the divergent meanings of the terms used in the laws as well as the form of the entire law. The terms אשם, מעל, and אשמה in Leviticus 5 belong to the religious domain: מעל signifies the offense against God committed by swearing a false oath; אשמה is the feeling of the sinner toward God as a result of this offense; אשם is the compensatory sacrifice, which is brought before the Lord so that the priest may atone for him and remove his guilt. In Numbers 5, these terms are given a clear moral-judicial content: the act of deceit is called "a breaking of faith with God" (מעל בה');[31] the focus of the guilt and the requirement of compensation are toward "him whom he has wronged" (לאשר אשם לו) (Num 5:7b), whereas the אשם refers not to the sacrifice but to the monetary compensation of the wronged man![32]

We witness here an important, systematic effort to integrate the laws of morality and social justice into the religious-cultic corpus. As a result of this process, the damage to a fellow man's property is considered a מעילה, a violation of sacred things. God becomes a party in the monetary claims and receives an אשם, through the monies of compensation, in the event that the victim of theft dies without leaving heirs (Num 5:8). The sacrifice of "the ram of expiation with which expiation is made on his behalf," which occupied the central position in PT's law in Leviticus, is thus shunted to the margins of the law of HS here.[33]

In the revised version of the guilt offering of theft, HS presents its innovative doctrine, that moral sins are a direct offense against God; this passage is reinforced by the express prohibitions against those acts, made in God's own name, in Leviticus 19, and their presentation as a profanation of the name of God. The deliberate linguistic affinities to the PT law of guilt offerings in Leviticus 5, on the one hand, and the infusion of

31. Although HS usually prefers the word חלל (see chapter 2, n. 164), here it used the expression למעל מעל בה', apparently in order to preserve the linguistic ties to Leviticus 5 (as we find also in the expression מכל חטאת האדם).

32. See chapter 2, n. 80. On the differing uses of the word אשם, see also A. Bertholet, *Leviticus* (HKAT; Tübingen, 1901); and Holzinger, *Numeri* (Tübingen-Leipzig, 1903) on Numbers 5. Although we do find the words אשם and השב אשם referring to monetary compensation (1 Sam 6:3, 4, 8, 17; see chapter 2, n. 81; cf. 2 Kgs 12:17), those passages refer to the guilt offering returned to God s compensation for the offense against him. Only in Numbers 5 do we find השב אשם referring to compensation paid to an injured person.

33. Jackson claims that the words מלבד איל הכפרים are a later addition (*Theft,* 173; see Excursus 2, n. 4; this was already suggested by A. Dillmann in his commentary [ad loc.]). I am of the opinion that, although the word מלבד is often an indicator of recensional addition and only appears in later biblical strata (see Excursus 2), this is not the case here. The entire law belongs to the later strata of the Pentateuch, and the use of מלבד alone is insufficient evidence for considering the words a later addition. The peripheral position of the sacrifice in the text of the law is evidence not of its secondary nature but of its marginality for the legislator.

new meaning into the old terms, on the other, express the innovative nature of HS's conception.[34] An additional innovation is the requirement that the thief confess his sin (Num 5:7).[35]

The attempt to integrate social-moral justice into the religious framework is also evident in HS's treatment of murderers; here, too, the profound difference between this school and PT is remarkable. In PT, the prohibition of murder appears in the Genesis period; after the flood, God addresses Noah and his sons, warning them: "Whoever sheds the blood of man, by man shall his blood be shed; for in his image did God make man" (Gen 9:6). The God of Genesis, who supervises the world order and the moral order is portrayed as claiming the victim's blood from his murderer: "of man, too, will I require a reckoning for human life, of every man for that of his fellow man!" (Gen 9:5). When, after the revelation of the name of Yahweh, God ordains his cultic laws on Mount Sinai and in the Tent of Meeting, the prohibition against murder is not mentioned, since, according to PT's view, the cultic sphere is completely detached from justice and social morality. HS, on the other hand, which recognizes no separation between the religious realm and the social-moral one, juxtaposes the law of the murderer to that of the blasphemer (Lev 24:16–17). As in the law of the sin offering for theft, here too, the ideological principle is expressed through legislation. But, whereas the PT law of guilt offerings could serve as the basis for HS in the case of monetary damages and could be rewritten in a way that would integrate social justice into the cultic system, here, where there was no PT precedent for cultic-Temple treatment of murder, a more radical procedure was required. The solution was found through the creation of a framework completely exterior to the Temple, functioning according to the principles of the Priestly cult. This framework is outlined in the HS passage of the cities of refuge (Num 35:9–34). The entire country is described as the sacred territory in which God dwells, and, as such, may not be defiled (v. 34). Just as the priests atone for the impurity of the Temple through the sprinkling of blood, so too may the land be atoned for from the impurity imparted to it by the murder victim's blood (v. 33). The return of the involuntary murderer to his town after the death of the high priest (v. 28) also has a parallel in the acts of atonement in the Temple: just as the high priest

34. Milgrom claims that, had the language of Num 5:6 been based on the texts of Leviticus 5, we should expect greater resemblance in terminology between the two sources (*Cult,* n. 388). The change in terminology—from אשם, as the name for the sacrifice in Leviticus to איל הכפרים in Numbers—is evidence, according to him, for the independence of the two laws. In my opinion, however, the change in terminology results from HS's ideology, which presents moral injustice as ritual guilt.

35. On the importance of confession in its moral and ritual context, see Milgrom, *Cult,* 106–28.

bore the sins of the people of Israel and atoned for them during his lifetime (see Lev 10:17; above, pp. 152–55), so too his death atones for the unintentional murder.[36]

Inclusive Sacredness

HS's removal of the barrier between morality and the cult is clearly expressed in the character and the extent of holiness. As we discussed earlier, in PT holiness is concentrated in ritual and applies primarily to the cultic enclosure. Although nonpriests may sanctify themselves through a vow of naziritism, this holiness vanishes at the end of the period of consecration. Only the priests, Aaron and his descendants, are sanctified for eternity at the time that they are initiated to serve in the Tabernacle (see above, p. 160).

HS expands the realm of holiness. In its view, the concept of holiness also encompasses the realm of social justice.[37] Holiness thus includes all areas of life and applies to the entire community of Israel and the land they inhabit. A striking expression of this concept is found in the Holiness Code, in Leviticus 19. The chapter opens with the address to the entire community of Israel: "You shall be holy, for I, the Lord your God am holy." This verse serves as the category that includes a large variety of detailed ordinances, covering a wide range of human activities, in the social realm as well as in the cultic. It would appear that through the observance of the entire range of these commandments, the Israelites may draw near to God and attain higher levels of holiness. For HS, there exists an intimate connection between the inclusion of justice and morality in the realm of holiness and the summons to the entire community of Israel to lead sanctified lives. When basic moral commandments like the honoring of one's parents and the prohibition of theft and deceit are included under the general ordinance of "you shall be holy," one may clearly not

36. See M. Greenberg, "The Biblical Conception of Asylum," *JBL* 78 (1959) 129–30; idem, "Cities of Refuge," *EM* 6:386.

37. The innovative nature of HS, as compared to the original Priestly conception, was documented by W. Eichrodt (*Theology of the Old Testament* [trans. J. Baker; London, 1961] 1:277–78). Compare Zimmerli, "Heiligkeit," 504–7. As H. Ringgren correctly remarked, the infusing of the concept of holiness with moral content is an uncommon phenomenon in biblical thought (*The Prophetical Conception of Holiness* [Uppsala, 1948] 23). For a discussion of this phenomenon in the history of religion, see N. Söderblom, "Holiness: General and Primitive," *ERE* 6:739-41; R. Otto, *The Idea of the Holy* (trans. J. W. Harvey; Oxford, 1958) 111–15; J. P. Reeder, "The Relation of the Moral and the Numinous in Otto's Notion of the Holy," in *Religion and Morality* (ed. G. Ukta and J. P. Reeder; New York, 1973) 255–92).

restrict holiness to the Temple and the priests.[38] The essence of holiness, according to Leviticus 19, is the perfection attained through the fulfillment of the commandments of God in all walks of life.

The view of the nation of Israel as a community called to the holy life finds clear expression in the laws concerning relations between Israel and the nations. Israel is demanded to separate itself from the surrounding nations and their ways: "You shall not follow the practices of the nation that I am driving out before you. . . . You shall be holy to Me, for I, the Lord am holy, and I have set you apart from other peoples to be mine" (Lev 20:23a, 26). We find prohibitions against the customs of the nations and their cult, directly related to the general commands calling for the sanctification incumbent upon Israel: in Leviticus 19, the prohibitions against turning to idols, divination, soothsaying, and inquiring of ghosts or familiar spirits are all enumerated under the category of "You shall be holy."[39] In Lev 20:7 we find the decree "you shall sanctify yourselves and be holy" immediately following the prohibitions against Molech worship and turning to ghosts and familiar spirits, and directly preceding the laws of incest and the prohibitions against bestiality. The call to sanctification that concludes the passage (v. 26) applies to the entire corpus of prohibitions listed in the chapter and not just to the laws of forbidden foods which immediately precede it.[40]

38. Note that it is possible to extend holiness to the entire Israelite community without infusing holiness with moral content. This conception may be seen in non-Priestly legal compilations of the Pentateuch: the Book of the Covenant commands Israel to be "men holy to Me" and to avoid eating carcasses (Exod 22:30); Deuteronomy calls Israel a "consecrated people," in its justification of the prohibitions against intermarriage with the nations of the land and as part of the obligation to completely destroy idolatrous cultic institutions (7:1–6) and the interdictions against gashing oneself, shaving the front of one's head, and abominable foods (14:1–21). The content of those injunctions indicates that the nature of holiness referred to there is purely ritual-cultic (J. Milgrom, "The Alleged 'Demythologization and Secularization' in Deuteronomy," *IEJ* 23 [1973] 158 already demonstrated this in the case of Deuteronomy).

Thus, in the legal compilations of the Pentateuch there are three different views: in PT holiness is ritual and restricted to the Temple and the priesthood. Although all Israelites are commanded to be ritually pure, their observance of purity does not endow them with the qualities of holiness. Non-Priestly sources extend holiness to all Israelites, but the practical expression of this holiness is limited to the ritual-cultic sphere (Exod 19:6; Deut 26:19; 28:9 lack a specific legal context, so that it is difficult to understand the nature of the holiness mentioned there). HS disagrees with both the non-Priestly sources and PT, and extends holiness of cultic and moral content to the entire Israelite community.

39. On the Bible's view of these customs as Gentile, see 2 Kgs 17:9–17; 21:2, 6; Isa 2:6.

40. Thus, we cannot accept M. Weinfeld's distinction between "the holiness of D, which expresses mainly national separateness and which demands isolation from the nations and their customs (and, as such, is mentioned in referring to separation from idolatry) (Deut 7:6) and the holiness of the Priestly Book, which extends only to the ritual sphere (Lev 11:43; 20:26) and is indifferent to the prohibitions against foreign worship and customs of the nations" (Lev 26:1; 18:1–5) ("The Change in the Conception of Religion in Deutero-

The struggle against corruption through the practices and cult of the nations holds a central place in PT's oeuvre. We find repeated warnings, backed by the punishment of "cutting off," against Molech worship, acts of sorcery, summoning of ghosts or familiar spirits, and soothsaying, as well as against idol worship and abominable sexual relations.[41] The Scriptures emphasize that these acts defile the sinners, the entire people, the land and the Sanctuary.[42] We should point out, in this context, that the essential distinction between the Israelite sphere of holiness and the Gentile-idolatrous sphere of impurity is not by any means a racial one. HS deals at length with the status of the alien, granting him equal cultic and judicial status with citizens (see chapter 2, n. 111). Leviticus 19, the chapter that most exhaustively forms the image of the community of Israel as a holy congregation, includes the instruction "the stranger that resides with you shall be to you as one of your citizens; you shall love him as yourself, for you were strangers in the land of Egypt: I the Lord am your God" (v. 34). The admonition to distance oneself from the abominations of the nations emphasizes the subjection of the stranger to these commands (Lev 18:26; 20:2). In other words, the stranger is a member with equal rights and obligations in the Israelite holy community, which includes all residents of the land who practice holiness and purity.

In HS, holiness is depicted not only as a basic fact and motivating force but also as the final aim of all the commandments. All the ordinances in Leviticus 19 appear under the category "You shall be holy, for I am holy"; similarly, chap. 22 closes with the words "You shall faithfully observe my commandments: I am the Lord. You shall not profane My holy name, that I may be sanctified in the midst of the Israelite people—I the Lord who sanctify you" (vv. 31–32). From these verses and similar ones in HS (Exod 31:13; Lev 11:44, 45; 20:7–8, 26; Num 15:40), we may draw the following picture: Yahweh, who is a holy God, has set Israel apart to be his. This act of separation creates a special relationship between God and his people, which is expressed through the commandments God gave to Israel, which serve to sanctify Israel. There is no one-time act in which God

nomy," *Tarbiz* 31 [1961] 1–8). It seems that, in this respect, there is no difference between D and HS, whose laws are included by Weinfeld under the inclusive term "Priestly Book." We may, however, distinguish between the position of HS and D, on the one hand, and the conception of PT, on the other. PT limits the realm of holiness to the Temple and the priesthood. Thus, it clearly does not apply this concept to relations between Israel and the nations, an issue barely discussed by this school. By contrast, HS and D, who extend holiness to the entire Israelite community, view separation from the nations and their cult as an obligation deriving from the holiness of the Israelite people.

41. On worship of Molech, see Lev 18:21; 20:1–5; on divination and soothsaying, turning to ghosts and inquiring of familiar spirits, see Lev 19:26, 31; 20:6, 27; on idols, see Lev 19:4; 25:1; Num 33:52; on incest, see Num 18:6–20, 22, 23; 20:10–21.

42. For warnings on impurity linked to the abominations and laws of the Gentiles, see Lev 18:24–30; 19:31; 20:3.

endows Israel with permanent holiness; there is, rather, a constant process of sanctification, which is realized through God's activities in the Temple and through the fulfillment of the commandments.[43] The commandments not only endow Israel with holiness but also increase the holiness of God: "that I may be sanctified in the midst of the Israelite people"! Just as the concept of holiness is far broader and more inclusive than in PT, so too are the terms signifying defilement of that holiness:

43. The justification given by HS for various ordinances is אני ה' מקדשכם, "I am the Lord who consecrates you" (Exod 31:13; Lev 20:7–8; 21:8; 22:31–32). This formula conveys the message that the sanctity bestowed by God upon Israel is a basic fact and first principle behind the observance of the commandments and the sanctification through them (cf. Zimmerli, "Heiligkeit," 305). I find difficult to accept the position of those scholars who insist on a sharp distinction between the position of D, in which the holiness of the Israelite is viewed as an unconditional inherent quality deriving from divine election, and the position of HS, which, in their opinion, views the holiness of the community not as a given condition but as a conditional goal dependent on the observance of the commandments (see Weinfeld, "Change in Conception," 8; idem, *Deuteronomy,* 226-28; "Demythologization," 232; but see also his reservations in "Currents," 132; see also Fishbane, *Interpretation,* 122 n. 47). It seems to me that the positions of the two schools are, as a whole, quite close: according to both of them, God sanctified Israel and chose them from among the nations to be his (D's formulation) or separated them from the nations to be his (HS's formation). (See Deut 7:6; 14:2, 26:18–19 // Lev 20:24–26). Both schools present very similar admonitions which derive from this holiness. In addition to the warnings against idolatry, we find the following prohibitions in both schools: forbidden foods (Deut 14:13–19 // Lev 11:41–45; 20:25–26); gashing oneself and shaving the front of one's head because of the dead in D (Deut 14:1) // rounding off the side-growth of one's head and making gashes in the flesh in HS (Lev 19:27–28; compare 21:5–6). Just as HS makes the continued holiness of Israel dependent on the observance of the commandments, so too D states: "The Lord will establish you as his holy people, as he swore to you, if you keep the commandments of the Lord your God and walk in his ways" (Deut 28:9). Milgrom already noted that holiness in D is conditional on observance of the commandments ("Profane Slaughter and a Formulaic Key to the Composition of Deuteronomy," *HUCA* 47 [1976] 5).

The difference in the approaches of D and HS is that, for D, the holiness of Israel is the basis and the reason for the prohibitions: "For you are a people consecrated to the Lord your God" (Deut 7:2–6; 14:1–2, 20), whereas in HS, the prohibitions are presented as a means to holiness (the difference between the two formulations is well documented in Weinfeld, *Deuteronomy,* 228; "Demythologization," 232; but, as discussed in n. 40 above, I believe that the conclusions that Weinfield derives from this are too strong). Furthermore, HS avoids stating outright that Israelites are holy, nor does it employ the verb בחר to designate their separation from the nations (see Weinfeld, *Deuteronomy,* 228; "Currents," 20). By contrast, D employs the present tense: "For you are a people consecrated to the Lord your God. . . . The Lord chose you" (Deut 7:6; 14:2). It would seem that HS intentionally avoids such formulations in order to preserve the difference between the holiness of the priests and the holiness of all Israelites (see below, pp. 183–92). D does not mention holiness in relation to the כהנים הלוים; apparently, this distinction is of no interest to its authors. This explains the difference between D and HS with respect to the prohibition against eating of animal carcasses: whereas in D, the prohibition applies to all Israelites, because of their holiness (Deut 14:21), in HS it applies only to the priests, who are especially holy (compare Lev 22:8–9 with 17:15). This distinction between D and HS was noted by Weinfeld, *Deuteronomy,* 226–28; "Change in Conception," 8).

the verbs חלל and even מעל, when they make their infrequent appearance in HS, are far richer in their range of reference in content than the word מעל in PT. In PT, the term מעל בה׳ refers to defilement of sacred things or false oaths;[44] in HS, the violation of any one of God's commandments is considered a defilement of his name.[45] The range of meanings conveyed by the verb מעל is also greater than in PT. In Num 5:6, מעל refers to social-moral injustice (see above, n. 3); in Num 31:16, it refers to the sin of idol worship, whereas in Deut 32:51 it refers to refraining from consecrating the name of God. Even a general violation of the commandments is called מעל, as it contains an element of violation of the ברית (see Lev 26:15, 40).[46]

The basis for these conceptions is summed up in the phrase that accompanies HS's laws and serves as their rationale—אני ה׳, "I am the Lord." Clearly, every violation of the law is a breaking of faith (מעל) with God and an insult to the name of the one who empowers the law. A succinct expression of this view appears at the conclusion of HS's law of sin offerings in Numbers 15: "But the person, be he citizen or stranger, who acts defiantly reviles the Lord; that person shall be cut off from among the people. Because he has spurned the word of the Lord and violated his commandment" (Num 15:30–31a).[47] Thus, we may comprehend the severity of the punishment—"cutting off"—for any transgression committed ביד רמה ("with upraised hand"), any sin committed intentionally, where no mitigating circumstances are present (see above, n. 46).

HS's expansion of the sacred realm is evident in the purity laws. Whereas in PT, the *zab* (someone having a seminal emission) or one defiled by corpse impurity may remain within the camp and only the

44. See Milgrom, *Cult,* 16ff.

45. The mention of the profanation of the name of God is found alongside certain prohibitions: the worship of Molech (Lev 18:21; 20:3); false oaths (Lev 19:12; see above, n. 24); special prohibitions applying to the priests (Lev 21:6); and the prohibition against eating sacred things while impure (Lev 22:2). Furthermore, we find the general warning that the violation of the commandments leads to the profanation of the name of God (Lev 22:31–32). This final group of verses form the conclusion of the group of commandments in Lev 19:1–22:31, as evidenced by the *inclusio* in Lev 22:26–30 (see above, p. 118).

46. This extension explains why HS prescribes a guilt offering even in cases not covered by the categories of PT. In addition to the cases of Num 5:5–8, we should mention the guilt offering in Lev 19:20–22. This sacrifice is brought because, in HS's view, every intentional sin is a trespass (מעל) against God, which may require a guilt offering (compare Milgrom, *Cult,* 35–36; Schwartz, "Slave-girl," 252 n. 49). In Num 15:30–31, HS provides a more extreme formulation, requiring the punishment of "cutting off" for sins committed "with upraised hand." But where there are mitigating circumstances, like in the case of a thief who regrets his deeds and confesses his sins (Num 5:6–7), or in the case of one who had intercourse with a betrothed slave girl (Lev 19:20–22), a guilt offering suffices (on the mitigating circumstances in this case, see Milgrom, *Cult,* 130–34; Schwartz, "Slave-girl," 248).

47. On the relation of Num 15:30–31 to the conception expressed in Numbers 19, see Toeg, "Halakhic Midrash," 18.

leper is sent out, in the law formulated by HS in Num 5:1–4, the *zab* and those impure with corpse impurity are sent out (above, p. 86). The reason for this regulation is "so that they do not defile the camp of those in whose midst I dwell." Here we arrive at the source of the disagreement between the two schools. According to PT, holiness, which results from God's presence, is restricted to the cultic enclosure. True, the people's impurity does lead, according to PT, to the defilement of the Tabernacle; therefore, Israelites must avoid impurity as far as possible and are even demanded to purify themselves of impurities that adhere to them and atone for them by bringing sacrifice (see above, chapter 3, n. 126). But the camp of Israel is of itself devoid of holiness. Thus, even severely impure persons such as the *zab* and those impure with corpse impurity may remain inside; only the leper is removed.

HS, on the other hand, believes that the holiness of God expands beyond the Sanctuary to encompass the settlements of the entire congregation of Israel, in whose midst God dwells.[48] Thus, a high level of purity must be maintained in the camp and the severely impure cannot remain inside it. Num 5:1–4 contains a reformulation of the purity laws, which reflects the widely differing ideology of HS on the subject of the domain of holiness.[49] (This phenomenon is similar to that found in the verses that immediately follow it, Num 5:5–8, in which the law of the sin offerings of theft was formulated to reflect HS's innovation: the erasure of the dividing lines between cult and morality.) The more severe enforcement of the demands for purification incumbent upon the Israelite community are linked to the threat of severe punishments of any Israelite, citizen or stranger, who does not purify himself from his impurity and thus defiles the Sanctuary of God "which is in their midst" (Lev 15:31; 17:16; Num 19:13, 20).[50] Such threats are never found in PT.

The principle of the expansion of the domain of holiness to the camp of Israel and its application to the land of Canaan require, in effect, that

48. The view that the holiness of God extends beyond the cultic realm may also be seen in other biblical strata; see S. E. Loewenstamm, "Nahalat Hashem," in *Studies in Bible* (Scripta Hierosolymitana 31; Jerusalem, 1986) 168–69. Especially noteworthy is Zech 2:14–16, in which the promise that God's presence will dwell within the "daughter of Zion" is accompanied by the promise that "the Lord will take Judah to himself as his portion in the Holy Land"; see also below, n. 55.

49. I do not claim that the demand to observe the purity of the Israelite camp is an innovation of HS. Perhaps Milgrom is correct in thinking that this is an early conception, which is also reflected in the law of the war camp in Deut 23:10–15 ("The Graduated Hattat of Leviticus 5:1–13," *JAOS* 103 [1983] 252). Unlike Milgrom, however, I believe that Numbers 5 is later than the PT purity laws. HS's and D's agreement on the issue of the preservation of the sanctity of the Israelite camp reflects their common consensus that ritual holiness is demanded of the entire congregation of Israel (see above, nn. 38, 44).

50. Lev 15:31 and Num 19:13, 20 are HS additions to PT legal scrolls (see above, pp. 68–70, 92–94).

the purity of the entire land be maintained. In fact, the warning that the land be kept pure is supported by a reason similar to that for the demand to observe the purity of the camp: "You shall not defile the land in which you live, in which I myself abide. For I the Lord abide among the Israelite people" (Num 35:34). In this passage, the encompassing of the entire land by the presence of God serves as the explanation for the punishment for the spilling of blood. In other biblical passages, HS warns against defilement of the land through the abominations of the nations (Lev 18:24–28; 20:22–24). In each case, we find explicit instructions applying the ordinances to the stranger (Lev 18:26; Num 35:15). Thus, if the special character of the land serves as the ground for the demand to separate from impurity, this demand must be imposed on all who dwell in it, both citizen and stranger.[51]

HS expresses the extension of the domain of holiness beyond the narrow confines of the Temple and the priesthood through the fringes law (Num 15:37–41; see also above, pp. 89–92). In these verses several principles of HS's thought are formulated: the main purpose of the fringes is to remind the people of Israel of all God's commandments and the requirement that they be observed. The remembering of *all* the commandments is repeatedly emphasized (Num 15:39a, 40a), as HS considers all divine commands to be of equal status. Verse 42 presents the view that Israel is consecrated to its God through the observance of the commandments. This is also a fundamental principle of HS. Aside from being a "reminder" of the commandments, the fringes symbolize the sanctity that Israel gains through their observance. In the course of our discussion of PT's laws, we called attention to the parallel between the ציץ נזר הקודש in the מצנפת (headpiece) of the anointed priest and the crown (נזר) of God on the nazirite's head. We remarked that PT allows those who have assumed nazirite vows of abstinence to adorn themselves temporarily with the trappings of holiness (see above, pp. 159–63). According to HS, which presents the holy life as the task and mission of the entire community, all Israel must wear this holy sign at all times. Just as in the headpiece, the gold frontlet (ציץ) tied with a cord of blue designates the anointed priest as "holy to God" (קדש לה') (Exod 28:36–37), so too the fringes (ציצית), which also contain a blue cord, testify to Israel's mission to be consecrated unto their God.[52]

51. See Ibn Ezra on Lev 18:26; J. Milgrom, "Religious Conversion and the Revolt Model for the Reformation of Israel," *JBL* 101 (1982) 171; M. Weinfeld, "Inheritance of the Land, Privilege versus Obligation: The Concept of 'The Promised Land' in the Sources of the First and Second Temple Periods," *Zion* 49 (1984) 115ff.

52. The relation between the ציץ (the headpiece) and ציצית (the fringes) was noted by Cassuto, *Exodus,* 383. Milgrom remarked ("Of Hems and Tassels," *BAR* 9 [1939] 65) that the common element in both the high priest's garments and the fringes—the permission to use

God, Sovereign of the People and the Land

The special relationship between God, Israel, and the land is not exhausted through the holiness that derives from the network of holiness laws. Many commandments emphasize God's sovereignty over the people, the land, and its produce.[53]

Israel is God's possession: "For it is to me that the Israelites are servants: they are my servants, whom I freed from the land of Egypt, I the Lord your God" (Lev 25:55). This proclamation appears at the conclusion of the slavery laws of HS (Lev 25:39–55) and eliminates the possibility that Israelites may become enslaved to each other: "For they are my servants whom I freed from the land of Egypt; they may not give themselves over into servitude" (v. 42). An Israelite sold to a fellow Israelite is considered hired labor: one may not subject him to the treatment of a slave nor rule over him ruthlessly; on the jubilee year, he leaves his employer and returns to his family (vv. 39–43). The citation of the events of the exodus as the basis for God's claim to the possession of Israel appears also in the Levite Tractate, which is of HS origin as well. Consecration of the Levites to service in the Tabernacle is presented as substitution for the Israelite firstborn, who are thus redeemed from their obligation to minister to God. The obligation of the firstborn was incurred when they were saved from the plague of the firstborn: "For every firstborn is mine: at the time that I smote every firstborn in the land of Egypt, I consecrated every firstborn in Israel, man and beast, to myself, to be mine, the Lord's" (Num 3:13; compare Num 8:17). The Levites were presented by Israel to God as a substitute for the firstborn (Num 3:12, 41; 8:16–18). The redemption of the firstborn was fixed as an everlasting commandment (Num 18:15, 16).[54]

Adjacent to the proclamation of God's possession of Israel are declarations of God's ownership of the land: "But the land must not be sold beyond reclaim, for the land is mine. You are but strangers resident with me" (Lev 25:23).[55] God's sovereignty over the land makes the Israelites

wool-linen blends—is an indication of their special sanctity (see M. Haran, *Temples and Temple Service in Ancient Israel* [Oxford, 1978] 160).

53. On the link between holiness and possession, see W. Robertson-Smith, *The Religion of the Semites* (New York, 1957) 92ff. and 140ff.

54. See Excursus 1. On the "giving" of the Levites, see E. A. Speiser, "An Unremarked Sanctification," in *Oz Ledavid: David Ben Gurion Jubilee Volume* (Jerusalem, 1974) 506–7; J. Milgrom, *Studies in Levitical Terminology* (Berkeley, 1970) nn. 103, 275; idem, "Alleged Wave-Offering," 146, M. Paran, "Two Types of 'Laying Hands Upon' in the Priestly Source," *Beer Sheva* 2 (1985) 117 n. 9.

55. On the sovereignty of God over the people and the land as the basis for the law of redemption of slaves and land in Leviticus 25, see S. Japhet, "The Laws of Manumission of Slaves and the Question of the Relationship Between the Collection of Laws in the Penta-

into residents lacking actual possession of their land; thus, they have no right to make any permanent sales of land. The limited possession of the land by Israelites is also evident in the laws of the sabbatical year. For every Israelite, the land is his to work for six years and the fruit his to enjoy, but in the seventh year the land must repose as a Sabbath to the Lord. On this year, the Israelite's rights of possession of the land are revoked; he may not farm it, nor does he have any prior rights to its produce: "It shall be a year of complete rest for the land. But you may eat whatever the land during its Sabbath will produce—you, your male and female slaves, the hired and bound laborers who live with you, and your cattle and the beasts in your land may eat all its yield" (Lev 25:6–7).

Even in the years in which the Israelite may work the land and enjoy its produce, he must recognize that as the possession of God, the produce too is a kind of הקדש, a consecrated item, and is not for profane use. Only after the gift of the firstfruits to God does the rest of the produce become "profaned," so that the farmer may use it for his own needs. This concept underlies the law of the *ʾomer* and the two loaves; only after they are waved before the Lord may the new grain be consumed (Lev 23:10–21).[56]

---

teuch," in *Studies in Bible and the Ancient Near East: Presented to S. E. Loewenstamm on his Seventieth Birthday* (Jerusalem, 1978) 246–47. An interesting parallel to HS's view may be found in the Song of the Sea: Israel is described there as "the people you redeemed" (Exod 15:13), "the people you have ransomed" (Exod 15:16); God has redeemed them from slavery to the Egyptians (see Cassuto, *Exodus,* 122). God brings his possession-people to his holy abode, the mountain of his inheritance (Exod 15:13, Loewenstamm, "Nahalat Hashem," 167–70). These phrases are metaphors for the land of Israel, which is God's inheritance and possession. The entire land has the virtue of holiness, as it is the residence of God and the place of his sanctuary (cf. "abode of righteousness, holy mountain" in Jer 31:23, which, as Loewenstamm has shown, also refers to the entire land). Thus, the verses of the song express a view very close to that of HS.

56. Although the Bible does not explicitly state that wheat of the new harvest may be enjoyed only after the two loaves are brought to the Temple, the resemblance of this law to the law of the *ʾomer* and the first grapes (הילולים) leads us to believe that this was the legislator's intention (see above, p. 27). The law was understood as such by the Dead Sea sect (see J. M. Baumgarten, "The Law of Hadash," *JJS* 27 [1976] 36–46). Philo (*Special Laws* 2.180) and several Karaite commentators (see L. Ginzberg, *Genizah Studies: In Memory of Doctor Solomon Schechter*, Vol. 2: *Geonic and Early Karaitic Halakah* [New York, 1929] 443, 444, 451).

In Lev 23:22, at the end of the passage discussing the *ʾomer* and the two loaves, HS orders donations to the poor. M. Greenberg sees this, too, as an expression of God's sovereignty over the land (*On the Bible and Judaism: A Collection of Writings* [Tel Aviv, 1985] 115). The landowner tells the tenant on his land: give the corners of the field and the gleanings to the poor and needy. Greenberg writes that the gift of the tithes to the Levites in Num 18:21–24 and the granting of towns to the Levites in Num 35:1–8 were instituted for similar reasons. Note that according to our classification, both Numbers 18 and Numbers 35 belong to HS. Note too that Ezekiel refers to the land allotted for the Temple and the inheritance of the priests and Levites as a sacred gift (תרומה) given to God (see Ezek 45:1–7; 48:8–14).

This applies equally to the law of the "fruit of jubilation"; only after it is consecrated to God, may the fruit of the tree be enjoyed (Lev 19:23–25).[57] Even after the grain is ground and baked, the first part of the dough must be presented as a heave offering to God (Num 15:18–21). The law that people must give God his part before enjoying the things of this world, applies not only to the fruit of the land. As we mentioned, HS prohibits the profane slaughtering of sheep or cattle and requires that they be brought as whole offerings and their fat be offered on the altar (see above, pp. 48–51). Although the Scriptures support this ordinance by prohibiting sacrifice to the goat-demons (Lev 17:7), the practical result is the prohibition of benefit from sheep or cattle until the first part, the fat, is consecrated to God (see HS's use of חלב ["fat"] as a parallel to the firstfruits of Num 18:12; cf. also Gen 4:4).[58] An offering to God is also raised from war booty (Num 31:25–47).[59]

The Holiness of the Congregation and the Holiness of the Priesthood

HS is of the opinion that the observance of the commandments dealing with relations between a man and his fellow man (such as respect for

57. As we said (chapter 1, n. 51), the simple meaning of Scripture is that the firstfruits of the vine (הילולים) be given to God, that is, to the priest.

58. Although the obligation to give a portion to God does not apply to game meat (see Lev 17:3), this loophole was closed in the *Temple Scroll* (see n. 59, below).

59. This was fixed as a permanent ordinance in the *Temple Scroll* 2:58, 60 (ed. Yadin, pp. 158, 191–92; see Yadin's introduction, 127–29). A thorough acquaintance with HS's laws, which permit enjoyment of things only after the proper sacred gifts have been made to the priests, leads us to question M. Haran's statement ("Priesthood, Priests" *EM* 4:44–45; idem, "Mekhes," *EM* 4:964–65) that the setting aside of a portion of the spoils of war for the priests has no ritual significance or element of holiness, but is merely a way of ensuring the rights of those priests who did not go to war. The fact (noted by Haran) that Scripture explicitly calls the tax מכס לה' or תרומה לה' (Num 31:28; 29, 39–41) is, in my opinion, sufficient evidence for viewing the tax as a sacred gift. Haran's proof—that the human captives and donkeys require no redemption—is inconclusive. Although the tribute was not meant to be sacrificed on the altar but was to be presented to the priests, there are other sacred gifts of similar status—the firstlings of the grain, the wine and the oil (Num 18:13) and the first grapes of the vine (see above, n. 57). The tension that exists between the gift of a part of the war booty to the priests and the command "you shall, however, have no territorial share among them or own any portion in their midst; I am your portion and your share among the Israelites" (Num 18:20) can only be resolved if the tribute is viewed as an offering to God, allotted to the priests. See also the *Sifre* (ad loc.): " 'and you shall have no share among them'—of the booty" (*Sifre Num* 119, ed. Horowitz, p. 142) and similar sayings in *Sifre Zuta* (ibid., 297) and *Sifre Dt* 153, (ed. Finkelstein, p. 213). This same explanation could serve to reconcile Num 18:20, 23–24, which states that the priests and Levites have no share in the land, with the granting of cities to the priests and Levites in Num 35:1–8 (see above, n. 56). In the *Temple Scroll,* the tribute of the spoils of war is enumerated among the sacred gifts, along with firstborn animals and first vintage grapes; based on the law of the tax of war spoils, the *Temple Scroll* also fixes a heave offering of hunted game (see *Temple Scroll,* 2:60 [ed. Yadin, pp. 191–92]).

one's father and mother and neighborly love), and the keeping of ceremonial commandments (such as observance of ritual purity and forbidden foods), are two parts of a single consecration, which increase the sanctity of God, who dwells among Israel. This doctrine imbues the daily life of every Israelite with something of the atmosphere of the Temple service: the Israelite who is sanctified with the holiness of the commandments and who wears the blue thread of the fringes is likened to a priest serving in the inner sanctum. The entire land of Israel is described as a holy place, and enjoyment of the produce of the fields and the possessions of this world, which are God's property, is comparable to partaking from the table of the Most High, like the priests' consumption of the offerings of God. HS does not, however, dispute the special status of the priests; alongside the call to consecration of the entire community and the emphasis on the indwelling of God's presence among Israel, the superior level of the priests—Aaron and his sons—is acknowledged.

HS connects the holiness of the priesthood to the special status of the entire nation. This is implied by the structure and content of the concluding verses of the daily offering pericope (Exod 29:42–46; see above, p. 65). The passage begins with an emphasis on God's meeting with the children of Israel and ends by declaring the purpose of the exodus as the indwelling of God among the community of Israel. In the middle of the passage we find the proclamation "I will sanctify the Tent of Meeting and the altar, and I will consecrate Aaron and his sons to serve me as Priests" (v. 44). The sanctification of the Tent of Meeting and the priesthood is viewed as an expression of God's dwelling among the community of Israel.

In the Holiness Code, we first find the ordinances dealing with purity and the holiness laws that pertain to the entire community (Lev 18:1–20:27), followed by special restrictions applying exclusively to those of greater holiness, the priests (Lev 21:1–22:9). Although certain parallels exist between the laws of holiness addressed to the Israelite community and those applying to the priests alone (compare Lev 19:26–28 with 21:5),[60] the Priestly laws are usually more severe: The eating of carcasses and animals that died of natural causes is permitted to the Israelite community, who are merely adjured to purify themselves from the resulting impurity, but it is completely forbidden to priests (see above, n. 43). Similarly, priests may not render themselves impure through contact with the dead, except in the case of close relatives (Lev 21:1–3). They are also forbidden to marry prostitutes, defiled women, or divorcees (Lev 21:7)—prohibitions that do not apply to Israelites at large. Scripture explains the greater sanctity of the priests by referring to their duties—the

60. See Milgrom, "Demythologization," 158.

offering of the bread of God (v. 6). This rationale is repeated in the address to the community of Israel: "You must treat them as holy, since they offer the food of your God; they shall be holy to you, for I the Lord who sanctify you am holy" (v. 8). Biblical scholars were bewildered at the connection with the final phrase אני ה׳ מקדשכם, which applies the sanctity of the priesthood to the entire nation. They thus considered it an error or a secondary interpolation.[61] But now that we understand the relation between the sanctity of the priesthood and the sanctity of Israel in HS, we may readily accept the text of this verse. God sanctifies Israel through dwelling among the people, and the Presence is concretized through the establishment of the sacred Priestly institutions in their midst.[62]

In HS's conception, the difference between the holiness of the priesthood and the holiness of the community of Israel is qualitative as well as quantitative. The special sanctity of the priesthood exists only in the ritual-ceremonial sphere, whereas the call to lead holy lives is addressed to all of Israel, including the priests. This demand includes the ritual as well as the moral spheres. Moreover, the holiness of the priests is presented as the basis from which the special prohibitions applying to them derive: "For they are holy to their God" (Lev 21:7). With respect to the congregation at large, on the other hand, HS does not state that they are holy and that their holiness is the basis for the commandments (see above, n. 43). It presents their sanctification as a constant process. The difference between the two levels of holiness is expressed in the narrative of the rebellion of the chieftains, which, as we saw above, was formulated by HS. In their complaint to Moses and Aaron, the chieftains disputed the superior status of the priests: "You have gone too far. For all the community are holy, all of them, and the Lord is in their midst. Why then do you raise yourselves above the Lord's congregation?" (Num 16:3). The chieftains' complaint would seem to be rooted in HS's view of the sanctified lives of the entire Israelite community and the indwelling of God among them; furthermore, the HS editors strengthened these claims by placing the fringes pericope directly before the rebellion narrative. As discussed above, this pericope emphasizes the sanctity of all Israelites, as symbolized through the blue thread of the fringes, fashioned like the high

61. Dillmann and Baentsch prefer the reading מקדשם, as in the Septuagint and the Samaritan version, instead of מקדשכם, as in the Masoretic version. Elliger is of the opinion that there is a recensional addition here and that it is difficult to know what the original form was.

62. See Ramban in his commentary (ad loc.). The same words, אני ה׳ מקדשכם, also serve as the reason for observing the Sabbath, which, according to HS, is also a holy institution that sanctifies Israel through observance of it (see Exod 31:13). As this is a standard formula in HS (see, e.g., Lev 20:8; 22-32), we should not wonder at the shift from the singular (וקדשתו, אלהיך, לך) in the first part of Lev 21:8 to the plural (אני ה׳ מקדשכם) at the end of the verse.

priest's garments. But it is through the narrative of the rebellion of the chieftains and the editorial stratum of the Levite revolt that HS reveals its entire model for holiness: in its opinion, the sanctification of all Israelites through the holiness of the Presence and the commandments cannot efface the difference between the congregation and the priests. The fire-pan and staff tests proved that only Aaron and his sons were chosen to serve before God (see Num 16:5, 7; 17:20); the verses on the test of the fire pans further emphasize that God's choice will reveal who his holy ones are. In his response to the complaint of the Levites, which was appended to the complaint of the chieftains, Moses says: "Is it not enough for you that the God of Israel has set you apart (הבדיל) from the community of Israel and given you access to him?" (v. 9). Moses' words give verbal expression to the difference between the two levels of holiness. As we mentioned (above, n. 43), the verb בחר (elect) appears in HS only in connection with the sanctity of the priests, the sons of Aaron; with respect to Israelites (including Levites), the word הבדיל (set apart) is employed (see Lev 20:24, 26; Num 8:14). The verb קדש (sanctified), too, never appears in the context of the Levites; its absence indicates that HS's intent was to stress the special sanctity of the priesthood.[63]

Thus, according to HS's model of holiness, we find three levels within the Israelite nation: All Israel is separated from the nations, and consecrated by the sanctity of the commandments, which include both the ceremonial and the cultic realms (Lev 11:44–45; 19:2; 20:7–8, 24–26; Num 15:40). The Levites are separated from the Israelites and dedicated to the service of the Tabernacle, in order to prevent the Israelites from entering the place of worship and to atone for them (Num 8:14–19; 16:9–10; 18:2–4, 6). The priests, Aaron and his sons, were elected to serve before the Lord—to guard משמרת הקודש, the holy enclosure—and the altar and to offer the bread of God. This election endows them with the highest grade of holiness, that emanating from the cult, in which Israelites and Levites may not participate (Exod 29:44; Lev 21:6, 8; Num 16:5–11; 17:20–23; 18:1, 5, 7).

The Relation of the People to the Temple and Its Worship

Even though HS accentuates the exclusive role of the priests in the cult, it does not seek to create the kind of separation between the Priestly-Temple sphere and the nation at large maintained by PT. On the contrary, throughout its writings, HS strives to create a deep affiliation between the congregation of Israel and the Tabernacle-Temple and its worship.

63. This was already noted by Milgrom, *Studies,* n. 103; see also chapter 2, n. 61.

It is this aim that results in the various additions made by HS to the Tabernacle ordinance scrolls of PT as well as the text describing the execution of these ordinances, which is also shaped by HS. These texts stress the role played by the Israelite people in erecting the Tabernacle and in the cult taking place there. The contrast is especially striking when viewed against the background of the PT ordinance scroll, in which Moses alone is responsible for the construction of the Tabernacle (see above, p. 65). The call "Let them make me a sanctuary that I may dwell among them" (Exod 25:8), which is of HS origin, is addressed to all Israelites. All of Israel, both men and women, contribute the materials needed for the construction of the Tabernacle and its vessels and for the clothes of the priests (Exod 25:2–7; 35:4–9, 21–29; 38:8). The construction is carried out by Bezalel, Oholiab, and other skilled persons among the Israelites (Exod 28:3–5; 31:1–11; 35:10–19, 30–35; 36:1–2, 8–38; 37:1–39:43). HS also legislates that the materials for the daily cult—the oil for the lamps, the spices for the incense, and the shewbread are to be taken from the community of Israel at large (Exod 25:6; 27:20–21; 35:28; 39:36–38; Lev 24:2, 8).

The all-Israelite character of the Tabernacle is articulated in a succinct formula in the concluding verse appended by HS to the ordinance concerning the altar of sacrifice (Exod 29:42–46). The purpose of the cultic framework is the creation of a strong, direct relationship between God and Israel: "I will abide among the Israelites, and I will be their God" (29:45). This explains the story of the chieftains' sacrifices, as formulated by HS (Num 7:2–88). If the primary aim of the Tabernacle is the indwelling of God among the Israelite people, it is fitting that it be dedicated through the sacrifices of the leaders of the nation. Furthermore, it seems that HS wishes to stress that the indwelling of God's Presence and his revelation in the Tent of Meeting precede the service of the priests and are independent of it. This is in marked contrast to PT. According to PT, God revealed himself in the Tent of Meeting only at the end of the days of ordination in which Aaron and his sons consecrated themselves to the priesthood, and only after Aaron offered up the sacrifices of the eighth day (see Leviticus 8–9). HS, on the other hand, stresses the sacrifices of the congregation and the chieftains, which, in its opinion, preceded the sacrifices of Aaron. In HS's view of things, those sacrifices, and not the sacrifice of Aaron, are the guarantor of the revelation of God in the Tent of Meeting. This idea is first expressed in the concluding verse of Exodus 29. Moses is ordered to offer up the daily sacrifice immediately upon the erection of the Tabernacle: "Now this is what you shall offer upon the altar: two yearling lambs, each day, regularly" (Exod 29:38).[64] There, the

64. The language of the second address, וזה אשר תעשה, reveals that this command was first addressed to Moses, who was ordered to bring the daily sacrifice on the days of ordination. See Ibn Ezra (ad loc.) and Ramban on Exod 40:27.

daily offering is the key to the communion of God with the community of Israel and to God's speaking with Moses in the Tent of Meeting (Exod 29:42).[65] In Exod 40:29, HS states that on the day that the Tabernacle was erected by Moses (which is the first of the days of ordination),[66] Moses indeed offered up the daily sacrifice, as God had commanded him.[67] When Moses completed the erection of the Tabernacle and the sacrificing on that day, the Presence of God filled the Tabernacle, as a sign of God's dwelling in it (Exod 40:34–35). In an adjacent verse, we find God calling to Moses from the Tent of Meeting and speaking with him (Lev 1:1).[68] HS repeatedly mentions, in its editorial additions to Lev 9:17 and Num 28:6, that the daily sacrifice was offered even before the completion of the ordination ceremonies on the eighth day.[69] On the day of the erection of the Tabernacle, the chieftains too bring their sacrifices (Num 7:1);[70] here again God speaks to Moses in close temporal proximity to the offering of the sacrifices brought by the people's representatives. At the end of the description of the sacrifices of the chieftains, it is written: "When Moses went into the Tent of Meeting to speak with him, he would hear the voice addressing him from above the cover that was on the top of the Ark of the Pact between the two cherubim; thus He spoke to him" (Num 7:89).[71] The common element in all these verses is the connection forged between the popular and public dimensions of the cult, which are performed prior to the priestly ceremonies, and the indwelling of God and his revelation to Israel and Moses. This connection is also expressed through the identity

65. "From where did the Presence speak with Moses? . . . From the altar of sacrifice, as it is written 'a regular burnt offering . . . at the entrance of the Tent of Meeting . . . for there . . . I will speak with you' (Exod 29:42)" (*Beraita deM'lekhet Hamishkan,* ed. Ish-Shalom, p. 84). On the relation between the sacrifice of the whole offering and the appearance of God, see B. A. Levine, *In the Presence of the Lord* (Leiden, 1974) 22–27.

66. As are the opinion of Rabbi Akiva (*Sifre Num,* ed. Horowitz, p. 67) and the conclusion of Ibn Ezra in his commentary on Exod 40:2.

67. ". . . And he sacrificed the whole offering in the morning—this refers to the daily whole offering; and he did likewise at twilight" (Ibn Ezra, ad loc.).

68. Lev 1:1 apparently originates with HS editors who used the verse to link the corpus of the establishment of the Tabernacle (Exodus 35–40) with the corpus of Leviticus 1–7. Cf. A. Kuenen, *A Historico-Critical Inquiry into the Origin and Composition of the Hexateuch* (trans. P. H. Wicksteed; London, 1886) 84 n. 18.

69. On Num 28:6 as an editorial interpolation of HS, see above, p. 30. On the relation of this verse to Exod 29:38; 40:29, which deal with the sacrifice of the daily offering during the days of ordination, see Ramban in his commentary on Exod 40:26 and A. Dillmann, *Die Bücher Exodus und Leviticus* (3rd ed.; Leipzig, 1897) 348; idem, *Die Bücher Numeri, Deuteronomium und Josua* (2nd ed.; Leipzig, 1866) 102. On Lev 9:17b, see Excursus 2 and n. 3.

70. On the date at the beginning of the pericope on the princes' sacrifices, see chapter 2, n. 71.

71. See also the discussion on this verse in J. Licht, *A Commentary on the Book of Numbers (I-X)* (Jerusalem, 1985) 111–12.

of the witnesses of God's revelation in the Tent of Meeting. We articulated earlier (p. 65, n. 17), that while PT stresses the exclusivity of the revelation to Moses (Exod 25:22; 30:6, 36), HS emphasizes the all-Israelite dimension of the revelation (Exod 29:42–43; Num 17:19).

HS's view of the Temple as the center of God's indwelling among the people highlights the interdependence of the holiness of the Temple and the deeds of each and every Israelite. As we discussed earlier (chapter 3, n. 126), the responsibility of every Israelite for the sanctity of the Temple is already implicit in the laws of PT. HS explicitly formulates this principle, which also serves as the basis for the more severe punishment inflicted on those who enter the Temple while impure. We first find this idea in the exhortation appended by HS at the conclusion of PT's purity laws: "You shall put the Israelites on guard against their uncleanness, lest they die through their uncleanness by defiling My Tabernacle which is among them" (Lev 15:31). We note a similar tone in the passages inserted by HS in the law of the waters of lustration: "Whoever touches a corpse, the body of a person who has died, and does not cleanse himself, defiles the Lord's Tabernacle; that person shall be cut off from Israel"; "If anyone who has become unclean fails to cleanse himself, that person shall be cut off from the congregation, for he has defiled the Lord's sanctuary. The water of lustration was not dashed on him: he is unclean." In the Holiness Code, we find the same conception applied to Molech worship: "And I will set my face against that man and will cut him off from among his people, because he gave of his offspring to Molech and so defiled my sanctuary and profaned my holy Name" (Lev 20:3).

HS's objective—to strengthen the bond between the people and the Temple—greatly affected its festival law; this is particularly evident when we compare it with the parallel law in PT. As we demonstrated in chapter 1, PT creates a complete separation between the festival cult of the priests in the Temple and popular customs, which it considers nonobligatory, since the priests take no part in them. This tendency is most blatant in the laws of the tenth day of the seventh month, where we find a total rupture between the atonement ceremony in the Temple and the popular fast day. The priests atone for the Holy through a long series of atonement procedures, but it is doubtful if the people, whose sins the priests atone for in the Sanctuary and whose transgressions are heaped upon the scapegoat sent out into the wilderness, have any idea that the ceremony is taking place. The people, who await God's grace and blessing, purify themselves and atone before God on the fast day, which takes place at another time, at the beginning of the rainy season. HS adopted the PT law scroll as the basis for its festival law, but enlarged and edited it, with the primary goal of integrating the Priestly and popular cults. The ceremony of the waving of the *ʾomer* and the two loaves, which expresses the people's expectation of a blessed harvest, are important Temple ceremonies, in which the priests play an important role. On the feast of Booths, the people come to the Temple and rejoice before the Lord with the four species, which express their desire for abundant rainfall. The blending of Priestly and popular worship created the "Day of Atonement," which joined the popular fast day with the Temple atonement ceremony and reflected the reciprocal relations between the priesthood and the Israelite community. HS explains the obligation to refrain from work and the affliction of one's soul which the people practice, by referring to the Priestly atonement ceremony taking place in the Temple on that day (see Lev 16:29–30; 23:28). The people take part in the purification and atonement taking place in the hidden inner sanctum through abstaining from work and afflicting their souls. The performance of an atonement ceremony in the Temple at the beginning of the rainy season expresses the priests' participation in the hopes and worries of the people and their expectation of a positive divine judgment.[72]

In HS's treatment of the Sabbath, we also note its striving to blend the popular and Priestly cults. The exhortation to observe the Sabbath day, a popular creation, is adjoined by this school to instructions on the erection of the Tabernacle and reverence for the Temple (see Exod 31:12–17; 35:1–3; Lev 19:30; 26:2). It would seem that HS sought not only to restore the honor of the Sabbath, which was neglected in PT, but also to call attention to the qualitative similarity between the Sabbath and the Temple.[73] The emphasis on the sanctity of the Sabbath, the severe punishment assigned to its violations, and the discussion of the details of the work prohibition give the Sabbath some of the grave atmosphere of holiness that surrounds the cultic enclosure. According to HS, the Sabbath is a sign of the holiness of Israel (Exod 31:13), and Israelites who keep the Sabbath are like priests serving in the Temple. The view of the Sabbath as a "Temple in time"[74] is also reflected by HS's use of the verb חלל to designate the violation of the sanctity of the Sabbath as well as the defilement of the sanctity of the Temple (Exod 31:14; Lev 21:12, 23).

72. In the Second Temple period, this partnership is expressed also in the high priest's Day of Atonement prayer for the needs of Israel. The priest recited this prayer after bringing the incense offering in the Holy of Holies; see I. Knohl, "The Priestly Torah Versus the Holiness School: Sabbath and the Festivals," *HUCA* 58 (1987) 105 and n. 123.

73. On the broader relation of the Sabbath to the Temple and its cultic expression, see M. Weinfeld, "Sabbath, Temple and Enthronement of the Lord—The Problem of the Sitz im Leben of Genesis 1:1–2:3," in *Mélanges Bibliques et Orientaux en l'Honneur de M. Henri Cazelles* (Paris, 1981) 501–12.

74. Compare A. Heschel's description of the Sabbath as a "palace in time" (*The Sabbath: Its Meaning for Modern Man* [New York, 1951] 21).

The Significance and Purpose of the Blending of Beliefs and Cultic Practices in HS

The life of faith has many facets. Sometimes people are engulfed by the cares of their daily lives and raise their eyes to the God who is near to those who call out to him, awaiting grace and salvation. Sometimes people lose sight of their profane needs and their entire beings thirst for spiritual elevation, to approach the holy, hidden and mysterious. If this is so for individuals, how, then, is it possible to give uniform, systematic expression to the varied religious and cultic experiences of an entire nation?

PT approached this problem by separating two levels of faith: the faith of Genesis and the patriarchs and the faith of Moses. For PT, this distinction corresponds, more or less, to the difference between the popular experience of faith, which PT considers preliminary, and the Priestly faith experience, which it considers the higher level of faith (see above, pp. 145–48, 159). On the deepest level, this distinction reflects a duality in the nature of God and in the relationship between God and humanity, as experienced by the religious person. The faith of Genesis and the patriarchs is correlated with the rational moral aspects of the divinity. It is expressed through the conception of God as Creator, overseer, and legislator of the moral law, whose primary concern is his creation, and especially human beings. The faith of Moses, on the other hand, is focused on the numinous essence, essentially detached from morality or the principles of providence and recompense.[75] PT represents the first conception as אלהים and the second as Yahweh. Its thought permanently isolates the two elements and completely divorces the faith consciousnesses corresponding to each of them. While PT is forced to compromise with certain popular elements in the cult, these are not openly expressed in the purely Priestly worship in the Temple (see above, p. 163).

HS opposed PT's total bifurcation on both ideological and practical levels. In the course of our discussion of HS's conceptions, we became aware of the all-out effort to weave the very different strands of faith principles and cultic institutions into a single cloth. We find, in HS, impersonal descriptions of God and his actions, along with anthropomorphic imagery and expressions of a direct and close relation between God and the people of Israel. Although HS's cultic laws are based on PT's Priestly-cultic corpus and draw much material from it, HS is also influ-

75. For the distinction between the numinous and the rational-moral dimensions, see Otto, *Idea of the Holy*, 1–40; see also his statement (p. 20) that the conception of God as creator and overseer of the world and the consequent feeling of dependence belong to the rational dimension of the divinity.

enced by popular tradition. Therefore, its cultic forms express the individual's and the nation's expectation of God's blessing and salvation or serve as the means of offering thanks for God's historical-national deeds and blessing of crops. HS even removes the barrier between the cultic and the judicial-moral spheres by giving cultic expression to moral elements: social injustices are called "מעל בה'"—a "breaking of faith with God" and require atonement by priests in the Temple. The spilling of blood must be atoned for ritually. Just as profane needs enter into the Temple realm, so too holiness is apportioned to daily life. Although HS assigns "cultic holiness" exclusively to the priests, holiness is no longer limited to the narrow confines of the Temple and the priesthood but emerges from the Priestly center, radiating out to all sectors of society and to all walks of life and encompassing the entire land. Israelites are called to realize the challenge of the holy life in their eating and drinking, in their relations to their families and to the stranger dwelling in the land, in their work in the fields and commerce, on the seat of judgment and in the company of friends.

The revolutionary project of HS was guided by its vision—to create a broad, all-inclusive framework of faith and cult, in which the multifarious values of the religious experience would be combined: it would express both the reflections of the priests serving in the Sanctuary and the innermost needs of the people in the fields. HS conjoins the name אלהים to the name of Yahweh; this expresses its ambition to integrate the diverse elements of the divinity in its conception.[76] The creation of the infrastructure for this all-inclusive world of faith is the fundamental transformation of the concept of holiness. Through absorbing morality and social justice into the concept of holiness, and through extending the demand to live a life of holiness to the entire community, it combines the many streams of faith and cult present in the Israelite nation. For HS, the primary mission of the entire nation is the attainment of holiness; it is this that separates Israel from the nations.

76. Otto calls such integration "rationalization and moralization of the numinous" (*Idea of the Holy,* 109–11). According to Otto, the integration of the numinous and the rational-moral is one of the striking characteristics of biblical faith (pp. 75, 110). This claim needs to be investigated further; as we saw, there are very few cases in the Bible outside of HS of the infusion of the concept of holiness with moral content. See above chapter 3, n. 113 and this chapter, nn. 37–38; compare below, chapter 5, n. 50.

CHAPTER

5

The Historical Framework for the Activities of the Priestly School

In previous chapters, the argument between PT and HS was presented as an abstract argument over the emphases on the various dimensions of God and the faith and cultic experiences related to them. When we discussed their respective ideas earlier, we deliberately avoided any reference to the historical background for the activities of these two schools; this was done in order to avoid the fallacy inherent in explaining the unique nature of the Priestly literature in the Pentateuch based on assumptions about its date of composition. A prime example of the fallacy in this approach may be seen in J. Wellhausen's *Prolegomena to a History of Israel.* While Wellhausen correctly identified many of the unique characteristics of PT's cultic system (see chapter 1, nn. 98, 99), he explained this uniqueness by claiming that PT was composed after the destruction of the First Temple and the Babylonian exile. Not only is the assumption as to the late date of composition of PT not borne out by critical inquiry (see Introduction, nn. 13-15), but Wellhausen's approach suffers from a fundamental flaw: whoever seeks to explain religious phenomena, and spiritual phenomena in general, through historical circumstances, ignores the power of spiritual creativity, which can never be completely explained through an understanding of its time and place of inception. We may, however, acknowledge that religious and spiritual phenomena are not created *ex nihilo* but are grounded in a particular historical, cultural, and social reality.[1] We may, thus, investigate the historical conditions surrounding developments in the spiritual world of the Israelite

1. See Y. Kaufmann's general remarks in *Exile and Foreign Land* (Tel Aviv, 1929) 1:15-17, as well as his comments on the historical background pertaining to the rise of classical prophecy (*A History of the Religion of Israel* [Jerusalem/Tel Aviv, 1960] 3:11).

priesthood, though we do not claim that in doing so we determine the "causes" of those developments.

Our study has shown that HS grew out of PT and drew on PT in many areas; but alongside the exploitation of PT's riches, which is evident in all levels of HS's writings, we find many striking changes and innovations. This two-sided relationship may best be understood if we assume that HS reflects a profound ideological change occurring within PT circles. As a result of this change, a new Priestly ideology was created, one that drew upon the early Priestly traditions and their cultic expressions but sought to infuse these expressions with new meaning. We need ask: In which historical frame was PT active? What was the background for the tremendous change in the Priestly ideology? And in what historical situation did HS originate and develop?

THE TIME RANGE OF THE PRIESTLY WRITINGS

As is well known, the question of the dating of the "Priestly source" is the focus of heated argument in biblical scholarship. We do not intend here to review this question, but we wish to mention an important observation arising from our study that should advance the research methods applied to this question.

In the course of our discussion of the writings of the two Priestly schools, we noted that each of them comprises several strata which appear alongside each other, sometimes intertwined.[2] This indicates that the Priestly corpus results from a long, multileveled process that began with the composition of the various PT strata, continued with the various stages in HS's creative activity, and terminated with the final editing of the "Priestly source" and the Pentateuch as a whole.[3] Thus, the Priestly source—that is, the combined works of PT and HS—is the result of literary activity spanning the course of several centuries.[4]

2. On the various strata in PT, see chapter 1, n. 60; Excursus 1, nn. 11, 27; chapter 2, n. 9. On stratification in HS's composition, see our comments on Exod 6:14–30 (above, p. 18); Exod 12:18–20 and Lev 23:32 (above, pp. 20–21); Lev 23:37–38 (chapter 1, n. 82); Num 9:1–14 (above, p. 90); the Levite Treatise and the rebellion of Korah (above, pp. 73–85).

3. On HS's role in the editing of the Pentateuch, see above, pp. 100–103.

4. See E. A. Speiser, *Genesis* (AB 1; New York, 1964) introduction, p. xvii; H. C. Brichto, "On Slaughter and Sacrifice, Blood and Atonement," *HUCA* 47 (1976) 19–37; compare S. R. Driver, *An Introduction to the Literature of the Old Testament* (Edinburgh, 1913) 154. The complexity and great stratification of the Priestly writings leads me to reject M. Haran's opinion, which confines the entire activity of the Priestly school to the period of Ahaz-Hezekiah (*Ages and Institutions in the Bible* [Tel Aviv, 1972] 187–88; idem, *Temples and Temple Service in Ancient Israel* [Oxford, 1978] 146–47). Elsewhere Haran also dates the composition of the Holiness Code, which, in his opinion, preceded the "Priestly source" (PT) to this same period (Haran, "The Holiness Code," *EM* 5:1098). If we accept Haran's

This understanding leads us to examine the issue of the historical framework of Priestly literary production in a different light. We no longer need to determine if the Priestly source was created before the destruction of the First Temple, as held by Kaufmann and his followers, or afterwards, as maintained by Wellhausen and his sympathizers. Both of them are right! Certain sections of the Priestly writings were composed during the First Temple period, whereas others were written during the Babylonian exile and at the time of the return to Zion—when the Pentateuch was edited.[5]

---

view, we would have to compress the composition of the Holiness Code, the emergence of PT, and all of PT's literary activity into the period of Ahaz and Hezekiah, which is less than fifty years. This seems unlikely to me. It is hard to accept that such a wide-ranging and complex body of material could be composed in such a short period. Nevertheless, I agree with Haran's identification of the reign of Ahaz and Hezekiah as a decisive period in the history of the Priestly writings.

5. See above, p. 103 and n. 152. Kaufmann, too, admits that the Pentateuch was edited in this period (*History*, 4:340–46), but, in his opinion, no new legislation was added at this time, and the project was restricted to compilation and editing (see *History*, 1:78–80, 215–20). Kaufmann bases his argument on the mixture of styles in the narrative sections of the Pentateuch, as opposed to the careful separation of sources in the legal material. Since the editors did not hesitate to integrate different sources of different styles in the narrative sections, Kaufmann concludes that they failed to notice or, at the least, failed to admit the differences among the sources: "For them, it was in its entirety the word of God. All was given by 'one sole Shepherd.' They felt no need to avoid mixing a 'novella' written in the spirit and language of P from the laws and 'novellas' of the Covenant Book or D, and vice-versa" (*History*, 1:79). The only theory that can explain the editors' behavior is that, at that time, "the development of the legal collections *had been completed.* The texts of all three collections [Covenant Book, P and D] were already completed and *finalized*" (ibid., pp. 79–80). I find Kaufmann's arguments incorrect. One cannot compare narrative and legislation in this way: the mix of styles in narrative portions is unavoidable; only so could the different traditions of the deluge, the Ten Plagues, and so on be utilized to form a single, continuous story. Could one imagine, for example, a presentation of the integral JE deluge tradition, followed by the entire Priestly version? In the legislative portions, on the other hand, the unique style of each of the sources could be preserved, and the sources placed alongside. Moreover, our study reveals a picture of the editors' activity very different from that presented by Kaufmann. While the HS editors did not intervene in the non-Priestly legal collections—the Covenant Book and D (see above, pp. 100–103 and n. 144)—they acted differently in their editing of the various Priestly writings. To the legal scrolls of PT they added hortatory verses, introductory and concluding phrases, and even legislative innovations (see Exod 25:1–9; 27:20–21; 28:3–5; 29:38–46; 31:1–17; Lev 3:17; 7:22–36; 10:6–11; 11:43–45; 14:34; 15:31; 16:29b–34; Num 5:21, 31;19:10b–13, 20–21a; 28:2, 6, etc.; see also chapter 2, n. 142). The editors added several items to their own legal compilation (the Holiness Code [H]) as well as to HS material outside of the Holiness Code (see above, n. 2). Thus, it seems that the editors recognized the specific character of each of the sources and related to each collection according to its origin: while they avoided tampering with the "outside" compilations (Covenant Book and D), as members of HS who viewed themselves as continuing the Priestly writings, they felt empowered to alter HS, and even intervened in the old PT legal scrolls.

Thus, several criteria employed by scholars in order to fix the date of the Priestly source provide only partial, sometimes contradictory, solutions. For example, some scholars claim that linguistic evidence indicates that the Priestly source was edited before the destruction, while others, using other linguistic criteria, arrive at the opposite hypothesis.[6] I believe there is merit in both claims and that the contradictory hypotheses result from a failure to discern the complexity of the material. If we examine the Priestly source as a single unit, without distinguishing between its different strata, and compare its language to that of the book of Ezekiel, we might conclude that Ezekiel's language is later than that of the Priestly source as a whole.[7] But this general conclusion still allows the possibility that certain strata in the Priestly source, especially in the last stages of HS's creative activity, are contemporary with, or even later than, Ezekiel. Thus, we may find evidence of Persian linguistic influence in the later parts of the Priestly writings.[8] The same result obtains from comparison of content and literary form. Ezekiel does, indeed, draw on the material of the Priestly sources of the Pentateuch, but may in turn have influenced the later strata of this composition.[9]

The same obtains for the comparative study of the book of Deuteronomy and the Priestly source. Recently several scholars drew attention to instances in which Deuteronomy clearly drew on the Priestly source.[10]

6. Whereas Horowitz uses linguistic analysis to prove the early date of the Priestly source, Polzin and Levine are of the opinion that the language of the Priestly source attests to its late date of composition. See Hurvitz, "Studies in the Vocabulary of the Priestly Code: The Use of "ראש" and "רכש" in the Book of Leviticus and Numbers," *Teʿuda* 2 (1982) 299-305; idem, "The Evidence of Language in Dating the Priestly Code," *RB* 81 (1974) 25-55; idem, *A Linguistic Study of the Relationship between the Priestly Source and the Book of Ezekiel* (CaRB 20; Rome, 1982); R. Polzin, *Late Biblical Hebrew: Toward an Historical Typology of Biblical Hebrew Prose* (Missoula, MT, 1976); B. A. Levine, "Research in the Priestly Source: The Linguistic Factor" (Hebrew), *Eretz Israel* 16 (1982) 124-31.

7. This is the method of analysis chosen by Hurvitz (above, n. 6). Compare D. Hoffmann's criticism of scholars' lack of discernment in ignoring the stratification and the gradual development of the Priestly oeuvre ("The Lexicography of P Document and the Problem Concerning It," *Teʿuda* 4 [1986] 22; see also the quote from Driver, *Introduction,* 156-57).

8. As argued by Levine, "Research."

9. The reciprocal influences of Ezekiel and the Priestly writings on each other were noted by Driver (*Introduction,* 145-51). Any detailed analysis of the relation of Ezekiel to the Priestly writings (PT and HS) is beyond the scope of this book. I hope to devote a separate study to this question at a later date.

10. See W. L. Moran, "The Literary Connection between Lv. 11, 13-19 and Dt. 14, 12-18," *CBQ* 28 (1966) 271-77; J. Milgrom, "Profane Slaughter and a Formulaic Key to the Composition of Deuteronomy," *HUCA* 47 (1976) 9-12; S. Japhet, "The Laws of Manumission of Slaves and the Question of the Relationship Between the Collection of Laws in the Pentateuch," in *Studies in Bible and the Ancient Near East: Presented to S. E. Loewenstamm on his Seventieth Birthday* (Jerusalem, 1978); I. L. Seeligmann, "Loans, Security and Interest in Biblical Law and in its World-View," in *Studies in the Bible and the Near East,* 183-205.

Nevertheless, Deuteronomy too might have had some influence on the latter stages of HS's writings. The fact that Deuteronomy is also apparently the product of a long process makes it even harder to determine the chronological relationship of D to the Priestly writings of the Pentateuch.[11]

Any study of the historical background of the Priestly source must be done by devoting strict attention to the particular nature of the source's components. There is an essential difference between PT and HS: PT concentrates on its own inner world and has little interest in what takes place outside the Temple and the cult, whereas HS is concerned with the broader life and problems of the Israelite congregation. The difference in the areas of concern of the two schools leads to differing ways of studying the historical background for their activities. In determining the historical framework of PT, Wellhausen cited the silence of the historical and prophetic writings on the cultic framework, described extensively in PT, as evidence for the late date of PT's cultic system. But the Priestly texts are, by their nature, the concern of a small circle of "professionals," and the silence of the non-Priestly sources may be explained by the detachment of those circles in which the prophetic and historical sources were created from the internal world of the priesthood.[12] Furthermore, PT has practically no contact with the exterior world; it isolates itself totally from the surrounding reality and the time period of its contemporaries.[13] Its thinking and energies are concentrated on the utopian account of the establishment of the desert sanctuary. Thus, other biblical sources are of no help in determining its date. HS, as we have written, is of a completely different nature. This school leaves the confines of the cultic enclosure and shows intimate contact with the broader popular literature and with everything taking place in all strata of Israelite society. HS's indebtedness to non-Priestly writings is evident in its style, its law, and its worship.[14] As a result, we may seek points of contact between HS writings and political

11. See Seeligmann ("Loans," n. 61) and his critique of the one-sided view of A. Cholewinski (*Heiligkeitsgesetz und Deuteronomium* [AnBib 66; Rome, 1976]).

12. On the complete independence of the language of PT from the language of non-Priestly sources, see above, p. 106; on the esotericism of the Priestly teachings, see chapter 3, n. 120; and Haran, *Temples,* 143. On esotericism as the reason for the lack of influence of PT on non-Priestly preexilic literature, see Driver, *Introduction,* 141–42; Haran, *Temples,* 10–12.

13. On the utopian nature of PT, see Driver, *Introduction;* see also Haran, as quoted in chapter 3, n. 131.

14. The difference between PT and HS on this matter was pointed out by M. Haran, "Behind the Scenes of History: Determining the Date of the Priestly Source," *JBL* 100 [1981] n. 12). On HS's relation to JE's language, see above, p. 196. See also our discussion of the relationship of the HS sabbatical year law to the parallel law in Exodus, below, n. 63. For the influence of popular cultic laws on HS, see above, pp. 174, 195–97; see also Excursus 1, n. 11.

and social processes and events described in historical or political literature. It is our opinion that these contact points are the key to determining the historical background for the growth of HS.

One of the main conclusions of our philological study was that HS is later than PT and is a continuation of PT. The evidence for this conclusion is extensive and unambiguous: there are many indications of HS editing of PT material but, to the best of our understanding, no evidence at all for influence in the opposite direction (see Excursus 3). The results of these findings are clear. HS was written after the end of PT's literary activity; thus, we find influence in one direction only. As an explanation for this phenomenon, we suggested that HS resulted from deep spiritual changes within PT circles. If so, the determination of the date of origin of HS will also provide us with the *terminus ad quem* for the literary activity of its predecessor, PT.[15]

The Search for a Historical Framework for the Origin of HS

The main corpus of PT is the Holiness Code; any research into the origins of this school must be made on the basis of a careful study of this collection. We believe that HS grows out of a radical change that takes place in PT circles; therefore, we will concentrate on the main points in which the Holiness Code differs from PT.

This scroll opens with the prohibitions against profane slaughter and sacrifice away from "the entrance of the Tent of Meeting" (Lev 17:1–9). This is a clear order to centralize the cult, whose explicit aim is war against the idolatrous sacrifice to the שעירים, "goat-demons" (Lev 17:7).[16] The innovation of this command is striking when seen against the lack of any explicit mention of this issue in PT (see Excursus 1, n. 10).

The next portion of the Holiness Code (chap. 18 and its parallel, chap. 20) ordains separation from the ways of the nations. Besides the prohibitions against the abominations of incest and abominable sexual relations,

15. I refer here to the composition transmitted to us in the Pentateuch. Of course, it is entirely possible that even after the great changes that took place in Priestly circles, some groups continued to uphold the older views of PT, and perhaps even created and disseminated new writings. For the possibility that PT's ideas continued to be a source of inspiration in later generations, see I. Knohl, "The Priestly Tora Versus the Holiness School: Sabbath and the Festivals," *HUCA* 58 (1987) n. 130; idem, "Post-Biblical Sectarianism and Priesly Scrolls of the Pentateuch: The Issue of Popular Participation in the Temple Cult on Festivals," *Proceedings of the International Congress on the Dead Sea Scrolls, Madrid, 18–21 March 1991* (Leiden, 1993) 601–10.

16. On the centralization of the cult, as commanded in Leviticus 16, and on the entire chapter's origins in HS, see Excursus 3.

the text emphasizes interdictions of Molech worship and warnings against soothsaying and conjuring of familiar spirits.[17] This is also an innovation, because PT does not deal at all with the question of contact with non-Israelite cultures.

Leviticus 19 presents a comprehensive collection of moral and cultic commands, all collected under the demand "You shall be holy." The innovative nature of this chapter is striking when compared with the separation of morality from the cult and the restriction of the concept of holiness to the cultic realm that we find in PT.

In Leviticus 23, HS incorporates PT's festival code in its broader law of festivals. As we showed, the main innovation of HS is the blending of the "pure" Priestly cult with popular festival customs which express the agricultural life. We suggested that HS incorporated in its law of firstfruits the popular law reflecting the customs of local sanctuaries preceding the centralization of the cult (see above, pp. 24–26).

In Leviticus 25 we find the laws of sabbatical and jubilee years—laws not even mentioned in PT. The fundamental principle of God's sovereignty over the people and the land serves as the basis for a wide-ranging agrarian and social reform whose aim is the rehabilitation of a social class whose financial status had been eroded and who had been uprooted from their land.

Chapter 26 concludes the Holiness Code with a set of blessings and curses. These elements are absent from PT (which is not edited as a covenant book) and are foreign to its conception of worship of God as the fulfillment of the divine command without expectation of recompense. At their climax, the curses warn of the destruction of the land and the exile of its inhabitants to the land of the enemy.

Based on this survey, we may propose that the origin of HS and the composition of the Holiness Code were a response to the following developments: the incursion of idolatrous practices into Israel, especially the worship of Molech and soothsaying and conjuring of familiar spirits; the development of social polarization leading to the uprooting of farmers from their lands and their enslavement to the rich; and the detachment of morality from the cult. We may notice that the formation of HS is linked to the centralization and purification of the cult; however, the traditions of popular worship are not invalidated. Finally, the curses at the conclusion of the Holiness Code reflect the impact of forced mass exile on the people.

I believe that through investigation of the prophetic and historical sources we may successfully pinpoint the period in which the questions

17. For the prohibition against Molech worship, see Lev 18:21; 20:2–5; against necromancy and conjuring of familiar spirits, see Lev 20:6, 27 (this prohibition also appears in Lev 19:31); against soothsaying and divination, see Lev 19:26.

handled by the Holiness Code were at the focus of the religious and social life. Those sources indicate that Molech worship was introduced to Israel during the reign of Ahaz and Manasseh and that soothsaying and inquiry of familiar spirits were also popular under those kings.[18] Their heirs, Hezekiah and Josiah, introduced reforms to purify and centralize the cult.[19] During the reign of Ahaz and Hezekiah, Isaiah and Micah prophesy in Judea; we find in their prophecy—as in Amos, who prophesied several years earlier in the kingdom of Israel—clear evidence of the severe social and financial polarization, which led to the uprooting of many farmers from their land and their being sold into slavery.[20] These prophets polemicize against those among the people who strictly perform the smallest details of rituals but distort social and moral justice.[21] During the reign of Ahaz and Hezekiah in Judea, the neighboring kingdom of Israel collapsed, and many of its inhabitants were exiled from their land.[22]

18. See 2 Kgs 16:3; 21:6; 23:10, 24; 2 Chr 28:3; 33:6; cf. also Isa 2:6; 8:19; Mic 5:11; 6:7. On the use of this evidence in dating HS, see L. Elliott-Binns, "Some Problems of the Holiness Code," *ZAW* 67 (1955) 38, 27; Haran, "Holiness Code," 1098 (note especially Haran's comments on the references to Molech worship in Jeremiah and Ezekiel).

19. On the destruction of the altars and the high places during the reign of Hezekiah, see 2 Kgs 18:4, 22; 2 Chr 30:14; 31:1. On the actions of Josiah, see 2 Kgs 23:8–9, 15–20; 2 Chr 34:3–7.

20. See Amos 2:6; 4:1; 5:11; 8:4–6; Isa 3:13–15; 5:8; Micah 2:2, 9; 3:1–3; 6:10–12. Scholars have noted HS's relation to the social circumstances described by these prophets; see C. Feucht, *Untersuchungen zum Heiligkeitsgesetz* (Berlin, 1964) 166–67.

21. See Amos 2:6–8; 5:4–15, 21–25; Isa 1:10–27; Micah 3:9–12; 6:1–8.

22. See 2 Kgs 15:29; 17:6, 23; 18:11. For the synchronization of the dates of the kings of Judea and Israel in this period, see H. Tadmor, "Chronology," *EM* 4:277–78.

Wellhausen rejects the possibility that the exile reflected in Leviticus 26 is that of the northern kingdom of Samaria (*Prolegomena,* 382–83). He argues as follows: (1) If this chapter of Leviticus had been written at the time of the exile of Samaria, we ought to find similarities to Isaiah. The linguistic similarities between this chapter and Ezekiel prove that it was composed around the time of that prophet. (2) It is unlikely that the destruction of Samaria had such a great impact on the people of Judea. (3) The hope for revival and renewal expressed in Lev 26:42–46 indicates that the author lived around the time of the end of the Babylonian exile. How else could he have received the vision of revival?

I believe we may refute each of Wellhausen's arguments in turn: (1) Although the ideological links to Isaiah's prophecy are not evident in Leviticus 26 (with the exception of the image of the remnant returning to God [see below, p. 213] and the mention of the חמנים [see below, n. 49]), we do find them clearly expressed in other parts of HS, which, as Wellhausen forcefully claims, are inseparable from chap. 26. On the other hand, linguistic affinities to the language of Ezekiel do not necessarily attest to a contemporary date of composition. Ezekiel may have borrowed literary expressions from HS. (2) The argument that the people of Judea were not concerned by the fall of Samaria is unfounded. Archaeological evidence indicates that many refugees from the kingdom of Samaria escaped to Jerusalem (see below, n. 35). Undoubtedly, the refugees' tales of the horrors of the destruction and the exile shocked the inhabitants of Judea, who feared a similar fate (see Isa 10:11; 36:19–20). (3) Just as the preexilic prophets Amos and Isaiah foresaw the revival that would

Most of the phenomena mentioned here apply both to the period of Ahaz and Hezekiah and to the period of Manasseh and Josiah; but during the reign of Manasseh and Josiah we no longer hear of the acute social polarization that leads to the uprooting of farmers from their lands and their enslavement to the rich.[23] Furthermore, idolatrous worship became widespread in Judea during the period of Manasseh (see 2 Kgs 21:3–5; 2 Chr 33:3–5; Zeph 1:4–5); had the Holiness Code been composed during this period, we would expect to find many warnings against idolatry, as we find in the book of Deuteronomy, which was published under Josiah's reign. The Holiness Code, on the other hand, struggles with Molech worship, soothsaying, and sorcery, whereas the warnings against idolatry are of secondary importance. This corresponds to the reign of Ahaz: at that time the worship of Molech and various forms of divining and magic were prevalent, but no institutionalized idolatry existed.[24] An additional factor which points to the period of Hezekiah is the correspondence of that king's reforms to the laws of HS.[25] As we saw, Leviticus 17 legislates the centralization of the cult as viewed by HS. These passages emphasize that sacrifices are to be made before the Tabernacle of God and the blood sprinkled "against the altar of the Lord at the entrance of the Tent of

---

take place after the exile, so too the idea of revival arose in the writings of the members of HS.

23. See Kaufmann, *History*, 3:14, 372–74, 448–49.

24. The account of the deeds of Ahaz, as described in the book of Chronicles, is tendentious. See S. Japhet, *The Ideology of the Book of Chronicles and Its Place in Biblical Thought* (Eng. trans. A. Barber; Frankfurt, 1989) 168; J. McKay, *Religion in Judah under the Assyrians* (SBT 26 2nd series; London, 1973) 6. On the orthodoxy of the altar erected by Ahaz and the sacrifices offered upon it, see Haran, *Ages*, 178 n. 48; idem, *Temples*, 135 n. 6; J. McKay, *Religion*, 7–8; M. Cogan, *Imperialism and Religion* (SBLMS 19; Missoula, MT, 1974) 73–77; idem, "The Ahaz Altar: The Problem of Assyrian Cult in Judah," in *Proceedings of the Sixth World Congress of Jewish Studies* 1 (Jerusalem, 1977) 122–24.

25. Although the link between the Holiness Code and Hezekiah's reforms was already proposed by P. Heinisch (*Das Buch Leviticus* [HS; Bonn, 1935] 11–13), he dated the main body of H to a period several generations earlier. To Hezekiah's reign he assigned the composition of chaps. 26 and 27 and the editing of the collected material.

Haran (*Ages*, 183–90; *Temples*, 141–48) concluded that Hezekiah's reforms were guided by the ideology of P and that P was also composed at this time. As we stated earlier, PT (P) does not even mention the question of the centralization of the cult, and the ordinances in Leviticus 17 are all of HS origin (see above, p. 112). While I accept Haran's argument that Hezekiah's reforms were executed under Priestly influence and were not based on D, I disagree on the identity of the school responsible for the development of this ideology. Furthermore, I disagree with him on the date of the Priestly writings as a whole. As I explained above (n. 4), Haran compresses the composition of the entire Priestly opus into the period of Ahaz-Hezekiah, whereas I believe that this period marks the beginning of the activity of HS. PT, which I believe is prior to HS, was formulated at an earlier time. Nor do I believe it possible to limit the writings of HS to the period of Ahaz-Hezekiah: this school continued to be active in later generations (see above, pp. 199–201; nn. 2–4 above).

Meeting" (vv. 5–6a). We find a similar formation in the passage on the altar on the other side of the Jordan in Joshua 22, a passage deeply imprinted by the language and style of HS.[26] The emphasis is on the prohibition against building an altar: "Far be it from us to rebel against the Lord, or to turn away this day from the Lord and build an altar for burnt offerings, meal offerings, and sacrifices other than the altar of the Lord our God which stands before his Tabernacle" (v. 29). In both Leviticus 17 and Joshua 22 there is an emphasis on the difference between legitimate sacrifice on the designated altar at the entrance of the Tent of Meeting and all other sacrifice, considered illegitimate. But we find no explicit contrast between the Tent of Meeting and other places of worship.[27] The contrast between the one legitimate altar and the other illegitimate ones is repeated in the reference to the reforms of Hezekiah in the words of the Rabshakeh: "He is the very one whose shrines and altars Hezekiah did away with, telling Judah and Jerusalem, 'You must worship only at this altar in Jerusalem'" (2 Kgs 18:22; cf. Isa 36:7); or as formulated in 2 Chronicles: "Before this one altar you shall prostrate yourselves, and upon it make your burnt offerings" (32:12).[28]

In Deuteronomy's understanding of the centralization of the cult, it is not the uniqueness of the altar that is stressed but rather "the site that the Lord shall choose" as opposed to "the sites at which the nations worshiped" or "in any place you like" (see Deut 12:2, 5, 11, 13–14). It seems that the differences in the understanding of the centralization of the cult between HS and D are expressed in the execution of the reforms of Hezekiah and Josiah. Under Hezekiah's reform, based on HS's conception, the high places and the altars were removed but the cult places outside Jerusalem retained their sanctity. Under Josiah's reform, which was shaped by the ideology of HS, these cult sites were completely destroyed and defiled.[29] Archaeological evidence of the difference between the two conceptions was revealed in the Arad excavations, with the discovery of an Israelite temple with a sacrificial altar in its courtyard. Archaeologists determined that while the altar of sacrifice was destroyed under Hezekiah, the Temple itself continued to function until its destruction by

26. To clarify the relation to HS's language, compare Josh 22:17 with Num 31:16; Josh 22:18 with Num 32:13; the phrase בתוכנו ה' in v. 31 with ובתוכם ה' in Num 16:3. The phrases משכן ה' and מזבח ה' in v. 19 are typical of HS language; see chapter 2, nn. 30, 130.

27. Compare Kaufmann, *History,* 1:131; idem, *The Book of Joshua* (Jerusalem, 1977) 240.

28. Recently, E. Ben Zvi has claimed that the text of Hezekiah's reforms in Rabshakeh's speech is Deuteronomic in character ("Who Wrote the Speech of Rabshakeh and When?," *JBL* 109 [1990] 84–85, 91). Our study cast doubts on his findings. Even if it is true that the language reflects the description of Hezekiah's actions in 2 Kgs 18:4–5, nevertheless, the emphasis on the one altar is never found in Deuteronomic literature but corresponds closely to HS's conceptions (see below).

29. See Haran, *Ages,* 180–82; *Temples,* 138–40.

Josiah. The evidence may be accounted for by the differing nature of the two reforms:[30] whereas Hezekiah's reforms were limited to enforcing the prohibition against sacrifice by destroying the altars and the high places, the reforms under Josiah led to the total destruction of cultic places outside of Jerusalem.[31]

It would seem, thus, that the religious, social, and political conditions under the reign of Ahaz and Hezekiah in Judea most closely correspond to the picture that emerges from the Holiness Code. It would seem that the change in Priestly circles that led to the rise of HS took place at this time.

If Hezekiah's centralization of the cult was made under the influence of HS and its rules, as detailed in the Holiness Code, we may place the period of its composition after Ahaz's rise to power (Ahaz became a co-ruler in 743 B.C.E.)[32] but preceding Hezekiah's reforms. We do not know when Hezekiah's reforms were carried out. 2 Chr 29:3 says that the reforms took place in the first year of Hezekiah's reign, but scholars suspect that this date may be tendentious and may not reflect historical fact.[33] We know that Hezekiah's reform is mentioned in the speech of the Rabshakeh, dated to 701 B.C.E., during Sennacherib's campaign against Hezekiah. Thus, we may determine that the Holiness Code was composed sometime between the years 743 and 701 B.C.E. The relationship of the Holiness Code to the reforms of Hezekiah would point to Jerusalem as the place of composition.

I believe that the events of the period of Ahaz and Hezekiah also provide us with the background for the hierarchical and functional distinction between priests and Levites, which is an innovation of HS (see above, p. 85). In the second half of the eighth century B.C.E., the kingdom of Israel collapsed, and many refugees from the northern kingdom–in-

30. See Y. Aharoni, "Arad: Its Inscriptions and Temple," *BA* 31 (1968) 26; idem, "An Altar of Jahweh in the Land of Egypt and a *Masseba* to Yahweh by its Border," in *Studies in the Book of Isaiah* (Jerusalem, 1980) 154–55.

31. H. L. Ginsberg (*The Israelite Heritage of Judaism* [New York, 1982] 115–16) argues against any Priestly influence on Hezekiah's reform. He claims that the mention of the cutting down of the *ashera* among the acts of Hezekiah, described in 2 Kgs 18:4 proves that the reform was inspired by D, since the prohibition of the *asherot* and the command to cut them down are mentioned specifically in D but not in the Priestly writings. But, as Ginsberg himself admits (n. 144), we could "prove," using the same method that Josiah's reforms were inspired by HS, since the destruction of the high places, which plays a central role in Josiah's reform, is mentioned specifically in HS (Lev 26:30; Num 33:52) but never in D!

32. See Tadmor, "Chronology," 301.

33. Cogan, "Tendentious Chronology in the Book of Chronicles," *Zion* 45 (1980) 168–69. Rainey, on the other hand, accepts the Chronicles tradition ("Arad in the Latter Days of the Judean Monarchy," *Cathedra* 42 [1987] 19). This study is not the appropriate framework for an exhaustive discussion of the historical accuracy of the Chronicles account of Hezekiah's reforms (see also below, n. 40).

cluding members of the tribe of Levi, who lived in Israel and served in part at cultic sites there[34]—streamed into Jerusalem.[35] We may surmise that the cult centralization reforms of the time of Hezekiah also encouraged the emigration of Levite families, formerly serving in the temples of the towns of Judea, to Jerusalem.[36] This made the question of the status of non-Jerusalemite Levite families a pressing issue: Should they be allowed to serve in the Temple in Jerusalem or not? According to the dominant conception in non-Priestly sources, all sons of Levi may serve in the cult.[37] PT, on the other hand, restricts participation in the cult to the "sons of Aaron"— a title apparently reserved for Priestly families serving in Jerusalem.[38] Naturally, this question also had social ramifications:

34. According to 2 Chr 11:14, all the Levites left the northern kingdom of Samaria at the time of Jeroboam. This tradition is, however, of no historical value; see Haran, *Ages,* 160 n. 30; *Temples,* 83 n. 34.

35. The emigration of the refugees from the north resulted in the rapid expansion of Jerusalem in this period; see M. Broshi, "The Expansion of Jerusalem in the Reign of Hezekiah and Manasseh," *IEJ* 24 (1974) 21-26.

36. While we do not possess sufficient information on the image of the priests serving at temples outside of Jerusalem, it appears that most traced their origins to the tribe of Levi (see Haran, *Ages,* 155-61; *Temples,* 76-83).

37. See Haran, *Ages,* 166; *Temples,* 89.

38. Haran and A. Cody argue that in the Priestly writings the term בני אהרן refers to all Levites residing in Judea; their main supporting evidence is the list of Priestly cities in Joshua 21, which apportions thirteen Judean towns of the total forty-eight Levite towns in the entire country for the residence of the sons of Aaron (Haran, *Ages,* 162-64; *Temples,* 84-89; A. Cody, *A History of Old Testament Priesthood* [AnBib 35; Rome, 1969] 159-66). I believe that this claim is at odds with the arrangements fixed by HS for the apportioning of sacred gifts. The main sacred gift, the tithe, is given to the Levites, who are obliged to separate a tithe of their share for the priests, the sons of Aaron (Num 18:21-32). From a financial point of view, an analysis of the distribution of resources under this arrangement indicates that the priests, the sons of Aaron, would make up 10 percent of the sons of Levi. Even if we include the other sacred gifts, to which the Levites are not entitled, it would still seem that the number of Levites is several times the number of Aaronide priests. According to Haran's theory, which claims that the "Sons of Aaron" were the Levites of Judean origin and the "Levites" were Levite families who emigrated from the north (see *Ages,* 188-89; *Temples,* 147-48), we should expect a very different numerical proportion: it is not possible that the number of northern refugees of the tribe of Levi was several times greater than the number of Levite tribe members in Judea and Jerusalem. If, on the other hand, the "Sons of Aaron" were the priests of the Jerusalem Temple and the "Levites" were all other members of the tribe of Levi in Judea and in the northern kingdom, then it is very likely that there were many more "Levites" than "Sons of Aaron." Haran's evidence from Joshua 21 is also inconclusive. Even if we accept the opinion of those scholars who claim that the geographic situation expressed in this list reflects the territorial situation at the time of the United Kingdom, this, as Haran admits, does not permit us to determine the date of composition of the written account (see Haran, *Ages,* 189 and n. 81; *Temples,* 148). Although the term "Levite towns" is mentioned in the HS jubilee law (Lev 25:32-34), and the law on the assignment of the towns to the Levites (Numbers 35) is also of HS origin, neither law distinguishes between Levite and Priestly towns. This distinction first surfaces in Joshua 21 and apparently belongs to a later stage in the development of the town lists (see Z. Kalai,

Would the Jerusalem priests allow the Levite families of Judah and Israel to participate in the Temple cult, thus giving up their exclusive rights as priests of the king's Temple of Jerusalem? And how should the Temple revenues henceforth be divided among the various Levite families?

HS sought to resolve this question by distinguishing between the Aaronide priests—that is, the ancient families of the Jerusalem priesthood—who retained the exclusive privilege of serving in the inner areas of the Temple, and the other Levite families, who are assigned the guardianship of the sacred enclosure and other service tasks. In order to provide a livelihood for this social class, HS determined that the tithe, formerly given entirely to the priests of the Jerusalem Temple, the Aaronides, should henceforth be given to Levites.[39] Thus, the Jerusalem priests gave up part of their livelihood to the benefit of Levite families arriving from Judea and Israel, but did not compromise their exclusive status.[40]

In order to lend legal validity to the cultic innovations, HS anchored them in the period of Moses, which is the founding period of the cult.[41] The separation of the Levites and their training for the cult are attributed to Moses and linked to the period of Israel's wandering in the desert: following the rebellion of the chieftains and the consequent plague, the Levites are appointed to protect the Tabernacle from intrusion of foreigners. This seems to reflect the events of the period of the monarchy, especially the period proximate to the composition of HS: the chieftains, in Priestly terminology, represent the political leadership of the Israelite people.[42] From other sources, we learn that the kings of Israel and Judah occasionally served in the cult, especially at dedication ceremonies for altars or temples.[43] According to the tradition of the book of Chronicles, Uzziah's desire to bring the incense offering in the Temple led to a clash between him and the Jerusalem Temple priests (2 Chr 26:16-21). Ahaz, Uzziah's grandson, sacrificed on the new altar built at his command

"The System of Levitic Cities," *Zion* 45 [1980] 20-21). It would seem that the schematic division of the towns between sons of Aaron and Levites is the product of late speculation, perhaps of the period following the canonization of the Pentateuch. It does not reflect the historical reality of the period of Ahaz and Hezekiah, in which, we believe, the functional distinction between Levites and Aaronide priests originated.

39. On the transfer of the gift of tithes from the priests to the Levites, see chapter 2, n. 60.

40. The reapportionement of sacred gifts to cult professionals at the time of Hezekiah is mentioned in 2 Chr 31:4-19. While I doubt that all the details of the narrative are historically accurate, I do believe that they are based on a reliable account of the changes in collection and distribution of the tithes and heave offerings that took place at this time.

41. On the Pentateuch's conception of the period of Moses as the formative period of the cult, see Japhet, *Ideology,* 199-200.

42. See Kaufmann, *History,* 1:139-40.

43. See J. Morgenstern, "A Chapter in the History of the High-Priesthood, *AJSL* 55 (1938) 1-5; R. de Vaux, *Ancient Israel* (New York, 1961) 1:124-25; Cody, *History,* 100-107.

(2 Kgs 16:12–13).[44] It would seem that the story of the rebellion of the chieftains and the test of the fire pans was composed against the background of the tensions between the priesthood and the royalty, which resulted from the king's intervention in the cult.[45]

It seems likely that the story of the Levites' revolt, led by Korah, which, as we noted, belongs to a later stage of HS's activity, also reflects the struggles of that period. The rebelling Levites oppose the distinction made between them and Aaron and his descendants and their removal from the inner cultic functions. It is reasonable to view this as an expression of protest on the part of Levites who served in the provinces against HS's decree that they may not approach the altar to bring sacrifice or incense.[46] This protest also surfaces in the book of Deuteronomy, which was composed at about the same time. Deuteronomy pleads the cause of the Levites of the provinces, declaring: "If a Levite would go, from any of the settlements throughout Israel where he has been residing, to the place that the Lord has chosen, he may do so whenever he pleases. He may serve in the name of the Lord his God like all his fellow Levites who are there in attendance before the Lord" (Deut 18:6-7).[47]

Thus, we see that the Levite laws of HS, including the story of the rebellion of the chieftains and the dispute of Korah, are constituted from the strands of the historical and social reality of the period of the school's formation.

Isaiah and the Holiness School

Supporting evidence for the theory that HS reflects the great changes in Priestly circles that took place in the second half of the eighth century

44. This altar served for lawful worship of God; see Cogan, *Imperialism,* 74–75; "Ahaz Altar," 120–21.

45. The connection between the actions of Uzziah and the revolt of the chieftains was already made in midrashic homilies (see *Tanhuma Zav* 11, 13; *Midrash Psalms* 118, 7). Cogan notes that the book of Kings does not censure Ahaz for infringing on the rights of the priests in offering "upon the altar" (*Imperialism,* 74–75 n. 44a; "Ahaz Altar," 121 n. 9). I think that Priestly circles disapproved of this action and that their criticism was cloaked in the narrative of the chieftains' rebellion.

46. It would seem that the character of Korah represents the Levite family known as the "sons of Korah." Scholars disagree on the origins of this family. Whereas some emphasize the northern elements in the psalms ascribed to the "sons of Korah," others point out the ties between the sons of Korah and the southern part of Judea; see N. Sarna, "The Psalm Superscriptions and the Guilds," in *Studies in Jewish Religion and Intellectual History* (ed. N. Stein and R. Lowe; University, AL, 1979) n. 64; S. E. Loewenstamm thinks that the sons of Korah originally enjoyed a high status among the Levites but lost their prominence as a result of their attempt to rise into the ranks of the priesthood ("Korah, Sons of Korah, Korahites," *EM* 7:258).

47. Compare also Jer 33:18. A discussion of the identity and status of the Levites in the law of the book of Ezekiel is not within the frame of our study. I hope to devote attention to this matter elsewhere.

B.C.E. is provided by the prophecy of Isaiah son of Amoz, who prophesied in Jerusalem at this time and whose message is related to HS's thinking. Although there is some link to other contemporary prophets, those links are restricted to Leviticus 26, which ends the Holiness Code.[48] The relation to Isaiah, on the other hand, is also evident in other sections of HS, which constitute the main body of HS's thinking. Let us mention at the outset, that we will not discuss literary or linguistic relations[49] (which might be accounted for through literary influence), but restrict our view to common central ideas that are formulated differently in the prophecy of Isaiah and in the writings of HS. This relation points to a living, direct relationship between the prophet and contemporary Priestly circles living in the area of Isaiah's preaching.

In his prophetic vision, Isaiah declares: "Holy, holy, holy! The Lord of Hosts! His presence fills all the earth!" (Isa 6:3). As in HS, the idea of God's holiness is of central importance. Isaiah often refers to God as "the Holy One of Israel," an expression exemplifying the connection between the holy God Yahweh and his people, Israel. The Israelites who sin incite against the "Holy One of Israel" and his word (Isa 1:4; 5:24). The prophet envisions a time when Israel will sanctify the name of God: "Men will hallow the Holy One of Jacob" (Isa 29:23, cf. 8:13). This closely resembles HS's view that through sinning Israel blasphemes God, profanes his holy Name and despises his word (Lev 20:3; Num 16:30–31). Through their observance of the commandments, on the other hand, God is sanctified in their midst (Lev 22:31–32). HS is of the opinion that God sanctifies Israel in potential and that the requirement of continuous sanctification applies to the entire people. In his vision, Isaiah ascribes the holiness of the remnant of Israel to their being a "holy seed," refined through the purifying action of God (Isa 4:2–4; 6:13). The theme of the return of the remnant of Israel to God is common to both Isaiah and HS (Isa 10:20–22; Lev 26:39–45).

The most important link between Isaiah and HS lies in the nature and characteristics of the concept of holiness. We have demonstrated that one of the unique features of HS is that it infuses the concept of holiness with moral content (see chapter 4, n. 37). Now, Isaiah is the only prophet who unequivocally expresses the moral dimension of holiness.[50] Isaiah sees

48. We find in Amos the phrase חלל את שם קדשי, "profane my holy Name" (2:7), which also appears in HS's writings (cf. Lev 20:3; 22:32); cf. also Amos 5:21; Amos 9:13 to Lev 26:59. Compare also Micah 5:12–13 with Lev 26:30–31; Micah 6:14a,15a with Lev 26:16b, 26b; compare also Hos 2:25 with Lev 26:12. Note the chiastic parallel between Hos 2:20, 23–24 and Lev 26:4–6. The great concentration of parallels in Leviticus 26 may be explained by the "prophetic" character of this chapter (see Elliott-Binns, "Problems," 39).

49. For example, the use of the word חמנים (Lev 26:30; Isa 17:8; 27:9). On the nature of the חמנים, see M. Greenberg, *Ezekiel 1–20* (AB 22; New York, 1983) 132.

50. Some scholars generalize, claiming that through prophecy the notion of holiness

social-moral injustice as blasphemy against the Holy One of Israel and his word (Isa 1:4; 5:23–24) and expects that God will judge the wicked among the nation and save the poor and oppressed (Isa 3:14; 5:17). The prophet states that by judging the wicked and restoring social justice, God is exalted and sanctified: "The Lord of Hosts is exalted by judgment, the Holy God proved holy by justice" (Isa 5:16). Isaiah and HS share the view that sanctity is expressed through the performance of righteousness and justice.[51]

There is, however, a fundamental disagreement between Isaiah and HS on the relation of morality to the cult. In HS, the demand to live a life of sanctity includes and combines the cultic and moral realms. Under the title "You shall be holy, for I, the Lord your God, am holy," HS includes injunctions on Sabbath observance and the sacrifice of the whole offerings, along with the command to take care of the poor and the prohibition against robbery, fraud, and showing partiality in justice (Lev 19:2–15). Isaiah, on the other hand, claims that God desires not the offerings of Israel and their Sabbaths but the correction of social-moral injustice and the upholding of the cause of the orphan and the widow (Isa 1:11–17).

It seems that the points of agreement, along with the grounds of contention between HS and Isaiah (as well as the other prophets of the period) give us the key to the understanding of the religious struggle that precipitated the development of this school.

The Reaction of the Priesthood to the Prophetic Critique

The period we have fixed for the origin of HS is also the time of the appearance of classical prophecy;[52] this is no coincidence. Classical prophecy grew out of a deep social and religious crisis.[53] The prophets of the

---

took on moral meaning (see, e.g., W. Eichrodt, *Theology of the Old Testament* [trans. J. Baker; London, 1961] 1:278), but this claim is unfounded. As N. H. Snaith remarked, Isaiah is the only one of the eighth-century prophets who infuses holiness with moral content (*The Distinctive Ideas of the Old Testament* [New York, 1964] 53). H. Ringgren points out that the idea of moral holiness is rare even in the preaching of later prophets (*The Prophetical Conception of Holiness* [Uppsala, 1948] 23).

51. The close relation between Isaiah and HS in this area was noted by Eichrodt (*Theology,* 1:280; see also p. 278, for the prophetic influence on the change in the Priestly concept of holiness).

52. Although classical prophecy began in the mid-eighth century B.C.E., or slightly before the time we posited for the origin of HS, there is, nevertheless, a considerable time overlap between the two. Under the reign of Ahaz and Hezekiah, when HS came into being, Isaiah and Micah were prophesying in Judea.

53. See Kaufmann, *History,* 3:11–13.

period decry the sharp social cleavages and condemn the rich for their abandonment of social justice and their valueless devotion to the cult. The extreme solution of classical prophecy to these phenomena is the rejection of ritual service and the insistence on moral purity as God's highest command.[54] This position is a slap in the face of the priesthood as their ideals are formulated in PT. At the core of PT's writings are the establishment of the cultic framework and the sacrificial worship in the Sinai desert.[55] The prophet Amos mocks this conception, saying: "Did you offer sacrifice and oblation to me those forty years in the wilderness, O House of Israel?" (Amos 5:25).[56] PT believes that the relationship between Israel and its God is exemplified through the observance of the עדות, the cultic demands God makes of Israel. The prophets, on the other hand, uphold social injustice as God's main demand of his people, and as the criterion that will determine the nation's fate.[57]

The prophets broadcast their message in public and did not hesitate to criticize the cult even in the Temple courtyards. Undoubtedly their words shocked their listeners and caused an uproar in Priestly circles. Witness the dispute between Amos and Amaziah (Amos 7:10–17) or the deep impression of Micah's prophecies of destruction on the people of his generation (Micah 3:9–12; Jer 26:17–19). Of course, the priesthood could not adopt the prophetic view, which completely delegitimizes the Temple framework; at the same time, they could not ignore the truth in the prophetic criticism of the nation's spiritual state and its reverberations among the people. No longer could they take refuge behind the Temple walls; they had to provide an answer for the questions of the day.

The theological framework of the priesthood, as formulated in PT, was incapable of responding to prophetic criticism or providing a solution for the generation's problems. As we remember, PT does not ignore moral law but sees it as a universal law incumbent on Israel since the Genesis period. But the insistence on the cult as the main focus of God's revelation to Moses and the sharp division between morality and the cult

54. Ibid., 3:71–81; Greenberg, *On the Bible and Judaism: A Collection of Writings* (Tel Aviv, 1985) 198–99.

55. See Lev 7:38 and Num 28:6.

56. On the tension between the prophecy of Amos and the conception of PT, see M. Haran, "Amos, Book of Amos," *EM* 6:284–85 (as for Jer 7:21–23, scholars disagree as to the relationship between these verses and the Priestly Torah); see Haran, "Amos"; M. Weinfeld, "Jeremiah and the Spiritual Metamorphosis of Israel," *ZAW* 88 (1976) 53–54; J. Milgrom, "Concerning Jeremiah's Repudiation of Sacrifice," *ZAW* 89 (1977) 272–75. As J. Begrich ("Die priesterliche Torah," in *Werden und Wesen des alten Testament* [BZAW 66; Berlin, 1936] 76–78) and R. Rentdorff remarked ("Priesterliche Kulttheologie und prophetische Kultpolemik," *TLZ* 81 [1956] 339–42), the prophets use Priestly terminology in their polemic against the Temple cult.

57. See Kaufmann, *History*, 3:76–81.

might easily be understood as a preference for cultic fervor over the performance of social justice.[58] There was an urgent need to reformulate the theological and legal framework of the priesthood in response to the moral criticism of the prophets, but in a way that would preserve the principles of the cultic tradition. So arose the change in direction of Priestly thinking, as expressed in the writings of HS.

On the one hand, HS preserves the centrality of cultic institutions. The Temple, the sacrifices, and the status of the priests are discussed at great length and are accorded a great measure of holiness; likewise, much emphasis is placed on the Sabbath and the festivals. On the other hand, HS assigns great importance to the practice of morality and social justice. It eliminates the barrier, set up by PT, between morality and the cult, incorporating both under the broadened rubric of holiness. The call "You shall be holy, for I am holy" can only be realized through observance of the cultic laws along with practice of just ways of love of the neighbor and the stranger. We thus find a moral refinement of the purely cultic conception, stemming from Priestly circles themselves, under the influence of the prophetic critique.[59]

The Practical and Ideological Solutions of HS to the Problems of the Day

The new Priestly school did not limit its activity to combining existing ideas and creating new theoretical constructs; it developed practical solutions to the contemporary crises as part of its theological cultic framework.

The Social Message of HS

HS originates in a generation that says:

> If only the new moon were over, so that we could sell grain; the Sabbath, so that we could offer wheat for sale, using an ephah that is too small, and a

58. I do not wish to argue that PT's conception was one of the causes of that generation's corruption. The Priestly Torah was mainly esoteric (see above, nn. 12–13), so that it is difficult to assign it any public influence at all. In any case, this conception could certainly offer no solution to the urgent contemporary problems.

59. Greenberg claims that because of the prophets' total negation of the cult, "the prophets' rebukes had no effect on the development of sensitivity towards the essential problems of the cult. We would be hard pressed to find any prophetic influence on the refinement of the cult and much of what was often identified as such, ought to be considered as an internal process in the development of cultic institutions" (*On the Bible,* 199). It would seem that HS's writings are a good example of a process of refinement of the cultic system, in response to the prophetic critique—even if it did not result in refinement of the cultic practices themselves (as was the case in the psalms discussed by Greenberg).

shekel that is too big, tilting a dishonest scale, and selling grain refuse as grain! We will buy the poor for silver, the needy for a pair of sandals. (Amos 8:5–6)

To those of distorted views, who are meticulous in observing the Sabbath but do not hesitate to use false scales and measures, HS commands "You shall be holy!" Holiness includes both the ordinance "You shall keep my Sabbaths" (Lev 19:3a) and the warning "You shall not falsify measures of length, weight, or capacity. You shall have an honest balance, honest weights, an honest *ephah,* and an honest *hin*" (Lev 19:35–36a).

Aside from the commands to walk in the ways of righteousness and practice social justice, which are frequent in HS (see Lev 19:9–18, 33–36; 23:22; 24:17–22), this corpus offers a program of comprehensive social reform in response to the problems of the time. This program, described in the jubilee law of Leviticus 25, is unique in that it is shaped by a theological-cultic model. The program is constructed of ancient elements: the Mesopotamian institution of דרור (liberty)[60] and the concept of God's sovereignty over the nation and the land, already mentioned in the Song of the Sea (see chapter 4, n. 56). These elements are woven by HS into a legal-religious platform, which eliminates, *de facto,* all slavery within Israelite society and assures the agrarian rehabilitation of dispossessed farmers ("It shall be a jubilee for you; each of you shall return to his holding and each of you shall return to his family," Lev 25:10b). To those who buy the righteous for silver and the needy for a pair of sandals, HS declares: "For it is to me that the Israelites are servants" (Lev 25:55a); "they may not give themselves over into servitude" (Lev 25:42b). And to "those who add house to house and join field to field" (Isa 5:8a), HS announces: "But the land must not be sold beyond reclaim, for the land is mine; you are but strangers resident with me. Throughout the land that you hold, you must provide for the redemption of the land" (Lev 25:23–24).

The jubilee year is a holy year,[61] the climax of seven sabbatical years[62]—a year of repose from agricultural work for the land and its inhabitants and the revocation of private ownership of its produce.[63] The sabbatical year is called here שבת שבתון, שבת לה' (Lev 25:2, 4); the proclamation of the jubilee year is made by blowing the ram's horn on the Day of Atonement,

60. See, recently, M. Weinfeld, *Justice and Righteousness in Israel and the Nations* (Jerusalem, 1985) 54–56 and the literature listed there.

61. The sanctity of the jubilee year is stressed in Lev 25:10, 12.

62. On the different views concerning the counting of the sabbatical and jubilee years, see B. Uffenheimer, "Utopia and Reality in Biblical Thought," *Immanuel* 9 (1979) 9.

63. The sabbatical year law already appears in the Covenant Book (Exod 23:10–11). The linguistic affinities between the two laws (compare Lev 25:3 with Exod 23:10) indicate that HS was guided by the Covenant Book law but chose to emphasize the sacral overtones of the sabbatical year institution.

which is also called שבת שבתון in HS (see Lev 16:31; 23:32). It would seem that the laws of the sabbatical and jubilee years in the Holiness Code, including the emphasis on their holiness, were designed to counter the habitual practices of the people of that period. Thus, whoever meticulously observed the Sabbath would also see that the land's Sabbaths and jubilees were maintained. In other words, the theological-sacral overtones of HS's social reforms were designed to give them validity and make them more compelling to that generation of scrupulous observers of the cultic sacral laws.[64]

HS's Struggle against Foreign Cults

The period of HS's origin is one of massive influx of foreign cults into Judea and Israel (see above, pp. 206–7 and nn. 18 and 25). This influx of nonnative cults and customs is apparently linked to the rise of the Assyrian empire in the eighth century B.C.E. Assyria was strongly influenced by Aramean culture,[65] and the mixed Assyrian-Aramean culture ruled over the entire East and left its mark on Judea as well.[66] PT provides no response to this challenge, as it does not even relate to contact with idolatrous culture. Thus, new currents in Priestly thought were necessary, currents that would boldly struggle against foreign influence.

Here, too, the solution was found through changing and enlarging the concept of holiness. Holiness, according to HS, surpasses the limits of the Temple-Priestly framework; it must be present throughout the Israelite congregation and the land of Israel. The call to a life of holiness, directed toward the nation as a whole, is grounded in Israel's separation from the nations to be a possession of God: "You shall be holy to me, for I, the Lord am holy, and I have set you apart from other peoples to be mine"

64. M. Weinfield (*Deuteronomy,* 188) claims that the Priestly writer was interested in the taboo of the sabbatical year and the sacral implications of this taboo, whereas the Deuteronomic author was concerned with the social aspect of this law, and completely ignored its sacred aspect (*Deuteronomy and the Deuteronomic* [Oxford, 1972] 188). I think this distinction is imprecise. Although the language of the Priestly legislator is molded by sacral expressions, the practical implications of the jubilee and sabbatical laws are of great social import, and the text shows great concern with the financial results of the law (see Weinfeld, *Deuteronomy,* 233 n. 3). For an analysis of these results, see Soss, "Old Testament Law and Economic Society," *Journal of the History of Ideas* 34 (1973) 339–43.

65. H. Tadmor, "The Aramaization of Assyria: Aspect of Western Impact," in *Mesopotamien und seine Nachbarn* (ed . H. J. Nissen and J. Renger; Berlin, 1982).

66. See M. Weinfeld, "The Moloch Cult in Israel and its Background," in *Proceedings of the Fifth World Congress of Jewish Studies,* Vol. 1 (Jerusalem, 1969) 52–61, 154; Cogan, *Imperialism,* 81–96; M. Greenberg, "Religious Stability and Ferment," in *The Age of the Monarchies: Culture and Society* (ed. A. Malamat; Jerusalem, 1979) 85–86.

(Lev 20:26). From this derives the obligation to distance oneself from the laws of the nations and their practices; this plays a highly central role in the Holiness Code. In HS, the land is conceived of as a kind of pure, living body, which vomits in reaction to the impurity resulting from the laws of the nations: "So let not the land spew you out for defiling it, as it spewed out the nation that came before you" (Lev 18:28; cf. 20:22).

HS also combats the incursion of foreign cults through the promotion of its laws on the centralization of the cult. The ordinance on the centralization of the cult is supported by the words "that they may offer their sacrifices no more to the goat-demons after whom they stray" (Lev 17:7a). The goat-demons are part of the "staging" of the law, which HS painstakingly integrates into the narrative of the desert wanderings, in order to lend it binding authority.[67] But it would seem that behind the desert staging we may discern the concern with infiltration of idolatrous cultic practices into the Land of Israel in the eighth century B.C.E. The centralization of the cult facilitates full Priestly supervision over the cultic worship and ensures that idolatrous practices—"sacrifices to the goat-demons"—will not be incorporated into the worship of God.[68] The application of this

67. Grintz claims that the fact that the worship of the goat-demons was not included among the Pentateuch warnings against idolatry is an indication that these verses were, indeed, applicable to the generation of Israelites wandering through the desert, before their entry into the Land of Israel (*Studies in Early Biblical Ethnology and History* [Tel Aviv, 1969] 218). I find this argument difficult to accept; the language of these verses demonstrates that the legislator did not restrict himself to the conditions of the desert but sought to fix his prohibitions as a חקת עולם, "an everlasting law." Had the law only been applicable to the goat-demons of the desert, what reason would there be for applying it to future generations in the land of permanent settlement? We should not be misled by the desert "scenery," which is one of the hallmarks of Priestly writing (cf. the anchoring of the rebellions of the chieftains and the Levites in the desert wanderings period, above p. 211). The sacrificing to the goat-demons hints at the cult of the high places, which absorbed many of the foreign practices that spread throughout Israel in the eighth and seventh centuries B.C.E., especially Molech worship (compare J. Aloni, "The Place of Worship and the Place of Slaughter According to Leviticus: 17:3–9," *Shnaton—An Annual for Biblical and Ancient Near Eastern Studies* 7–8 [1983–84] 40–41). We find a similar use of the word שעירים in 2 Chr 11:15 and perhaps 2 Kgs 23:8 (see D. Hoffmann, "Kleinigkeiten," *ZAW* 2 [1882] 175). The same comment applies to Ps 106:37, "Their own sons and daughters they sacrificed to demons." This verse refers, apparently, to the worship of Molech, which is called sacrificing to the "demons" (שדים). As earlier exegetes already noted, there is a relation between the sacrifice to the demons (שדים) and the sacrifice to the goat-demons mentioned in Leviticus 17 (see *Sifra, Aharei-Mot* 9, 8; *Leviticus Rabbah* 22,8, ed. Margaliot., p. 517; Ibn Ezra's commentary on Lev 17:7). Sacrifice to the demons is also mentioned in Deut 32:17 (see Ibn Ezra and Rashbam, ad loc.); there too the reference may be to Molech worship.

68. For example, the sacrifice of sons, which, among certain groups among the people was seen as the fulfillment of God's commandment; see Greenberg, *Ezekiel,* 369–70; M. Fishbane, *Biblical Interpretation in Ancient Israel* (Oxford, 1985) 184–87.

law to the resident aliens as well (Lev 17:8), along with the granting of equal cultic and judicial status (Num 15:14–16), is an additional defense measure against the incursion of idolatrous practices into the land.[69]

We find, thus, at the beginning and at the end of the Holiness Code two programs of reform. The first is the centralization of the cult, designed to confront the influences of foreign worship; as we noted, this program was instituted under the reign of Hezekiah. The second reform program, the jubilee law, was planned to resolve the social and moral crisis. As we have no evidence for the implementation of the jubilee law, it seems that it remained a purely utopian vision.[70] In any case, these laws demonstrate the creative, innovative spirit of HS and its responsiveness to the pressing needs of the time.

The Historical Framework for PT's Activities

The fixing of the date of origin of HS gives us a *terminus ad quem* for the composition of PT (see above, p. 204 and n. 15). Since HS originated in the period from the rule of Ahaz to that of Hezekiah, the PT material in the Pentateuch must have been composed earlier. This material has no direct relation to historical reality, but it would seem that those scholars who claim that PT's model of the Tabernacle reflects a certain influence of the Solomonic Temple are correct.[71] Furthermore, an analysis of the components of the buildings reveals a correspondence between the functions of the Tabernacle and those of the Temple of Solomon, before changes were introduced under Ahaz and Hezekiah.[72] This supports our theory. Thus, PT must have originated at some time during the two-hundred-year period between the construction of Solomon's Temple and the reign of Ahaz-Hezekiah—between the mid-tenth century B.C.E. and the mid-eighth century B.C.E. This time period also accounts for the many strata in PT, which indicate a compilation made over a long period of time (see above, nn. 2, 4).

The theory that places the origins of PT at this period also comports

69. Compare SHaDaL's commentary on Num 15:15.

70. See S. E. Loewenstamm, "Jubilee," *EM* 3:580.

71. See Haran, *Temples,* 189–92. Nevertheless, it is possible that the basis for the plan of the Tabernacle may have been an early tradition from the wandering or settlement periods (see S. E. Loewenstamm, "Mishkan Hashem," *EM* 5:540–42; Haran, *Temples,* 197–204; Y. Aharoni, "The Solomonic Temple, the Tabernacle and the Arad Sanctuary," in *Orient and Occident: Essays presented to Cyrus H. Gordon on the occasion of his Sixty-Fifth Birthday* [ed. H. A. Hoffner; Neukirchen-Vluyn, 1973] 4–6). But this tradition was refashioned by PT, influenced by the plan of Solomon's Temple (Haran, *Temples*; Aharoni, "Solomonic Temple," 85–86).

72. Haran, *Temples,* 192–94.

with the image of the priests that arises from contemporary historical sources. The foundation of the Davidic kingship and the establishment of Solomon's Temple created a new situation in the Israelite nation. For the first time in their history a מקדש מלך, a royal sanctuary, was created, whose needs were paid from the royal treasury and whose priests were court subjects.[73] The early monarchic period was a flourishing time politically and materially for the Israelite people, and a productive spiritual and literary period as well.[74] But the gap between Priestly circles and non-Priestly writers continued to grow.[75] The priesthood retreated even further behind the Temple walls and avoided taking any part in the life of the people and society. Whereas prior to the monarchy, priests often fulfilled senior government posts (cf. the priests of Shiloh, Samuel) and, under David, the priests were involved in affairs of the kingdom and in court intrigues (see 2 Sam 15:35–36; 17:15–17; 19:12; 1 Kgs 1:7–8, 38–39), after Solomon ascended the throne, we no longer hear of any involvement of the priests in affairs of the kingdom, with the exception of Jehoiada the priest (2 Kgs 11:4–20). This singular exception probably was provoked by the religious threat posed by Athaliah's actions (see 2 Kgs 11:18). Even the traditional roles of the priesthood in wartime—the inquiry of the Urim and Thummim before going out to battle and the carrying of the ark to the battlefield—were no longer mentioned during or after the reign of Solomon.[76] The isolation from the people and their literary endeavors and their lack of participation in the judicial establishment and in battle are all hallmarks of the work of HS (see above, pp. 157–58). We may safely assume that the establishment of the "King's Temple" of Jerusalem and the creation of a closed, elitist Priestly class dependent on the royal court are all part of the background leading to the development

73. Compare G. von Rad, *Old Testament Theology* (trans. D. M. G. Stalken; Edinburgh, 1973) 43; Greenberg, "Religious Stability," 65.

74. See von Rad, *Theologie,* 1:49–55; Kaufmann, *History,* 2:195–211; E. E. Urbach, *Wüste und Gelobtes Land: Geschichte Israels von den Anfangen bis zum Tode Salomon* (Berlin, 1938) 279–85.

75. See von Rad, *Theologie,* 1:56 and see n. 5 to this chapter, on the lack of any connection between PT and the non-Priestly sources of the Pentateuch. Note especially the complete lack of points of contact between PT and the source J, which developed, according to many scholars, in the same place (Judea) and at the same time that we suggested for the creation of P—the beginning of the monarchic period.

76. The final mention of inquiry of God through the Urim and Thummim before battle is in the wars of David (see 1 Sam 30:7–8; 2 Sam 5:19, 23). In later generations, inquiry of the word of God is made through the prophets (see 1 Kgs 22:4–25; 2 Kgs 3:11; compare Greenberg, "Religious Stability," 69). The last mention of the carrying of the ark to the battlefield is in David's war against the Ammonites (2 Sam 11:11). Kaufmann suggested that the custom of taking the ark out to battle reflects the tradition of the House of Eli, while the contrary position was maintained by the House of Zadok, who controlled the Solomonic Temple (*History,* 2:471).

of PT. It is these circles that generate the ideal of a superior faith, completely detached from social, national, or material needs.

PT attains a level of abstraction and loftiness unequaled in the Bible (see chapter 3, n. 136). In fact, never in the history of Israel, until the contact between Judaism and the philosophical thought of the Middle Ages,[77] do we find a similar level of anti-anthropomorphic description of God. Unlike scholars who espouse a developmental model for Israelite faith, we do not believe that a high level of abstraction and a loftiness of ideals necessarily point to a late date of composition.[78] Research on other cultures has shown that literary and religious creativity sometimes attains its peak of glory at the very dawn of a new culture.[79] Our study shows that PT should be seen as an example of a cultural oeuvre that refutes the theory of gradual development in the realm of the spirit.

The Priesthood's Outreach to the People

In the eighth century B.C.E., Israel and Judea were shaken by political, social, cultural, and religious upheavals: the wars with the Arameans and the resulting social and economic polarization; the rise of the Assyrian

77. On the anthropomorphisms in postbiblical literature, see Kaufmann, *History,* 1:231–41.

78. This is primarily opposed to Driver (*Introduction,* 140–41), for whom loftiness and abstraction of PT's language at the beginning of the book of Genesis (as opposed to the anthropomorphic description of the Creation in J) are proof of the late date of PT. We believe that both PT and J came into existence at about the same time. The differences in religious language result from the very different atmosphere prevailing within the two different groups of authors: whereas PT expresses the abstract, lofty conception of God formulated within the inner circles of the priesthood, J reflects the popular, non-Priestly understanding of God. This, of course, in no way detracts from the literary power and spiritual level of the writings of J. On the contrary, I wholeheartedly accept Urbach's evaluation of the period of the United Kingdom as a religious high point, in no small measure thanks to the stature of the "Jahwistic composition" (see Urbach, *Wüste,* 282). The "popularity" of this work refers to the anthropomorphic image of God in this composition. As Urbach remarks, this in no way detracts from its high monotheistic level. If we add the flourishing of poetry, psalmody and wisdom literature (see Kaufmann, *History,* 2:195–206), we may generalize by saying that this was the peak period of all Israelite literature—in every genre.

79. See J. A. Wilson's comments on the theology of Memphis (*The Burden of Egypt* [Chicago, 1951] 59) and G. Sarton's composition (*A History of Science* [New York, 1965]) on the works of Homer (special thanks to M. Greenberg, who drew my attention to these scholars' writings). Compare W. Kaufmann's arguments (*Critique of Religion and Philosophy* [New York, 1961] 388–89) against the evolutionary biases in the study of biblical religion; Kaufmann's critique drew analogies to the histories of other religions, in which key figures, often unique in the history of that religion, appear already at that religion's very beginnings.

empire and the incursion of Aramaic-Assyrian culture; the destruction of the northern kingdom of Samaria; the exile of Israel to Assyria; and Sennacherib's war against Judea. These cataclysmic events gave birth to new spiritual forces among various strata of the people. In this period, the classical prophets arose, sharply attacked the Temple cult, and presented a new understanding of the pact between God and Israel. In the opinion of many scholars, the main corpus of Deuteronomy was formulated in the kingdom of Israel at this time.[80] After the destruction of the northern kingdom, many of its inhabitants migrated to Jerusalem, bringing their spiritual heritage with them. The immigration of the northern peoples to Jerusalem is confirmed by the rapid expansion of the city under Hezekiah.[81] The influence of the traditions of the refugees was felt in the amazing development of spiritual life in Judea.[82] The royal court became a focus of cultural activity, and the people of Hezekiah's court edited the wisdom literature.[83] These upheavals and changes drew the Jerusalem priesthood out of the shelter of the Temple and stimulated forces of renewal and creativity to resolve the immediate crises. The priesthood sought to grapple with the urgent religious and social problems and to respond to the challenge of the prophetic critique. This struggle shaped the creative activity of a new Priestly school—the Holiness School.[84]

The primary innovation in HS's thinking was the infusing of holiness with moral content and the application of holiness to the entire community of Israel and to the land they inhabited. From this derived the call to each and every Israelite, which is one of the hallmarks of HS.[85] The outreach to the people required compromise of the spiritual loftiness attained by HS, since HS, in its very nature, was directed toward a small chosen elite.[86] HS abandoned Priestly separatism and addressed the people, adopting elements of faith and worship popular among the nation at large. The religious language of HS is imbued with the spirit of popular faith: God is described in anthropomorphic language, and the

80. On the theories of the northern origins of the core of D, see Greenberg, "Religious Stability," n. 81.

81. See Broshi, "Expansion."

82. Compare Greenberg, "Religious Stability," 83.

83. Prov 25:1; in this connection, Ginzberg's theory ("Heritage," 34–37) on the northern origin of Proverbs is noteworthy. On literary activity in Hezekiah's court, see Weinfeld, *Deuteronomy*, 161–62.

84. In light of our theory on the influence of HS's teachings, as exemplified in the Holiness Code, on Hezekiah's program to purify and centralize the cult, we may surmise that the compilation and redaction of HS were carried out in connection with compiling and editing taking place in the royal court.

85. See Introduction, n. 3; above, pp. 101–3, 173.

86. See p. 153 and n. 120.

commandments are presented in the framework of a covenant of mutual obligation.[87] The cultic laws of this school also show influences of popular custom.[88]

HS's openness to popular creativity, combined with its profound knowledge of the Priestly heritage from which it originated, prepared it, in the course of time, for the gigantic task of editing the Pentateuch,[89] which consisted primarily of combining Priestly and popular material. This project, which profoundly impacted the further development of Judaism, was apparently accomplished during the Babylonian exile or during the period of the return to Zion.[90] But the historical task of HS did not end with the final redaction of the Pentateuch; it continued to influence later generations. Although this is not the place to analyze the concepts of faith and worship that prevailed in the Second Temple period and their relationship to the various schools in the Pentateuch, we might put forth our opinion that the central movement in Judaism in the Second Temple period, which began with Ezra and his circle and continued through the *haburot* of the Pharisees, mostly continued the popular Priestly heritage of HS.[91] The halakah of Qumran and the Sadducees,[92] on the other hand, preserve the hard core of the cultic conception prevalent in PT.[93] The verification of these claims, to which I intend to devote a separate study, will confirm the thesis put forth here—that the radical change that took place within the Jerusalem priesthood under Ahaz and Hezekiah, and which led to the development of HS, was a key point in the entire history of Israelite faith and worship.

87. See above, pp. 172–74.

88. See above, n. 14. This relation may derive from the entry of elements of the priesthood from the periphery into the ranks of the Holiness School.

89. See above, n. 3.

90. See chapter 2, n. 152; compare n. 5 in this chapter.

91. See Knohl, "Sabbath," 137–38.

92. On the relationship of Sadducee halakah to the halakah of the Qumran writings, see J. M. Baumgarten, "The Pharisaic–Sadducean Controversies about Purity and the Qumran Text," *JJS* 31 (1980) 157–70; Y. Susman, "The Study of the History of Halakha and the Dead Sea Scrolls," *Tarbiz* 59 (1990) 11–76.

93. I refer here to the emphasis on the Priestly elements of the cult and the suppression of popular ritual. In other areas, which are not strictly cultic, such as its concern with moral questions, the severity of its Sabbath laws, and others, the Qumran sect's position resembles that of HS. This may be the focus of the split between the Qumran sect and the Sadducees: whereas the Sadducees systematically followed PT, in both its severe and its lenient tendencies, the Qumran sect followed the more severe rulings and the ways of piety in all areas. Of course, this issue requires systematic treatment, and I can only raise several preliminary thoughts at this point.

EXCURSUS

5

A Response to Jacob Milgrom

In the introduction to his monumental commentary on the book of Leviticus (*Leviticus 1-16* [AB; New York, 1991), Jacob Milgrom devotes considerable space to a discussion of my doctoral thesis, upon which the present book is based. I cannot here respond in detail to all that Professor Milgrom wrote. Rather, I include verbatim the address I delivered at the special session that was held at the meeting of the Society of Biblical Literature in San Francisco in November 1992, on the occasion of the appearance of Professor Milgrom's book. In this address, I focused on the question of the relationship between morality and cult in the Priestly Torah, since it appeared to me that this was the main issue on which we differed. I have made no changes in the text of the address; it is presented here just as it was delivered.

I would like to begin my remarks by expressing my congratulations to Professor Milgrom on the fruits of his literary endeavors. I would like to express my thanks as well for the encouragement I received from him at the outset of my own efforts in biblical scholarship. At the time, ten years ago, I was a doctoral student in Talmud at the Hebrew University, and by chance I was drawn into the complex issues of Pentateuchal source criticism, which had until then been entirely foreign to me. I wanted to understand the nature of the relationship between the festival legislation in Leviticus 23 and the parallel list in Numbers 28-29. When I began to investigate this question using the philological tools I had acquired in the Talmud Department, I recognized that the accepted view assigning an earlier date to the H source than to P was fundamentally wrong, and that the earlier stratum of Priestly writings was in fact P. I saw also that the H material was much more extensive than had previously been perceived and was to be found in significant measure in Exodus and Numbers as well.

When I brought these observations to the attention of the central figures in the study of Priestly literature, I met with a distinctly dubious response: How could someone as young as I was, someone without the usual thorough training in biblical studies, have the audacity to cast doubt on the common conventions of the field?

Professor Milgrom's attitude was entirely different. A few years earlier, in his article in the *IDB Supplement,* he had staked out a position in support of the traditional view that H predates P, stating (p. 543): ". . . much of the language and some ideas in chs. 17–26 differ with the first part of Leviticus. Most probably P incorporated into these chapters an earlier document which might be called the Holiness Source." However, in the summer of 1983, when I shared with him the results of my study of the festival legislation (which appeared later in *HUCA* 58), Professor Milgrom was entirely open to reinvestigating the issue. When he became convinced of the correctness of my arguments in favor of an earlier date for P than for H, he adopted my view, as is evident from the introduction to his Leviticus volume. In fact, he accepted not only the predating of P but also my observation that the rise of the Holiness School occurred during the period of Ahaz and Hezekiah and that the cultic reforms of Hezekiah's reign were based on the writings of this school. I cite from the introduction to Professor Milgrom's commentary (pp. 26–27): "Knohl's thesis stands, and it reaches its zenith in the search for the Sitz-im-Leben, provenance, and date of H. . . . I accept fully his argumentation for setting H's terminus a quo in the days of Hezekiah (the end of the eighth century)."

Although, as I have said, Professor Milgrom has adopted my major arguments, there remains a certain disagreement between us at the edges of the chronology of the Priestly writings: Milgrom is of the opinion that the beginning of the P writings can be dated to the period of Shiloh, while I am convinced that this school commenced its literary activity with the construction of Solomon's Temple. We also disagree about the date of the conclusion of the Holiness School's literary production. Milgrom thinks the final stratum of H was created during the Babylonian exile; I have found evidence that I think indicates that this school concluded its activities with the final redaction of the Pentateuch at the beginning of the Persian period. This dispute is, in my opinion, quite secondary, and I would not like to engage the issue here. On this occasion, I would rather concentrate on the differences between us in our understanding of the theology and cultic outlook of the P school, or, as I prefer to call it, "the Priestly Torah" or "PT."

As I understand it, PT perceives a total separation between the ethical realm and the cultic. In its opinion, the ethical imperative is the basis for the existence of the universe and of human society. Moral law is essentially universal, and the world operates according to it during the primeval and patriarchal ages. In contrast, the revelation to Moses and Israel, symbolized by the appearance of the name YHWH, centers entirely on the numinous element of the divinity, an element beyond reason and ethics. The cultic system that becomes established after the revelation of the Tetragrammaton also reflects the numinous dimension of the divinity and of religion, and thus bears no connection to any concern for societal improvement or the establishment of justice or morality. Therefore, the legal system promulgated in Moses' time does not include a single command whose exclusive concern is the maintenance of morality and social justice.

Milgrom (*Leviticus,* introduction, 21–26) disagrees with me and tries to prove that the cultic legislation of PT encompasses the ethical elements as well. His basic arguments are two: (1) Various texts from Mesopotamia and other cultures of the ancient world indicate a worldview in which morality and social justice are a religious imperative indivisible from cultic law. Is it imaginable that PT, postdating these texts by at least half a millennium, did not also place ethics and cult in the same realm? (2) In Lev 16:21, PT prescribes, as part of the annual atonement rites, that the high priest confess the iniquities (Heb. עונת) of the Israelites over the head of the goat that is later sent to Azazel. In Milgrom's opinion, the semantic range of the term עונת in Priestly literature includes ethical sins, and thus the high priest's confession is intended to atone for the people's cultic and ethical sins as the same time.

I will respond to these points in order. It is true that in ancient Near Eastern law we find sensitivity to ethical and social issues, and one can discern in those laws an outlook in which the maintenance of social justice is under the direction of the gods. PT, too, does not deny the central importance to humanity of maintaining morality and social justice. In fact, as I mentioned earlier, in the view of PT, the ethical law, which God is concerned with upholding, is the sole basis for society's existence in the Genesis and patriarchal periods. The flood story dramatizes the point that "lawlessness" (Heb. חמס)—that is, the violation of the ethical imperative—can result in the destruction of humanity and of the entire universe. It is precisely because justice and morality were known and accepted in human society many generations before the emergence of the Israelite nation that PT portrays the innovation in Mosaic revelation as being in a realm beyond the ethical (see Y. Kaufmann, *The Religion of Israel,* 233ff.). According to the Priestly Torah, the essence of revelation at Sinai was the revelation of the numinous dimension of divinity, without which the religious personality could not attain wholeness.

In PT's outlook, the divine names current in the earlier periods, "Elohim" and "El Shaddai," signify the rational and moral dimension of divinity, while the Tetragrammaton, revealed to Moses, signifies the numinous dimension of divinity. PT insists on a consistent distinction between these names. With the appearance of the Tetragrammaton, all use of the earlier names ceases, and so the combinations ה' אלהים and ה' אלהיכם are absent from this school's writings. Similarly, as stated before, a distinction is maintained between morality, concentrated in the primeval period, and the cultic system established with the appearance of revelation in the name of YHWH. This distinction reflects no disregard for ethics, but rather a refined sensitivity to the multiple dimensions of divine revelation and to the variegated contents of human experience.

I will respond now to the argument about the ethical component of the high priest's confession on Yom Kippur, indicated, in Milgrom's view, by the use of the Hebrew term עונת. I regret that I cannot accept this argument. Milgrom cites the following five verses in order to prove that the word עונת in the Priestly Torah refers to ethical trangressions: Lev 5:1 and 5:17 and Num 5:15 and 16 and 30:16. It seems to me that none of the cited verses provides substantial proof of his argument.

(1) Lev 5:1 deals with a person who refuses to offer testimony:

ונפש כי־תחטא ושמעה קול אלה והוא עד או ראה או ידע אם־לוא יגיד ונשא עונו.

> If a person incurs guilt—
> When he has heard a public imprecation [JPS footnote: namely, against one who withholds testimony] and—although able to testify as one who has either seen or learned of the matter—he does not give information, he is subject to punishment.

This act is defined as an עון not because of its ethical dimension but because the one who commits it "has heard a public imprecation"—that is, he has impaired the sanctity of the divine name which, pronounced within his hearing, requires him to testify.

(2) There is no evidence that Lev 5:17 describes an ethical transgression.

ואם־נפש כי תחטא ועשתה אחת מכל מצות ה׳ אשר לא תעשינה ולא ידע ואשם ונשא עונו.

> And when a person, without knowing it, sins in regard to any of the Lord's commandments about things not to be done, and then realizes his guilt, he shall be subject to punishment.

The comprehensive language of "any of the Lord's commandments about things not to be done" refers only, I think, to the totality of *cultic* imperatives.

(3) Verses 15 and 31 in Numbers 5 do indeed define adultery as an עון. Verse 15, in the context of the trial by ordeal prescribed for a woman suspected of adultery, reads as follows:

והביא האיש את־אשתו אל־הכהן והביא את קרבנה עליה עשירת האיפה קמח שערים
לא־יצק עליו שמן ולא־יתן עליו לבנה כי מנחת קנאת הוא מנחת זכרון מזכרת עון.

> . . . the man shall bring his wife to the priest. And he shall bring as an offering for her one-tenth of an ephah of barley flour. No oil shall be poured upon it and no frankincense shall be laid on it, for it is a meal offering of jealousy, a meal offering of remembrance which recalls wrongdoing.

Verse 31, at the conclusion of the same pericope, reads as follows:

ונקה האיש מעון והאשה ההוא תשא את־עונה.

> The man shall be clear of guilt; but that woman shall suffer for her guilt.

While these verses categorize adultery as עון, many scholars have demonstrated that the Bible perceives adultery to be not so much an ethical evil as an affront to God. It will suffice in this context to cite Ps 51:6, in which David comments on the Bathsheba affair in these words:

לך לבדך חטאתי והרע בעיניך עשיתי.

> Against You alone have I sinned, and done what is evil in Your sight.

(4) Num 30:16 is the last verse cited as proof of Professor Milgrom's point. In the context of the annulment of vows and oaths made by women, the verse states:

ואם הפר יפר אתם אחרי שמעו ונשא את עונה.

> But if he annuls them after [the day] he finds out, he shall bear her guilt.

This verse sees the annulment of a vow as an עון because here too the sacredness of the name of God that was pronounced at the time of swearing the vow has been violated.

In summary, nowhere in the Priestly Torah are transgressions of commandments about human relations labeled "עון" unless accompanied by a cultic, sacral component. Therefore, I cannot accept the view that the high priest offers confession for moral transgressions over the goat on Yom Kippur. In the view of the Priestly Torah, such sins are not part of the cultic system, and thus the priests do not deal with them. The rectification of moral misconduct is effected by the return of stolen property to its owner, and not by the offering of a sacrifice or the sending out of a scapegoat.

This outlook finds clear expression in the law of the guilt offering (אשם) in Lev 5:20–26.

> The Lord spoke to Moses, saying: When a person sins and commits a trespass against the Lord by dealing deceitfully with his fellow in the matter of a deposit or a pledge, or through robbery, or by defrauding his fellow, or by finding something lost and lying about it; if he swears falsely regarding any one of the various things that one may do and sin thereby—when one has thus sinned and, realizing his guilt, would restore that which he got through robbery or fraud, or the deposit that was entrusted to him, or the lost thing that he found, or anything else about which he swore falsely, he shall repay the principal amount and add a fifth part to it. He shall pay it to its owner when he realizes his guilt. Then he shall bring to the priest, as his penalty to the Lord, a ram without blemish from the flock, or the equivalent, as a guilt offering. The priest shall make expiation on his behalf before the Lord, and he shall be forgiven for whatever he may have done to draw blame thereby.

As Professor Milgrom has correctly observed (in *Cult and Conscience,* p. 85), it is apparent from this law that the Priestly legislator regards only the combination of moral evil and a false oath as "a trespass against the Lord" (מעל בה'), requiring the bringing of a guilt offering to the Lord. Robbery or exploitation that is not associated with a false oath is not called "a trespass against the Lord" and does not require expiation through sin offering. Moral injustice itself is in the realm not of the Priestly cultic system but of the civil justice system.

Only with the appearance of the later Priestly school, the "Holiness School," do we find the interpenetration of ethical and cultic considerations. Out of the religious and social crisis of the period of Ahaz and Hezekiah, and as a reaction to the prophetic critique of cultic institutions, a new Priestly concept of holiness emerges, a concept composed both of cultic commandments and of ethical imperatives. The fullest exposition of that concept is in Leviticus 19, the central chapter of the Holiness Code. Our admiration for the innovations of the Holiness School should in no way blur our appreciation for the strength and uniqueness of its predecessor, the Priestly Torah.

Recognition of the unique outlook of PT emphasizes the sharp contrast between it and the views of classical prophecy. In prophetic thought, the God of Moses is the God of morality. God's major concern in this world is the maintenance of social justice, and the fate of the Israelite nation depends on upholding the ethical/social commandments. The content of Sinaitic revelation is seen by the prophets as solely ethical. Jeremiah says (7:22):

> כי לא־דברתי את־אבותיכם ולא צויתים ביום הוציא(י) אותם מארץ מצרים על־דברי עולה וזבח.
>
> For when I freed your fathers from the land of Egypt, I did not speak with them or command them concerning burnt offerings or sacrifice.

And because of that, they do not even imagine that the Israelites took part in cultic activities during the period of wandering in the wilderness of Sinai. As Amos asks rhetorically (5:25),

> הזבחים ומנחה הגשתם־לי במדבר ארבעים שנה בית ישראל
>
> Did you offer sacrifice and oblation to Me those forty years in the wilderness, O House of Israel?

At the opposite pole, the Priestly Torah sees the cultic command as the sole content of God's revelation to Moses and Israel. The main event that took place at Sinai was the erection of the Tabernacle and the establishment of the cultic system of sacrifices and priestly activities. In PT's portrayal, the people received unmediated divine revelation only from the time of the dedication of the Tabernacle, when fire appeared from the Lord and consumed the sacrifices on the altar. Not revelation at Sinai but revelation at the Tabernacle, associated with sacrificial worship, is the climactic moment in Israel's history. The possibility of experiencing through the cultic act nearness to the sacred and mysterious essence of divinity is seen here as the pinnacle of religious life.

The power of the Bible lies in the fact that it preserves within itself, in full force, contradictory conceptions of great depth and uniqueness. We would be ill-advised to blur such disagreements. We should instead attempt to understand each stance on its own, for, in the well-known rabbinic phrase, אלו ואלו דברי אלהים חיים ("Both these and those are the words of the living God," *b. Erubin* 13a).

Index of Modern Authors

Index of Biblical References